22

CLAMP

TRANSLATED AND ADAPTED BY
William Flanagan

LETTERED BY
Dana Hayward

BALLANTINE BOOKS • NEW YORK

A Del Rey Manga/Kodansha Trade Paperback Original

Tsubasa, volume 22 copyright © 2008 by CLAMP
English translation copyright © 2009 by CLAMP

Published in the United States by Del Rey Books, an imprint of The Random House Publishing Group, a division of Random House, Inc., New York.

DEL REY is a registered trademark and the Del Rey colophon is a trademark of Random House, Inc.

Publication rights arranged through Kodansha Ltd.

First published in Japan in 2008 by Kodansha Ltd., Tokyo

ISBN 978-0-345-51038-9

Printed in the United States of America

www.delreymanga.com

9 8 7 6 5 4 3 2 1

Translator/Adapter—William Flanagan
Lettering—Dana Hayward

Contents

Tsubasa crosses over with *xxxHOLiC*. Although it isn't necessary to read *xxxHOLiC* to understand the events in *Tsubasa*, you'll get to see the same events from different perspectives if you read both series!

Honorifics Explained

Throughout the Del Rey Manga books, you will find Japanese honorifics left intact in the translations. For those not familiar with how the Japanese use honorifics and, more important, how they differ from American honorifics, we present this brief overview.

Politeness has always been a critical facet of Japanese culture. Ever since the feudal era, when Japan was a highly stratified society, use of honorifics—which can be defined as polite speech that indicates relationship or status—has played an essential role in the Japanese language. When you address someone in Japanese, an honorific usually takes the form of a suffix attached to one's name (example: "Asuna-san"), is used as a title at the end of one's name, or appears in place of the name itself (example: "Negi-sensei," or simply "Sensei!").

Honorifics can be expressions of respect or endearment. In the context of manga and anime, honorifics give insight into the nature of the relationship between characters. Many English translations leave out these important honorifics and therefore distort the feel of the original Japanese. Because Japanese honorifics contain nuances that English honorifics lack, it is our policy at Del Rey not to translate them. Here, instead, is a guide to some of the honorifics you may encounter in Del Rey Manga.

-san: This is the most common honorific and is equivalent to Mr., Miss, Ms., or Mrs. It is the all-purpose honorific and can be used in any situation where politeness is required.

-sama: This is one level higher than "-san" and is used to confer great respect.

-dono: This comes from the word "tono," which means "lord." It is an even higher level than "-sama" and confers utmost respect.

-kun: This suffix is used at the end of boys' names to express familiarity or endearment. It is also sometimes used by men among friends, or when addressing someone younger or of a lower station.

-chan: This is used to express endearment, mostly toward girls. It is also used for little boys, pets, and even among lovers. It gives a sense of childish cuteness.

Bozu: This is an informal way to refer to a boy, similar to the English terms "kid" and "squirt."

Sempai/Senpai: This title suggests that the addressee is one's senior in a group or organization. It is most often used in a school setting, where underclassmen refer to their upperclassmen as "sempai." It can also be used in the workplace, such as when a newer employee addresses an employee who has seniority in the company.

Kohai: This is the opposite of "sempai" and is used toward underclassmen in school or newcomers in the workplace. It connotes that the addressee is of a lower station.

Sensei: Literally meaning "one who has come before," this title is used for teachers, doctors, or masters of any profession or art.

-[blank]: This is usually forgotten in these lists, but it is perhaps the most significant difference between Japanese and English. The lack of honorific means that the speaker has permission to address the person in a very intimate way. Usually, only family, spouses, or very close friends have this kind of permission. Known as *yobisute*, it can be gratifying when someone who has earned the intimacy starts to call one by one's name without an honorific. But when that intimacy hasn't been earned, it can be very insulting.

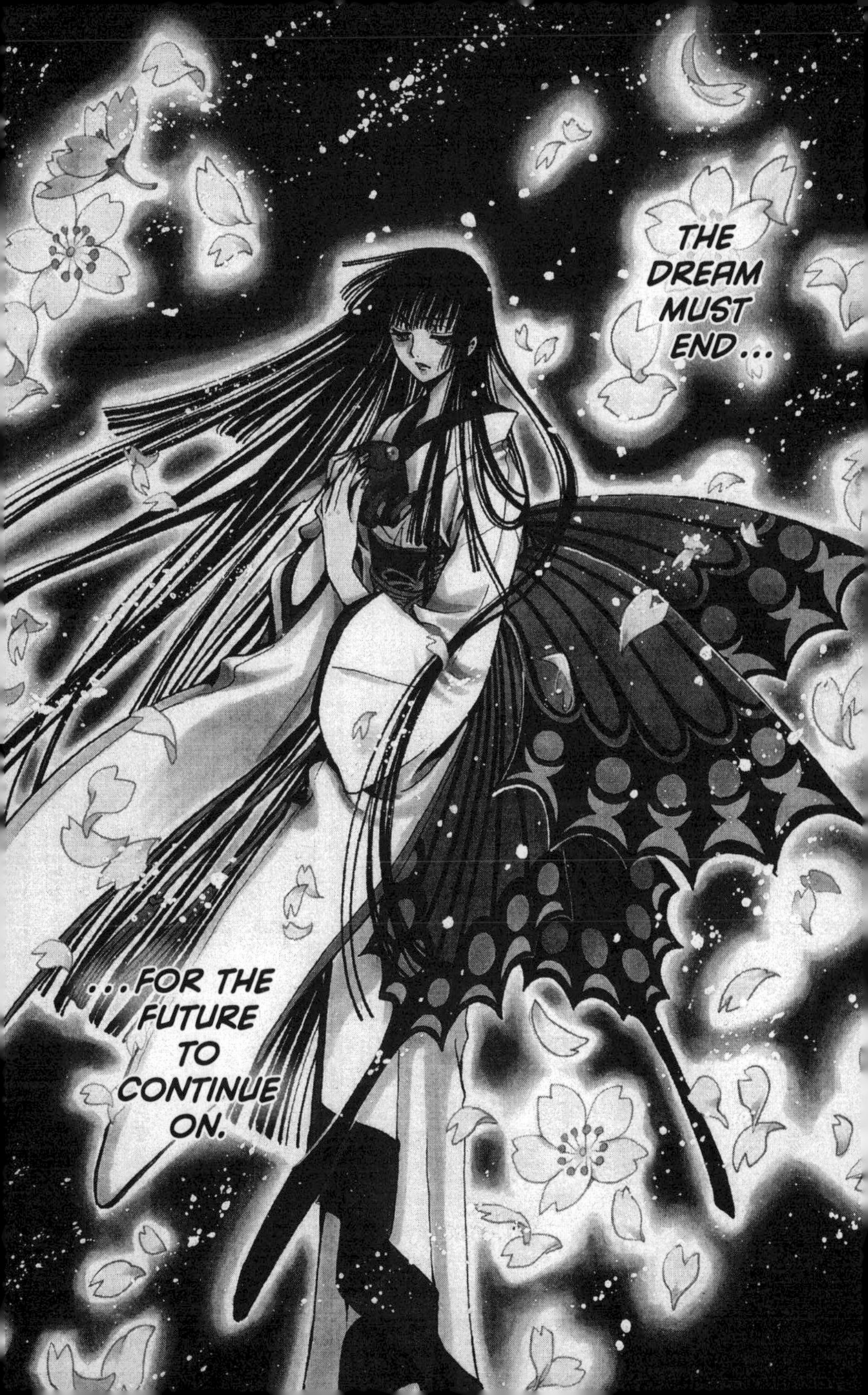
THE DREAM MUST END...
...FOR THE FUTURE TO CONTINUE ON.

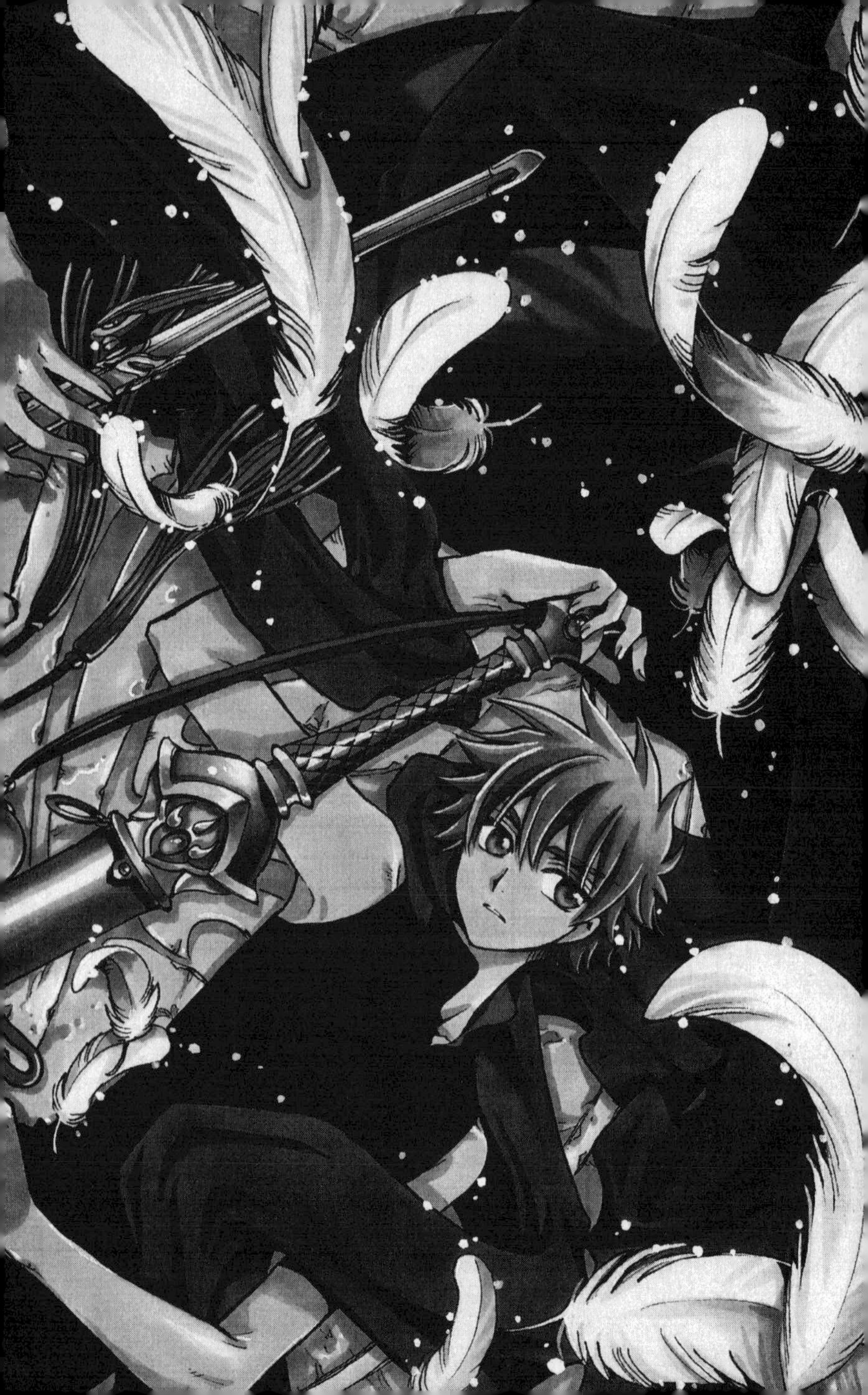

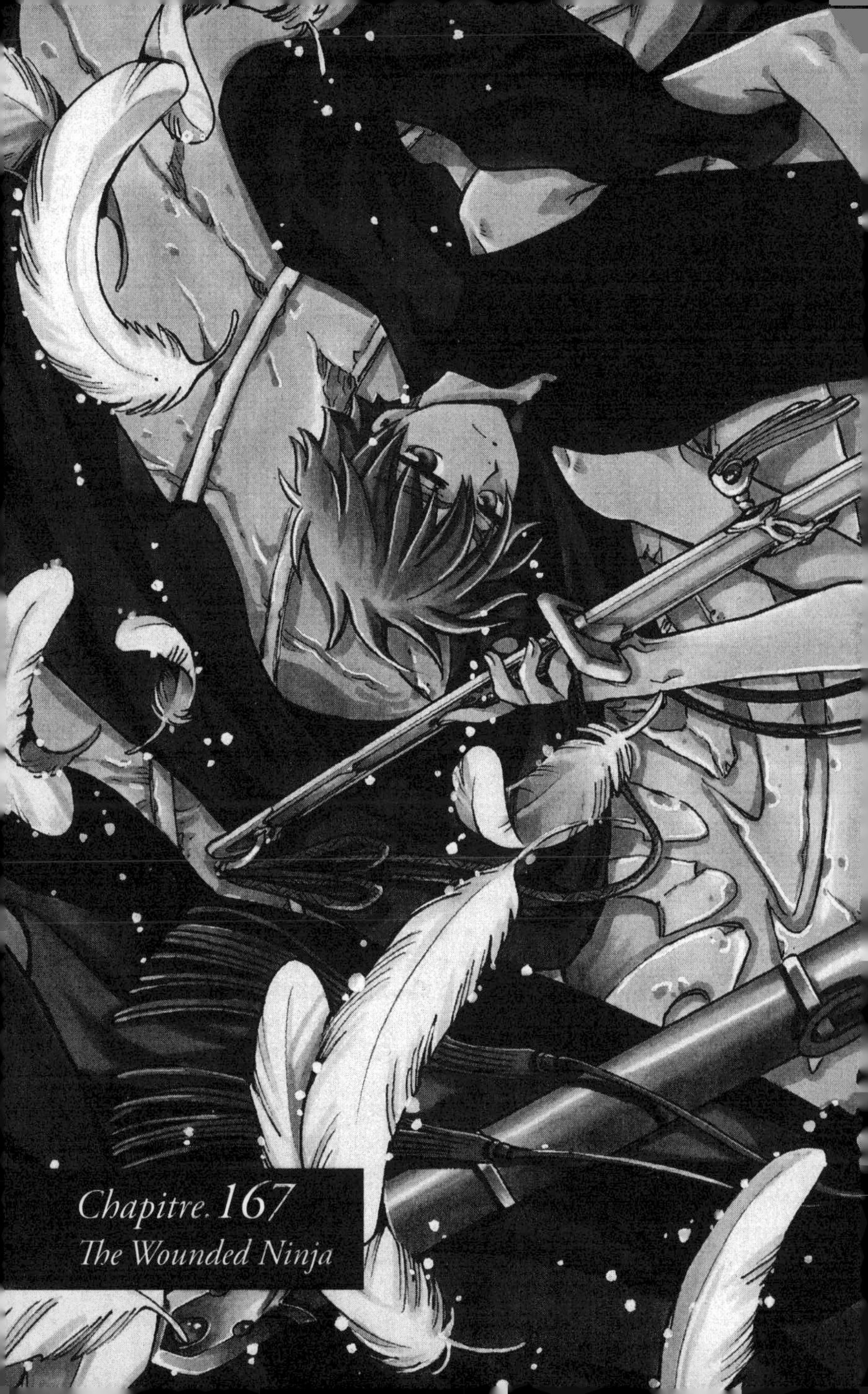

Chapitre. 167
The Wounded Ninja

ツバサ

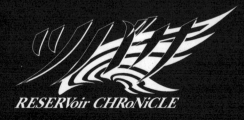

RESERVoir CHRoNiCLE

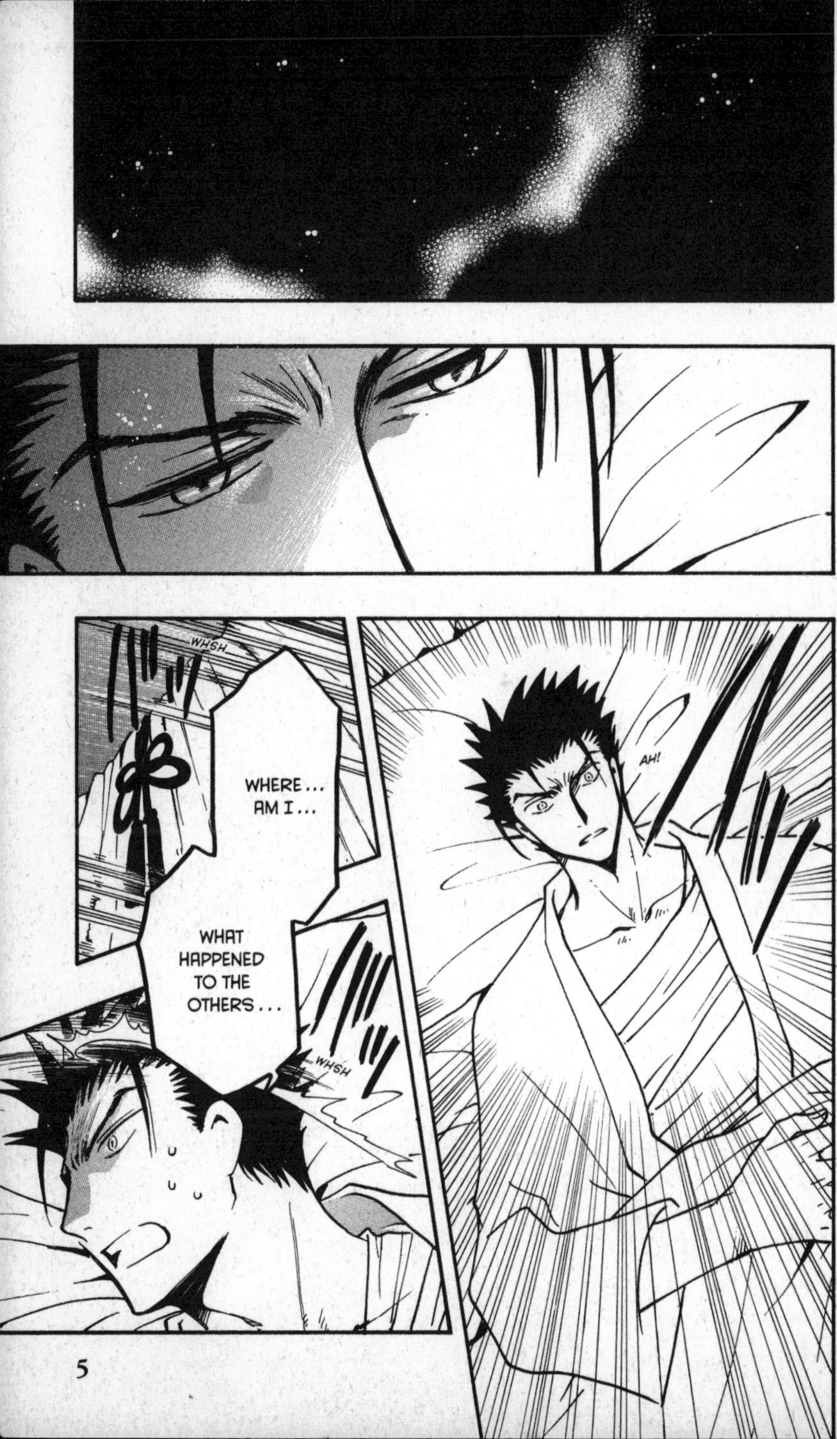
AH!
WHSH
WHERE... AM I...
WHAT HAPPENED TO THE OTHERS...
WHSH

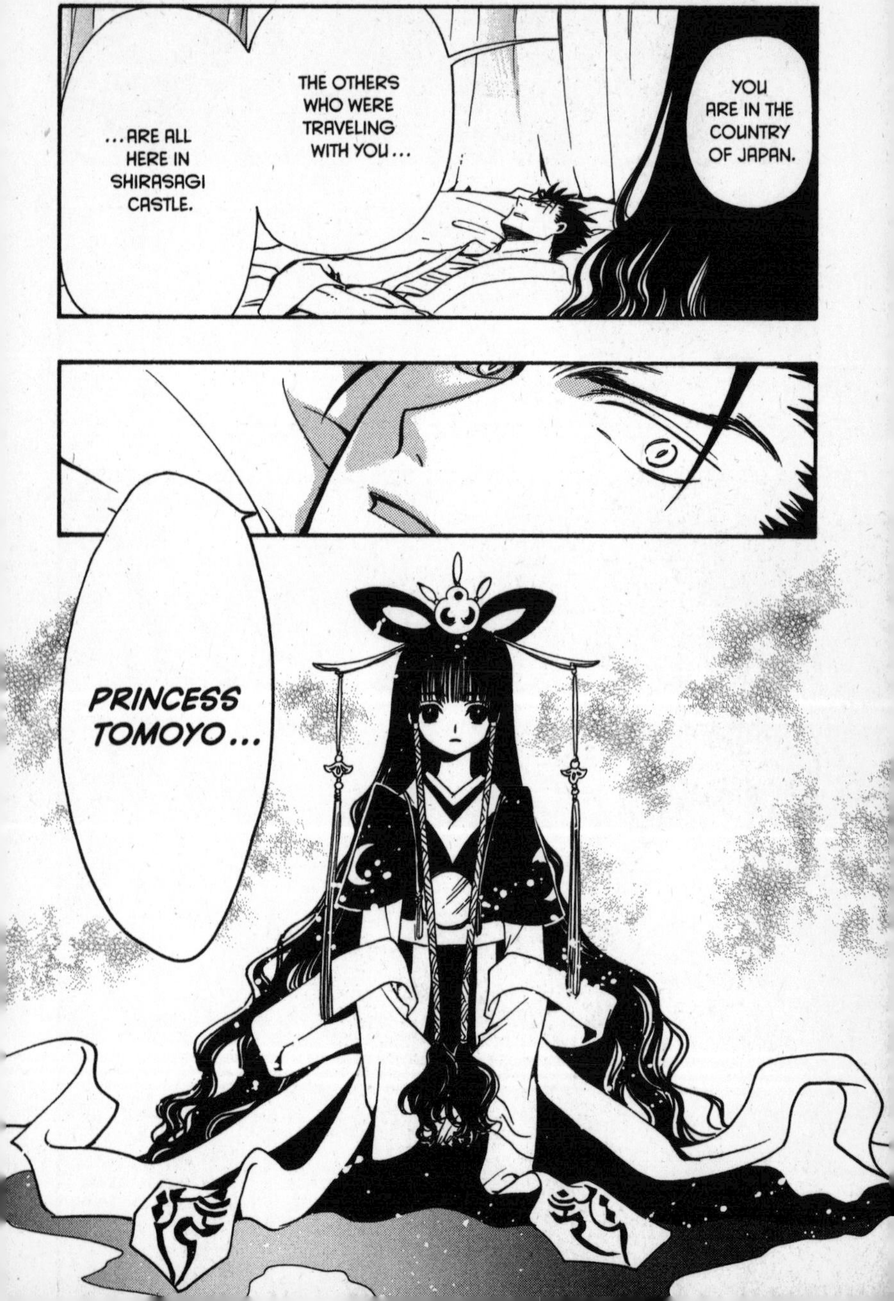
YOU ARE IN THE COUNTRY OF JAPAN.
THE OTHERS WHO WERE TRAVELING WITH YOU...
...ARE ALL HERE IN SHIRASAGI CASTLE.
PRINCESS TOMOYO...

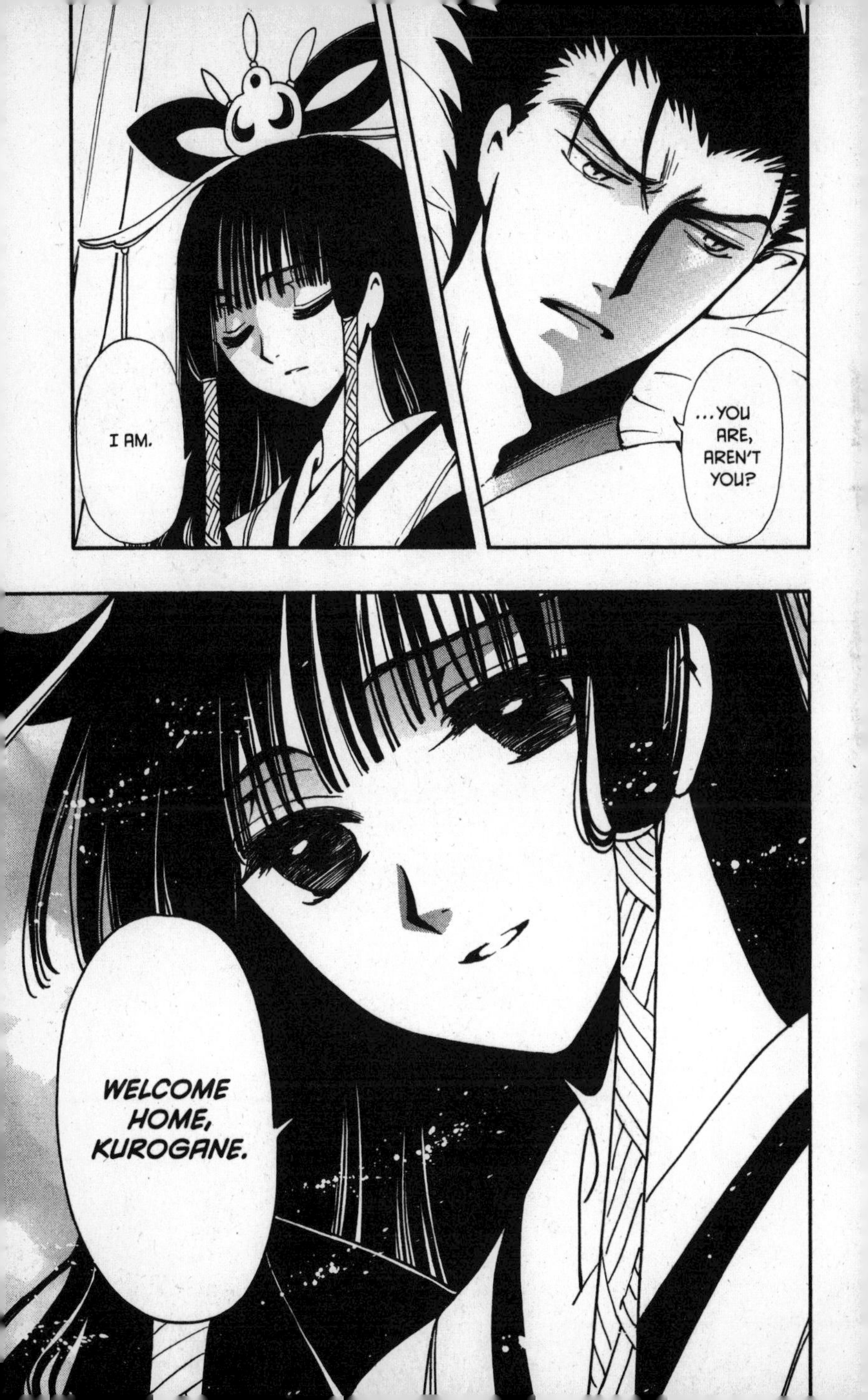
...YOU ARE, AREN'T YOU?
I AM.
WELCOME HOME, KUROGANE.

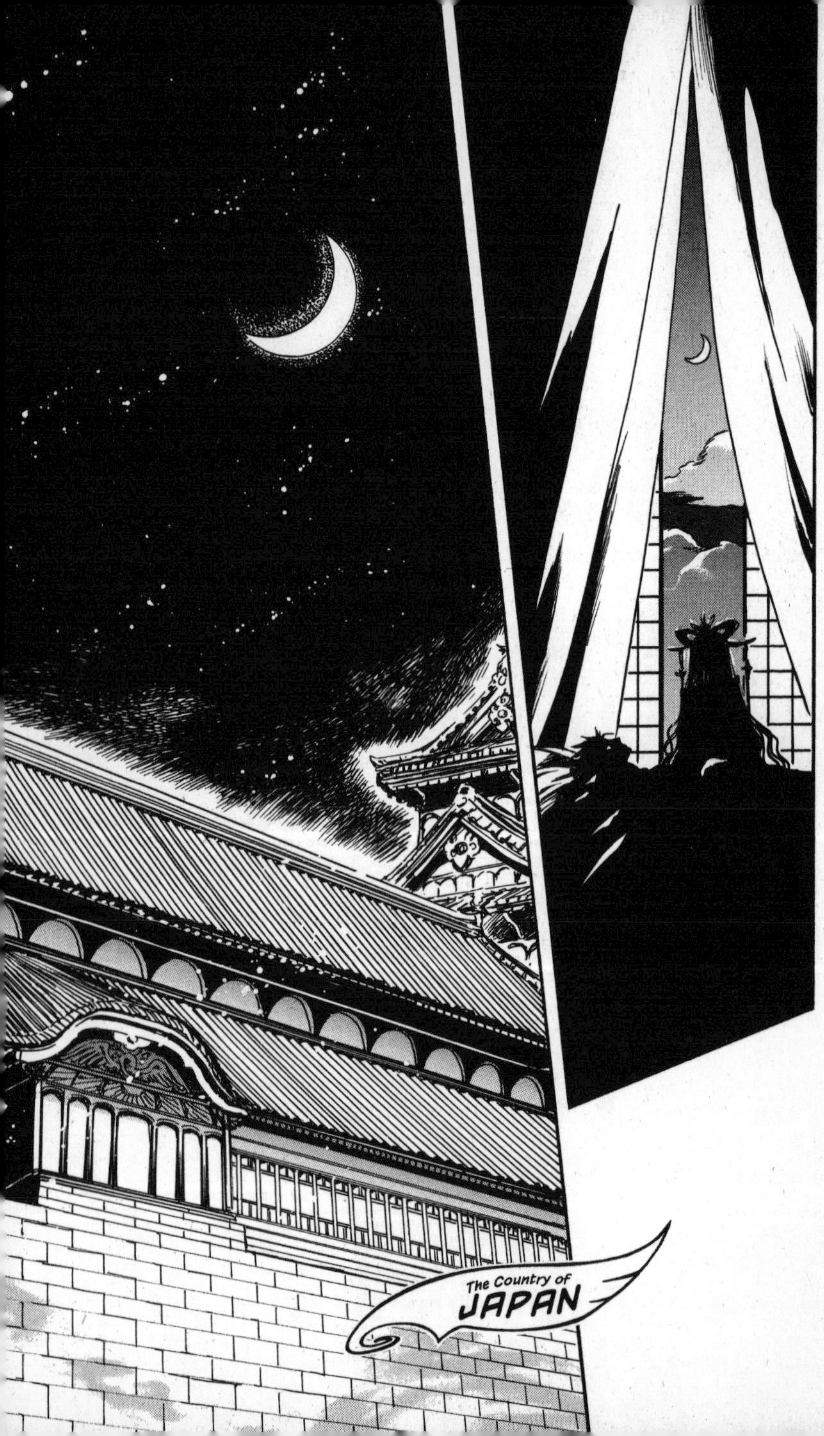
The Country of
JAPAN

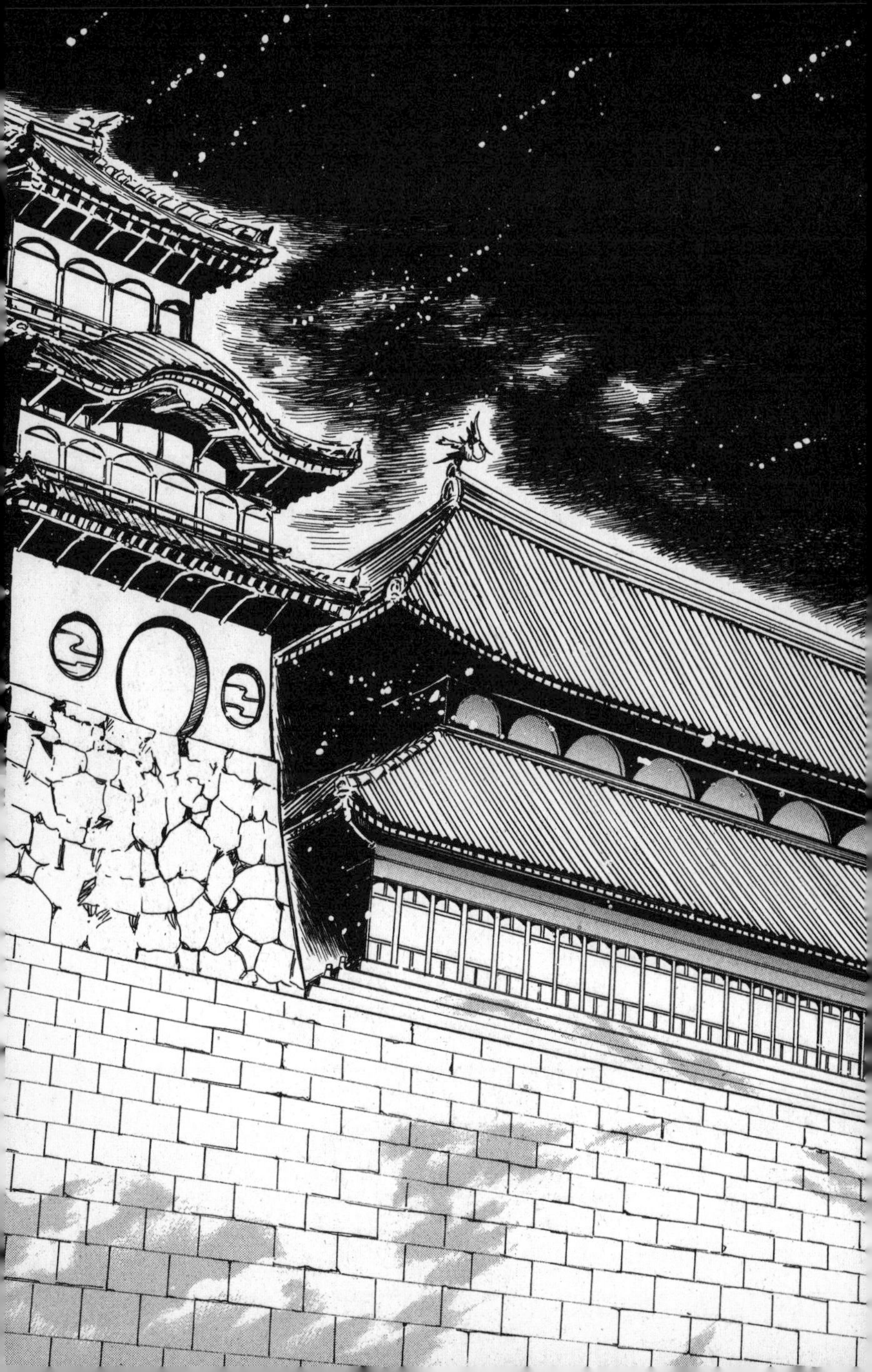

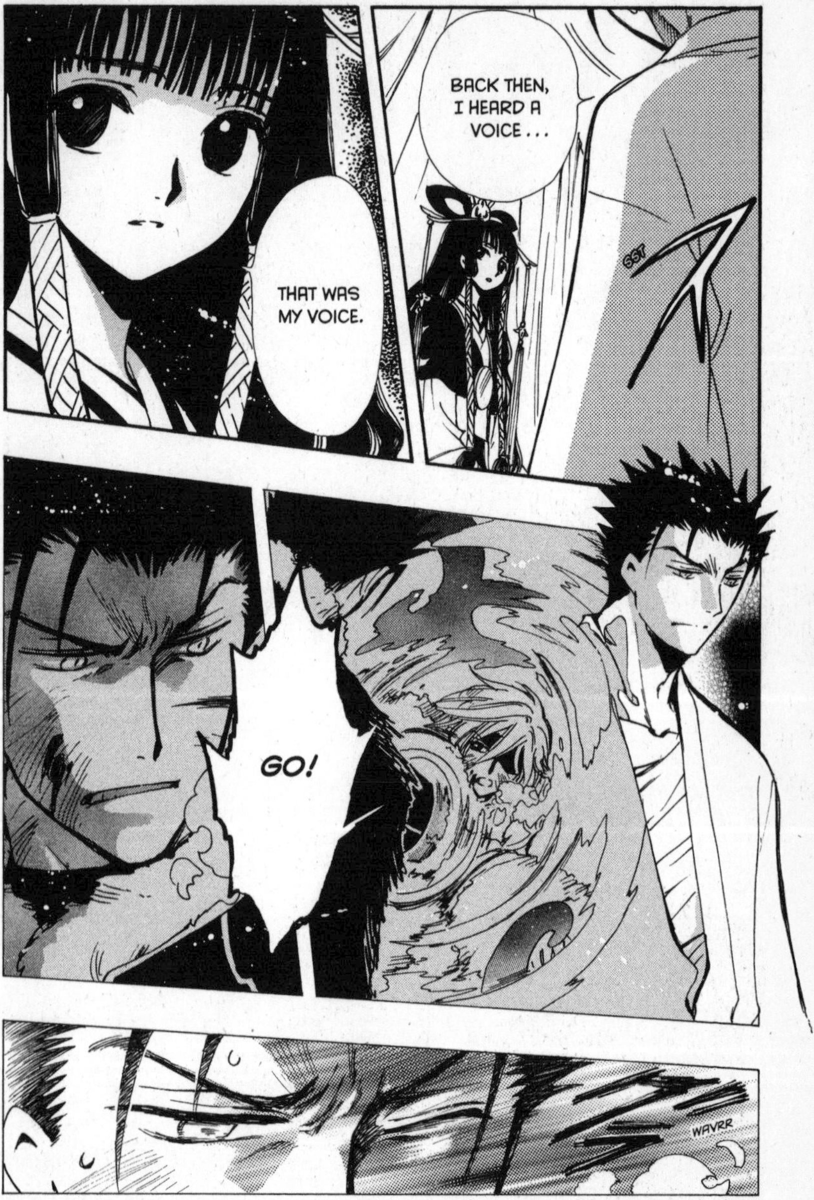
BACK THEN, I HEARD A VOICE . . .
SST
THAT WAS MY VOICE.
GO!
WAVRR

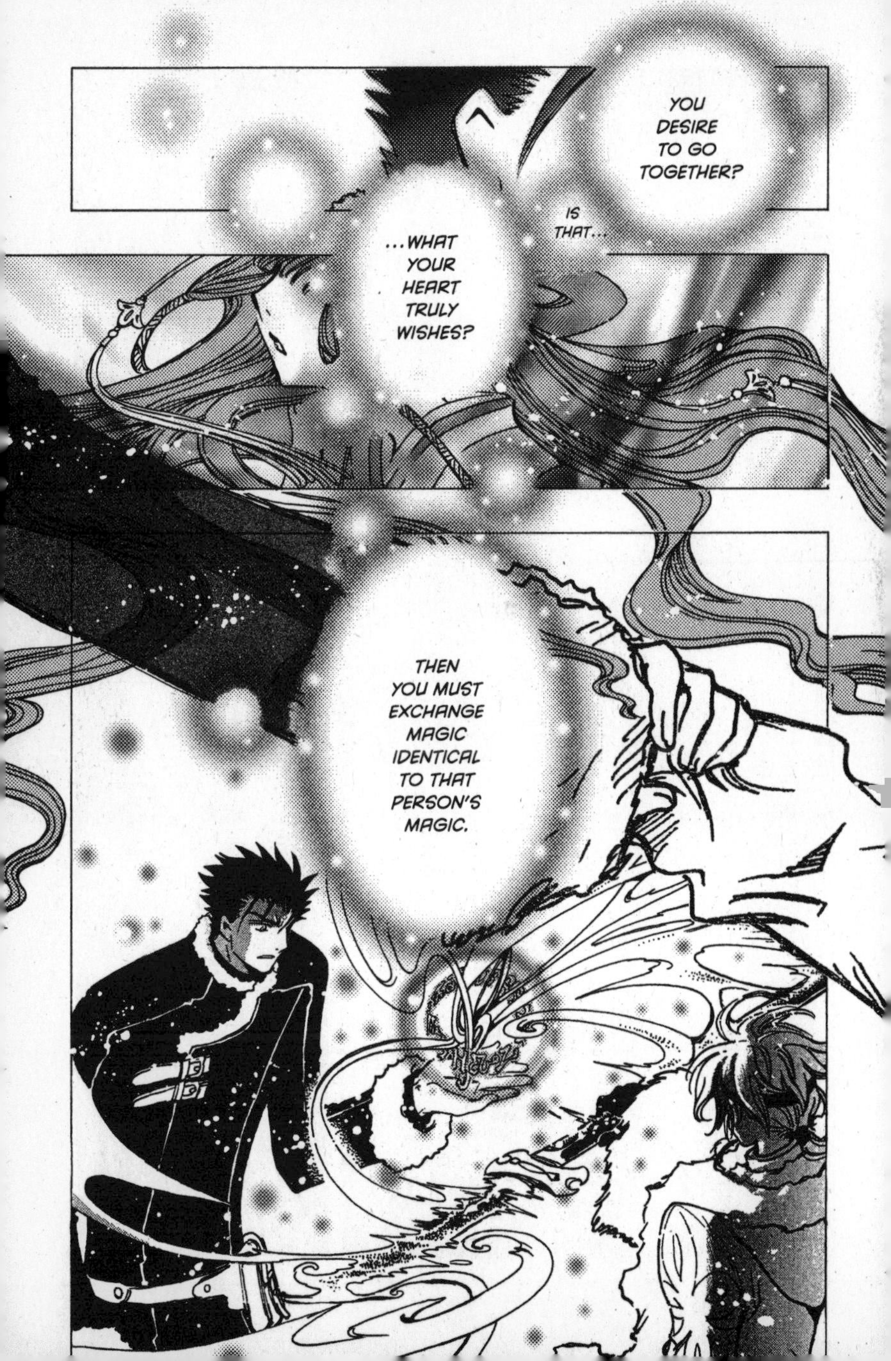
YOU DESIRE TO GO TOGETHER?
IS THAT...
...WHAT YOUR HEART TRULY WISHES?
THEN YOU MUST EXCHANGE MAGIC IDENTICAL TO THAT PERSON'S MAGIC.

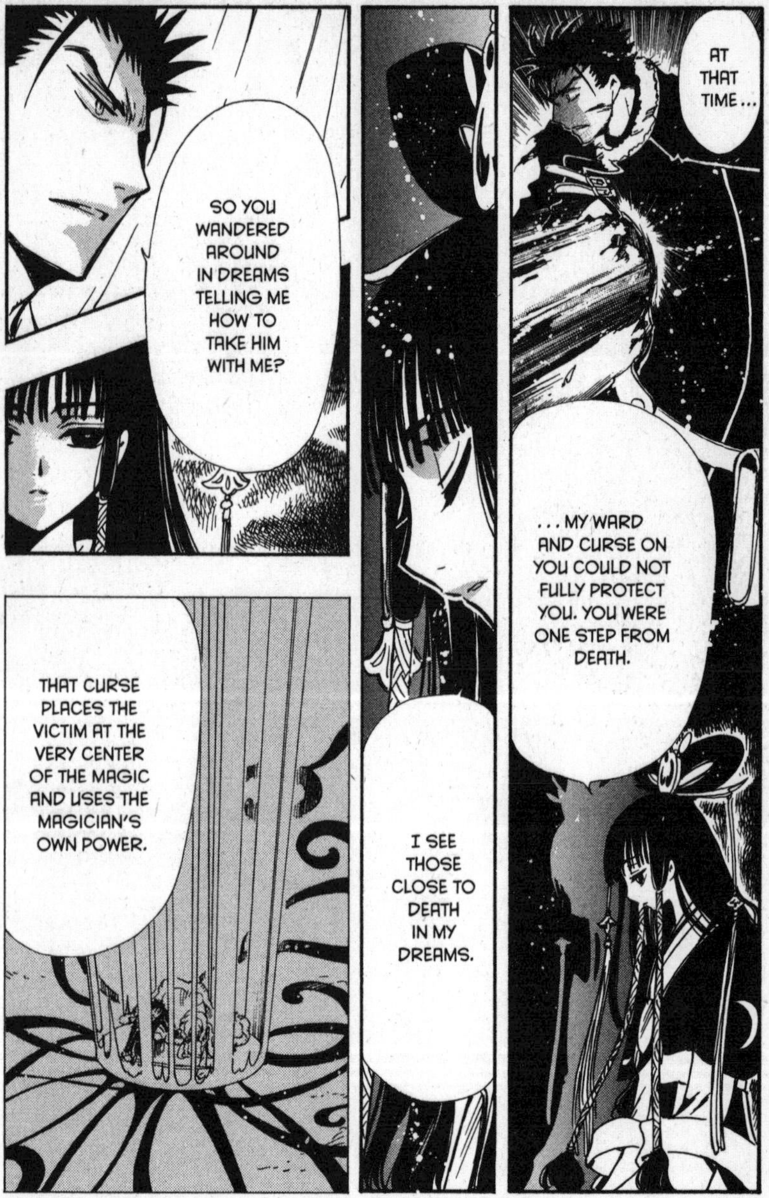

AT THAT TIME...
...MY WARD AND CURSE ON YOU COULD NOT FULLY PROTECT YOU. YOU WERE ONE STEP FROM DEATH.
I SEE THOSE CLOSE TO DEATH IN MY DREAMS.
SO YOU WANDERED AROUND IN DREAMS TELLING ME HOW TO TAKE HIM WITH ME?
THAT CURSE PLACES THE VICTIM AT THE VERY CENTER OF THE MAGIC AND USES THE MAGICIAN'S OWN POWER.

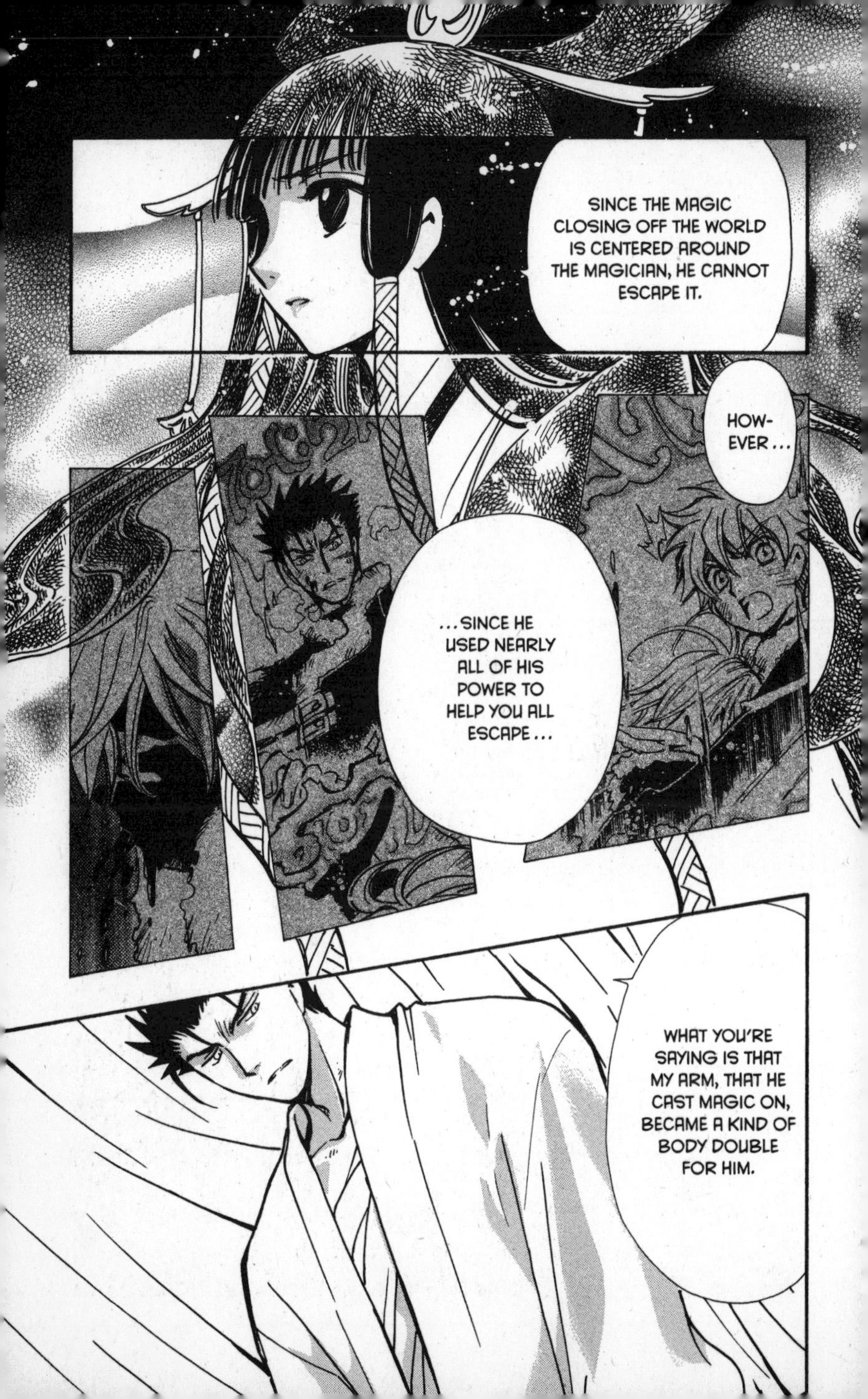
SINCE THE MAGIC CLOSING OFF THE WORLD IS CENTERED AROUND THE MAGICIAN, HE CANNOT ESCAPE IT.
HOW-EVER...
...SINCE HE USED NEARLY ALL OF HIS POWER TO HELP YOU ALL ESCAPE...
WHAT YOU'RE SAYING IS THAT MY ARM, THAT HE CAST MAGIC ON, BECAME A KIND OF BODY DOUBLE FOR HIM.

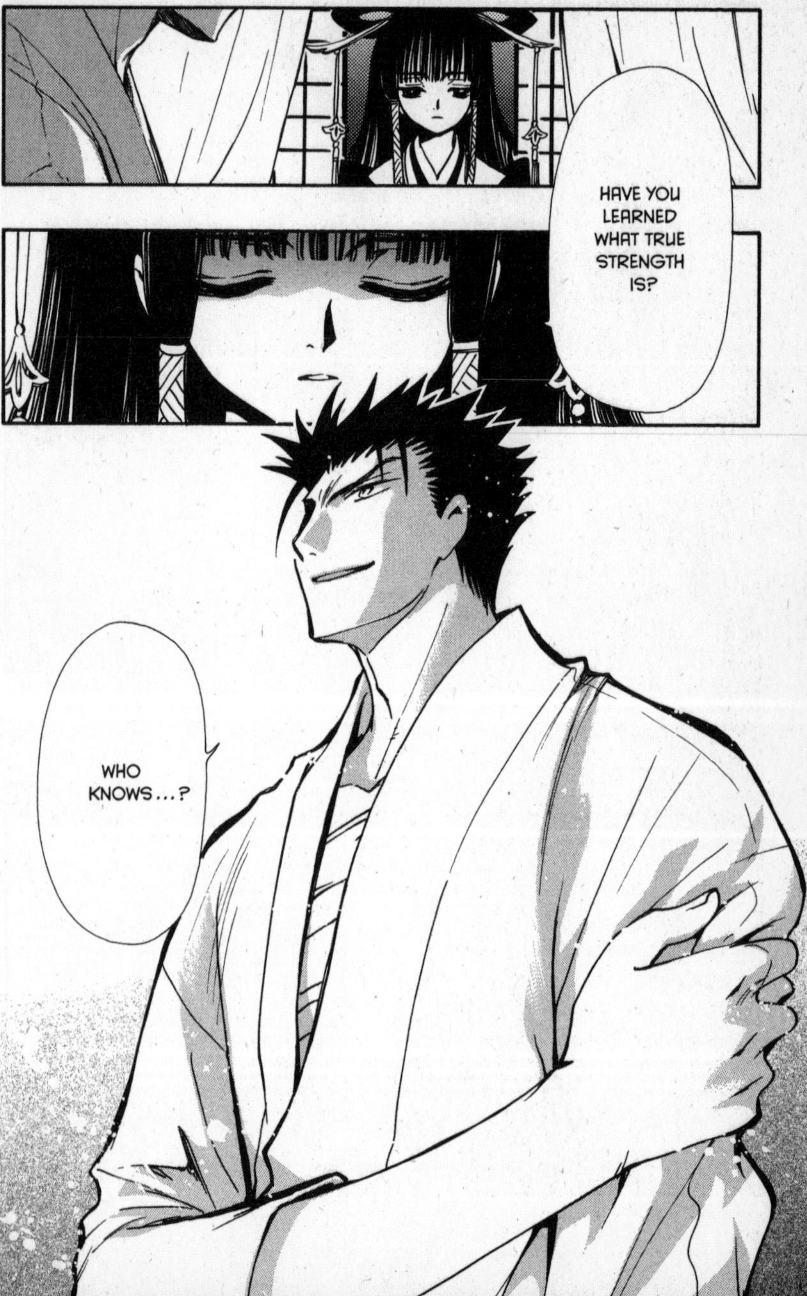
HAVE YOU LEARNED WHAT TRUE STRENGTH IS?
WHO KNOWS...?

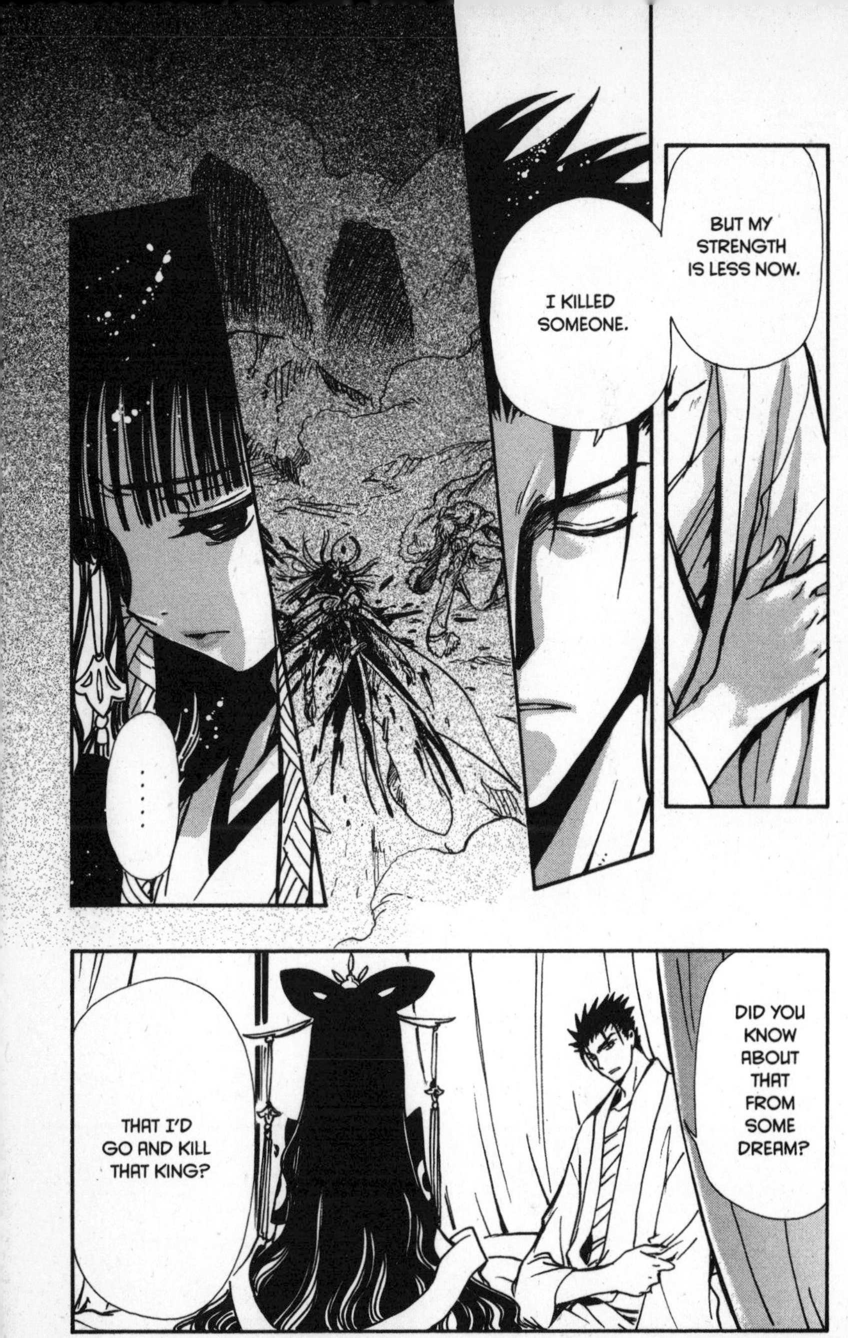
BUT MY STRENGTH IS LESS NOW.
I KILLED SOMEONE.
……
DID YOU KNOW ABOUT THAT FROM SOME DREAM?
THAT I'D GO AND KILL THAT KING?

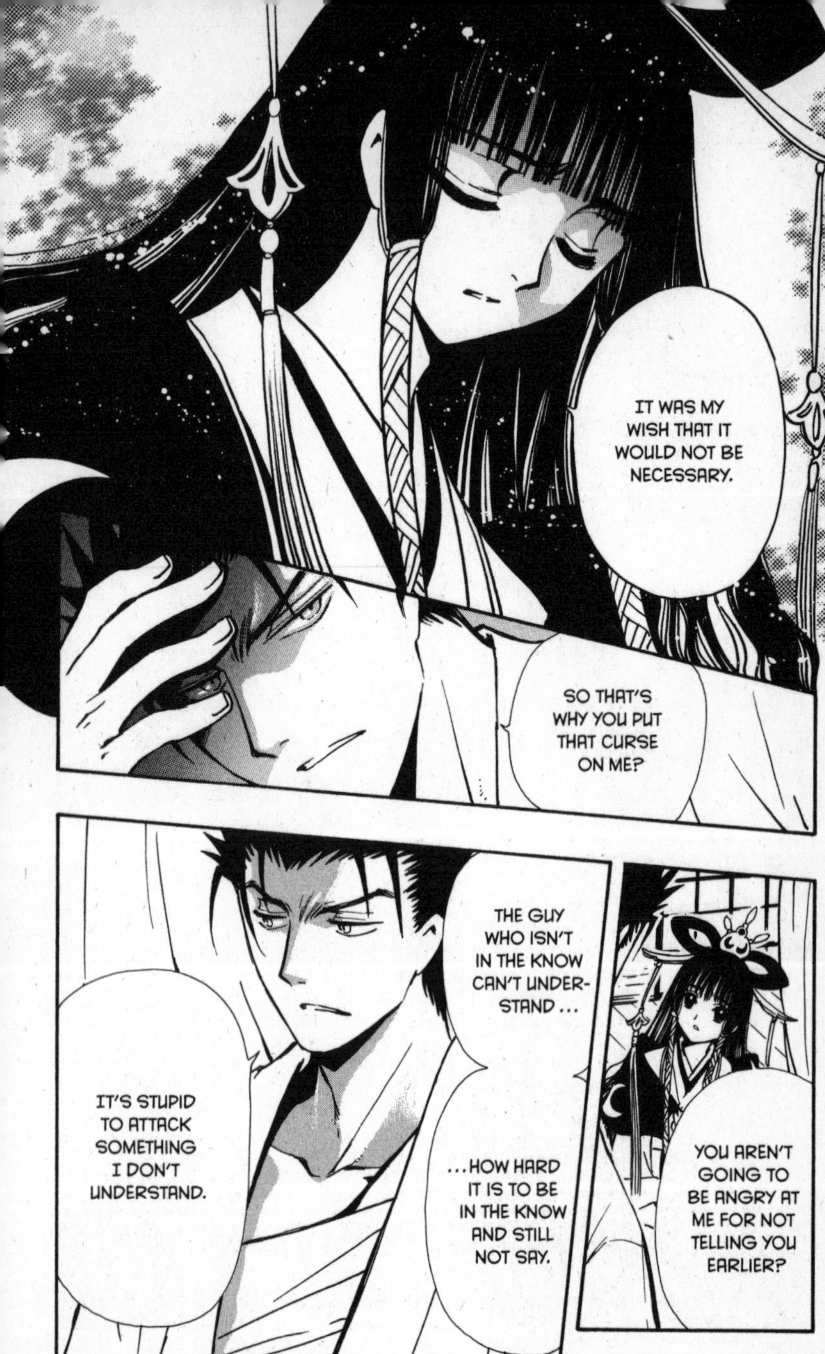
IT WAS MY WISH THAT IT WOULD NOT BE NECESSARY.
SO THAT'S WHY YOU PUT THAT CURSE ON ME?
YOU AREN'T GOING TO BE ANGRY AT ME FOR NOT TELLING YOU EARLIER?
THE GUY WHO ISN'T IN THE KNOW CAN'T UNDER-STAND...
...HOW HARD IT IS TO BE IN THE KNOW AND STILL NOT SAY.
IT'S STUPID TO ATTACK SOMETHING I DON'T UNDERSTAND.

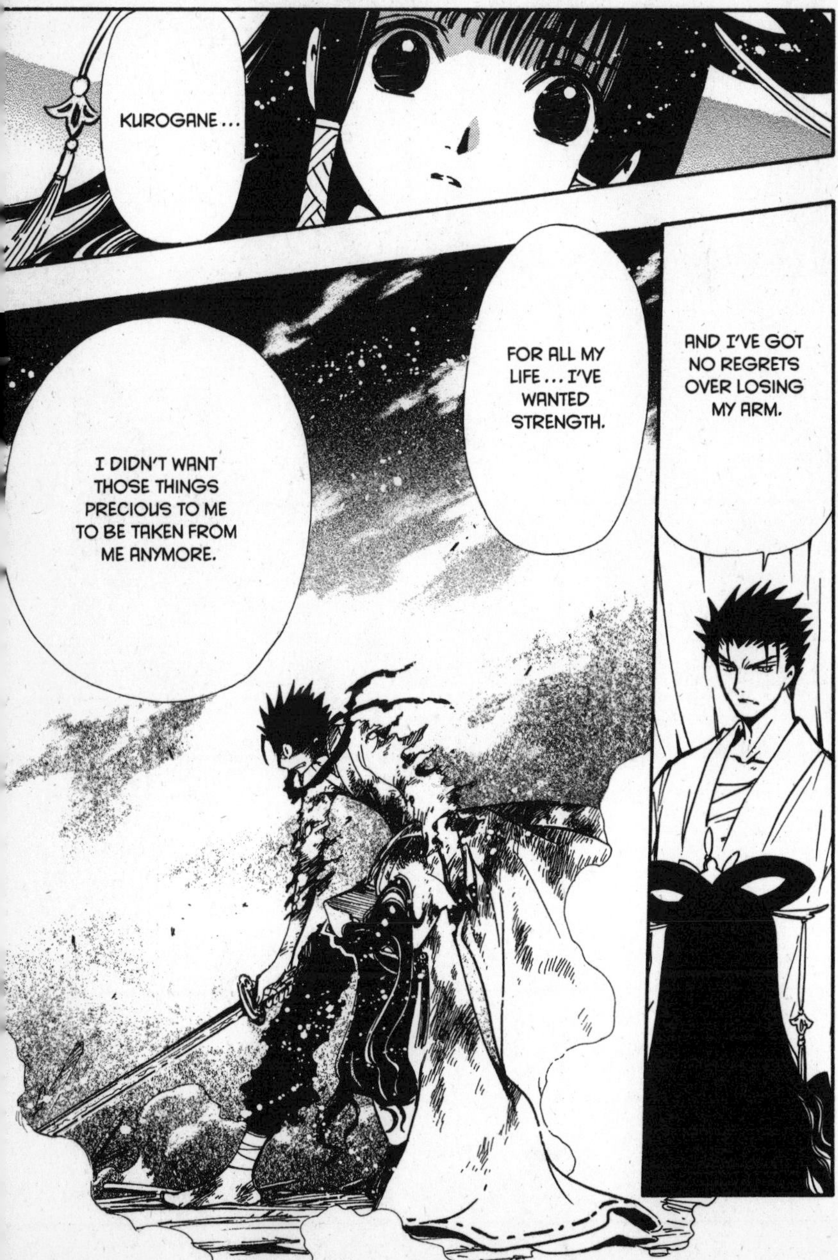
KUROGANE…
AND I'VE GOT NO REGRETS OVER LOSING MY ARM.
FOR ALL MY LIFE… I'VE WANTED STRENGTH.
I DIDN'T WANT THOSE THINGS PRECIOUS TO ME TO BE TAKEN FROM ME ANYMORE.

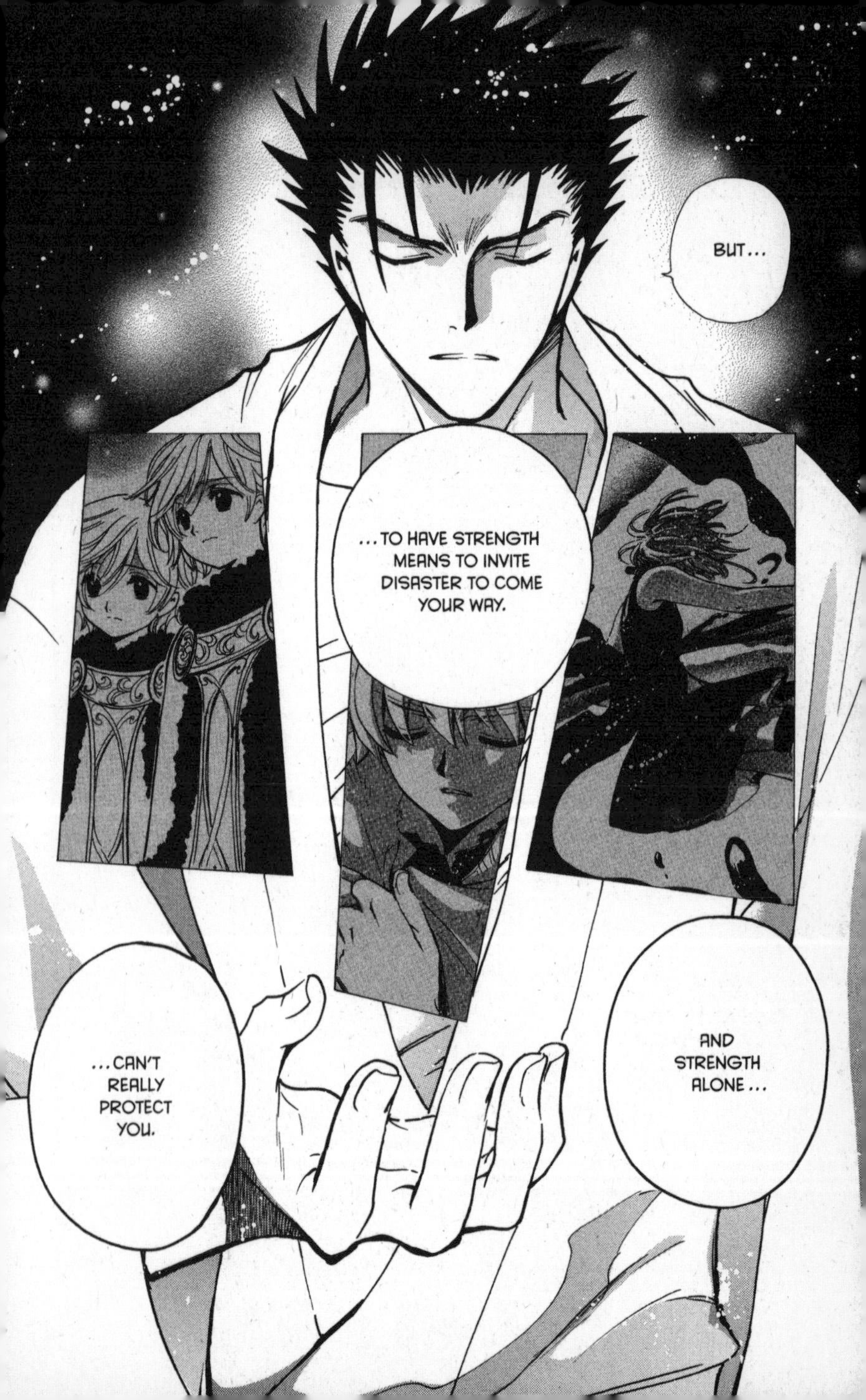
BUT...
...TO HAVE STRENGTH MEANS TO INVITE DISASTER TO COME YOUR WAY.
AND STRENGTH ALONE...
...CAN'T REALLY PROTECT YOU.

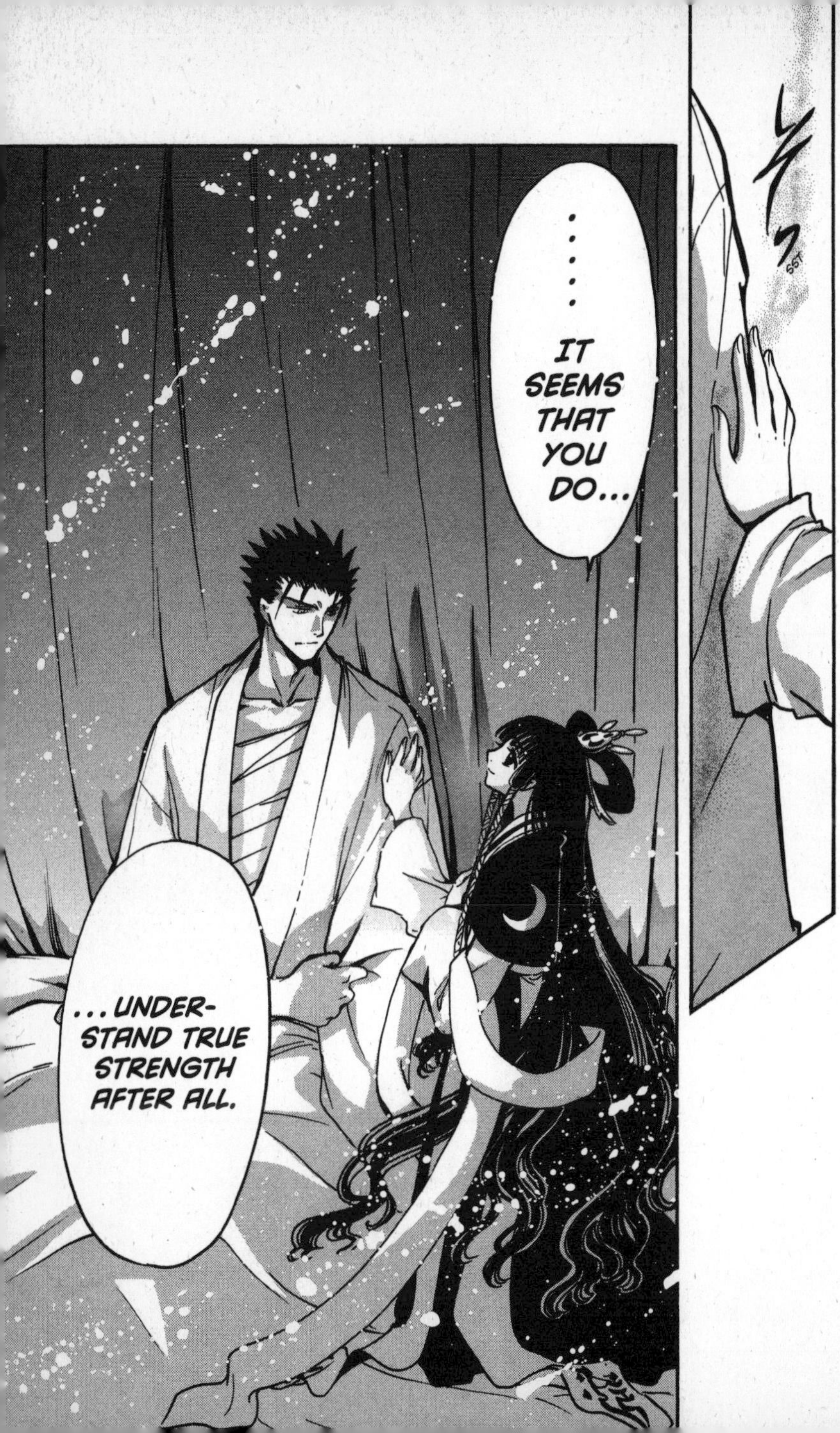
SST
...... IT SEEMS THAT YOU DO...
...UNDER-STAND TRUE STRENGTH AFTER ALL.

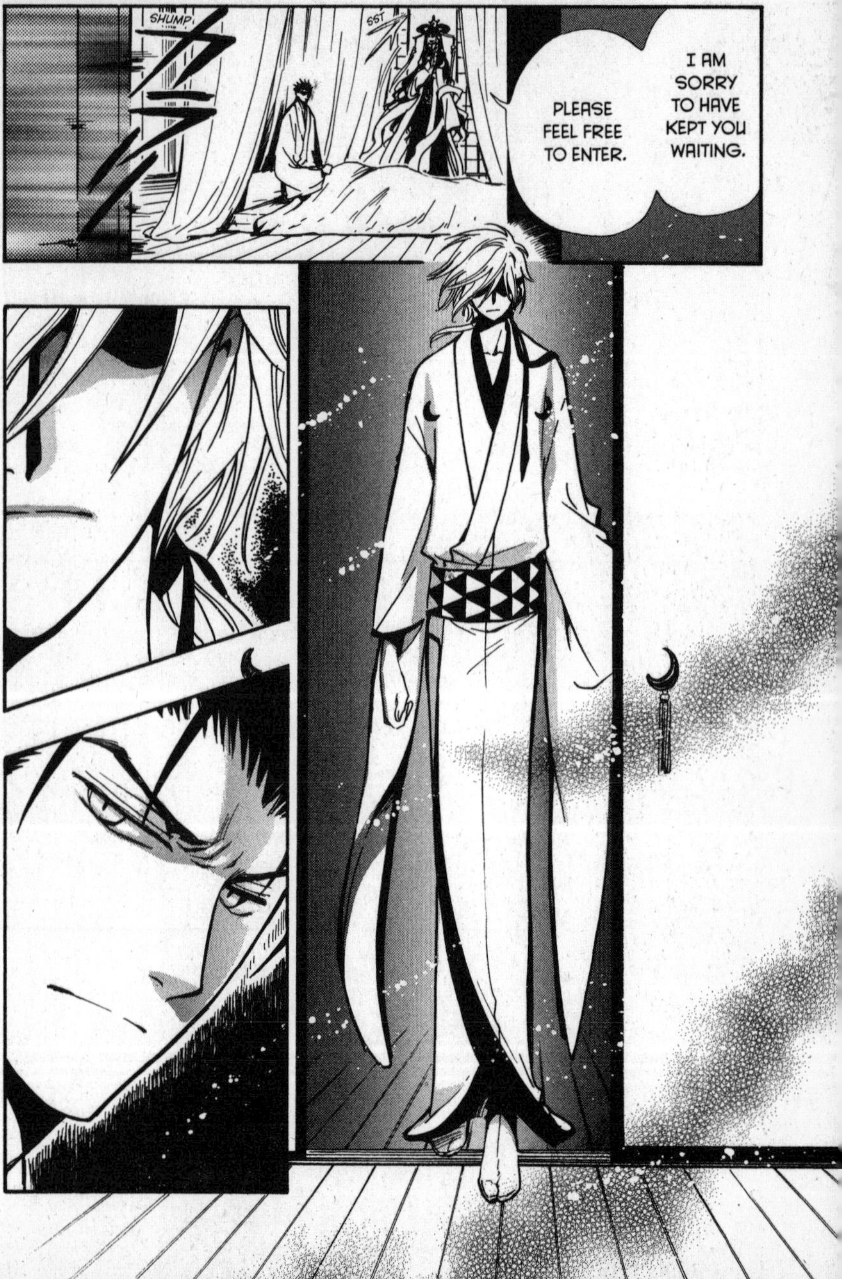
I AM SORRY TO HAVE KEPT YOU WAITING.
PLEASE FEEL FREE TO ENTER.
SST
SHUMP

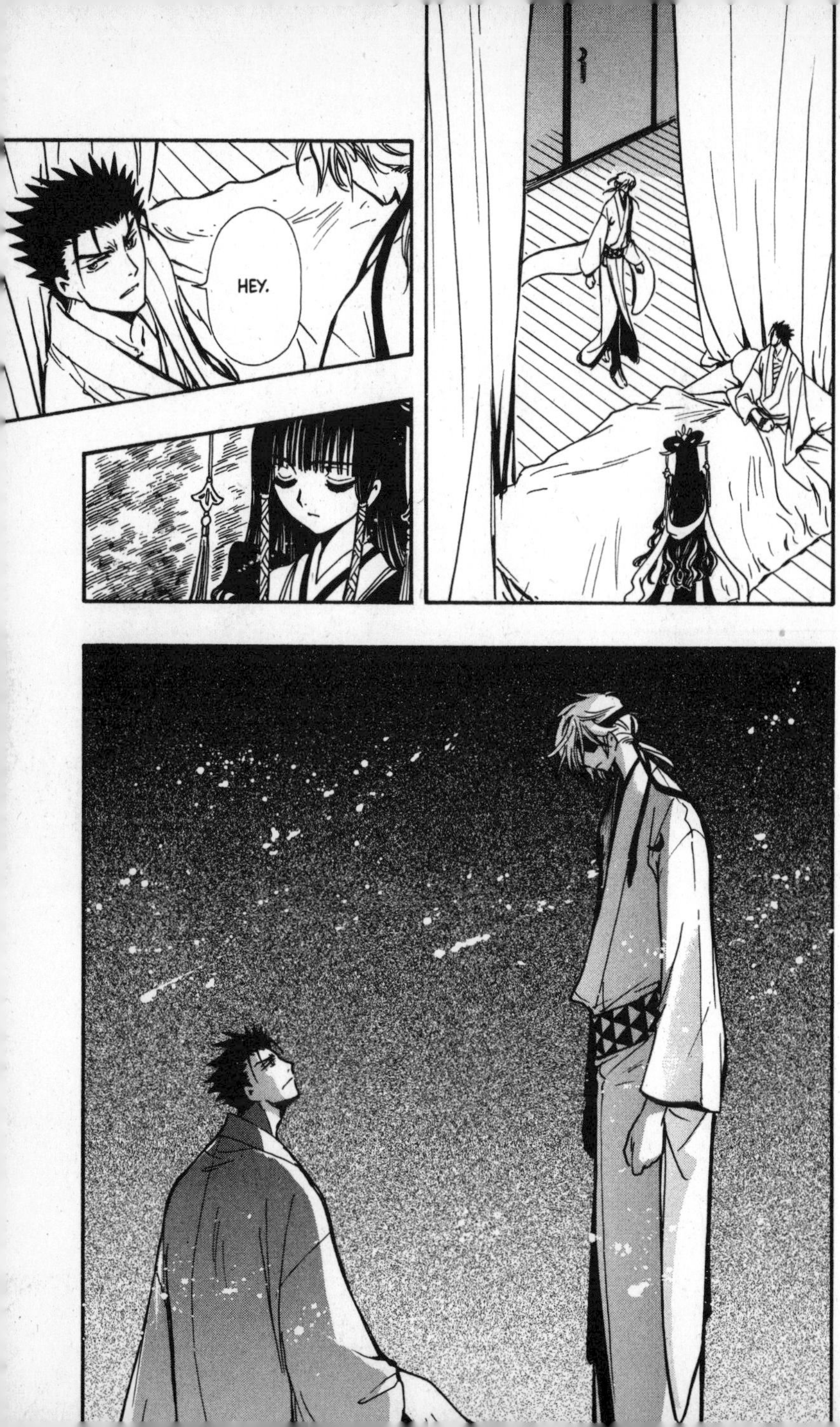
HEY.

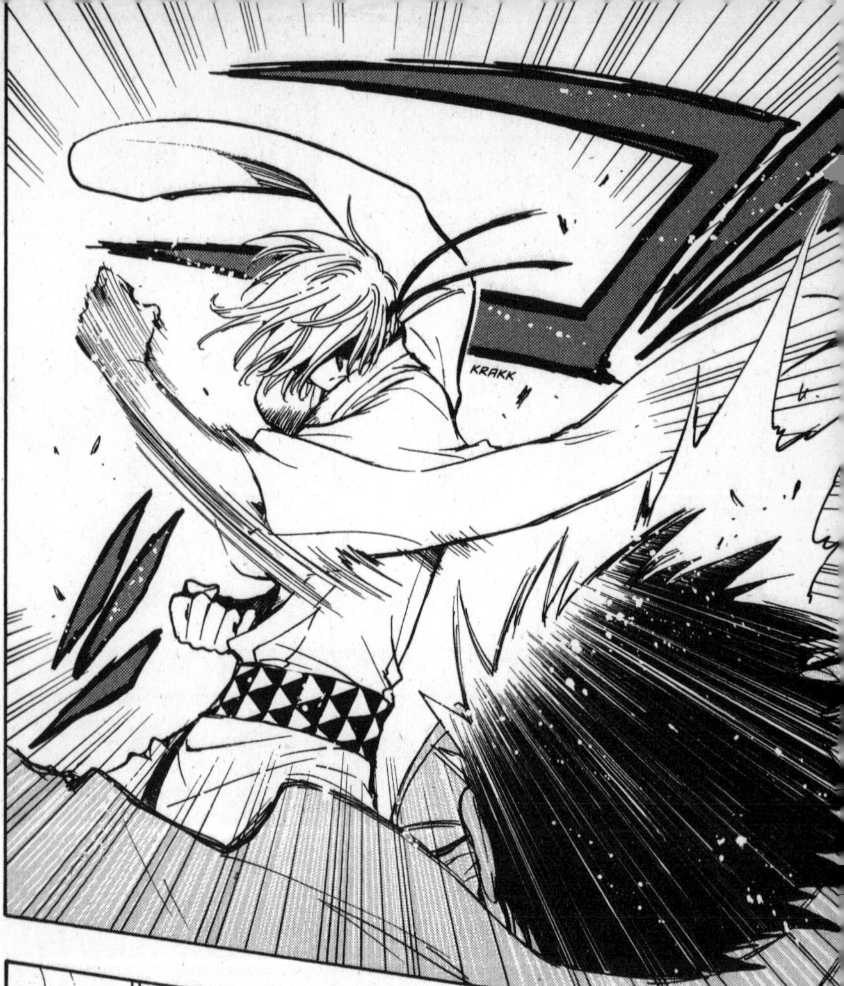
KRAKK

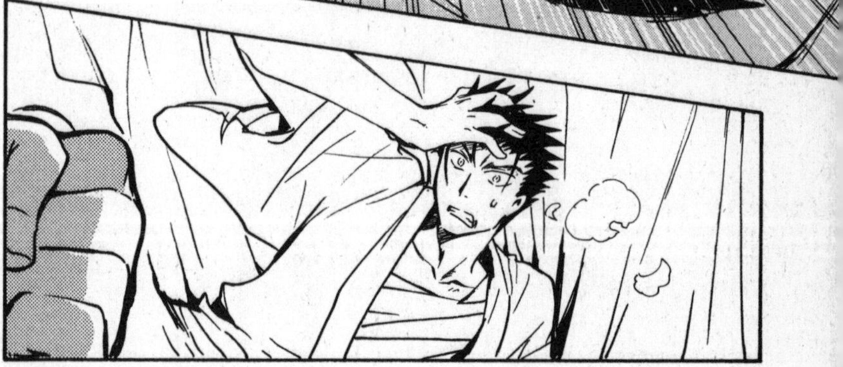

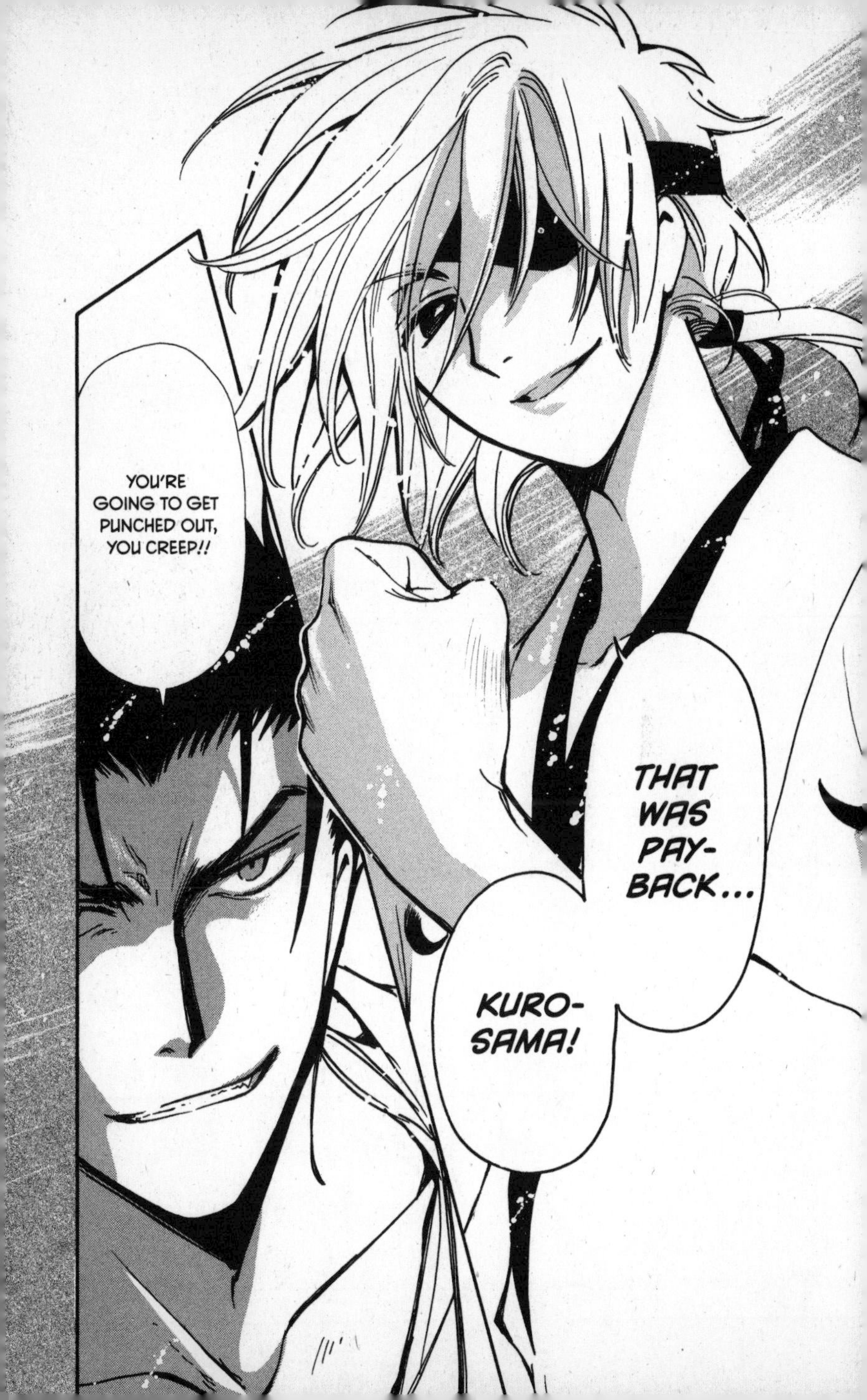
THAT WAS PAY-BACK...
KURO-SAMA!
YOU'RE GOING TO GET PUNCHED OUT, YOU CREEP!!

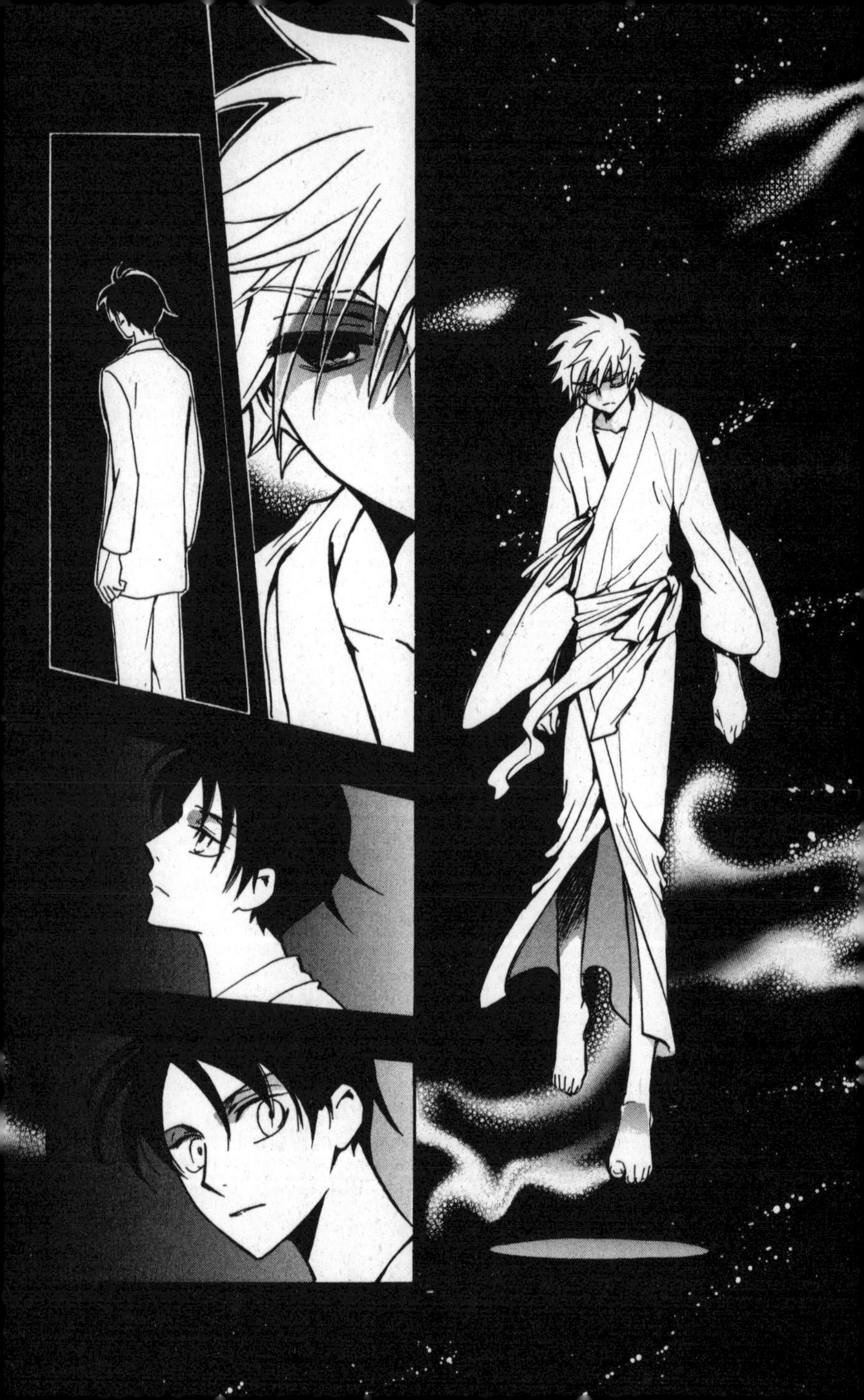

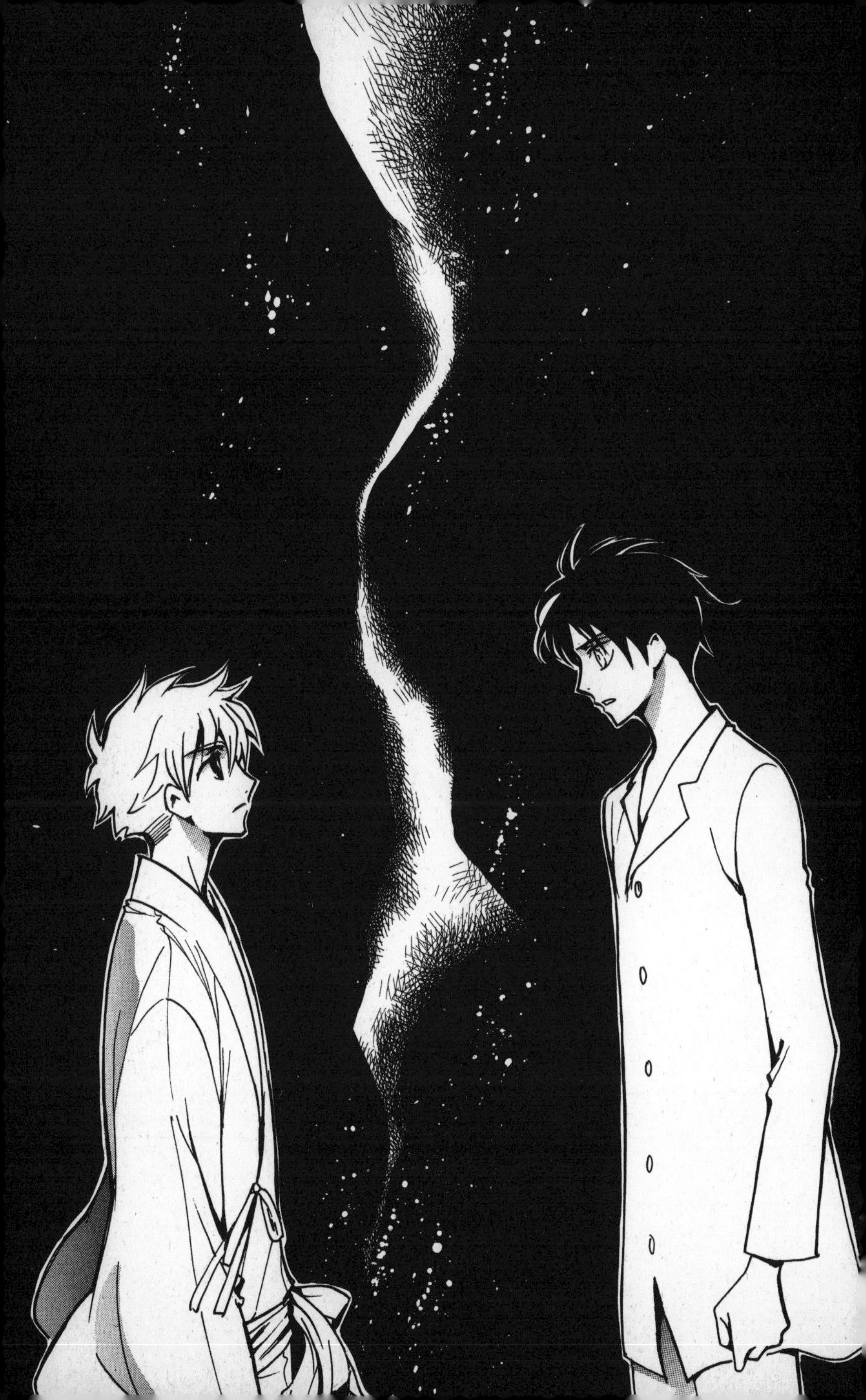

RESERVoir CHRoNiCLE

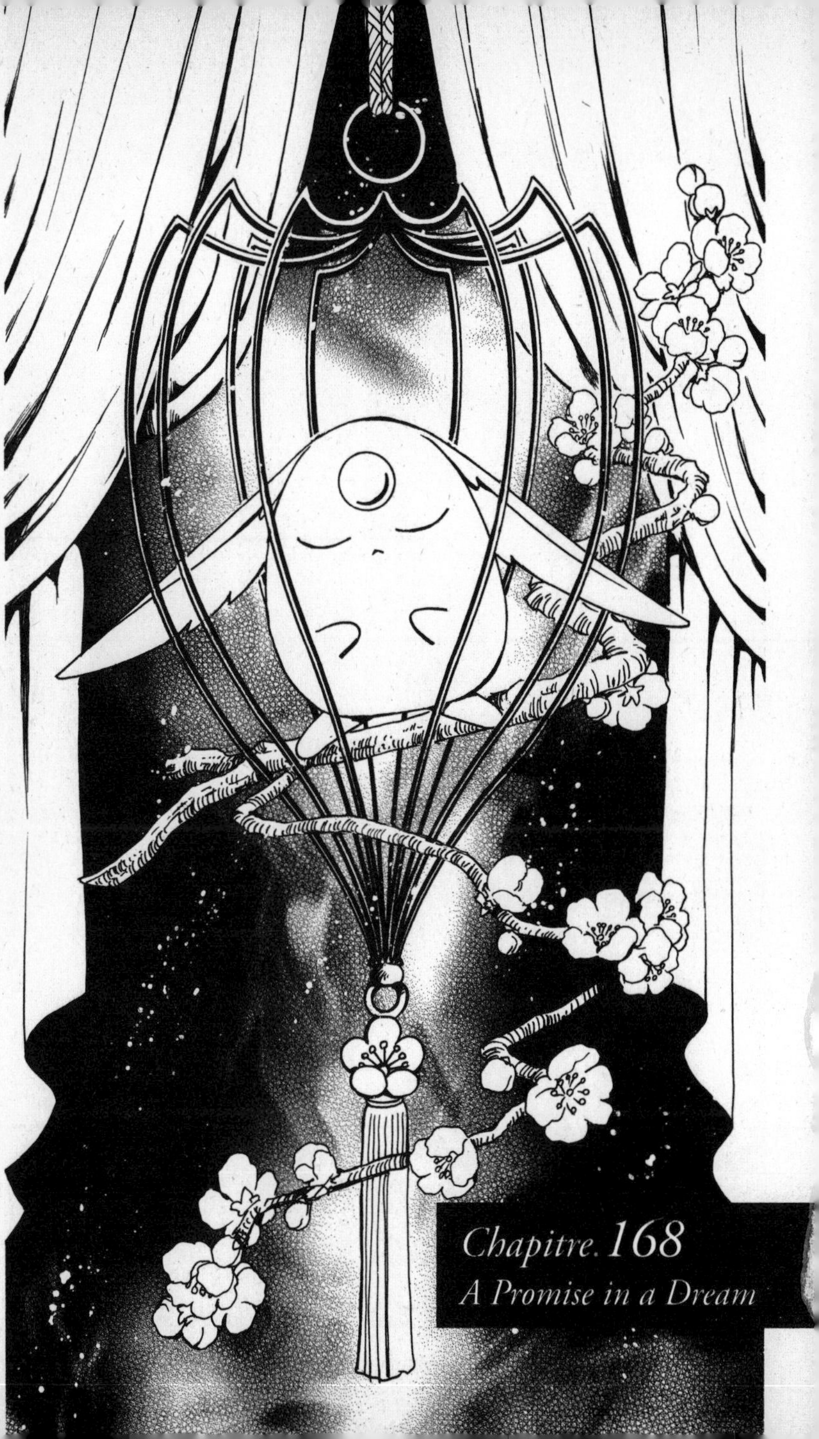

Chapitre. 168

A Promise in a Dream

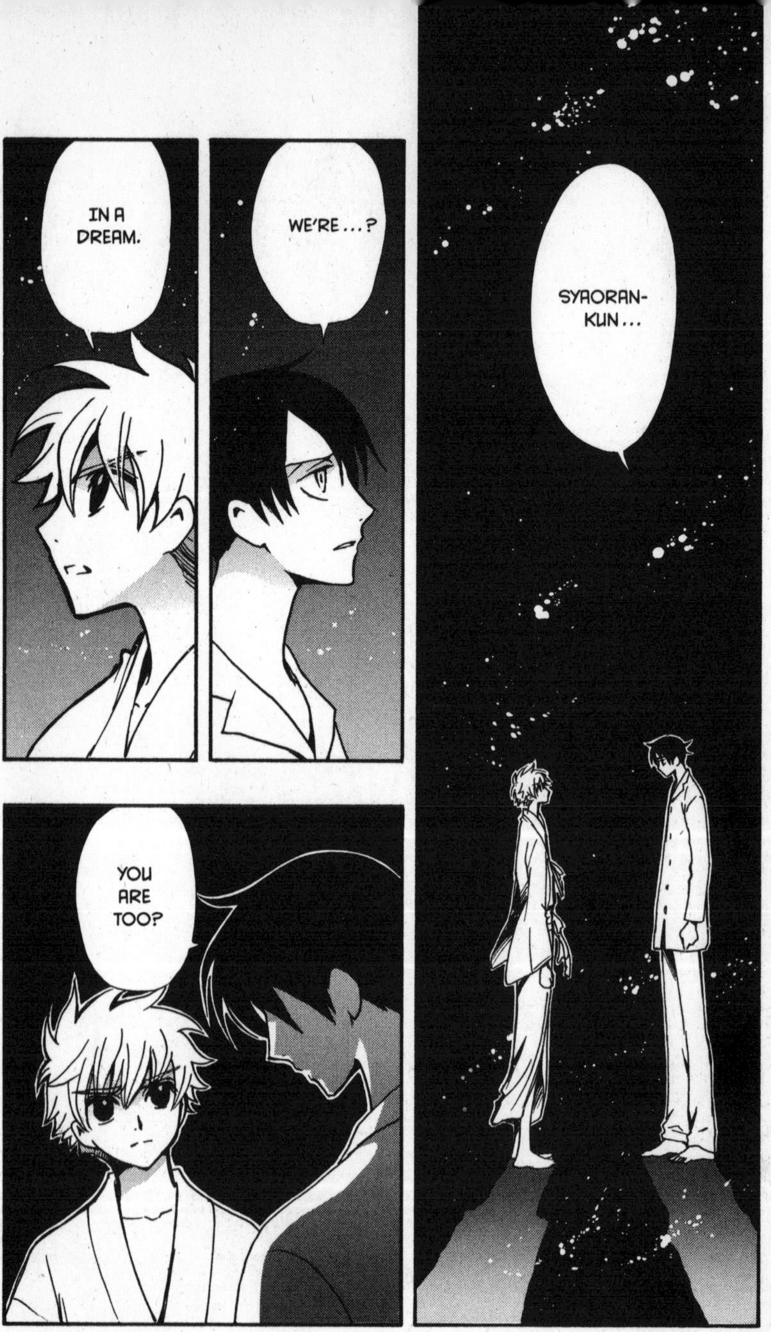
SYAORAN-KUN...
WE'RE...?
IN A DREAM.
YOU ARE TOO?

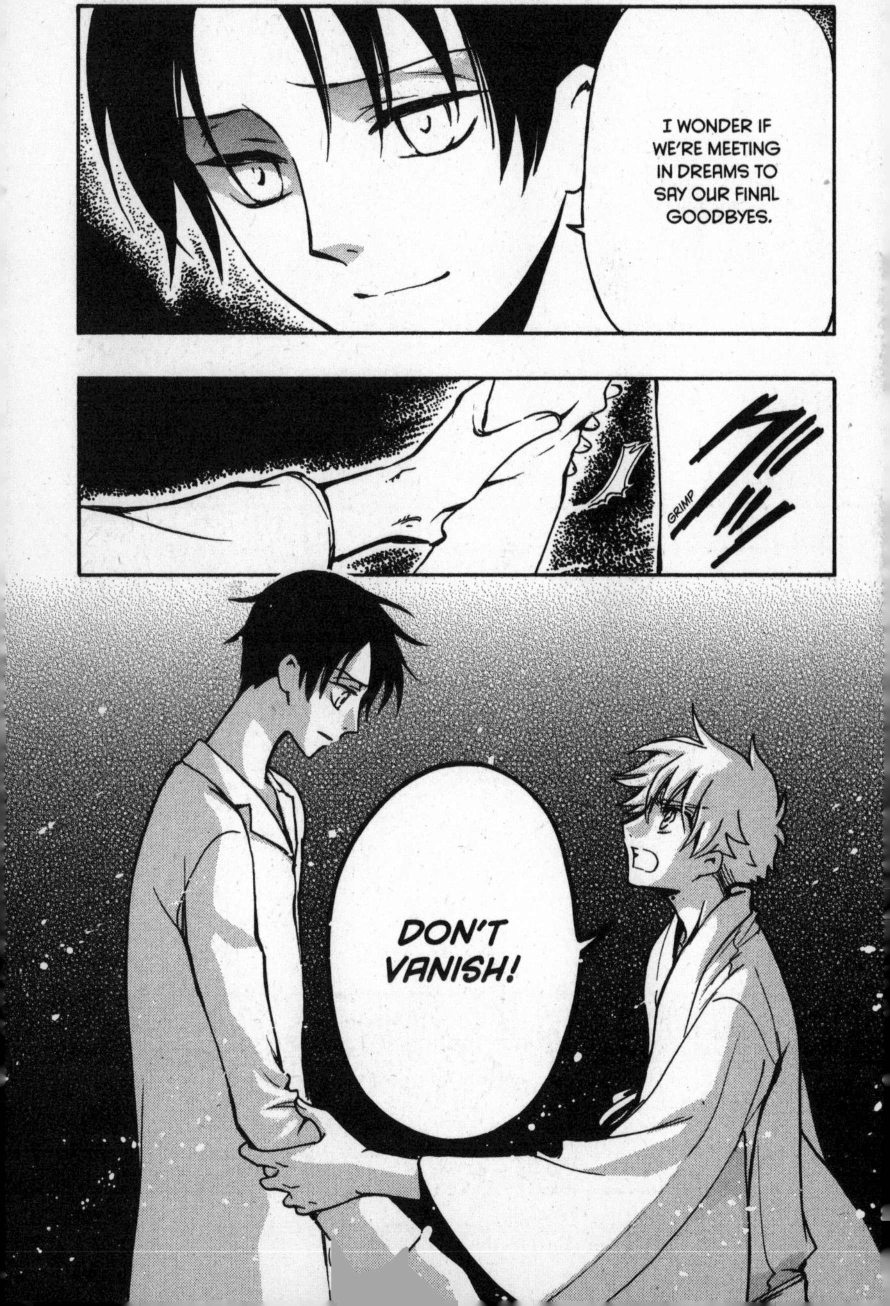
I WONDER IF WE'RE MEETING IN DREAMS TO SAY OUR FINAL GOODBYES.
GRIMP
DON'T VANISH!

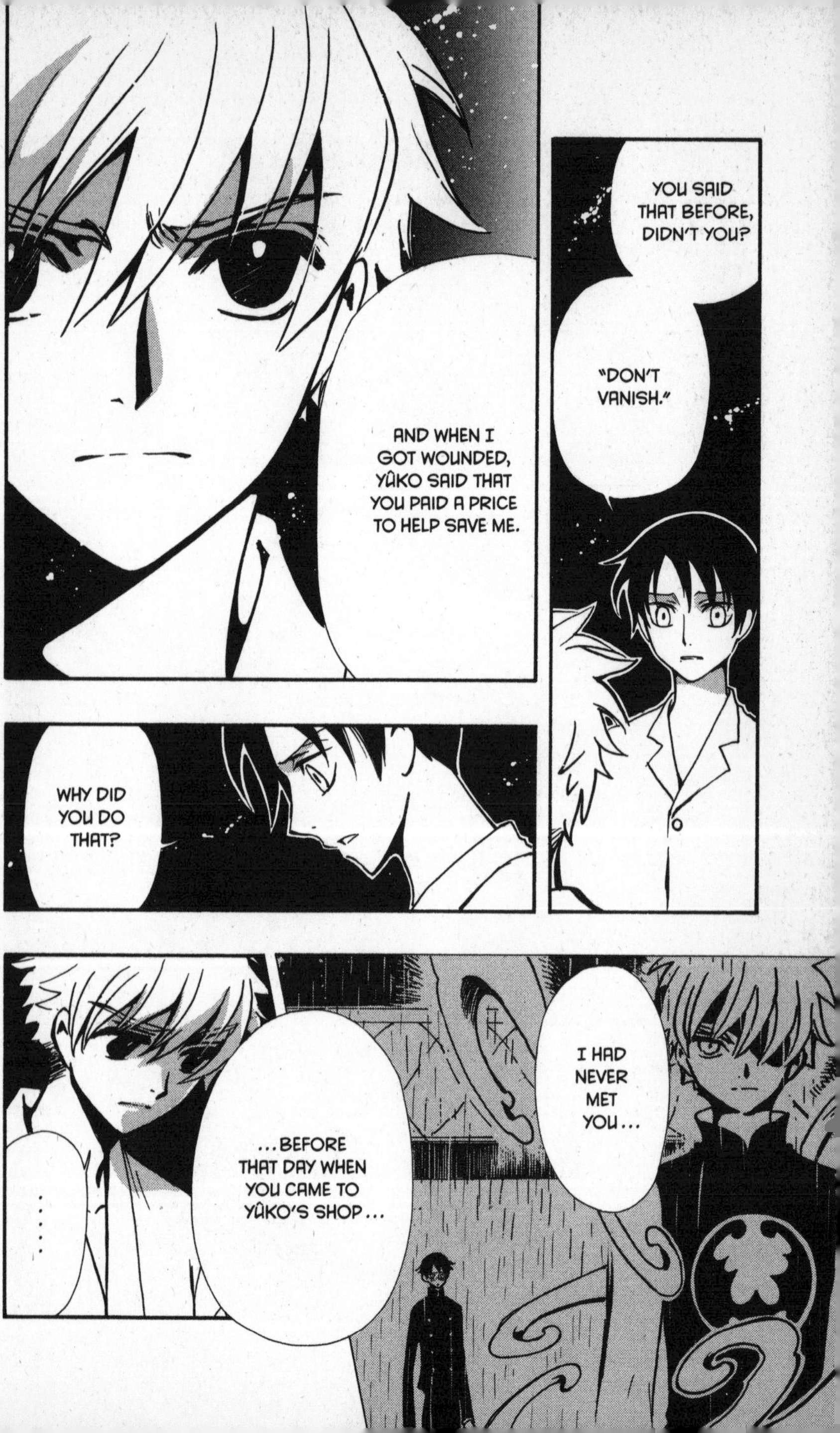
YOU SAID THAT BEFORE, DIDN'T YOU?
"DON'T VANISH."
AND WHEN I GOT WOUNDED, YÛKO SAID THAT YOU PAID A PRICE TO HELP SAVE ME.
WHY DID YOU DO THAT?
I HAD NEVER MET YOU...
...BEFORE THAT DAY WHEN YOU CAME TO YÛKO'S SHOP...
.....

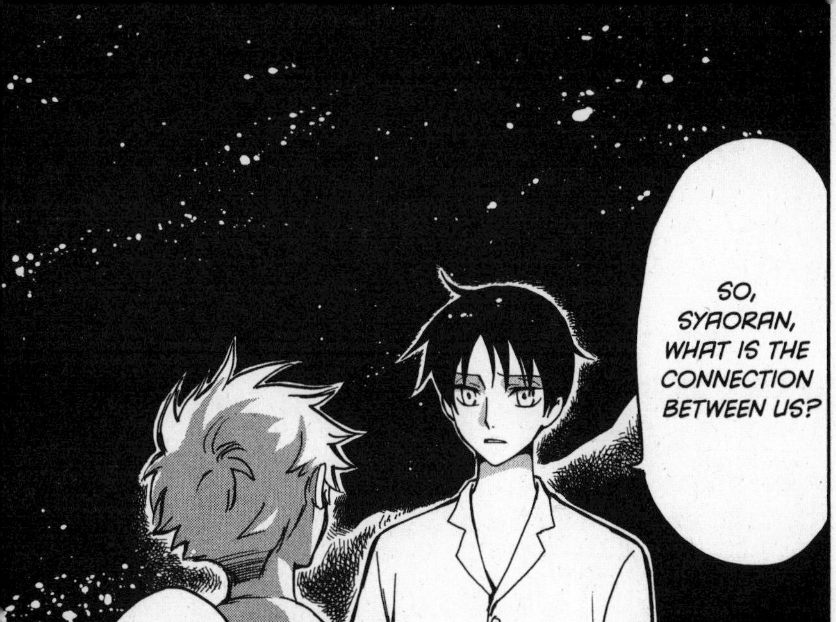
SO, SYAORAN, WHAT IS THE CONNECTION BETWEEN US?
DO YOU KNOW WHAT IT IS?

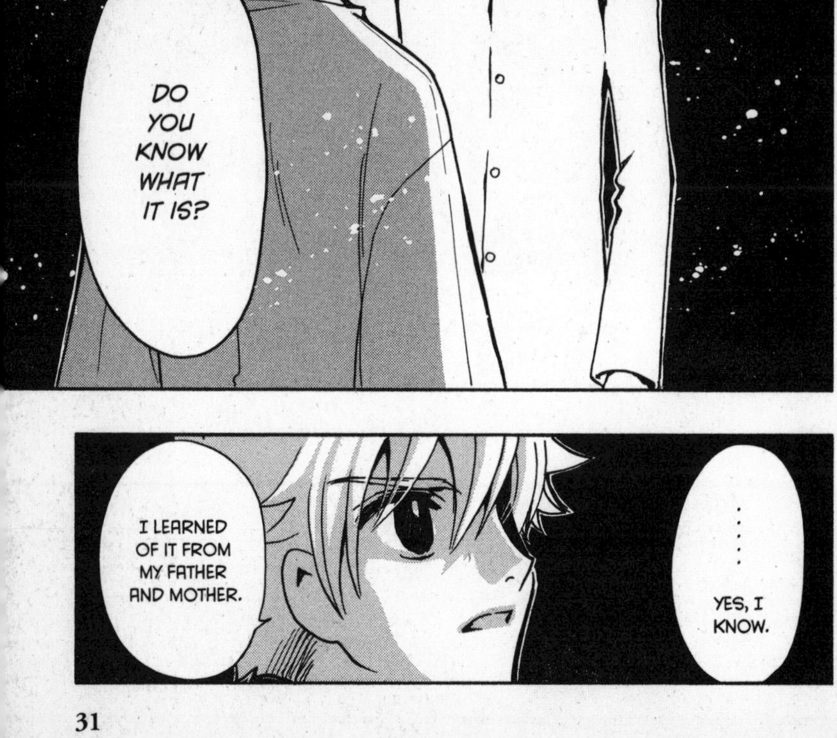
..... YES, I KNOW.
I LEARNED OF IT FROM MY FATHER AND MOTHER.

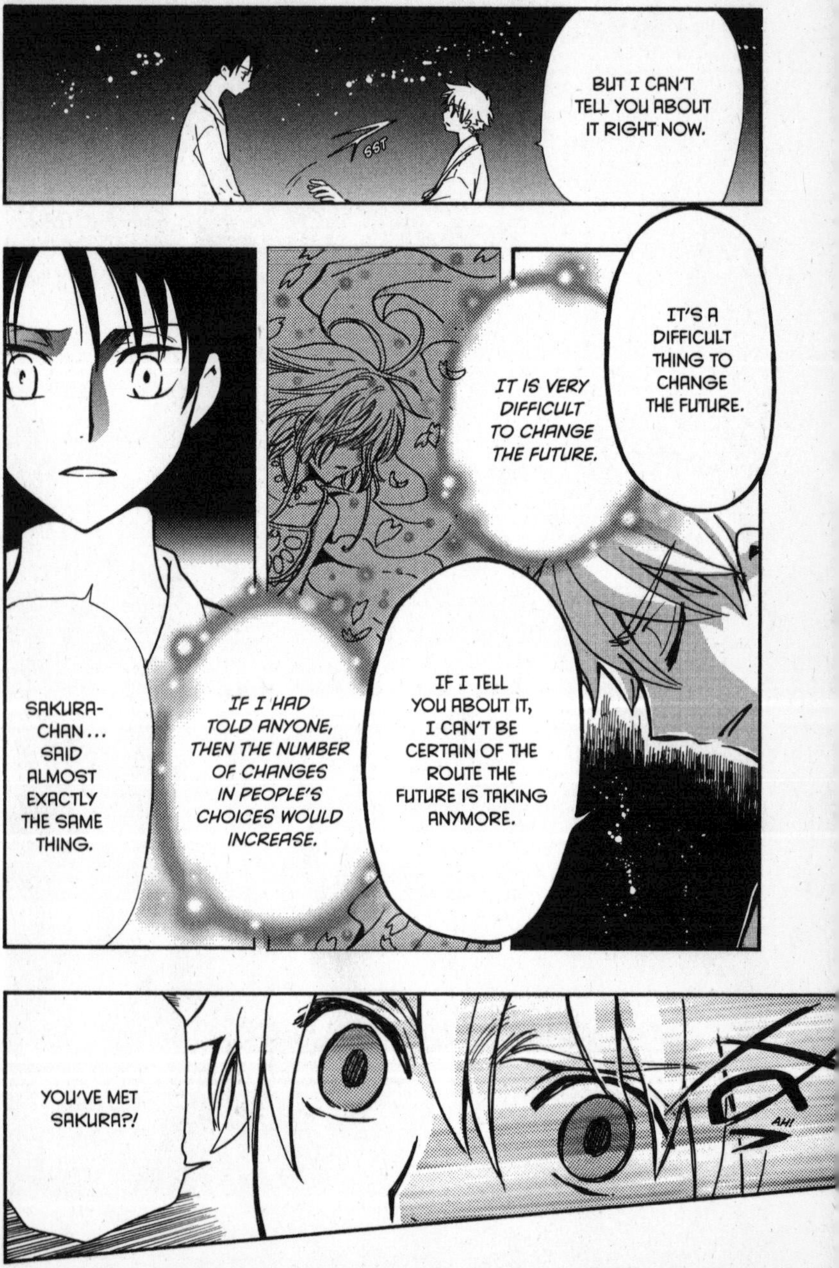
BUT I CAN'T TELL YOU ABOUT IT RIGHT NOW.
SST
IT'S A DIFFICULT THING TO CHANGE THE FUTURE.
IF I TELL YOU ABOUT IT, I CAN'T BE CERTAIN OF THE ROUTE THE FUTURE IS TAKING ANYMORE.
IT IS VERY DIFFICULT TO CHANGE THE FUTURE.
IF I HAD TOLD ANYONE, THEN THE NUMBER OF CHANGES IN PEOPLE'S CHOICES WOULD INCREASE.
SAKURA-CHAN... SAID ALMOST EXACTLY THE SAME THING.
AH!
YOU'VE MET SAKURA?!

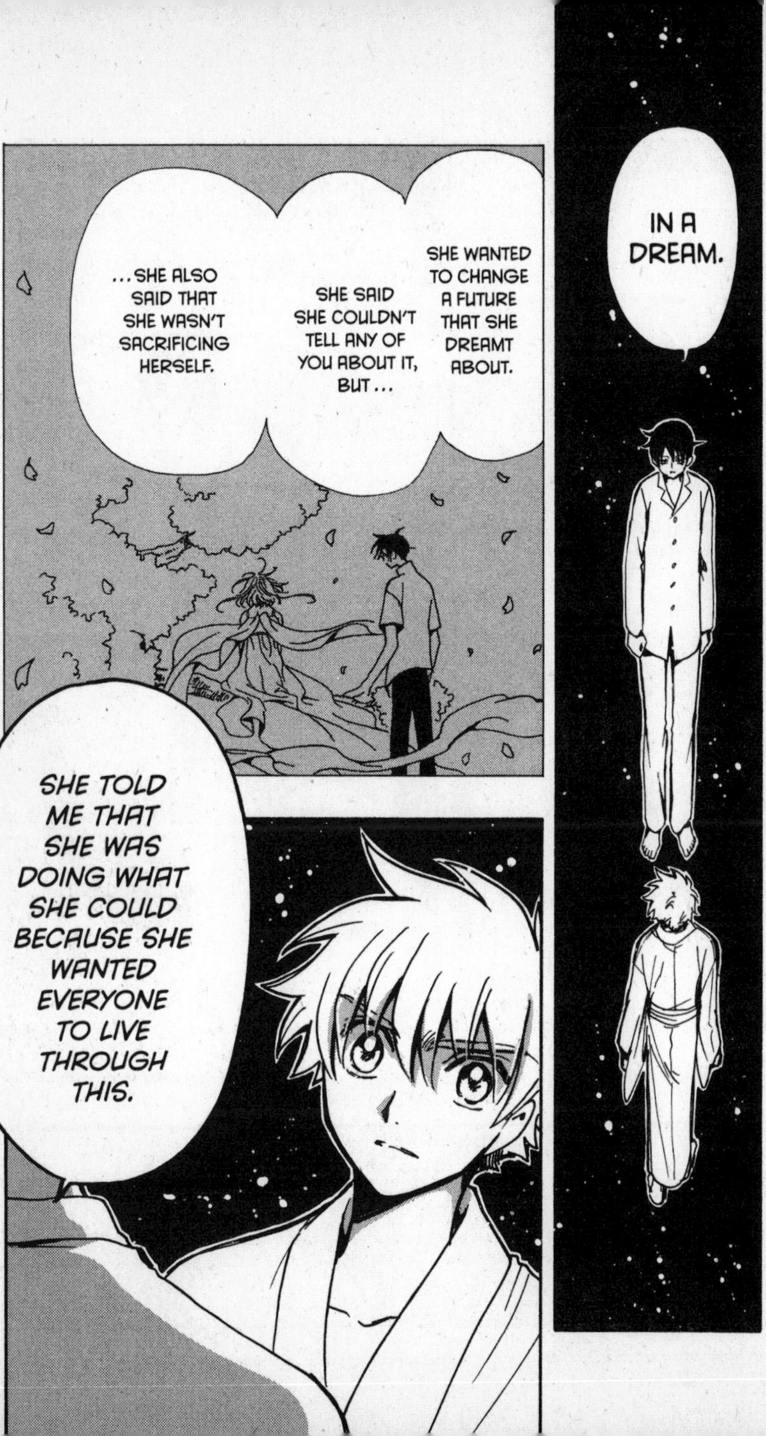
IN A DREAM.
SHE WANTED TO CHANGE A FUTURE THAT SHE DREAMT ABOUT.
SHE SAID SHE COULDN'T TELL ANY OF YOU ABOUT IT, BUT...
...SHE ALSO SAID THAT SHE WASN'T SACRIFICING HERSELF.
SHE TOLD ME THAT SHE WAS DOING WHAT SHE COULD BECAUSE SHE WANTED EVERYONE TO LIVE THROUGH THIS.

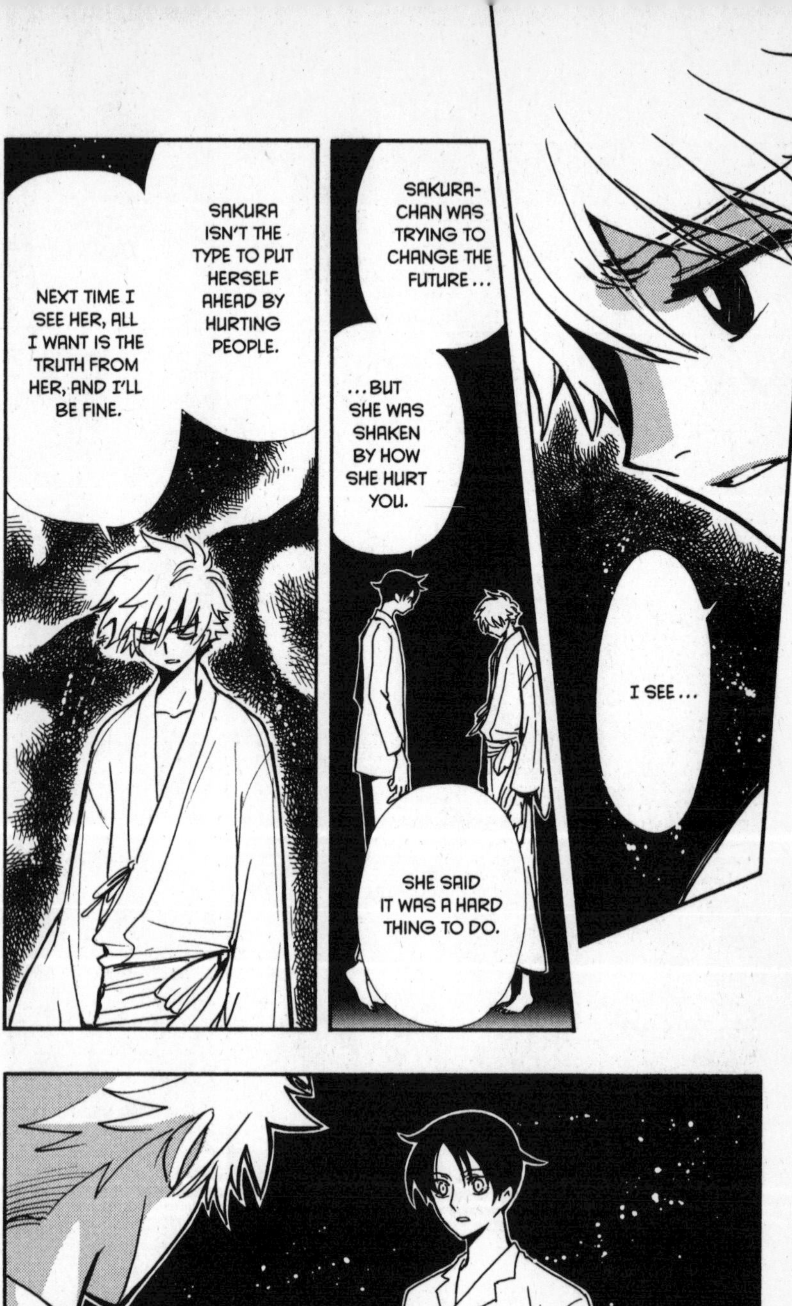
I SEE...
SAKURA-CHAN WAS TRYING TO CHANGE THE FUTURE...
...BUT SHE WAS SHAKEN BY HOW SHE HURT YOU.
SHE SAID IT WAS A HARD THING TO DO.
SAKURA ISN'T THE TYPE TO PUT HERSELF AHEAD BY HURTING PEOPLE.
NEXT TIME I SEE HER, ALL I WANT IS THE TRUTH FROM HER, AND I'LL BE FINE.

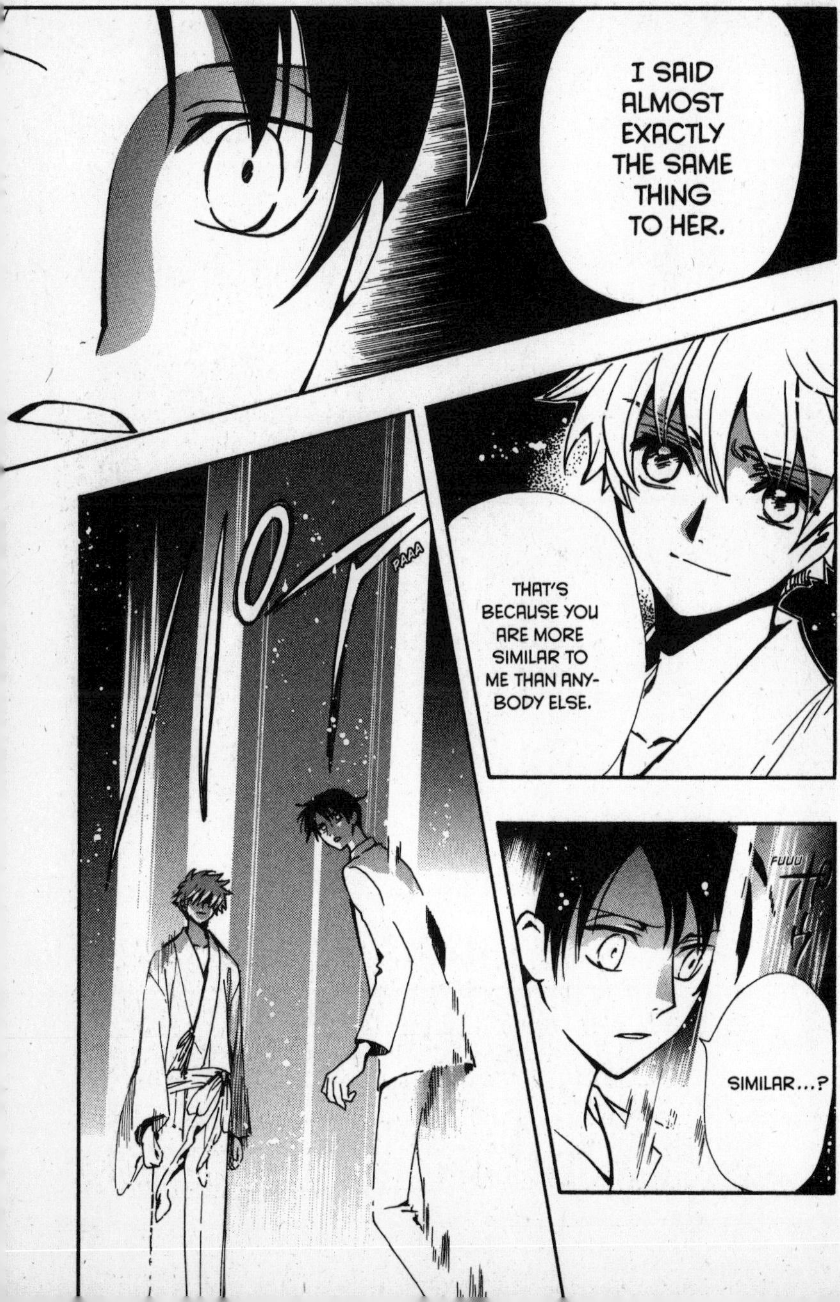
I SAID ALMOST EXACTLY THE SAME THING TO HER.
THAT'S BECAUSE YOU ARE MORE SIMILAR TO ME THAN ANY-BODY ELSE.
FUUU
SIMILAR...?
PAAA

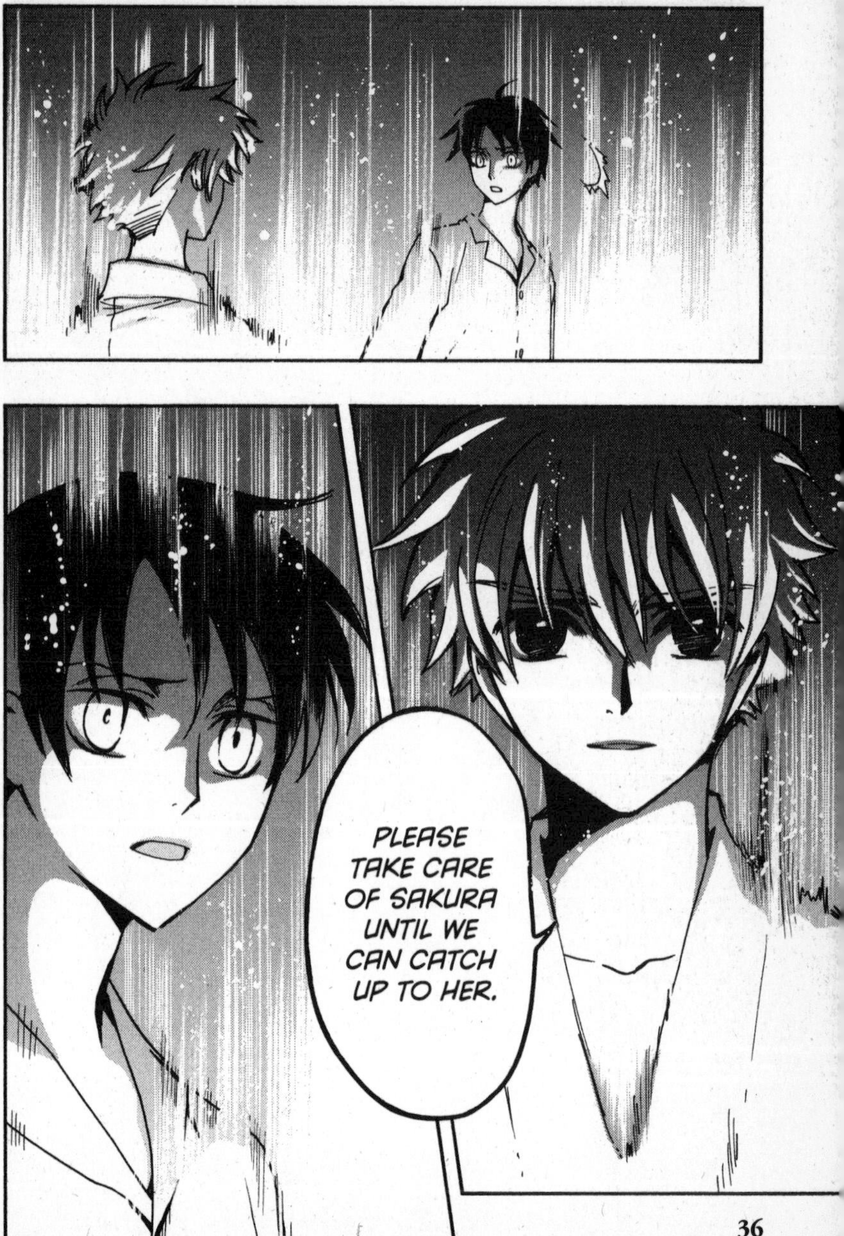
PLEASE TAKE CARE OF SAKURA UNTIL WE CAN CATCH UP TO HER.

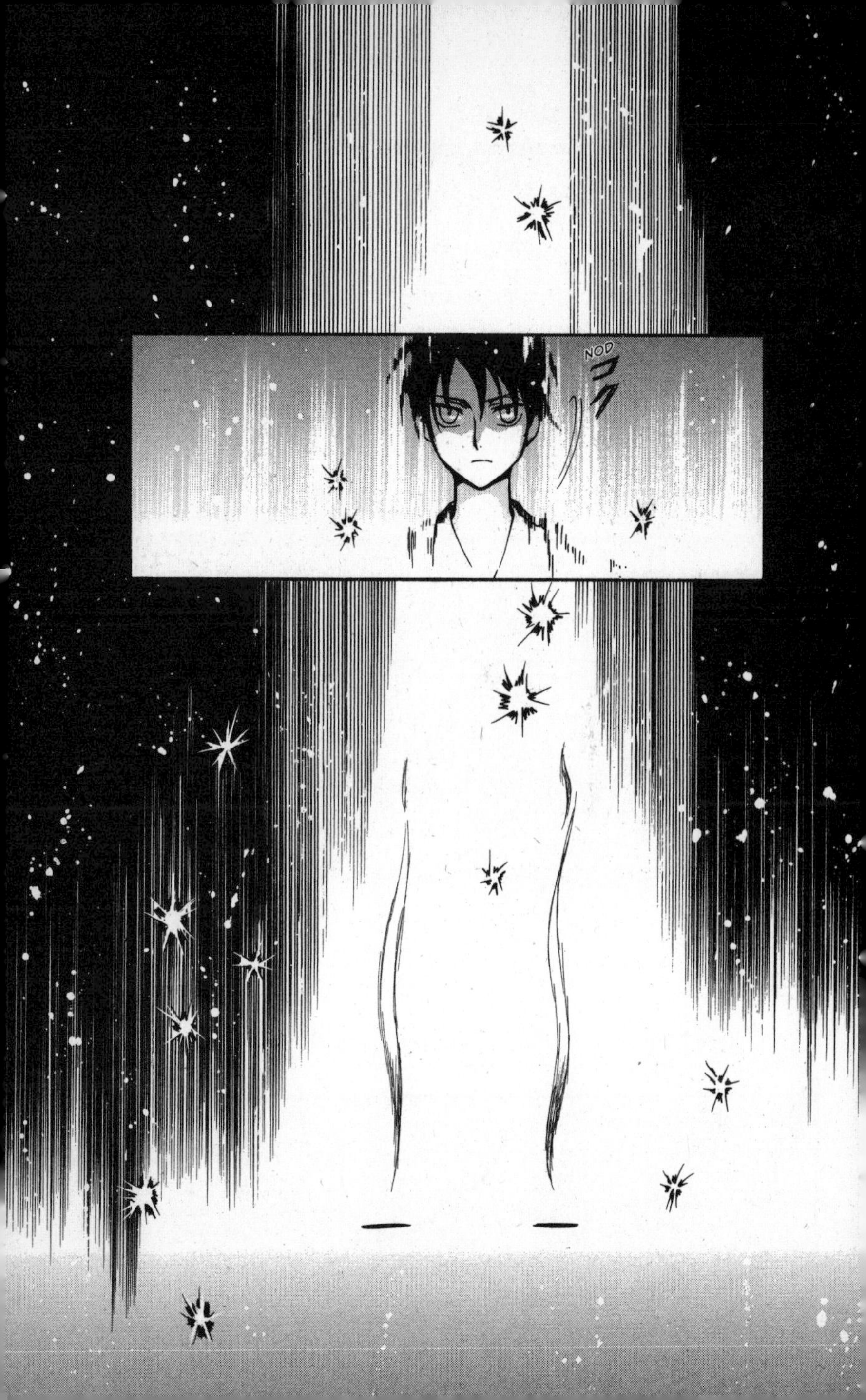
NOD
コク
...

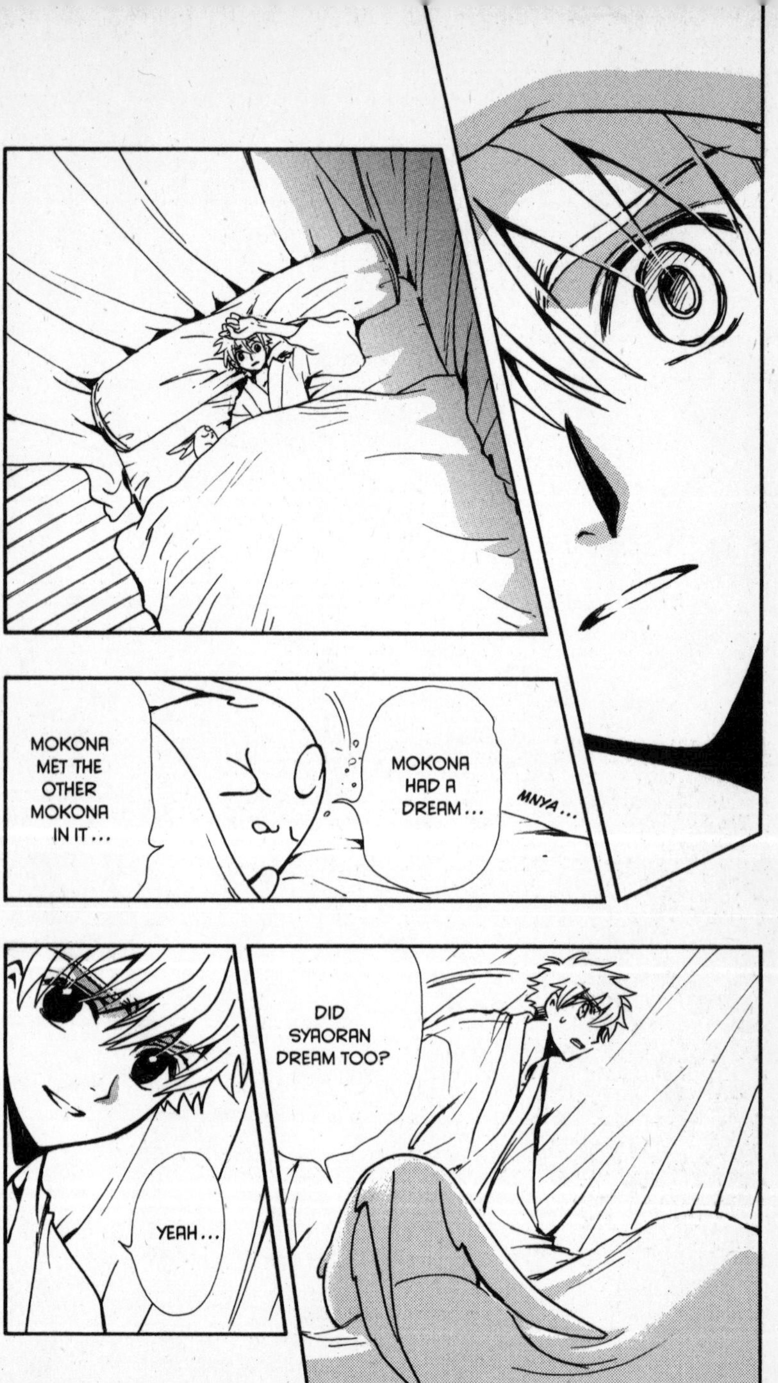
MNYA...
MOKONA HAD A DREAM...
MOKONA MET THE OTHER MOKONA IN IT...
DID SYAORAN DREAM TOO?
YEAH...

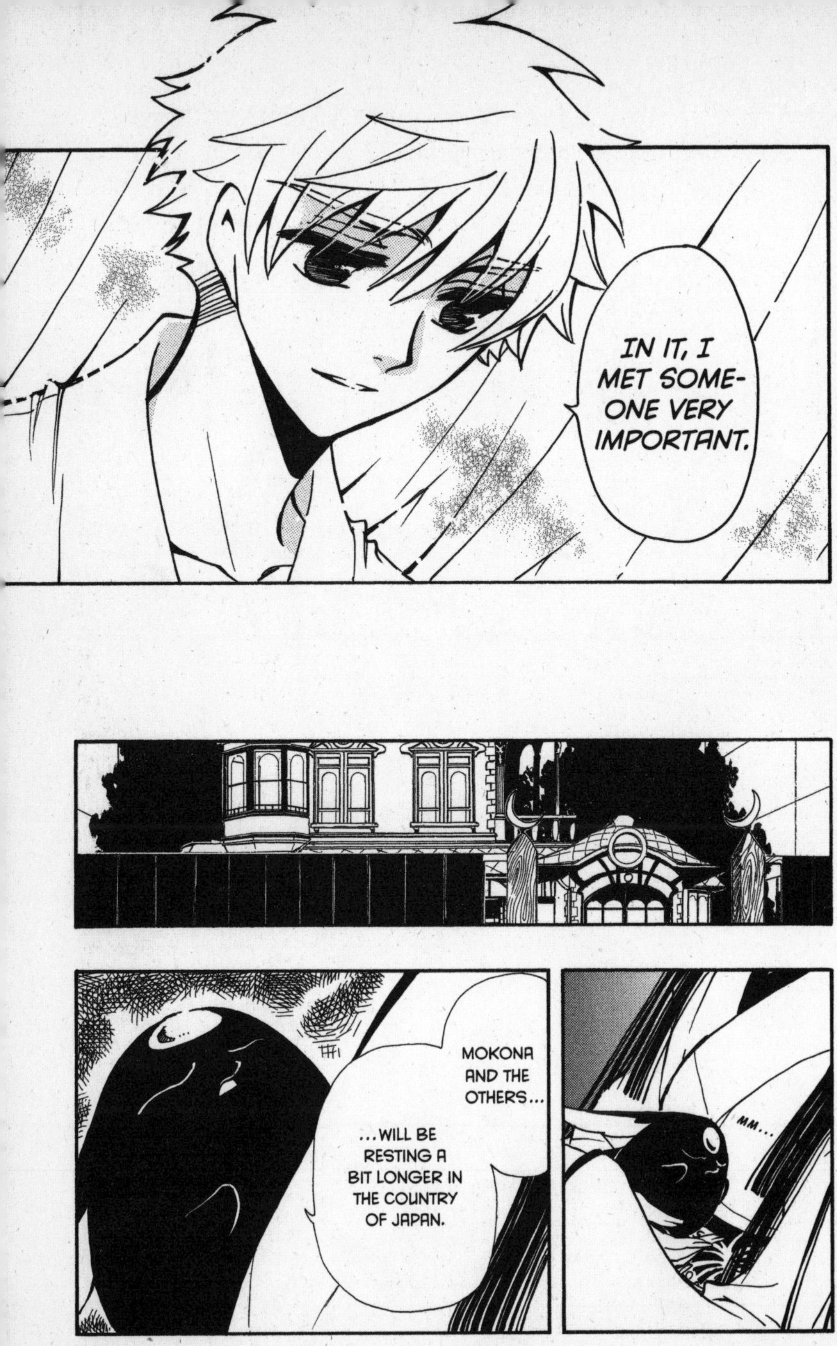
IN IT, I MET SOME-ONE VERY IMPORTANT.
MM...
MOKONA AND THE OTHERS...
...WILL BE RESTING A BIT LONGER IN THE COUNTRY OF JAPAN.

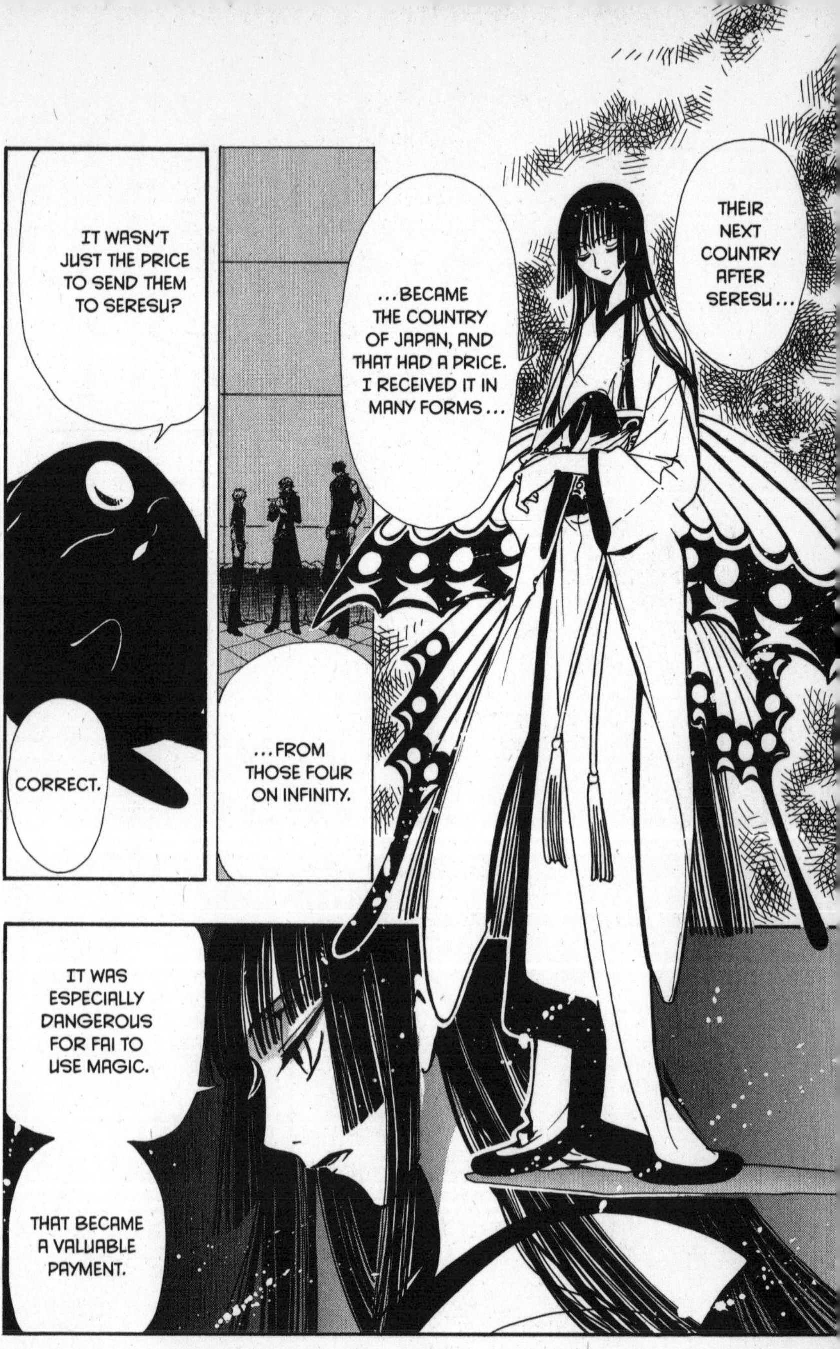
THEIR NEXT COUNTRY AFTER SERESU...
...BECAME THE COUNTRY OF JAPAN, AND THAT HAD A PRICE. I RECEIVED IT IN MANY FORMS...
...FROM THOSE FOUR ON INFINITY.
IT WASN'T JUST THE PRICE TO SEND THEM TO SERESU?
CORRECT.
IT WAS ESPECIALLY DANGEROUS FOR FAI TO USE MAGIC.
THAT BECAME A VALUABLE PAYMENT.

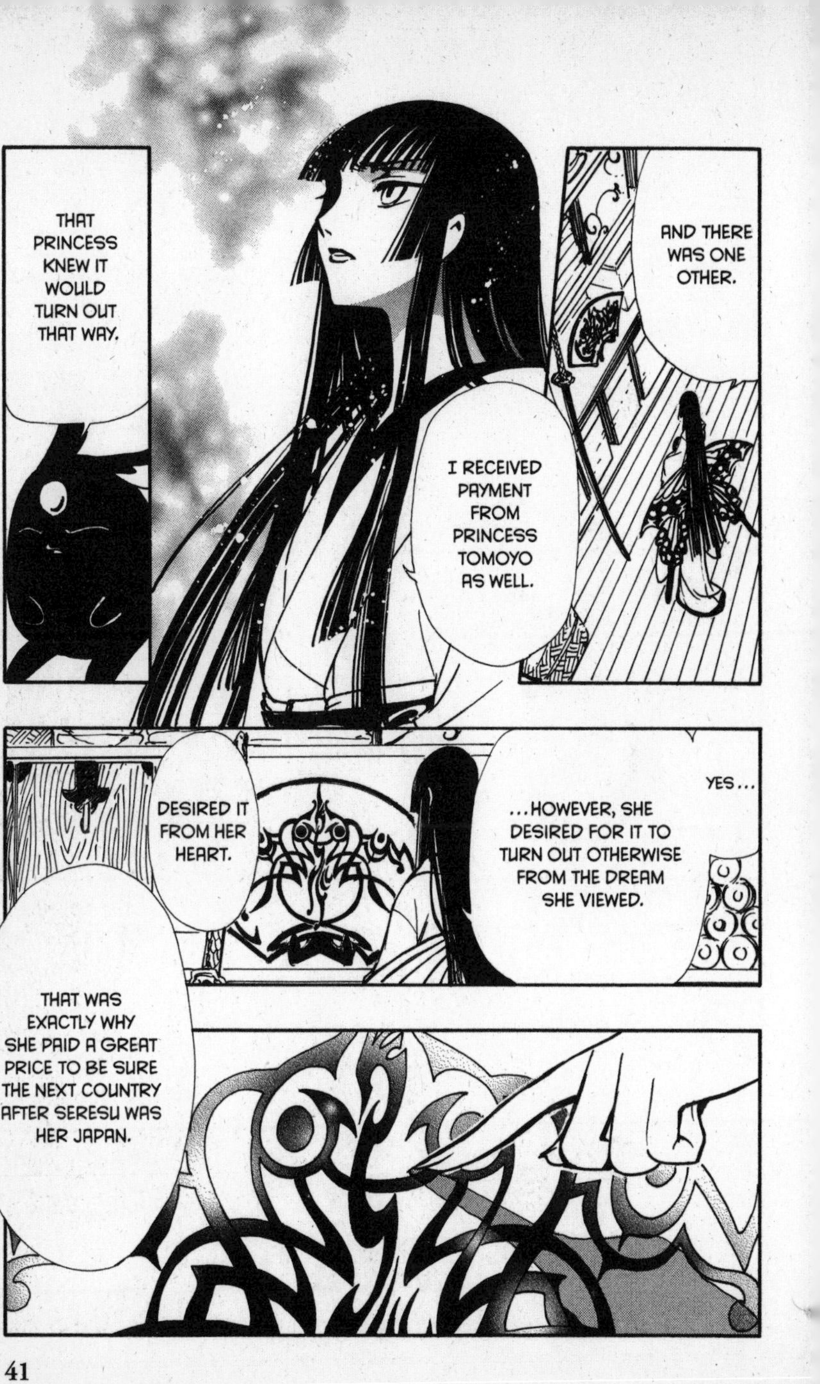
AND THERE WAS ONE OTHER.
I RECEIVED PAYMENT FROM PRINCESS TOMOYO AS WELL.
THAT PRINCESS KNEW IT WOULD TURN OUT THAT WAY.
YES...
...HOWEVER, SHE DESIRED FOR IT TO TURN OUT OTHERWISE FROM THE DREAM SHE VIEWED.
DESIRED IT FROM HER HEART.
THAT WAS EXACTLY WHY SHE PAID A GREAT PRICE TO BE SURE THE NEXT COUNTRY AFTER SERESU WAS HER JAPAN.

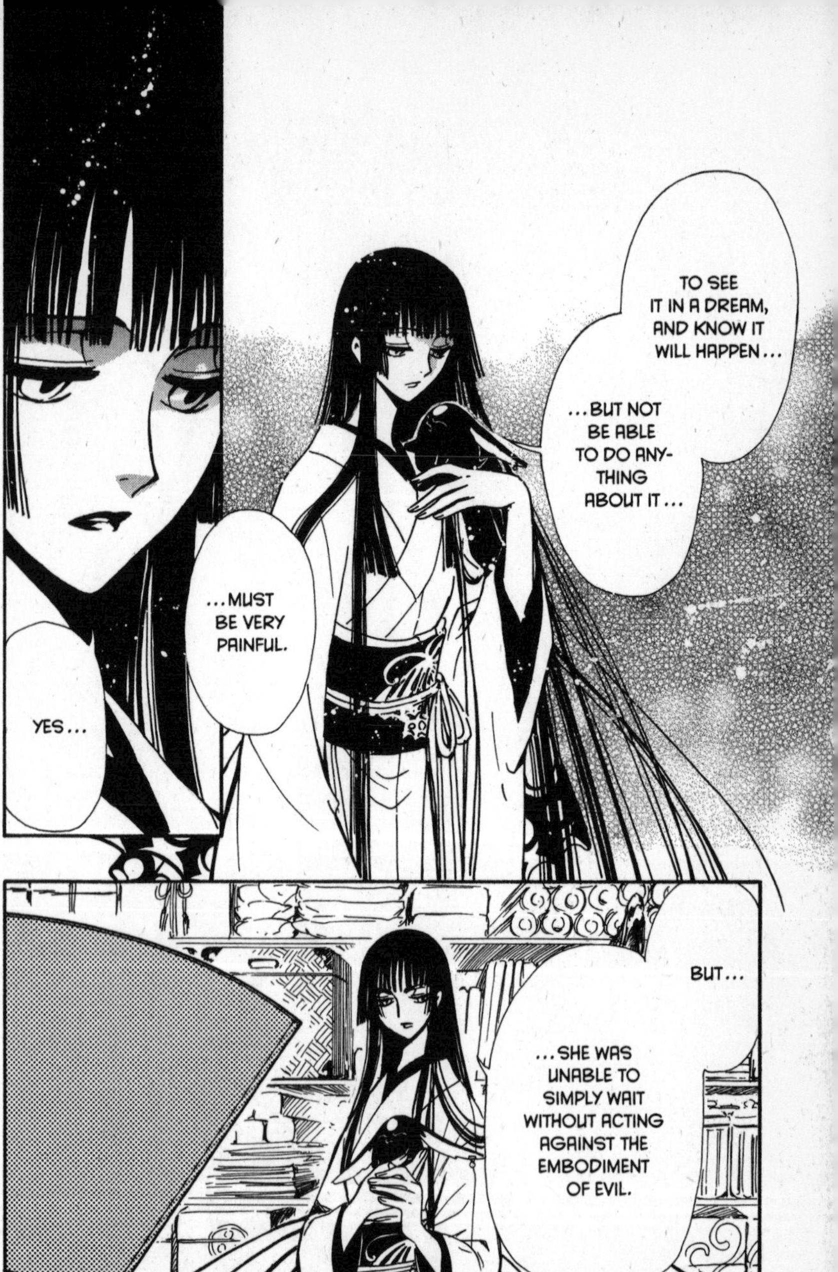
TO SEE IT IN A DREAM, AND KNOW IT WILL HAPPEN...
...BUT NOT BE ABLE TO DO ANY-THING ABOUT IT...
...MUST BE VERY PAINFUL.
YES...
BUT...
...SHE WAS UNABLE TO SIMPLY WAIT WITHOUT ACTING AGAINST THE EMBODIMENT OF EVIL.

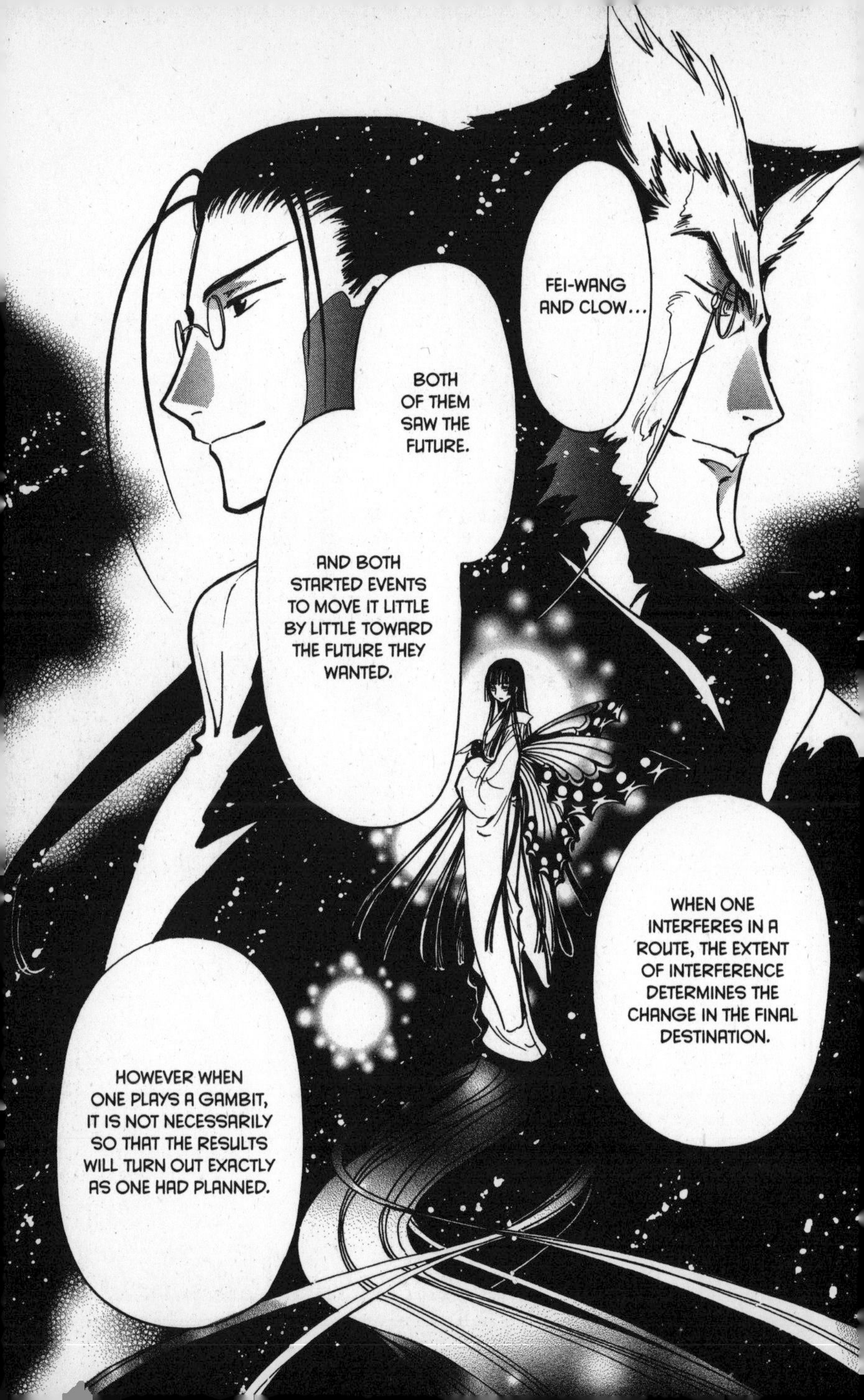
FEI-WANG AND CLOW...
BOTH OF THEM SAW THE FUTURE.
AND BOTH STARTED EVENTS TO MOVE IT LITTLE BY LITTLE TOWARD THE FUTURE THEY WANTED.
WHEN ONE INTERFERES IN A ROUTE, THE EXTENT OF INTERFERENCE DETERMINES THE CHANGE IN THE FINAL DESTINATION.
HOWEVER WHEN ONE PLAYS A GAMBIT, IT IS NOT NECESSARILY SO THAT THE RESULTS WILL TURN OUT EXACTLY AS ONE HAD PLANNED.

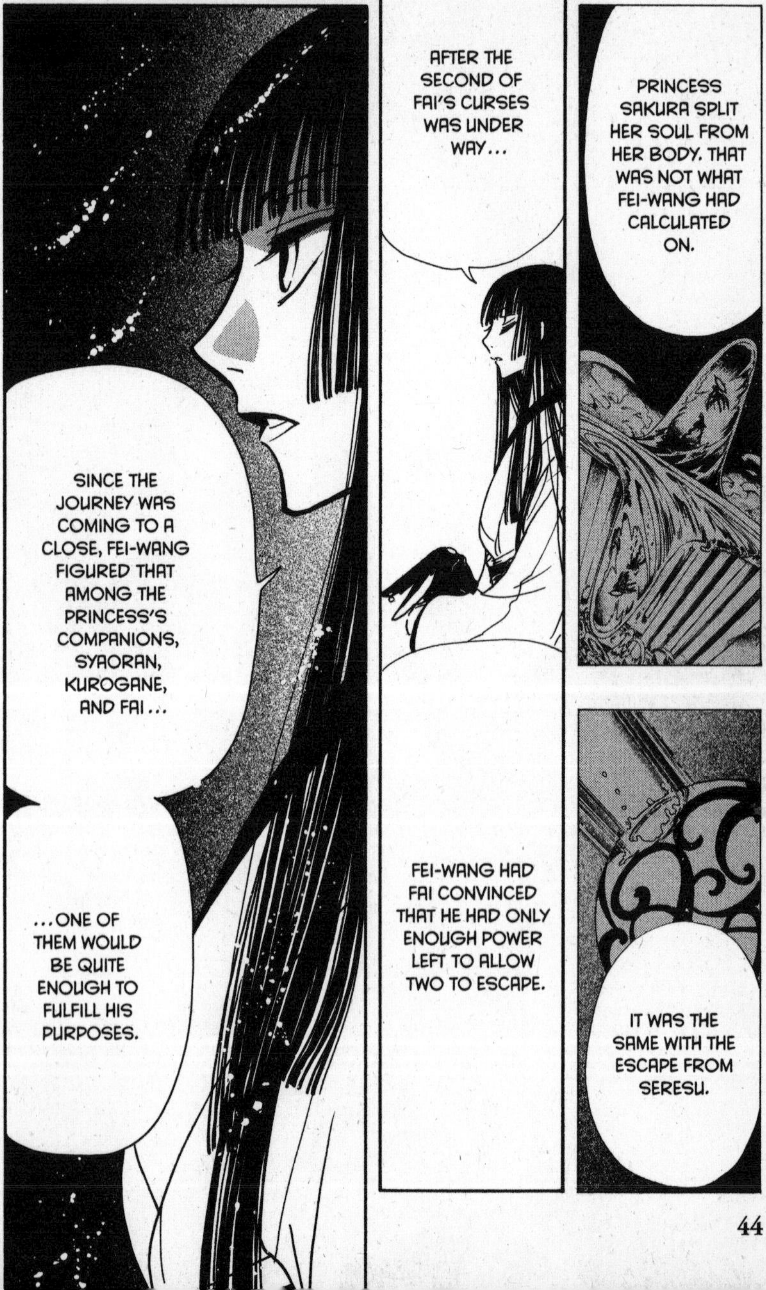
PRINCESS SAKURA SPLIT HER SOUL FROM HER BODY. THAT WAS NOT WHAT FEI-WANG HAD CALCULATED ON.
IT WAS THE SAME WITH THE ESCAPE FROM SERESU.
AFTER THE SECOND OF FAI'S CURSES WAS UNDER WAY...
FEI-WANG HAD FAI CONVINCED THAT HE HAD ONLY ENOUGH POWER LEFT TO ALLOW TWO TO ESCAPE.
SINCE THE JOURNEY WAS COMING TO A CLOSE, FEI-WANG FIGURED THAT AMONG THE PRINCESS'S COMPANIONS, SYAORAN, KUROGANE, AND FAI...
...ONE OF THEM WOULD BE QUITE ENOUGH TO FULFILL HIS PURPOSES.

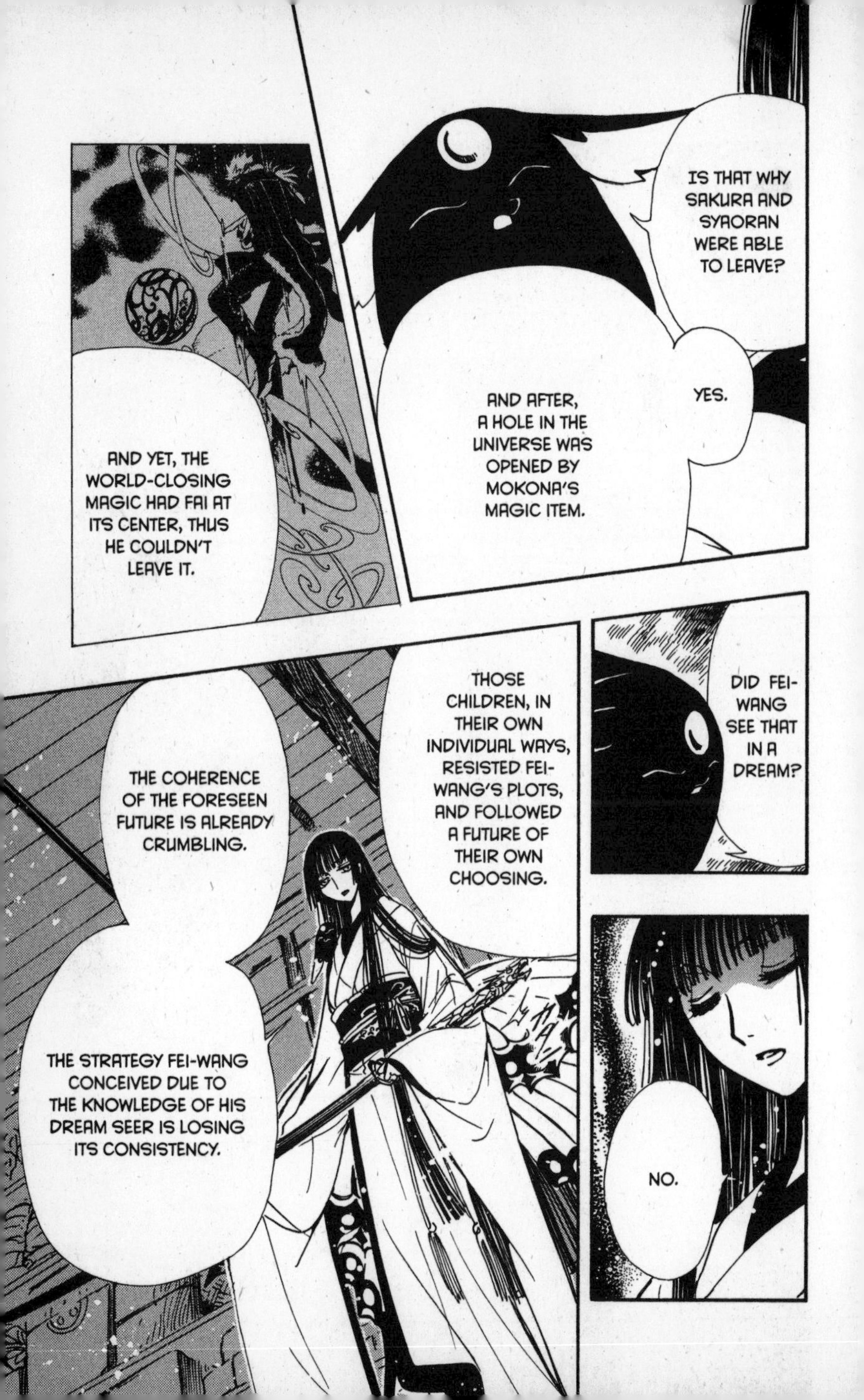
IS THAT WHY SAKURA AND SYAORAN WERE ABLE TO LEAVE?
YES.
AND AFTER, A HOLE IN THE UNIVERSE WAS OPENED BY MOKONA'S MAGIC ITEM.
AND YET, THE WORLD-CLOSING MAGIC HAD FAI AT ITS CENTER, THUS HE COULDN'T LEAVE IT.
DID FEI-WANG SEE THAT IN A DREAM?
NO.
THOSE CHILDREN, IN THEIR OWN INDIVIDUAL WAYS, RESISTED FEI-WANG'S PLOTS, AND FOLLOWED A FUTURE OF THEIR OWN CHOOSING.
THE COHERENCE OF THE FORESEEN FUTURE IS ALREADY CRUMBLING.
THE STRATEGY FEI-WANG CONCEIVED DUE TO THE KNOWLEDGE OF HIS DREAM SEER IS LOSING ITS CONSISTENCY.

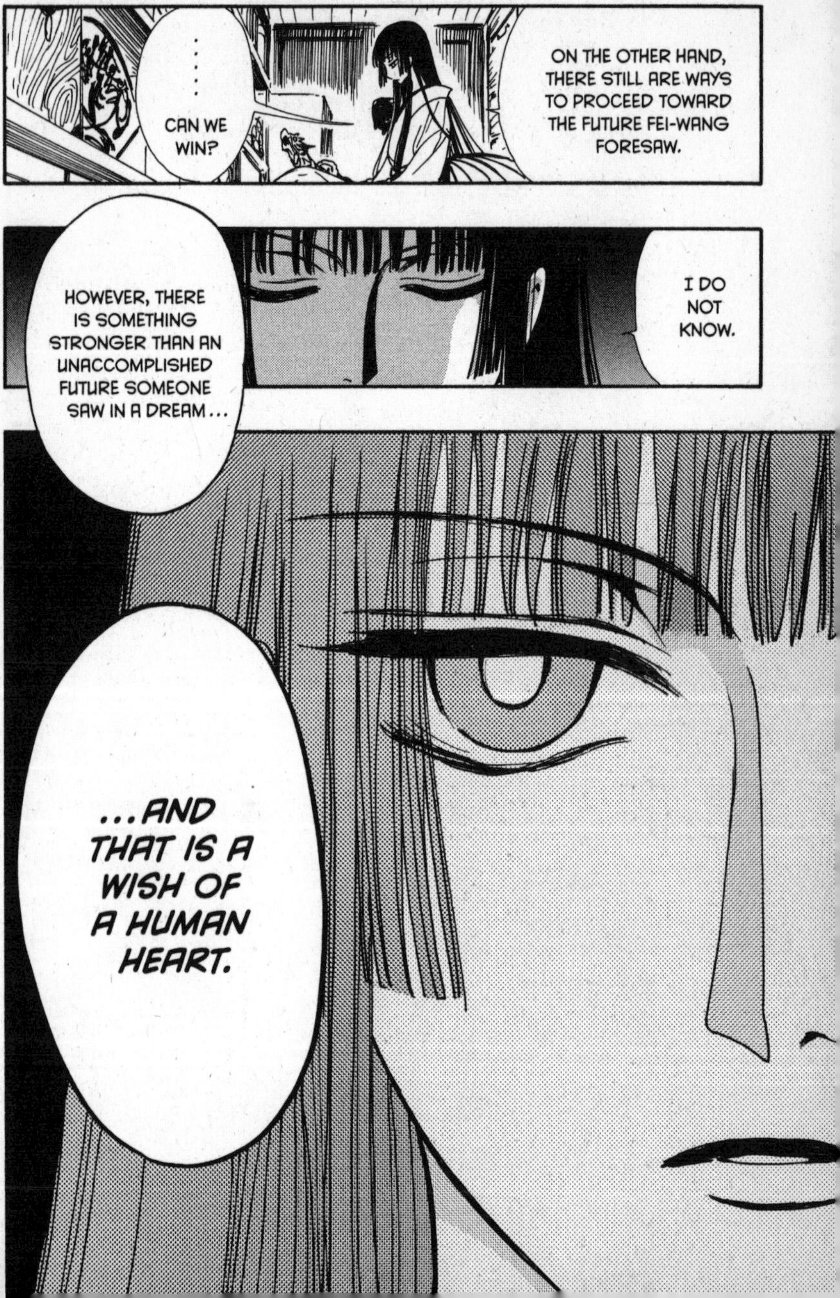
ON THE OTHER HAND, THERE STILL ARE WAYS TO PROCEED TOWARD THE FUTURE FEI-WANG FORESAW.
.... CAN WE WIN?
I DO NOT KNOW.
HOWEVER, THERE IS SOMETHING STRONGER THAN AN UNACCOMPLISHED FUTURE SOMEONE SAW IN A DREAM...
...AND THAT IS A WISH OF A HUMAN HEART.

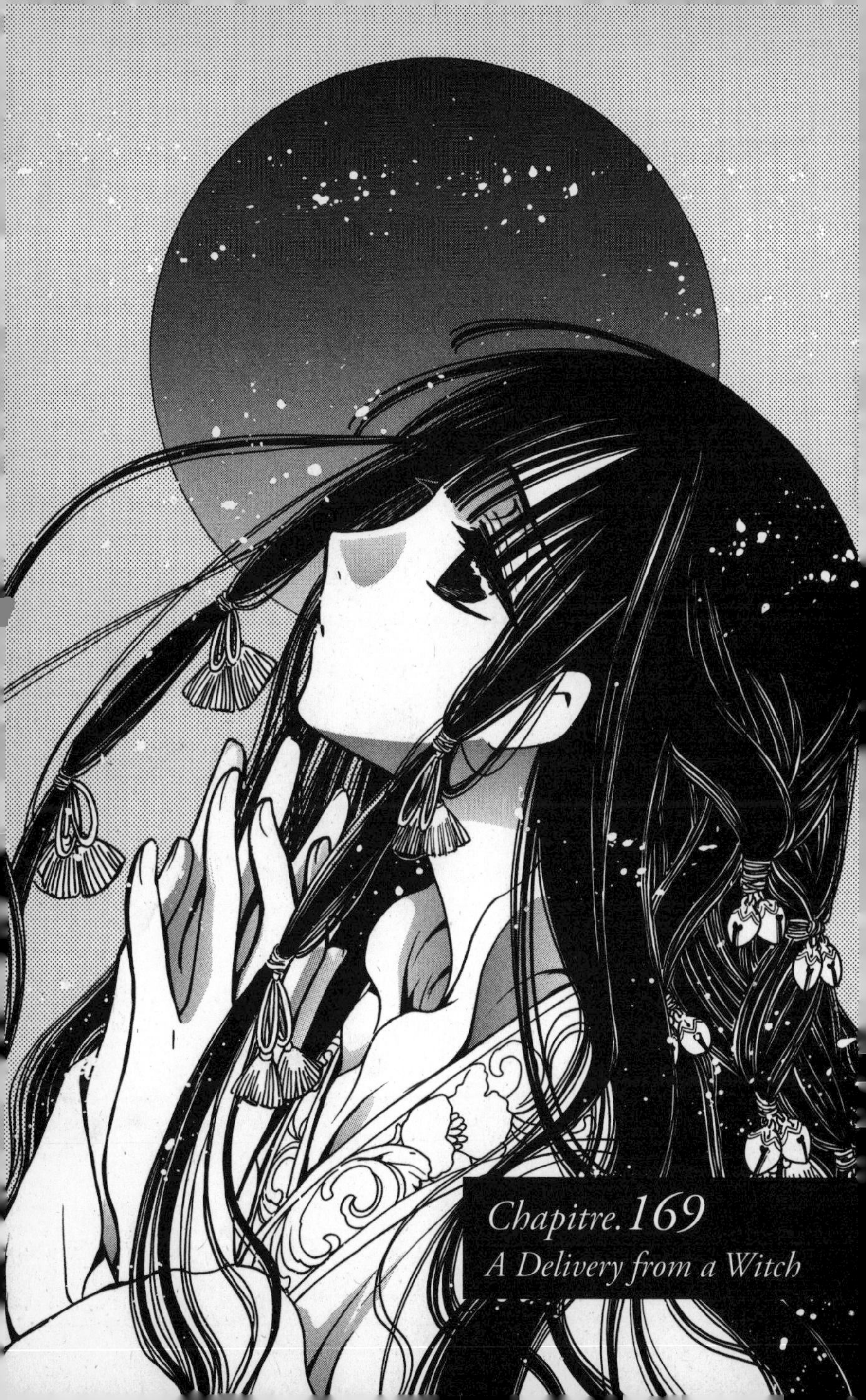
Chapitre. 169
A Delivery from a Witch

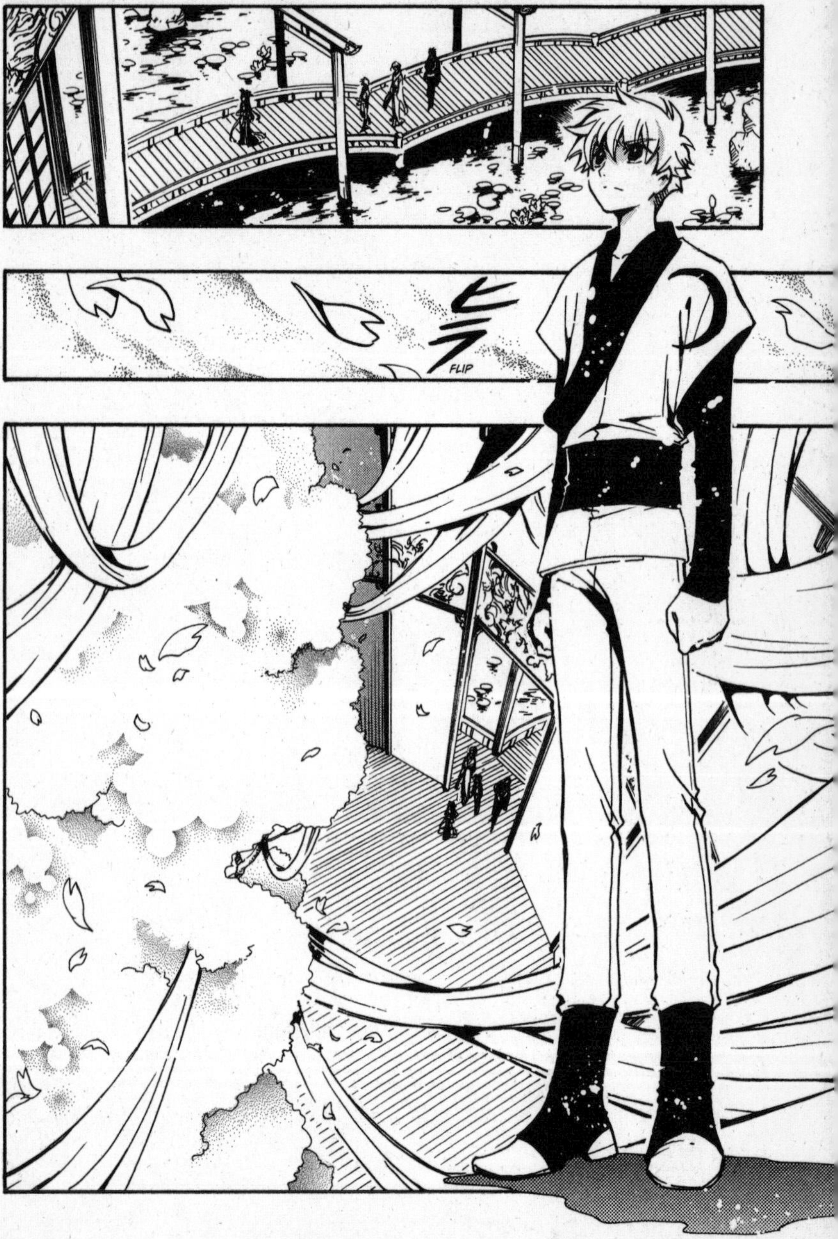
ヒラ
FLIP

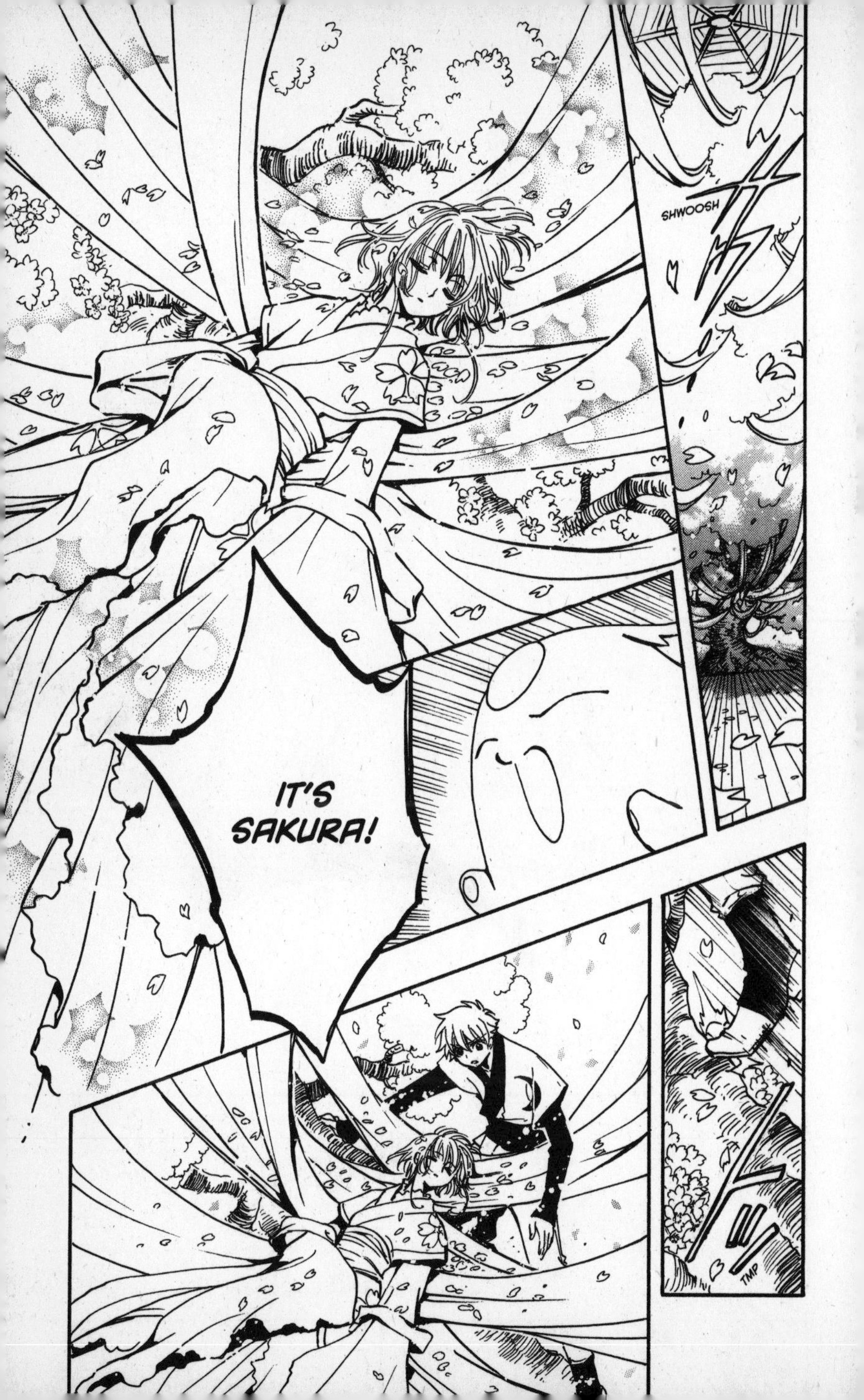
SHWOOSH
IT'S SAKURA!
TMP

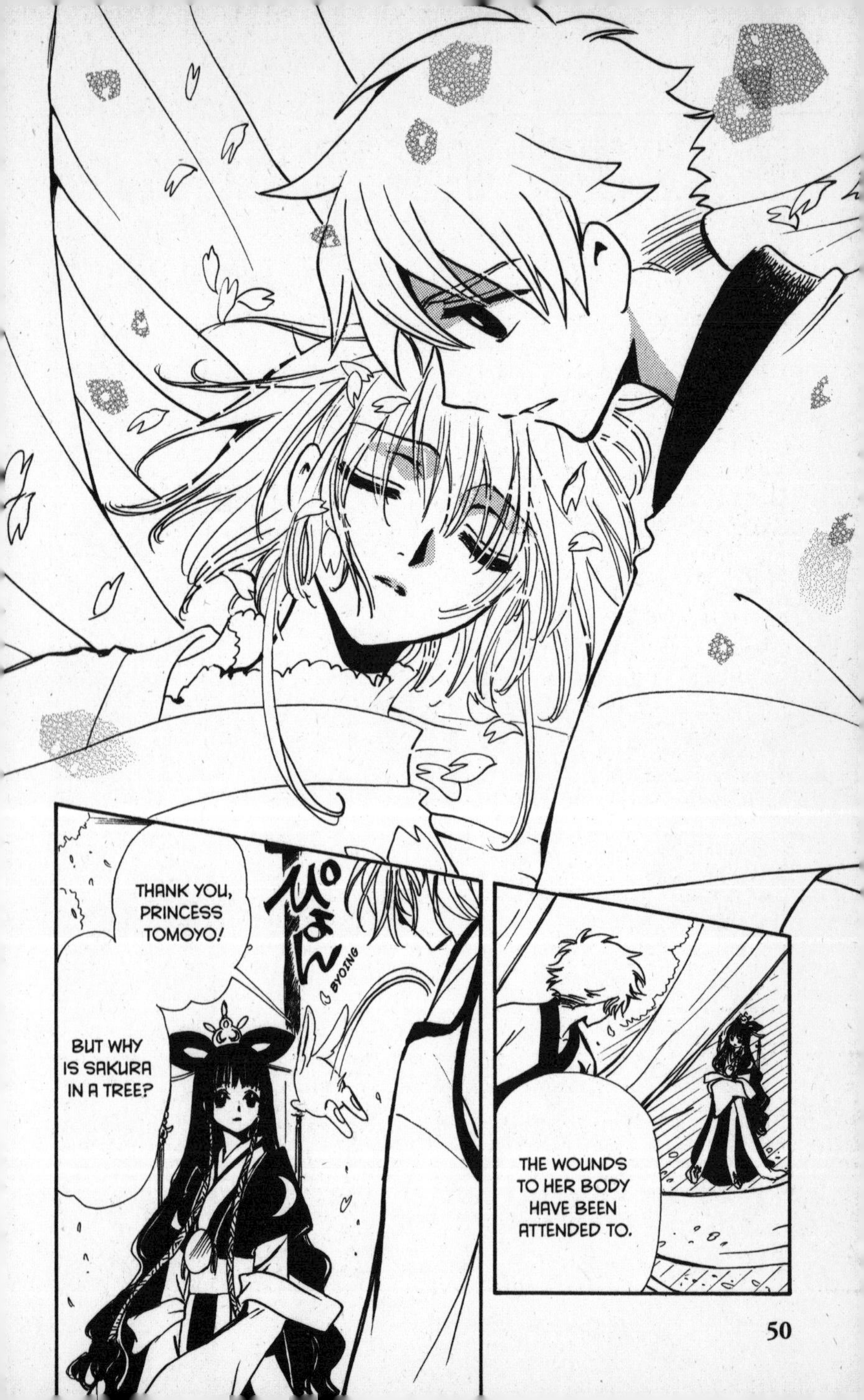
THE WOUNDS TO HER BODY HAVE BEEN ATTENDED TO.
ぴょん
BYOING
THANK YOU, PRINCESS TOMOYO!
BUT WHY IS SAKURA IN A TREE?

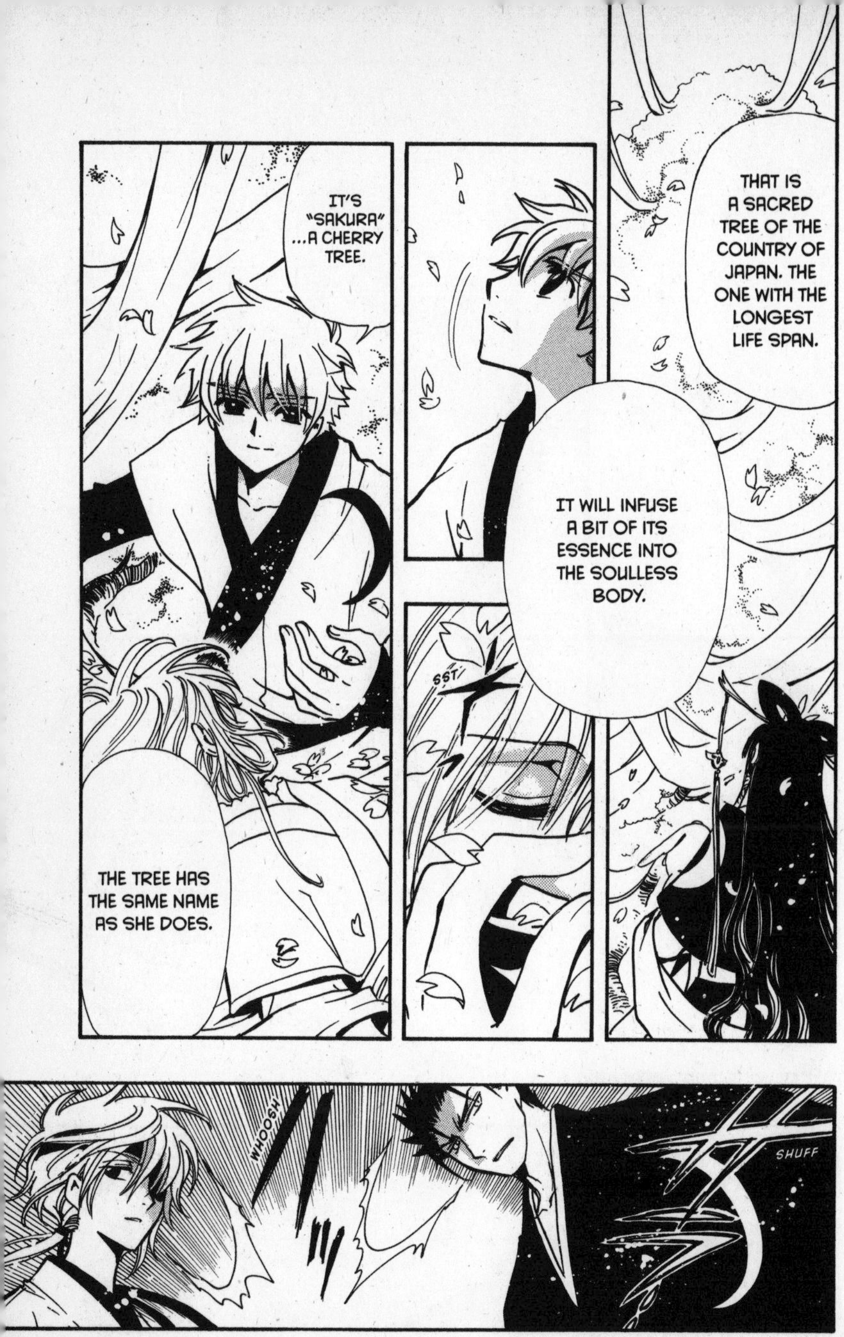
THAT IS A SACRED TREE OF THE COUNTRY OF JAPAN. THE ONE WITH THE LONGEST LIFE SPAN.
IT WILL INFUSE A BIT OF ITS ESSENCE INTO THE SOULLESS BODY.
SST
IT'S "SAKURA" ...A CHERRY TREE.
THE TREE HAS THE SAME NAME AS SHE DOES.
SHUFF
WHOOSH

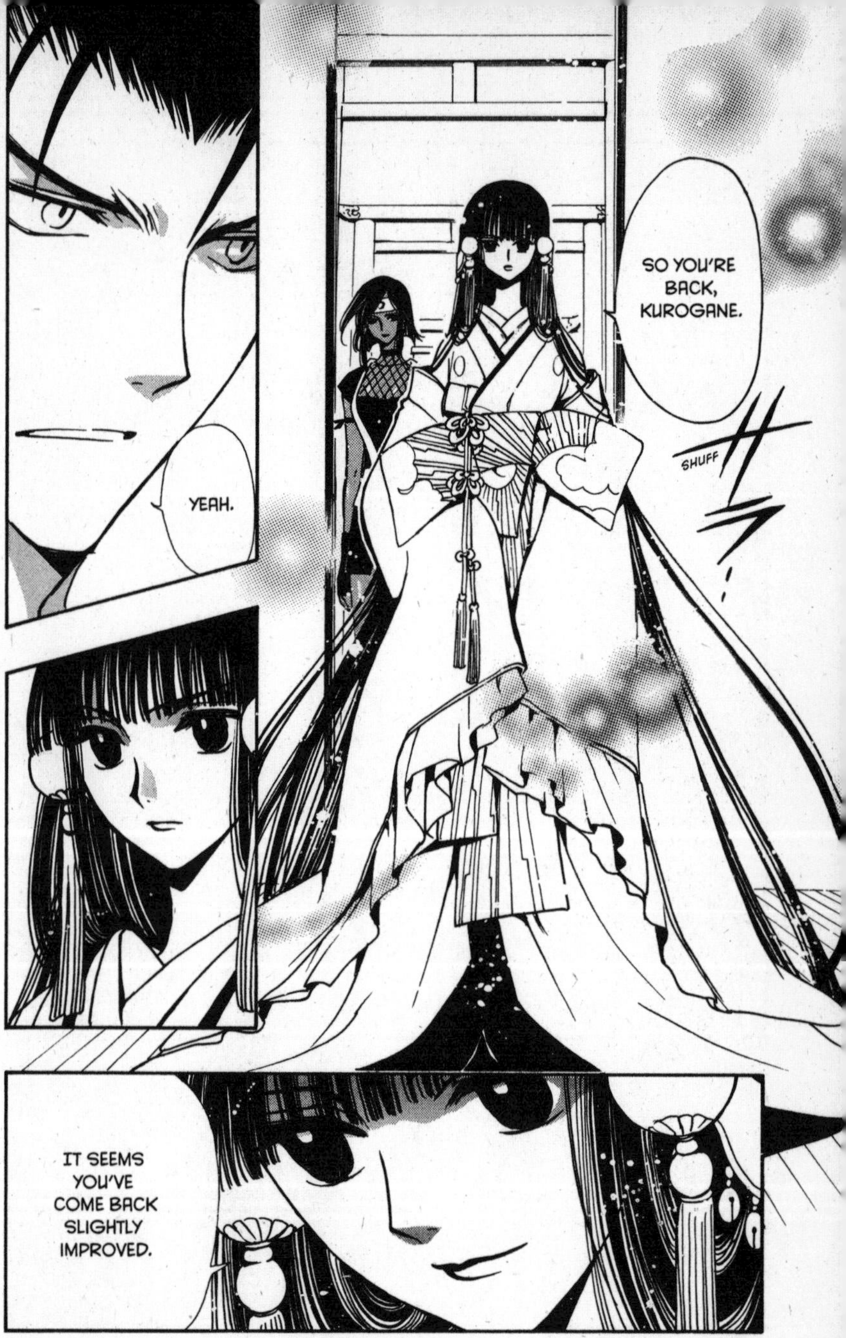
SO YOU'RE BACK, KUROGANE.
SHUFF
YEAH.
IT SEEMS YOU'VE COME BACK SLIGHTLY IMPROVED.

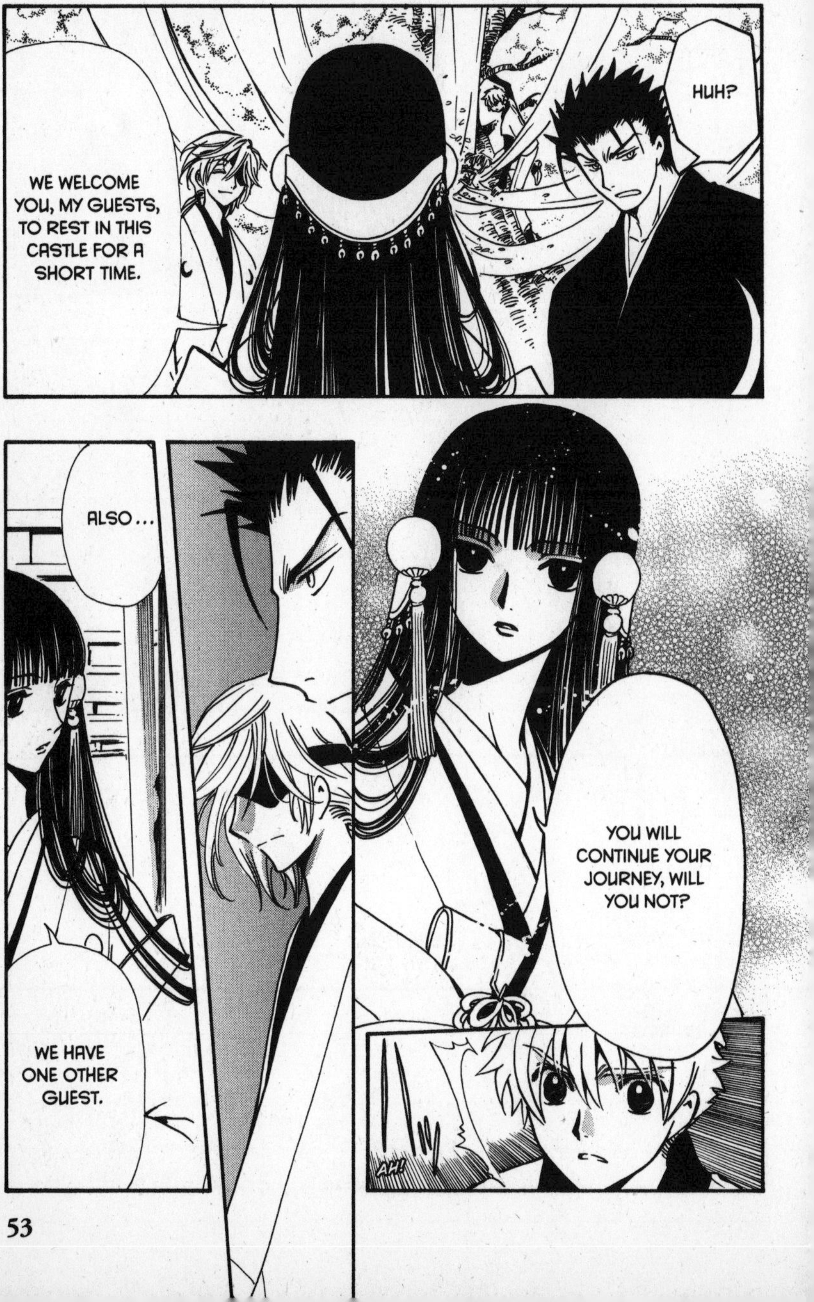
HUH?
WE WELCOME YOU, MY GUESTS, TO REST IN THIS CASTLE FOR A SHORT TIME.
YOU WILL CONTINUE YOUR JOURNEY, WILL YOU NOT?
AH!
ALSO...
WE HAVE ONE OTHER GUEST.

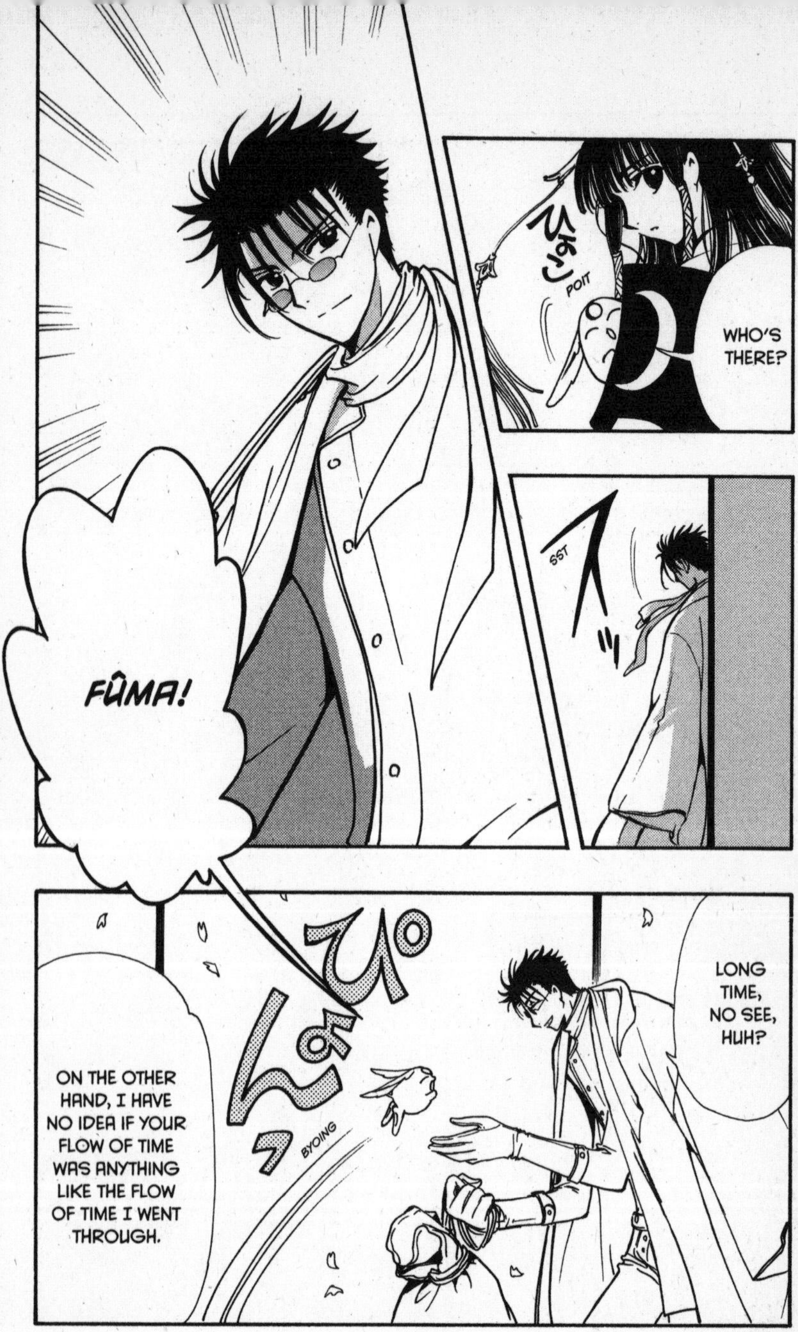
POIT
WHO'S THERE?
SST
FÛMA!
LONG TIME, NO SEE, HUH?
BYOING
ON THE OTHER HAND, I HAVE NO IDEA IF YOUR FLOW OF TIME WAS ANYTHING LIKE THE FLOW OF TIME I WENT THROUGH.

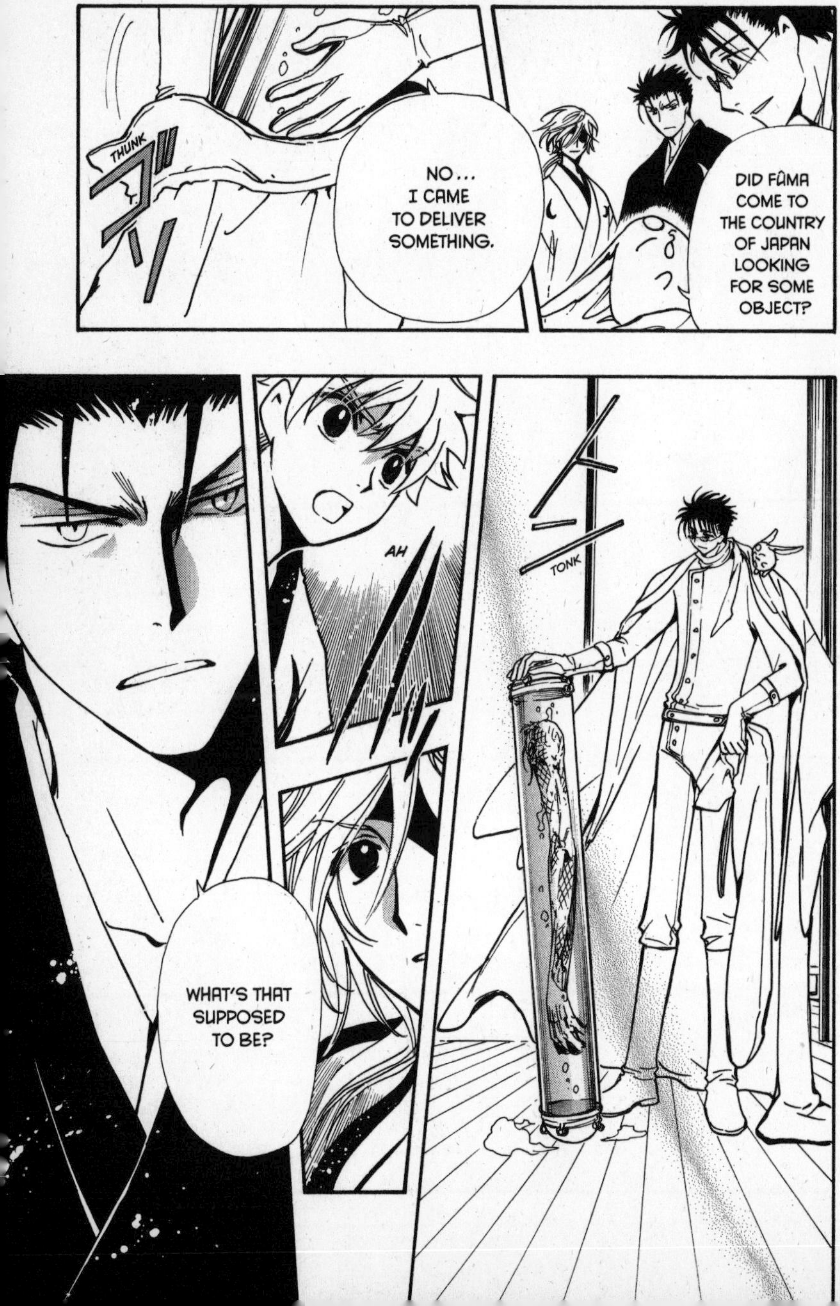
DID FÛMA COME TO THE COUNTRY OF JAPAN LOOKING FOR SOME OBJECT?
THUNK
NO... I CAME TO DELIVER SOMETHING.
TONK
AH
WHAT'S THAT SUPPOSED TO BE?

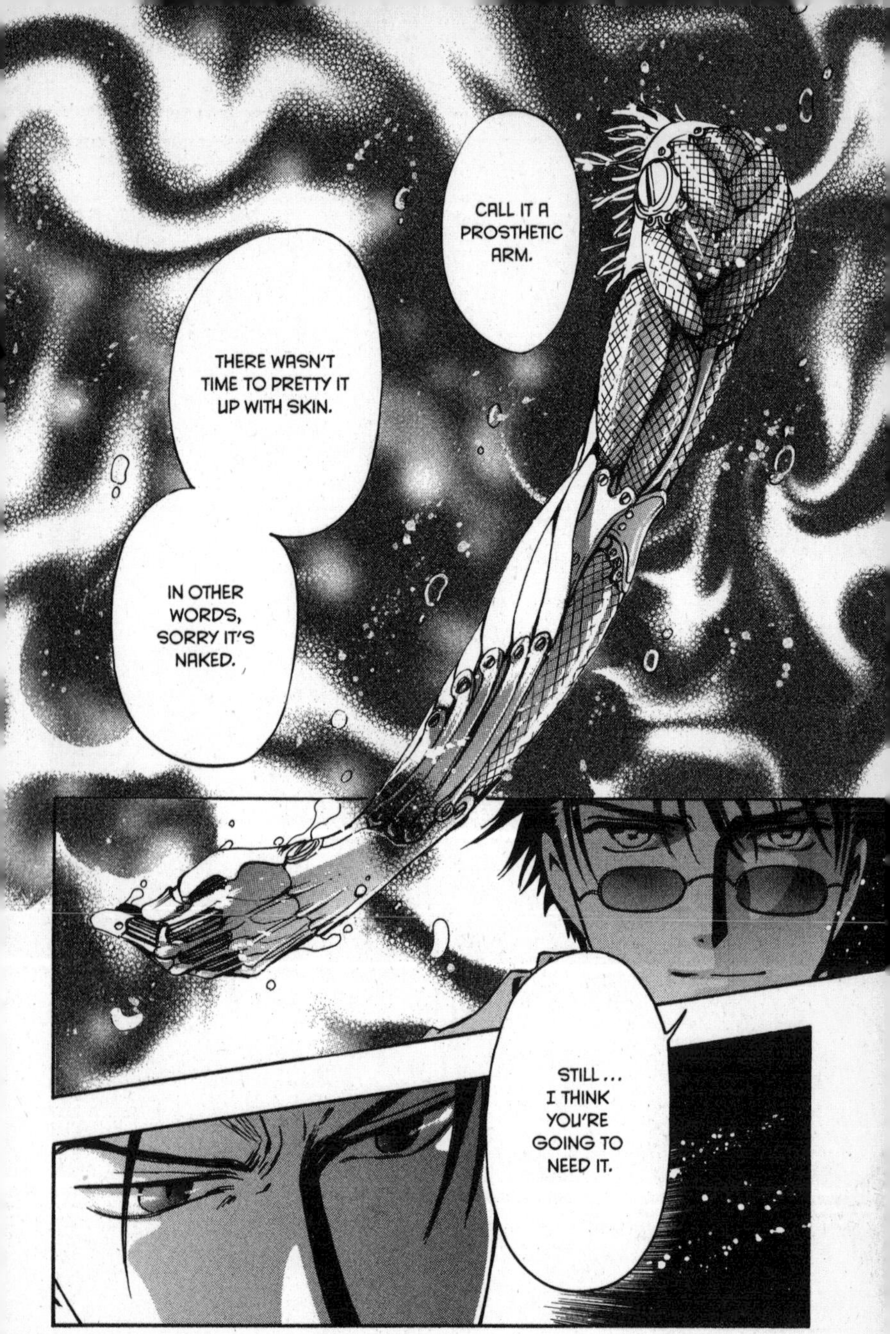
CALL IT A PROSTHETIC ARM.
THERE WASN'T TIME TO PRETTY IT UP WITH SKIN.
IN OTHER WORDS, SORRY IT'S NAKED.
STILL... I THINK YOU'RE GOING TO NEED IT.

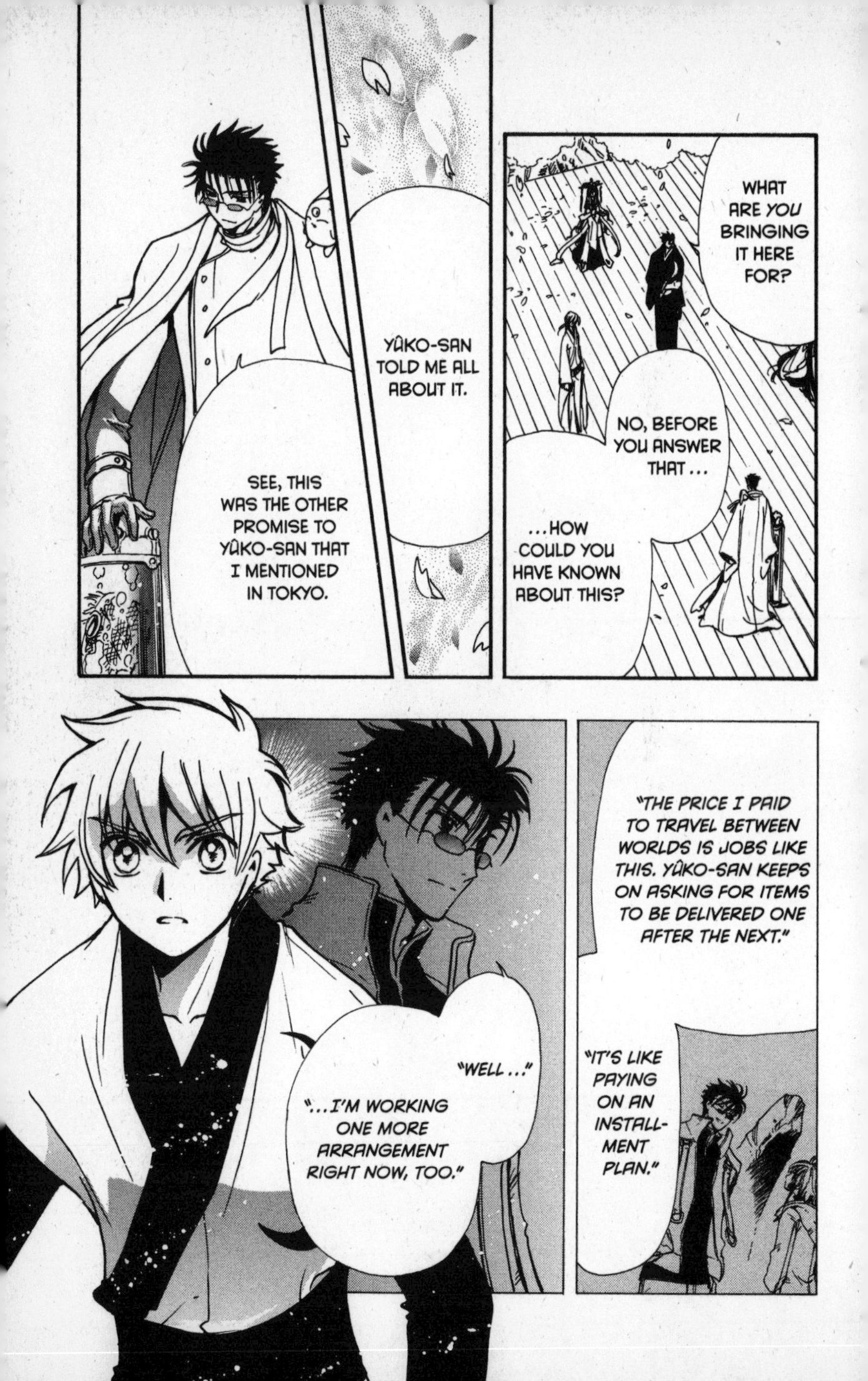
WHAT ARE YOU BRINGING IT HERE FOR?
NO, BEFORE YOU ANSWER THAT . . .
. . . HOW COULD YOU HAVE KNOWN ABOUT THIS?
YÛKO-SAN TOLD ME ALL ABOUT IT.
SEE, THIS WAS THE OTHER PROMISE TO YÛKO-SAN THAT I MENTIONED IN TOKYO.
"THE PRICE I PAID TO TRAVEL BETWEEN WORLDS IS JOBS LIKE THIS. YÛKO-SAN KEEPS ON ASKING FOR ITEMS TO BE DELIVERED ONE AFTER THE NEXT."
"IT'S LIKE PAYING ON AN INSTALL-MENT PLAN."
"WELL . . ."
". . . I'M WORKING ONE MORE ARRANGEMENT RIGHT NOW, TOO."

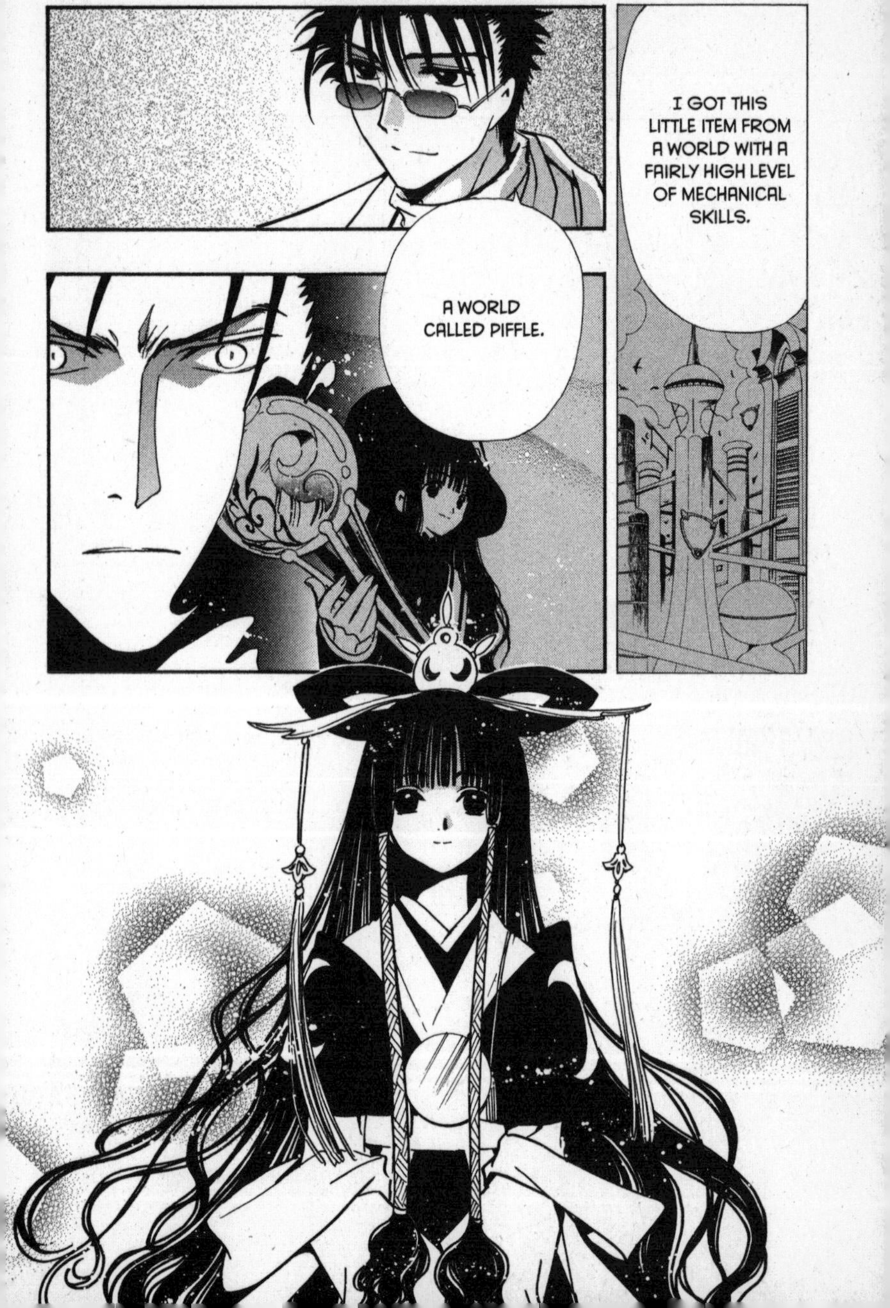
I GOT THIS LITTLE ITEM FROM A WORLD WITH A FAIRLY HIGH LEVEL OF MECHANICAL SKILLS.
A WORLD CALLED PIFFLE.

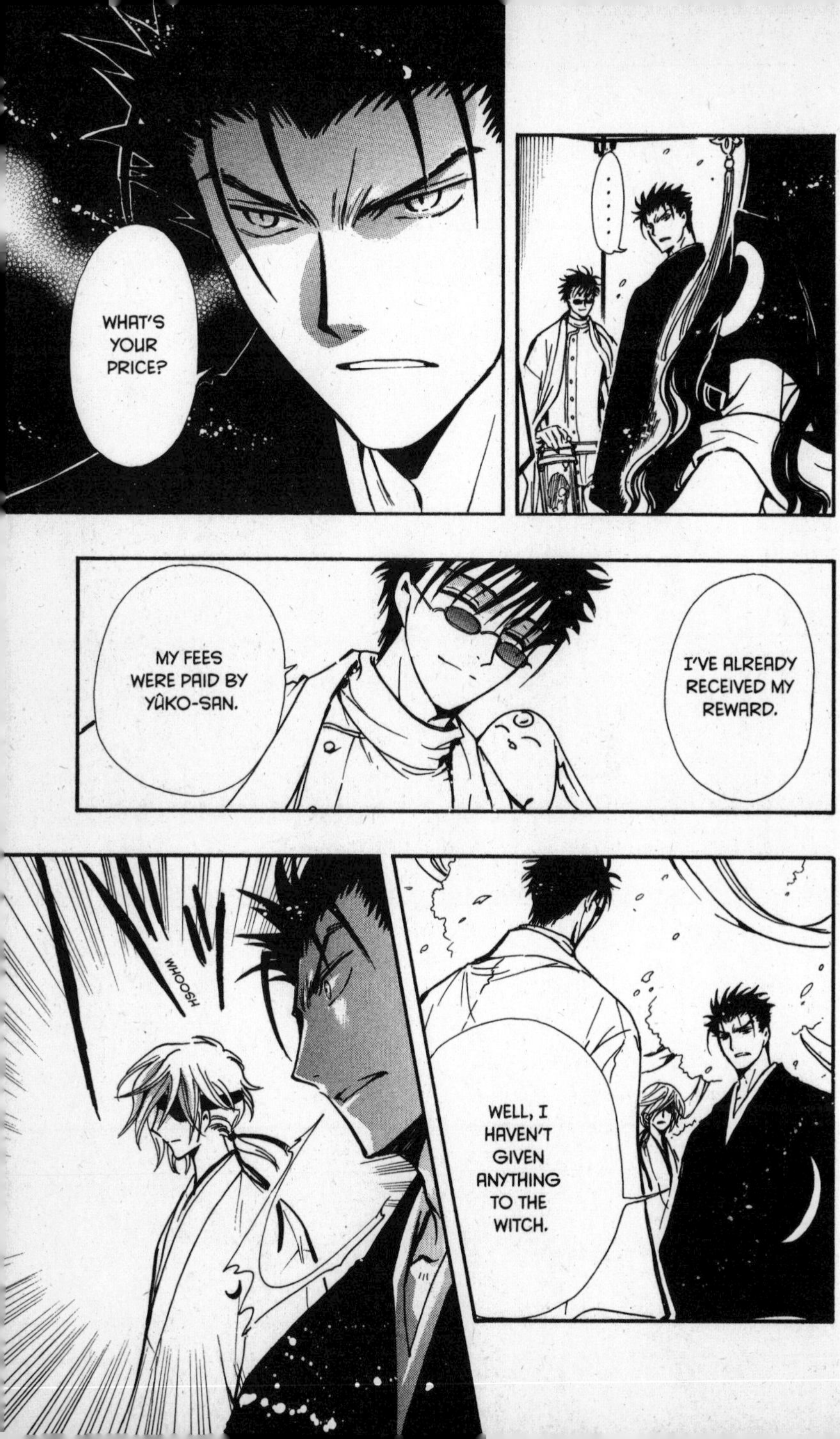
......
WHAT'S YOUR PRICE?
I'VE ALREADY RECEIVED MY REWARD.
MY FEES WERE PAID BY YÛKO-SAN.
WELL, I HAVEN'T GIVEN ANYTHING TO THE WITCH.
WHOOSH

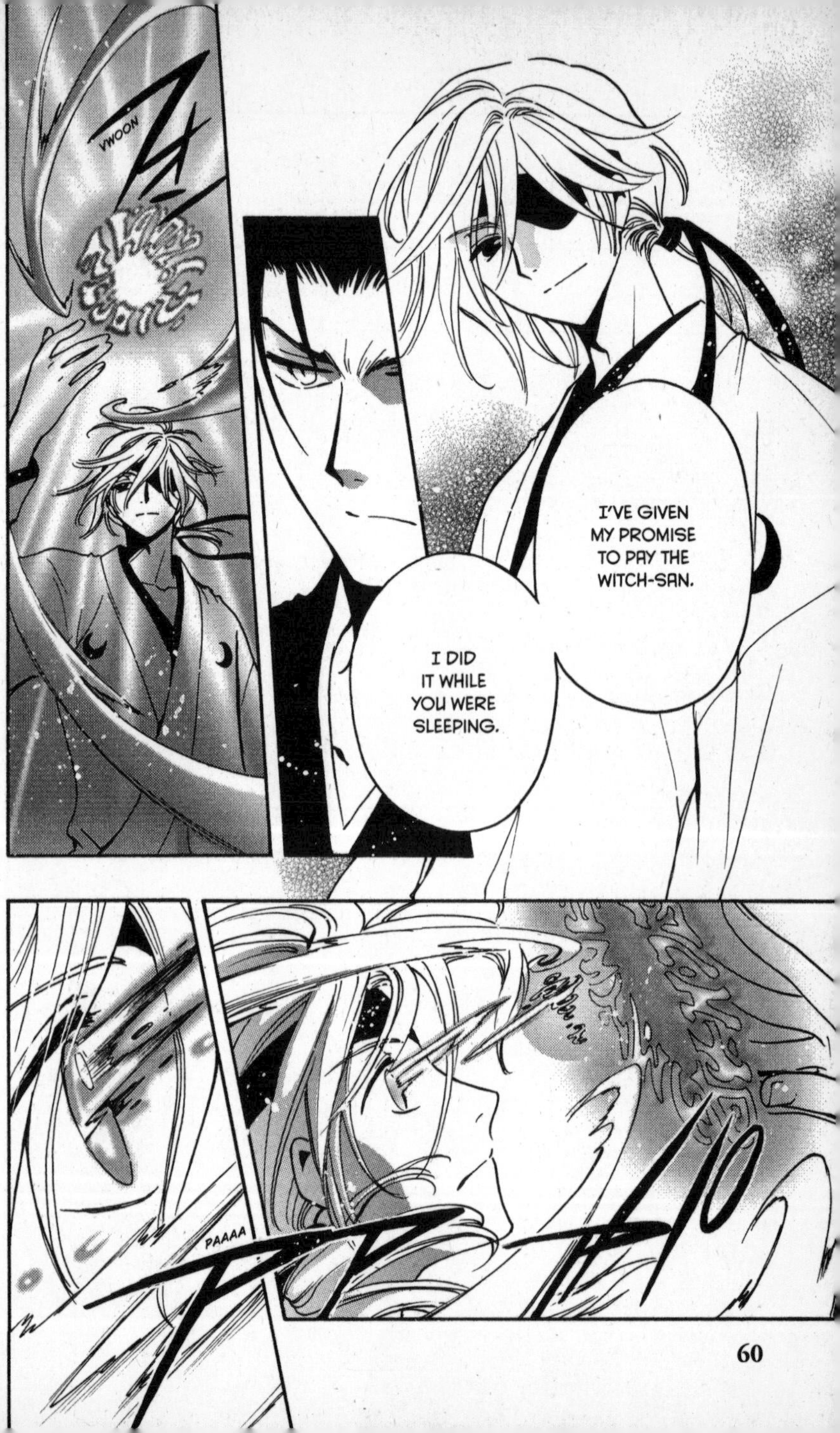
I'VE GIVEN MY PROMISE TO PAY THE WITCH-SAN.
I DID IT WHILE YOU WERE SLEEPING.
VWOON
PAAAA

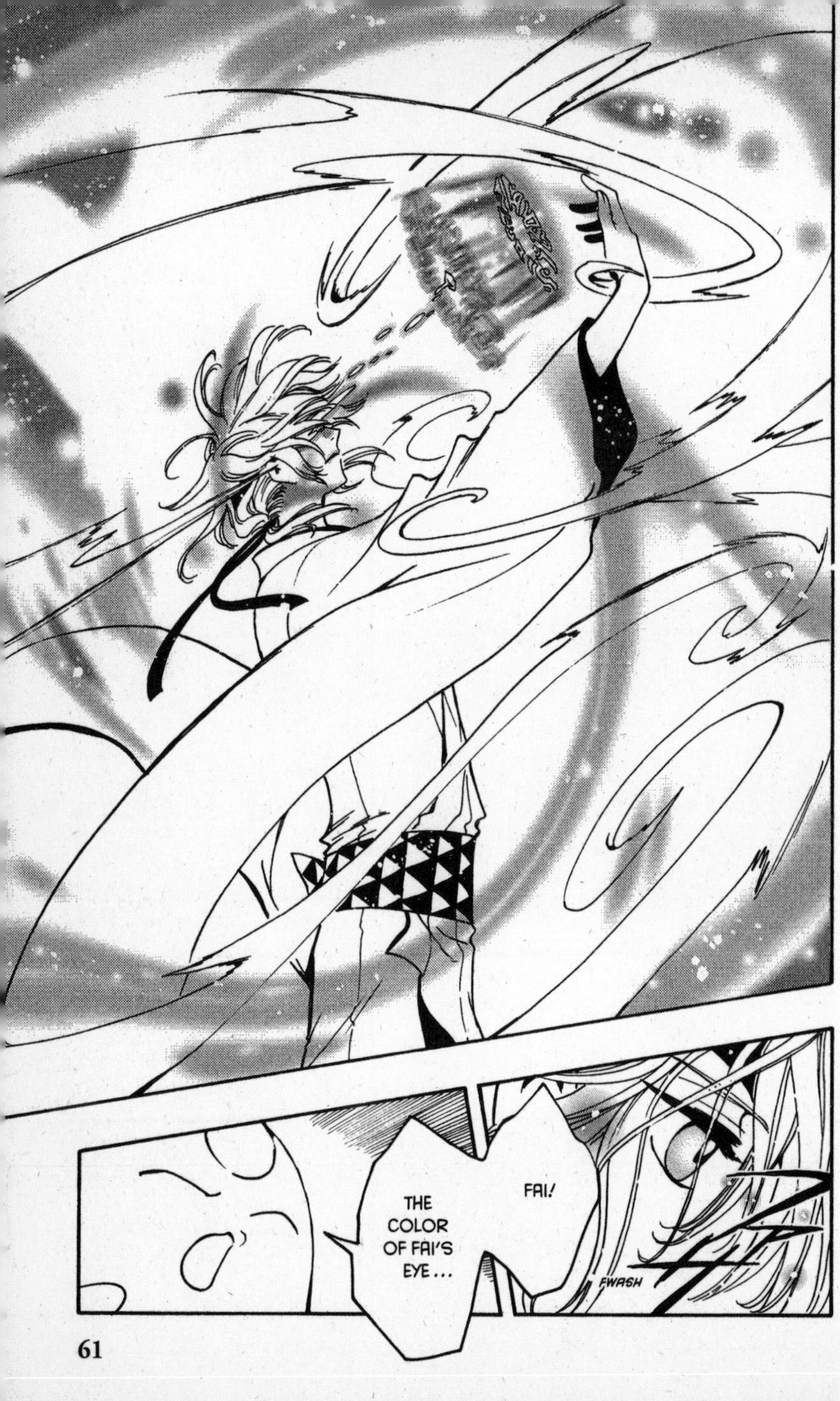
FAI!
FWASH
THE COLOR OF FAI'S EYE . . .

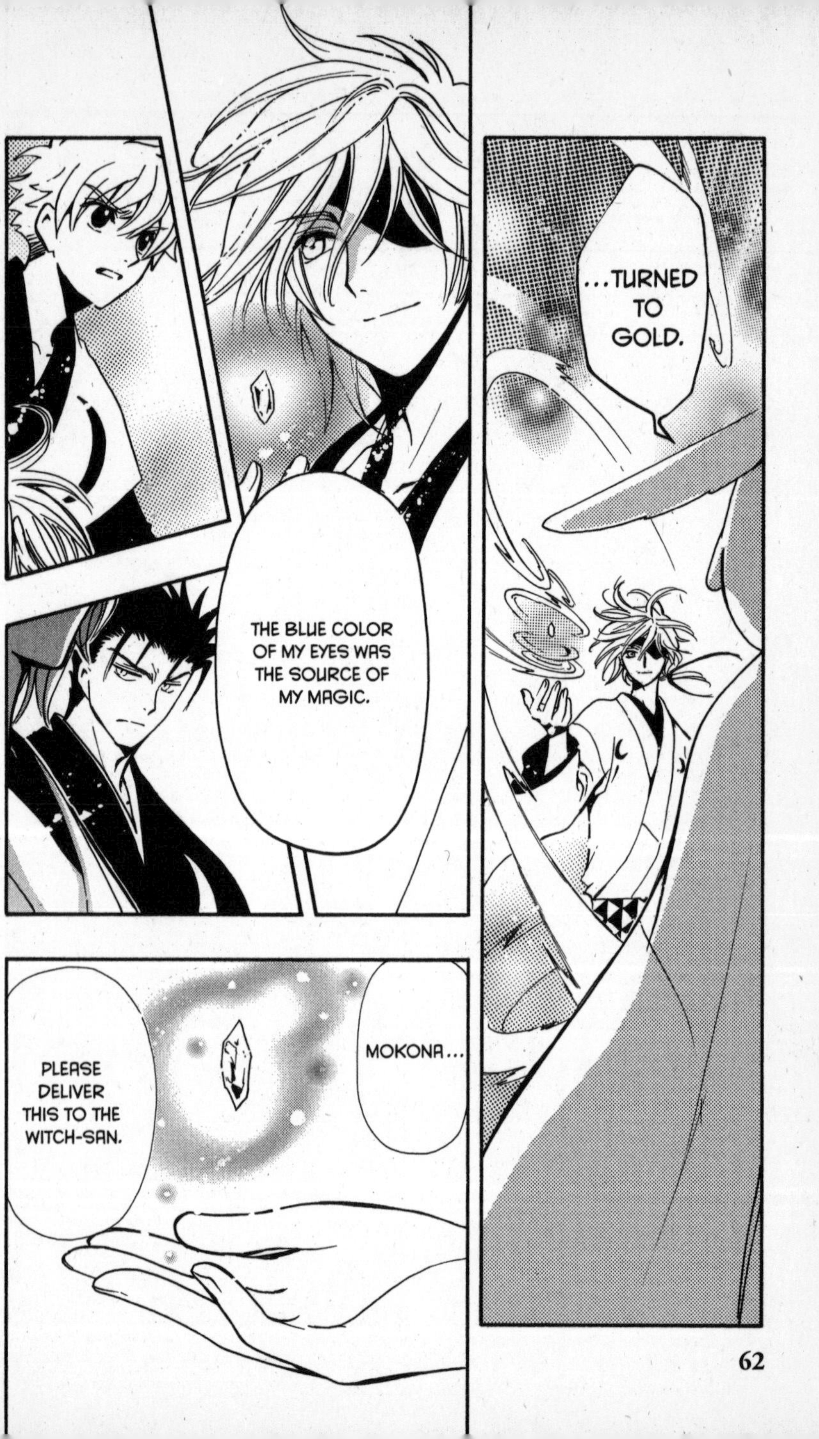
...TURNED TO GOLD.
THE BLUE COLOR OF MY EYES WAS THE SOURCE OF MY MAGIC.
MOKONA...
PLEASE DELIVER THIS TO THE WITCH-SAN.

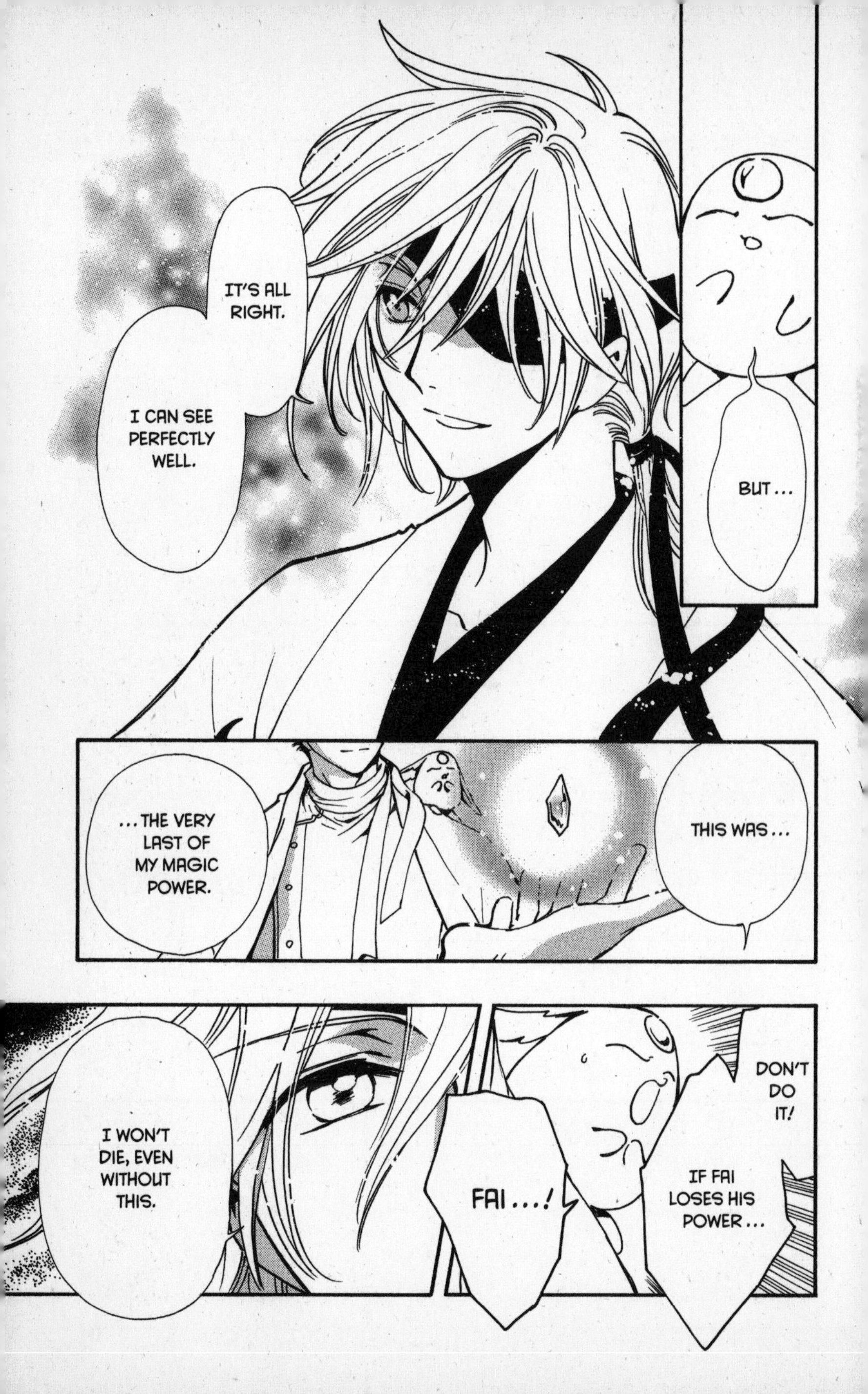
BUT...
IT'S ALL RIGHT.
I CAN SEE PERFECTLY WELL.
THIS WAS...
...THE VERY LAST OF MY MAGIC POWER.
DON'T DO IT!
IF FAI LOSES HIS POWER...
FAI...!
I WON'T DIE, EVEN WITHOUT THIS.

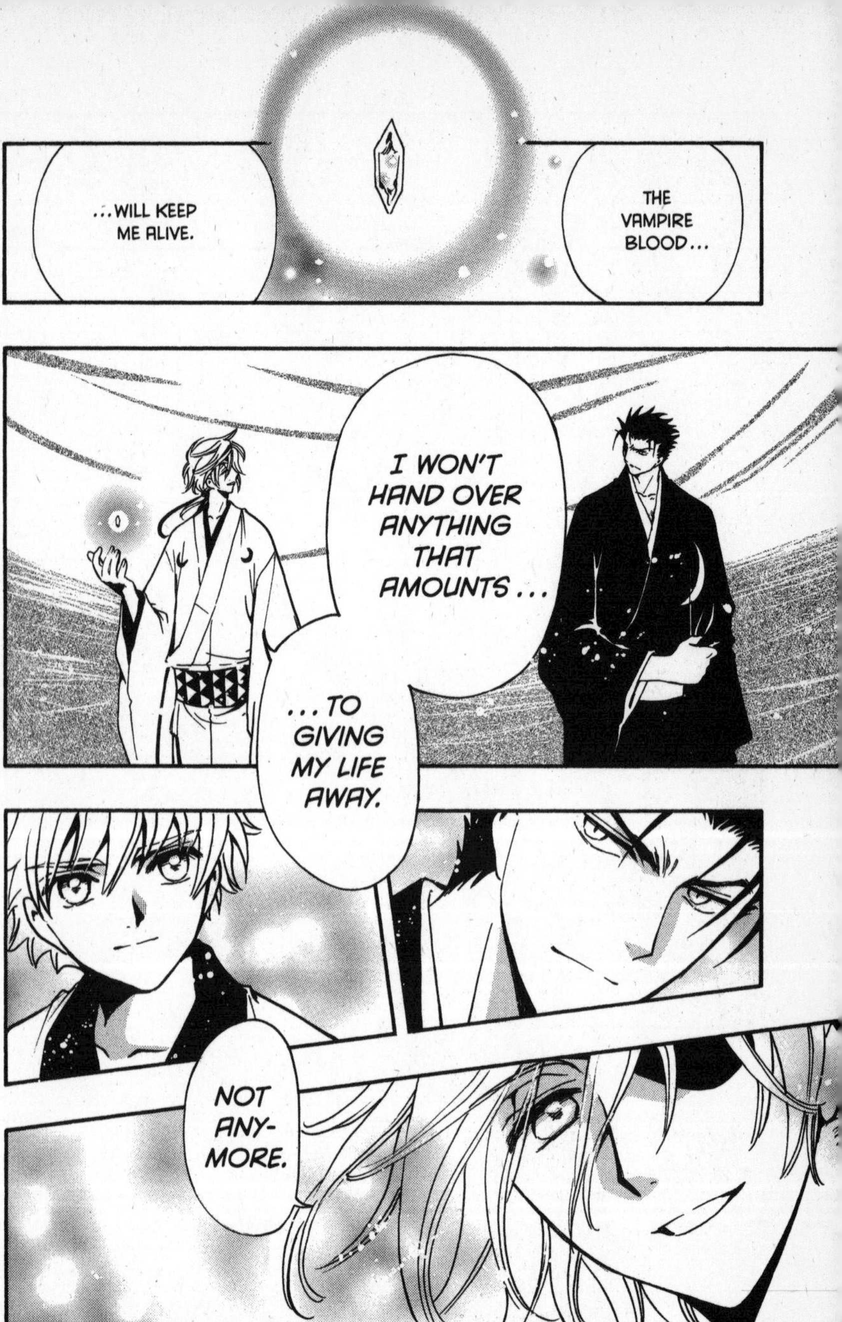
THE VAMPIRE BLOOD...
...WILL KEEP ME ALIVE.
I WON'T HAND OVER ANYTHING THAT AMOUNTS...
...TO GIVING MY LIFE AWAY.
NOT ANY-MORE.

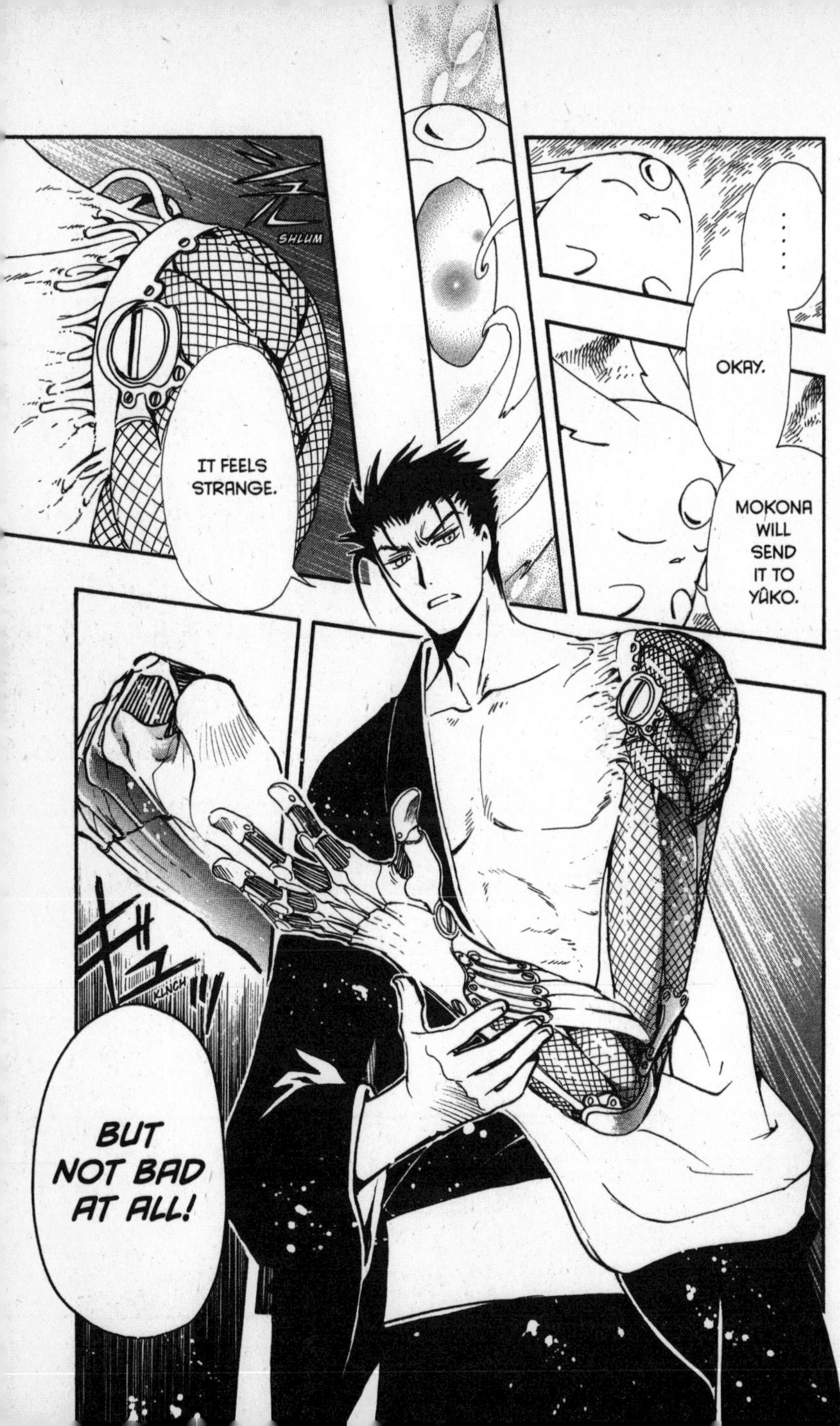
.....
OKAY.
MOKONA WILL SEND IT TO YŪKO.
SHLUM
IT FEELS STRANGE.
KLNCH
BUT NOT BAD AT ALL!

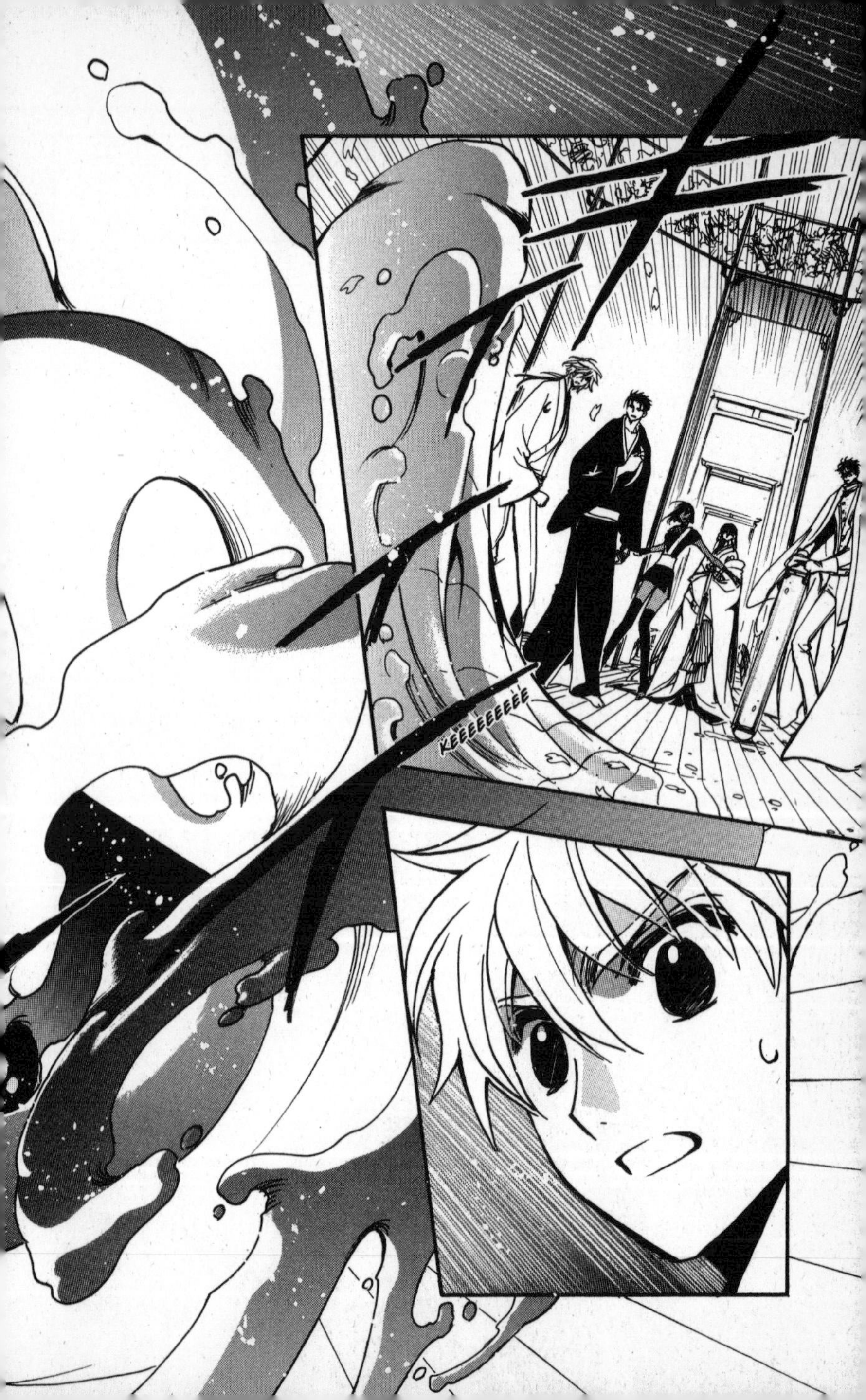
KEEEEEEEEEE

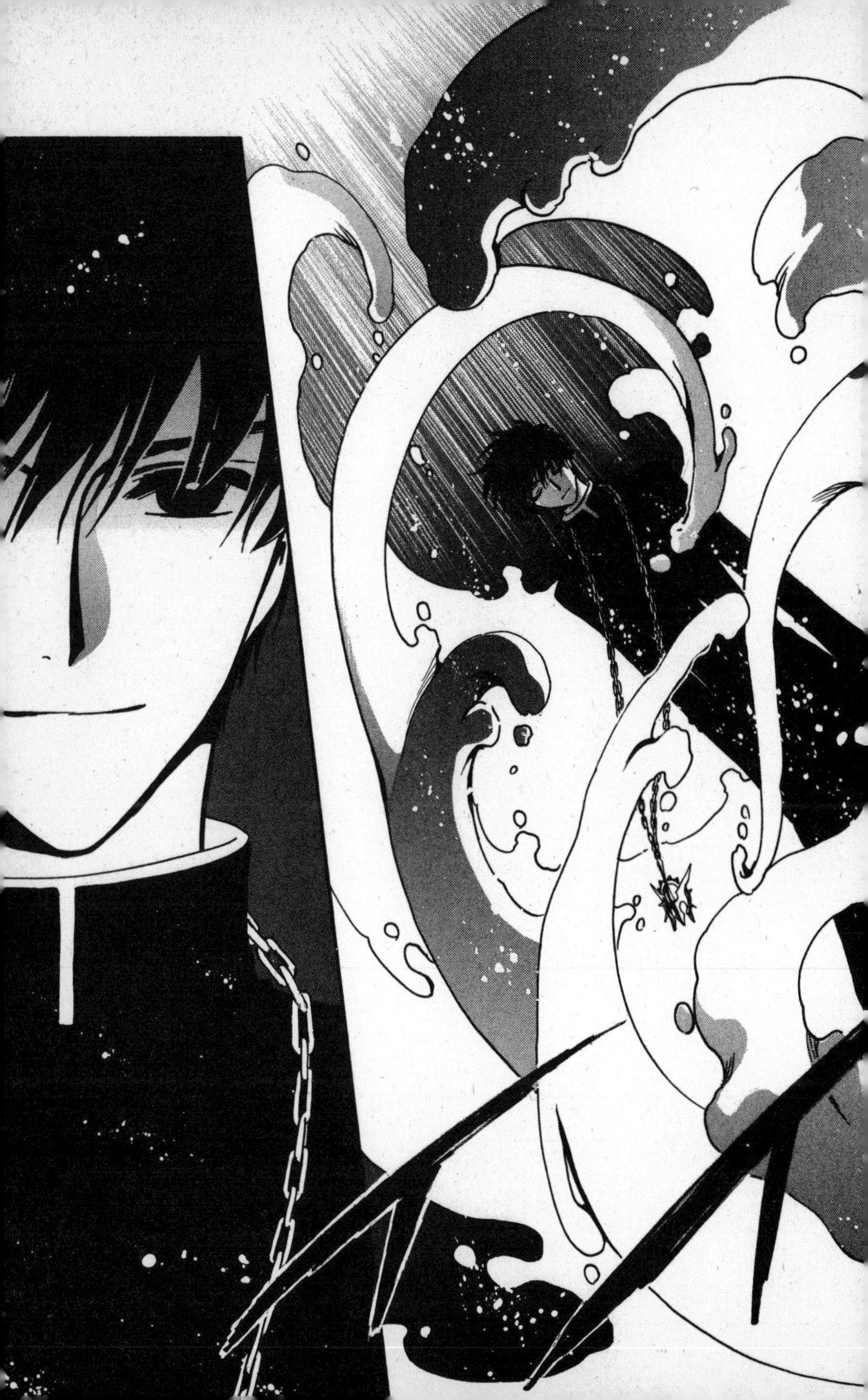

ツバサ

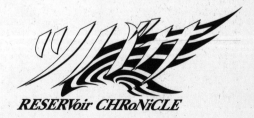

RESERVoir CHRoNiCLE

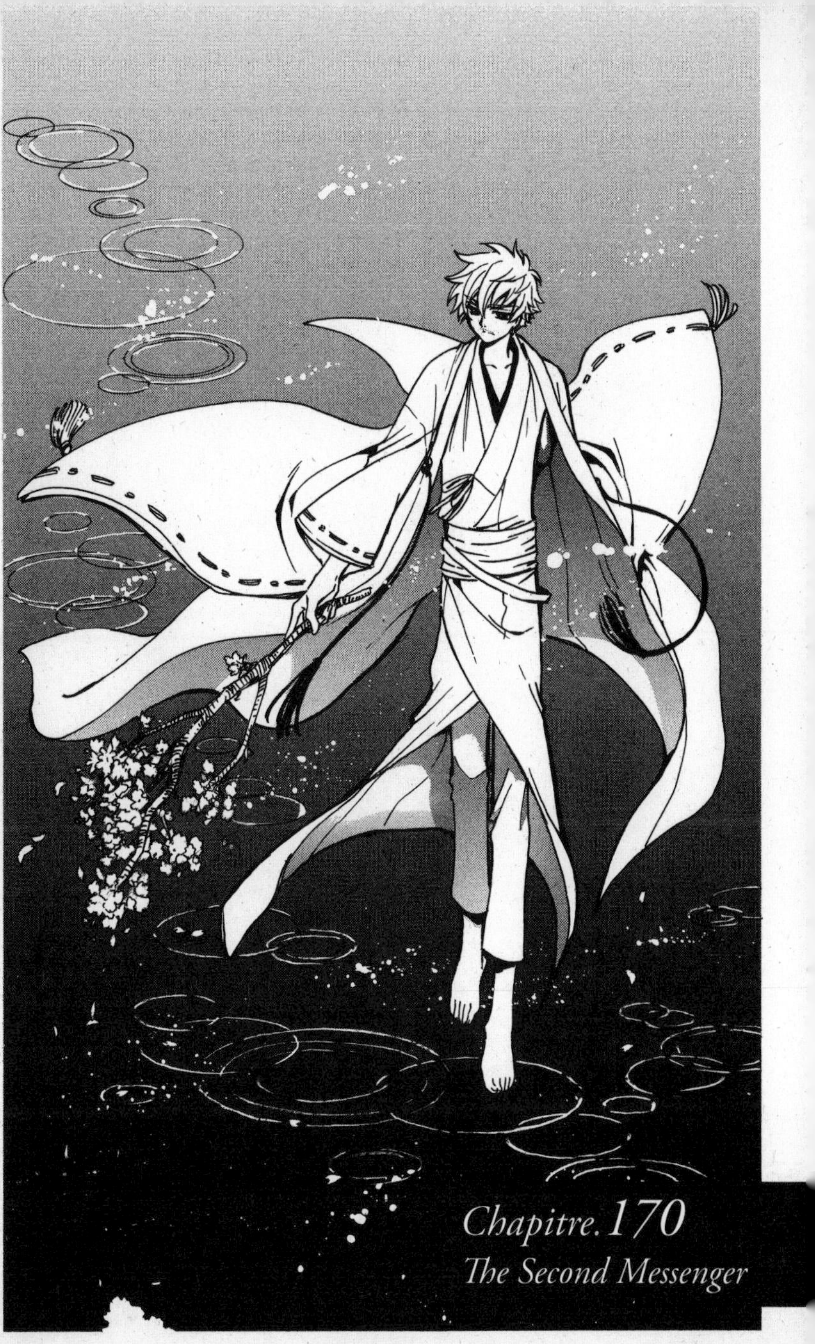
Chapitre. 170
The Second Messenger

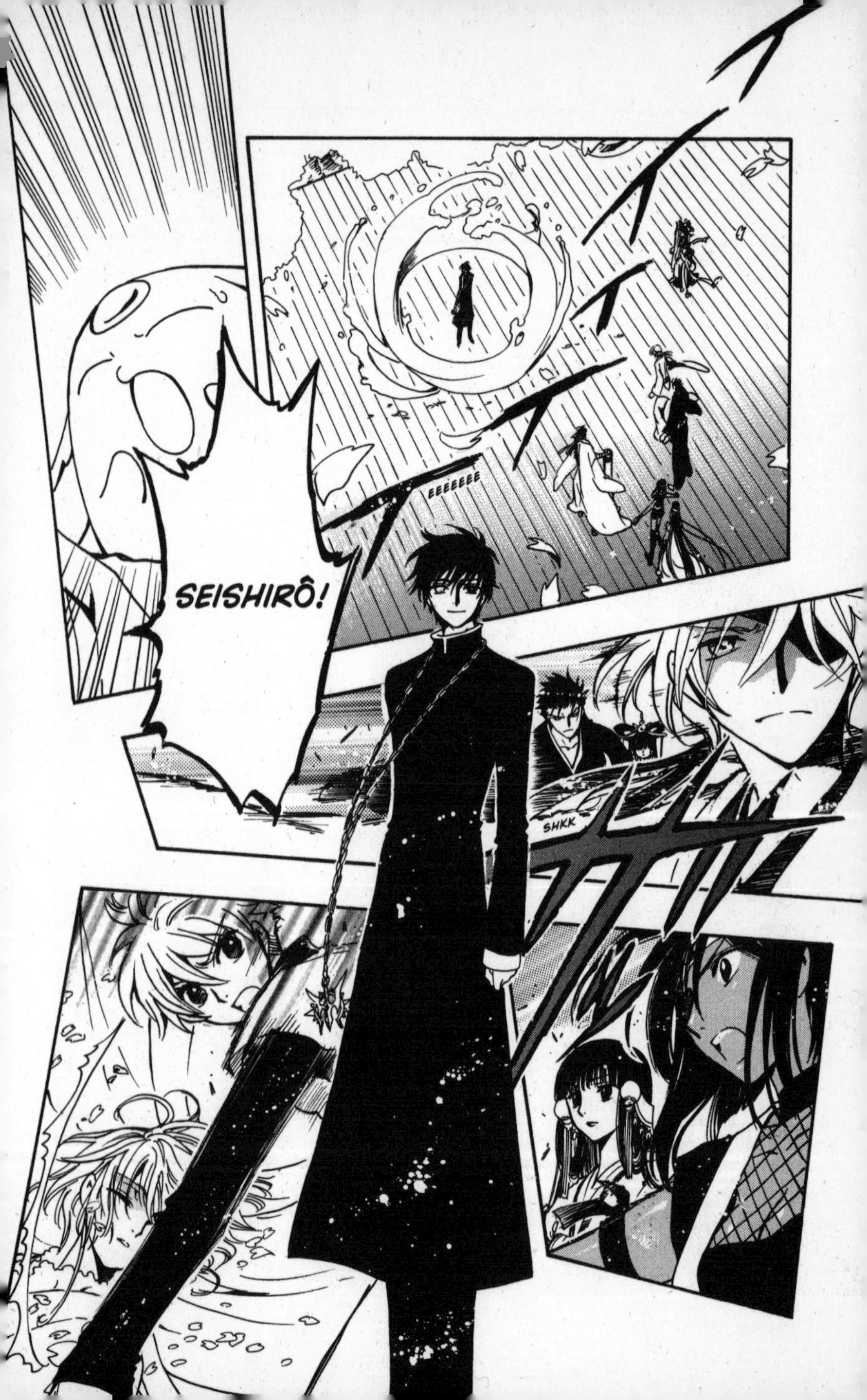
EEEEEEE
SEISHIRÔ!
SHKK

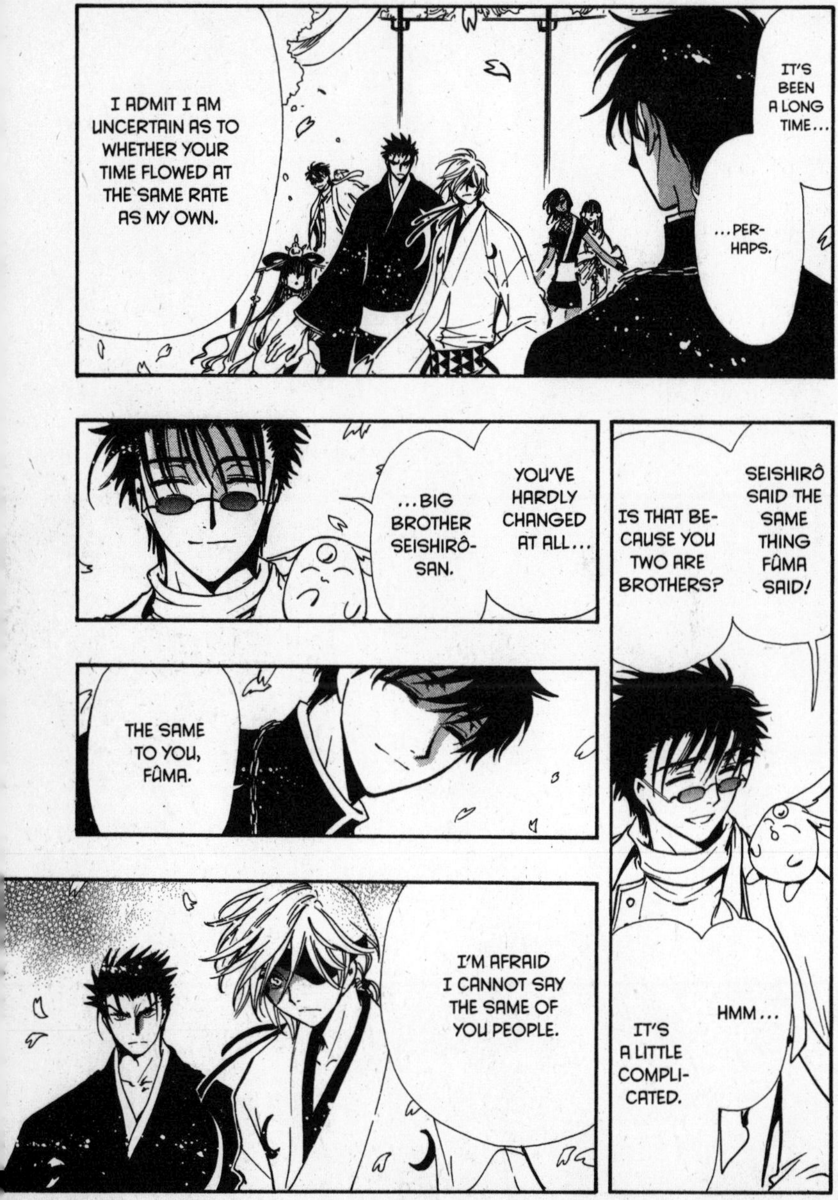
IT'S BEEN A LONG TIME...
...PERHAPS.
I ADMIT I AM UNCERTAIN AS TO WHETHER YOUR TIME FLOWED AT THE SAME RATE AS MY OWN.
SEISHIRÔ SAID THE SAME THING FÛMA SAID!
IS THAT BECAUSE YOU TWO ARE BROTHERS?
HMM...
IT'S A LITTLE COMPLICATED.
YOU'VE HARDLY CHANGED AT ALL...
...BIG BROTHER SEISHIRÔ-SAN.
THE SAME TO YOU, FÛMA.
I'M AFRAID I CANNOT SAY THE SAME OF YOU PEOPLE.

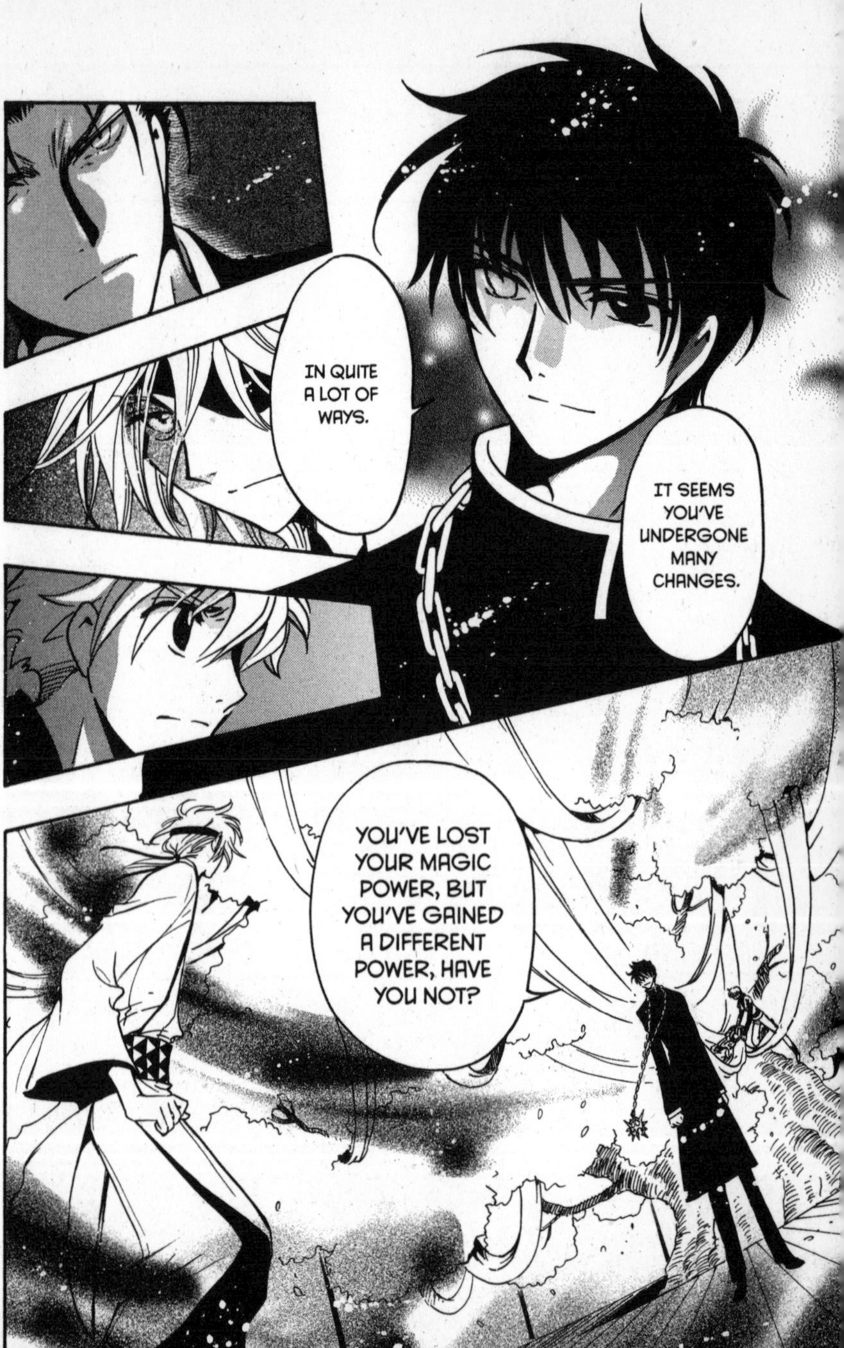
IT SEEMS YOU'VE UNDERGONE MANY CHANGES.
IN QUITE A LOT OF WAYS.
YOU'VE LOST YOUR MAGIC POWER, BUT YOU'VE GAINED A DIFFERENT POWER, HAVE YOU NOT?

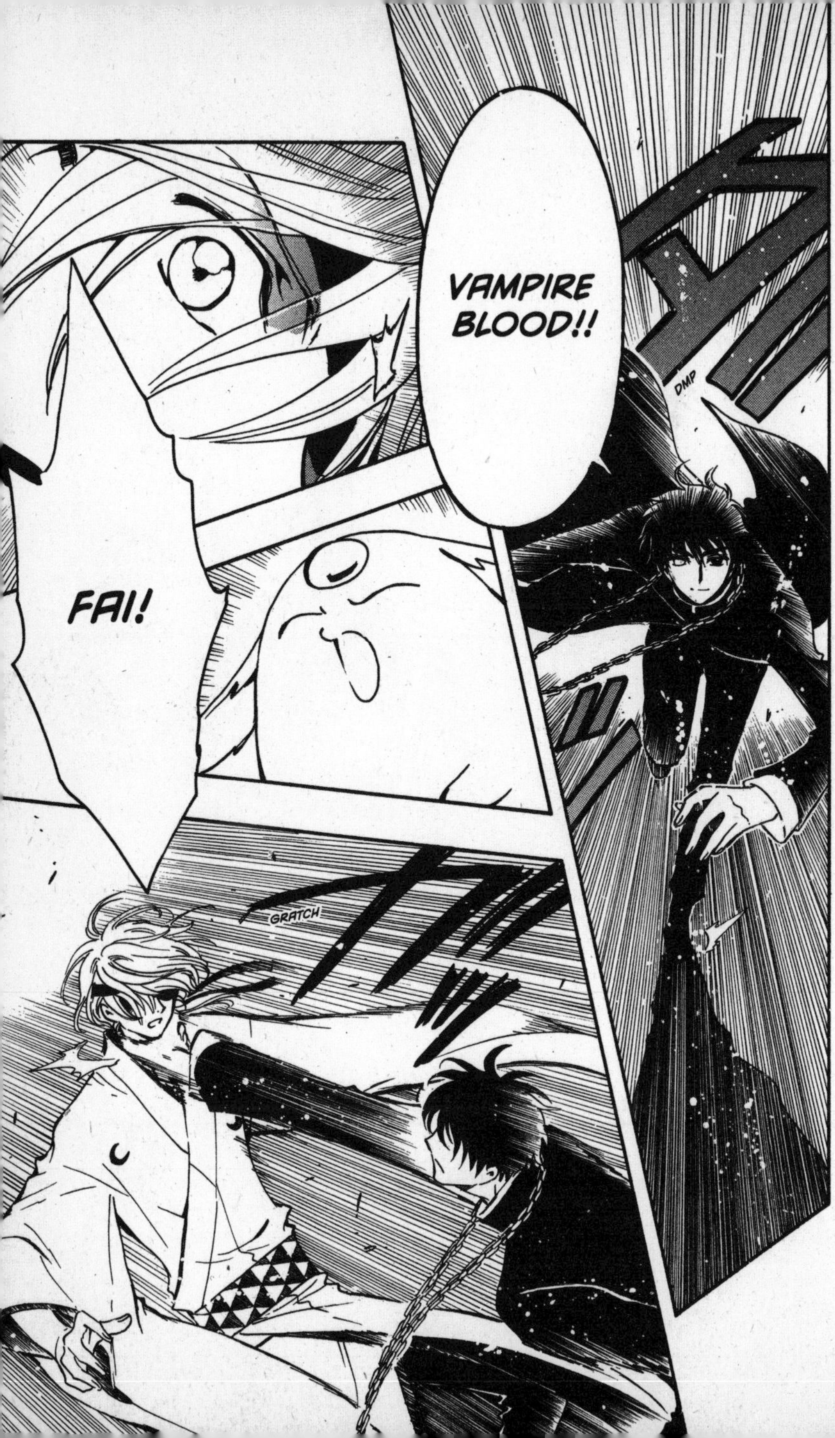
VAMPIRE BLOOD!!
DMP
FAI!
GRATCH

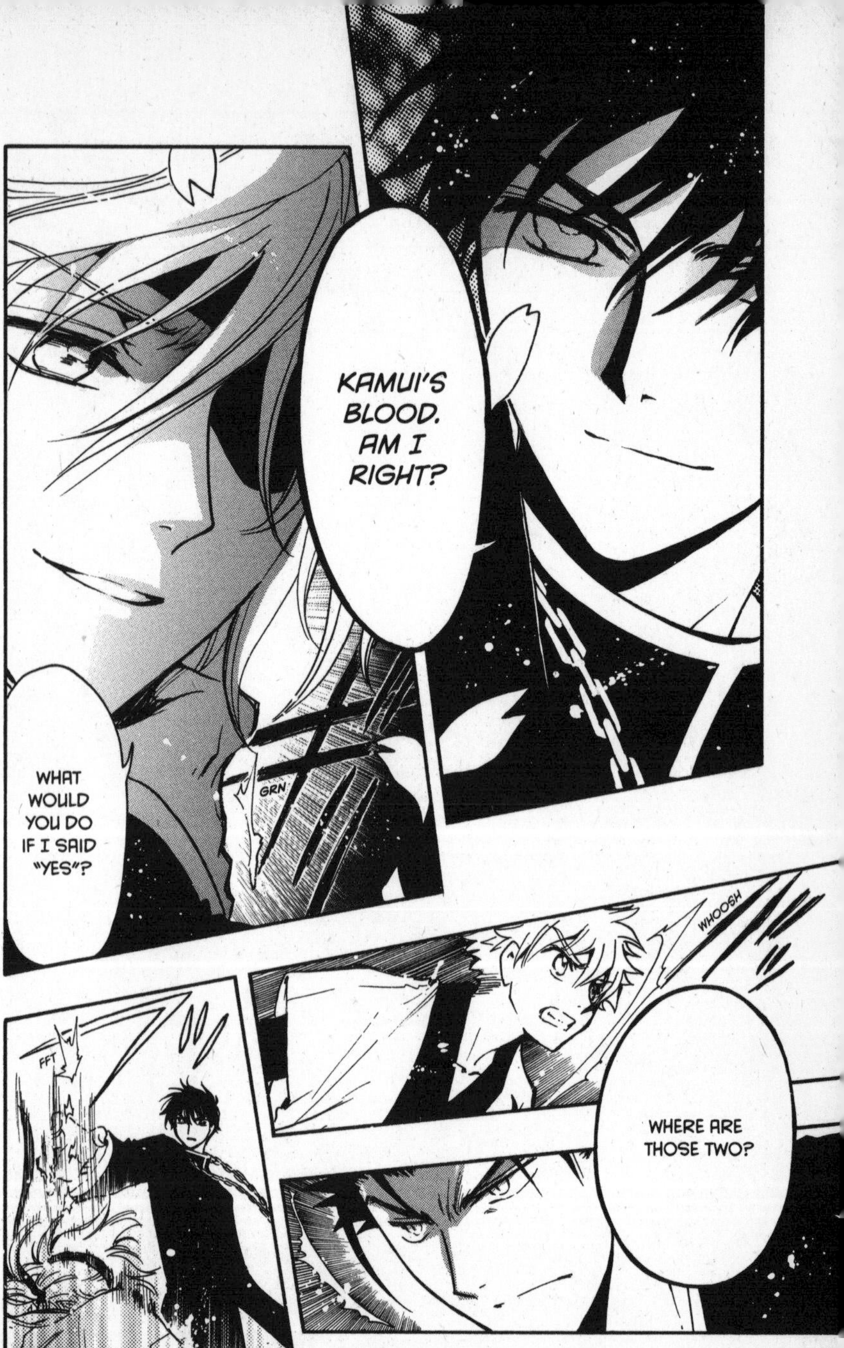
KAMUI'S BLOOD. AM I RIGHT?
WHAT WOULD YOU DO IF I SAID "YES"?
GRN
WHOOSH
WHERE ARE THOSE TWO?
FFT

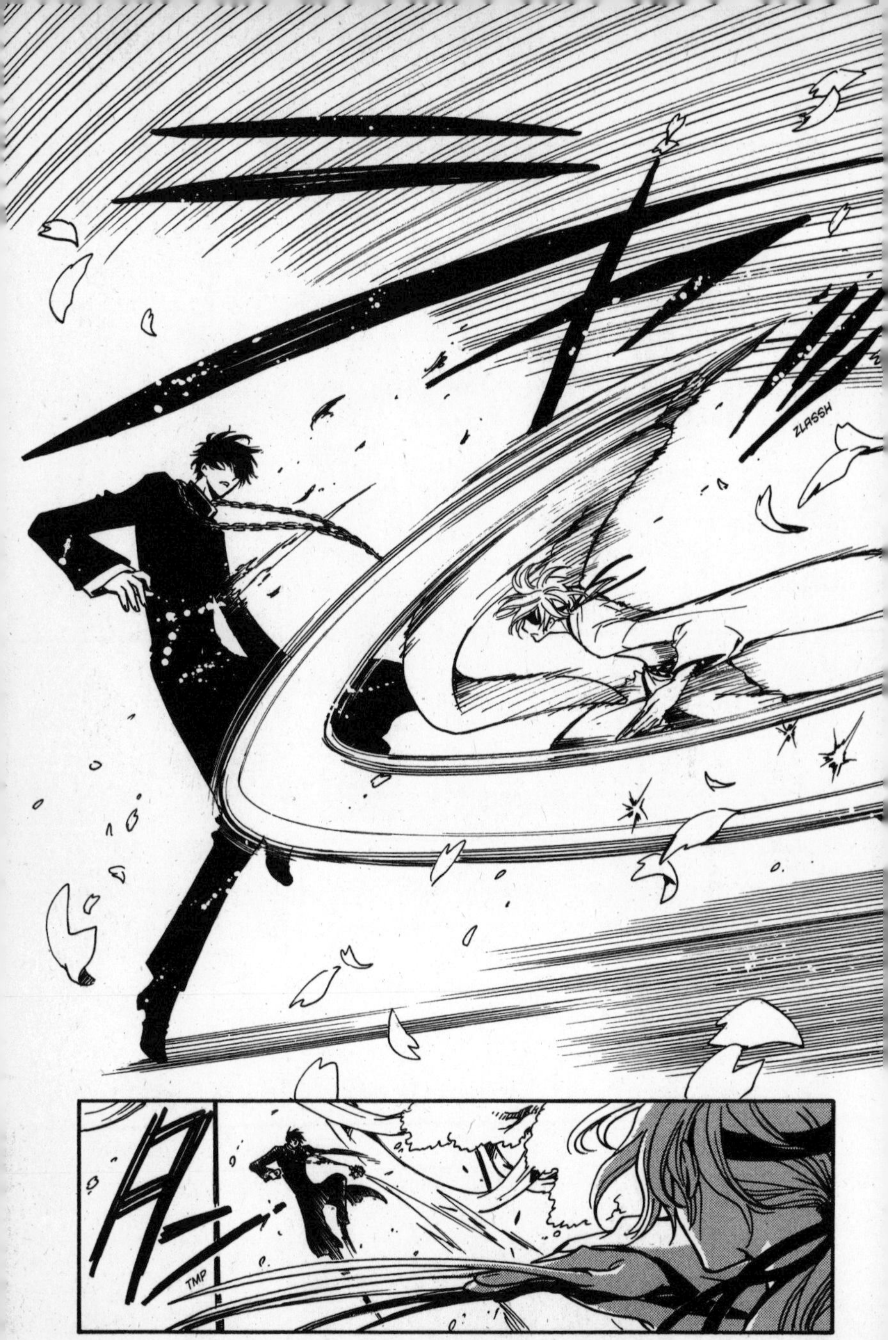
ZLASSH
TMP

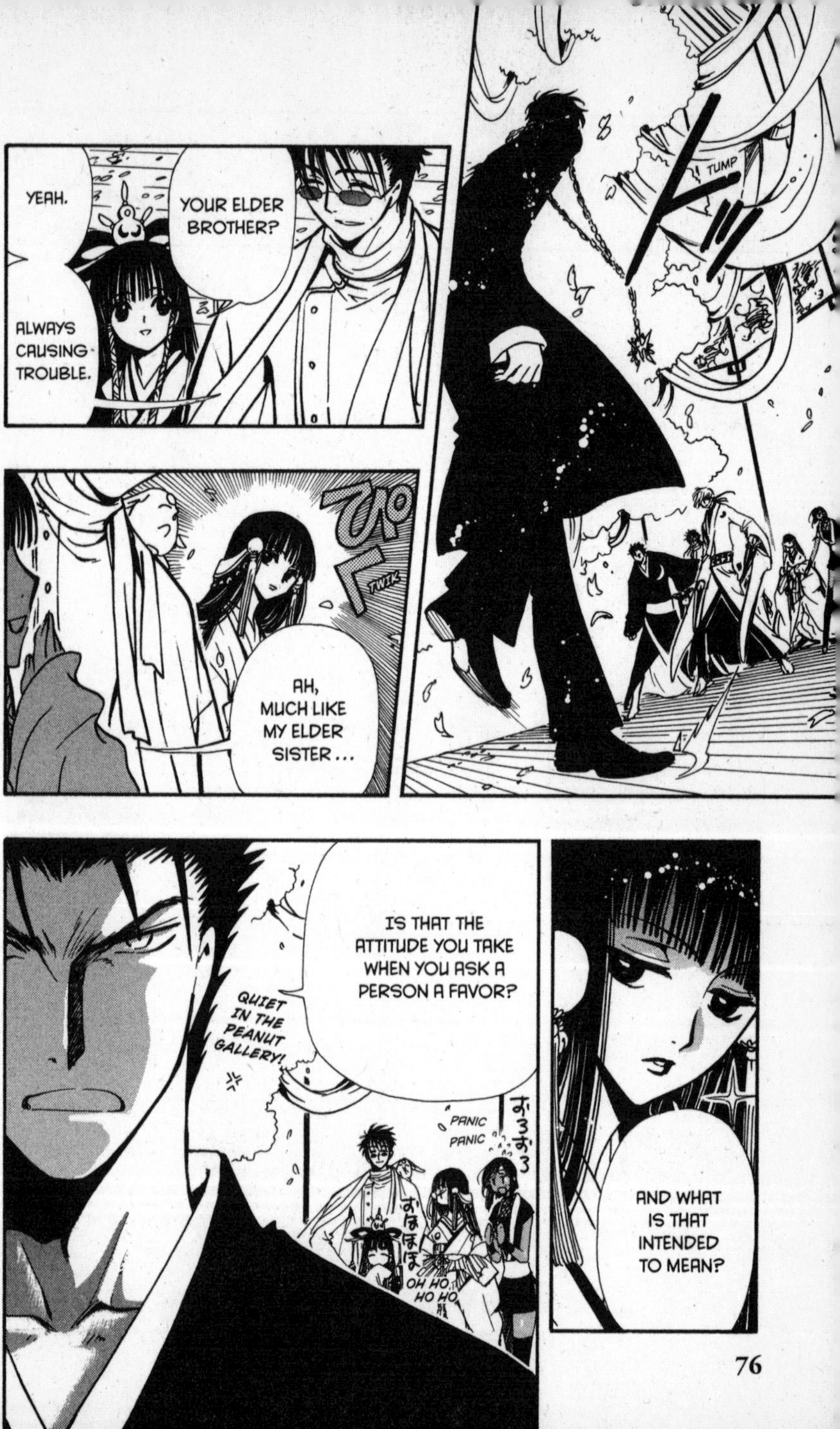
TUMP
YOUR ELDER BROTHER?
YEAH.
ALWAYS CAUSING TROUBLE.
TWIK
AH, MUCH LIKE MY ELDER SISTER...
AND WHAT IS THAT INTENDED TO MEAN?
IS THAT THE ATTITUDE YOU TAKE WHEN YOU ASK A PERSON A FAVOR?
QUIET IN THE PEANUT GALLERY!
おろおろ
PANIC PANIC
おほほほ
OH HO HO HO

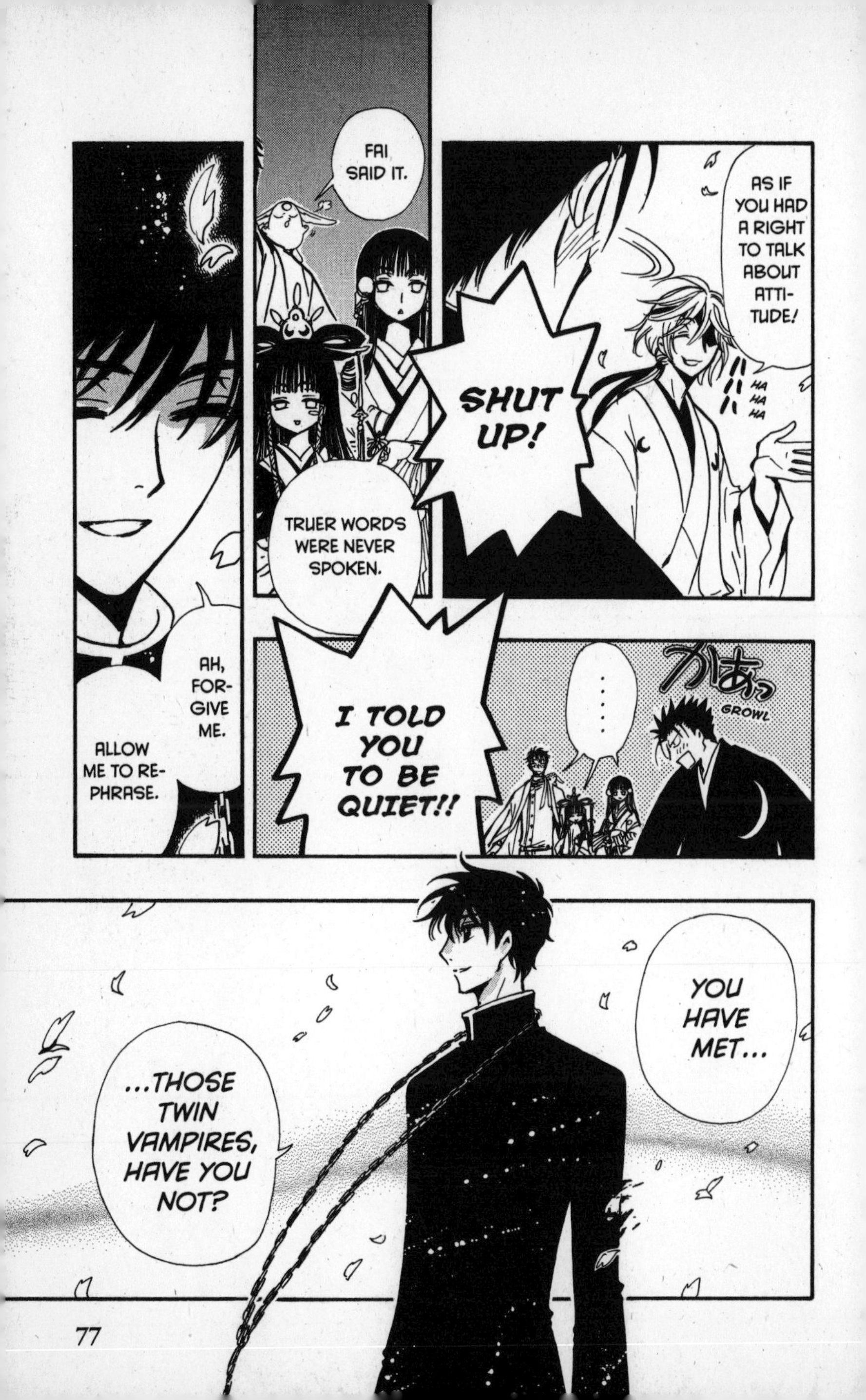
AS IF YOU HAD A RIGHT TO TALK ABOUT ATTI-TUDE!
HA HA HA
SHUT UP!
FAI SAID IT.
TRUER WORDS WERE NEVER SPOKEN.
かあっ
GROWL
.....
I TOLD YOU TO BE QUIET!!
AH, FOR-GIVE ME.
ALLOW ME TO RE-PHRASE.
YOU HAVE MET...
...THOSE TWIN VAMPIRES, HAVE YOU NOT?

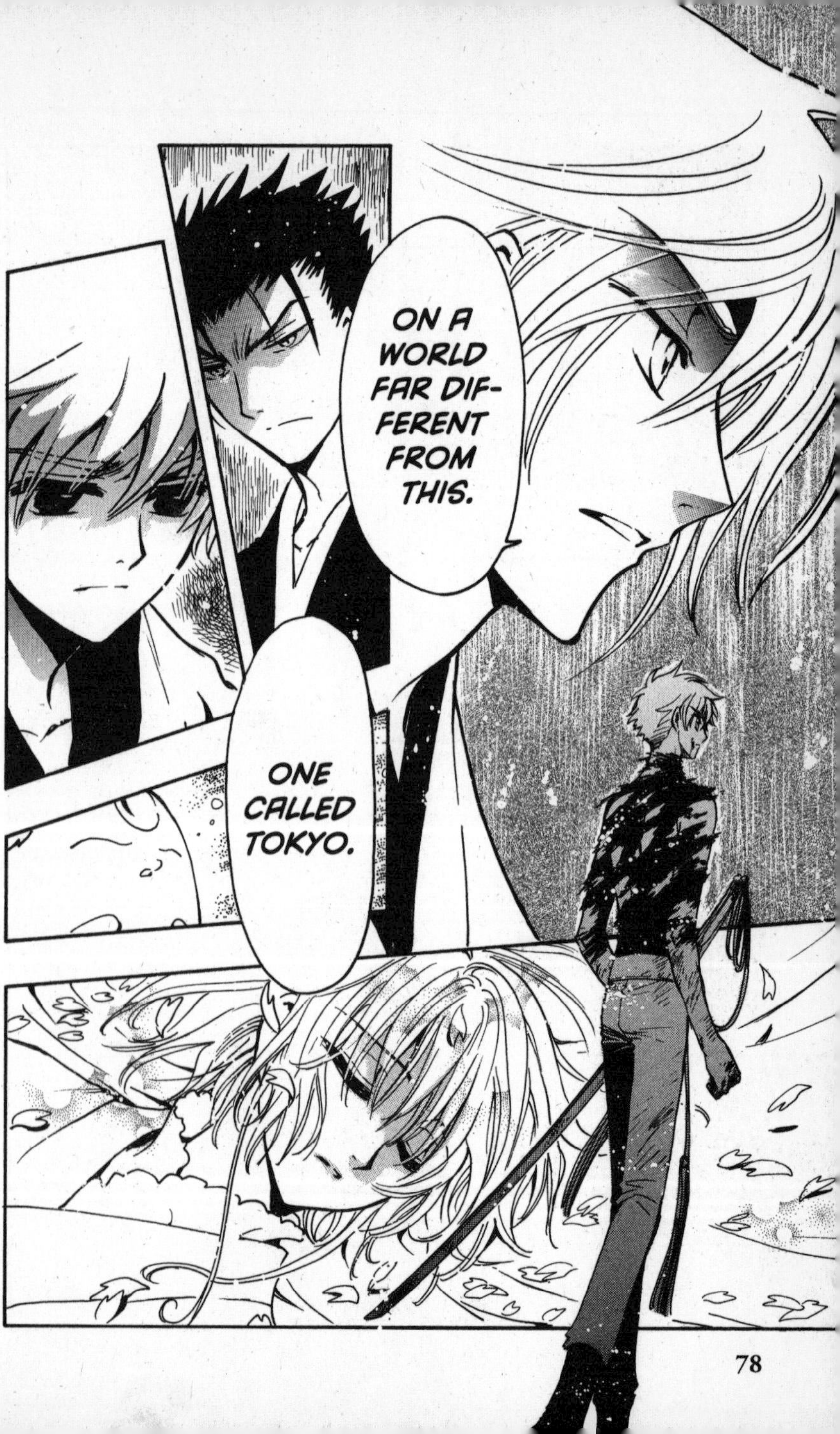
ON A WORLD FAR DIF-FERENT FROM THIS.
ONE CALLED TOKYO.

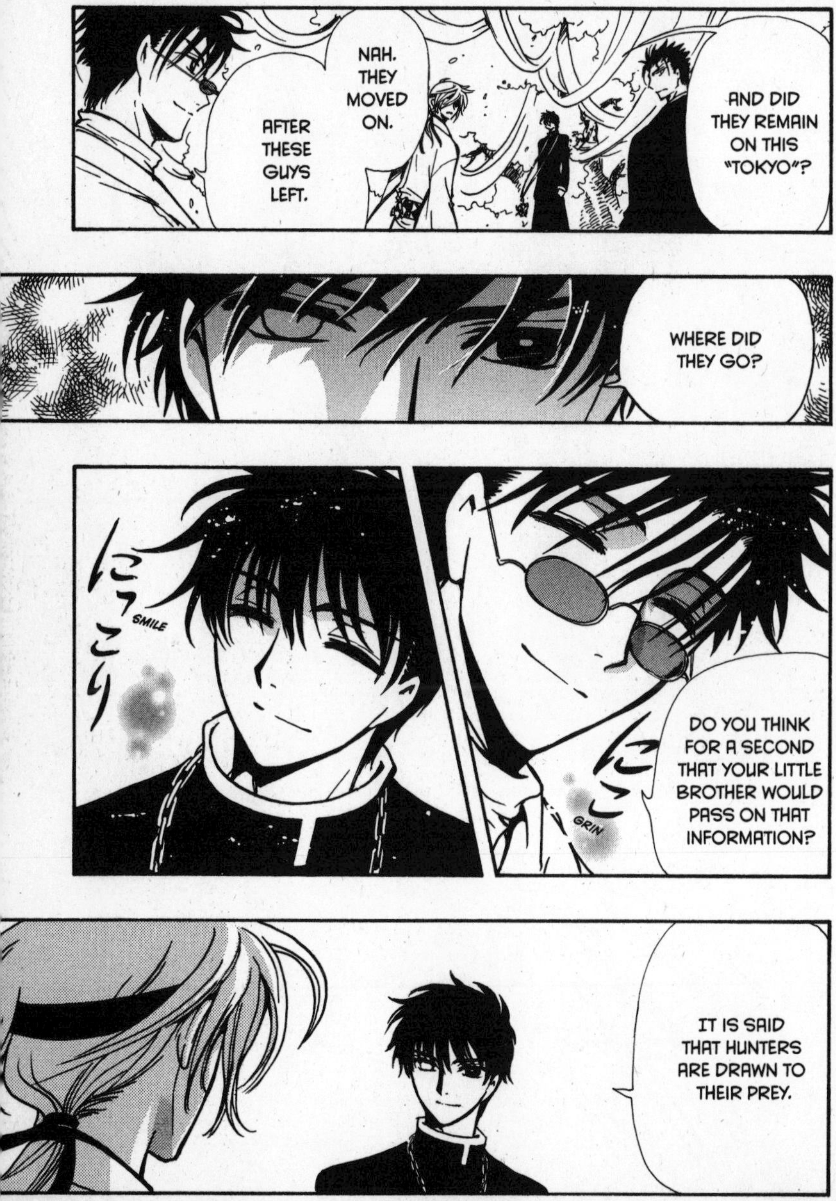
AND DID THEY REMAIN ON THIS "TOKYO"?
NAH. THEY MOVED ON.
AFTER THESE GUYS LEFT.
WHERE DID THEY GO?
DO YOU THINK FOR A SECOND THAT YOUR LITTLE BROTHER WOULD PASS ON THAT INFORMATION?
GRIN
にっこり
SMILE
IT IS SAID THAT HUNTERS ARE DRAWN TO THEIR PREY.

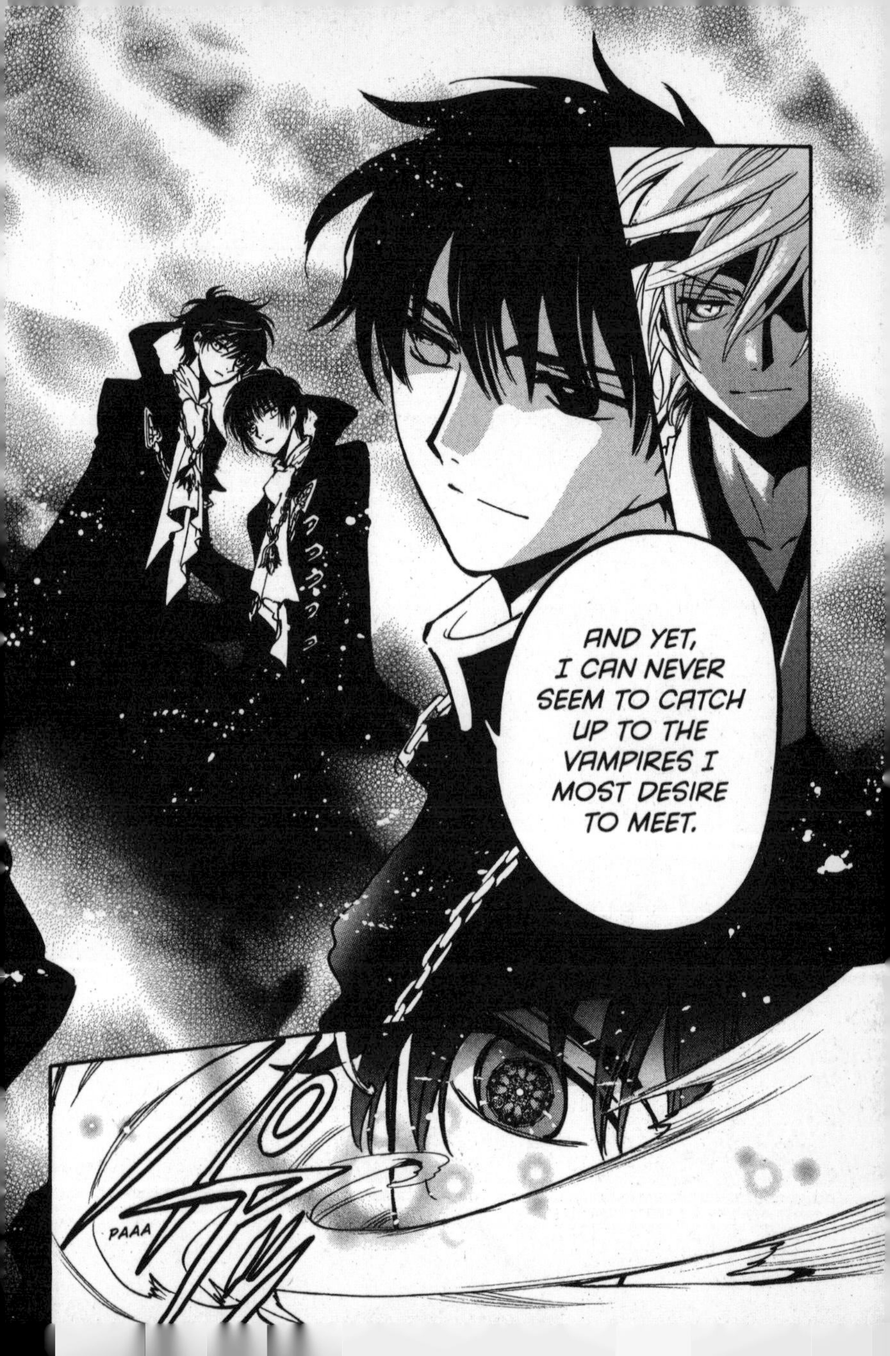
AND YET, I CAN NEVER SEEM TO CATCH UP TO THE VAMPIRES I MOST DESIRE TO MEET.
PAAA

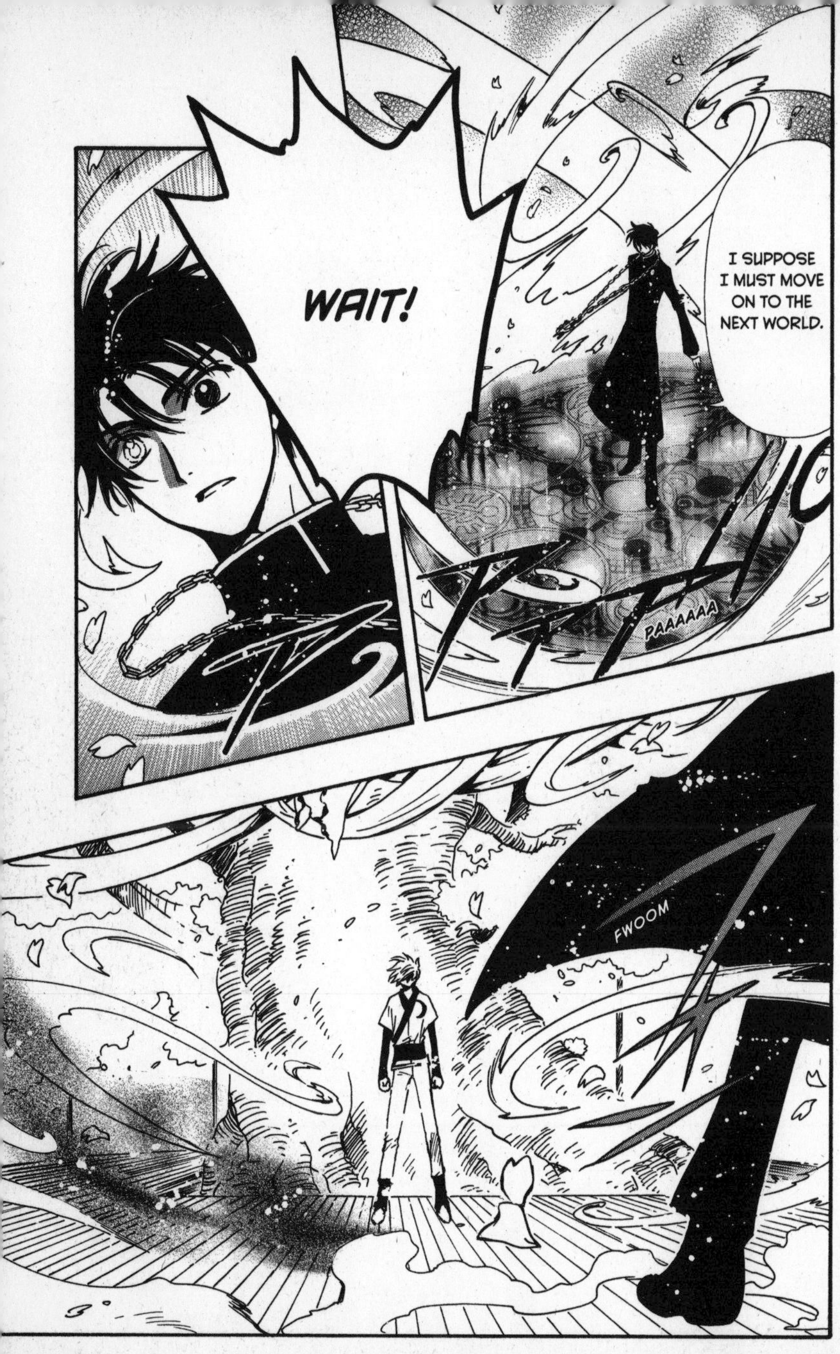
I SUPPOSE I MUST MOVE ON TO THE NEXT WORLD.
PAAAAAA
WAIT!
FWOOM

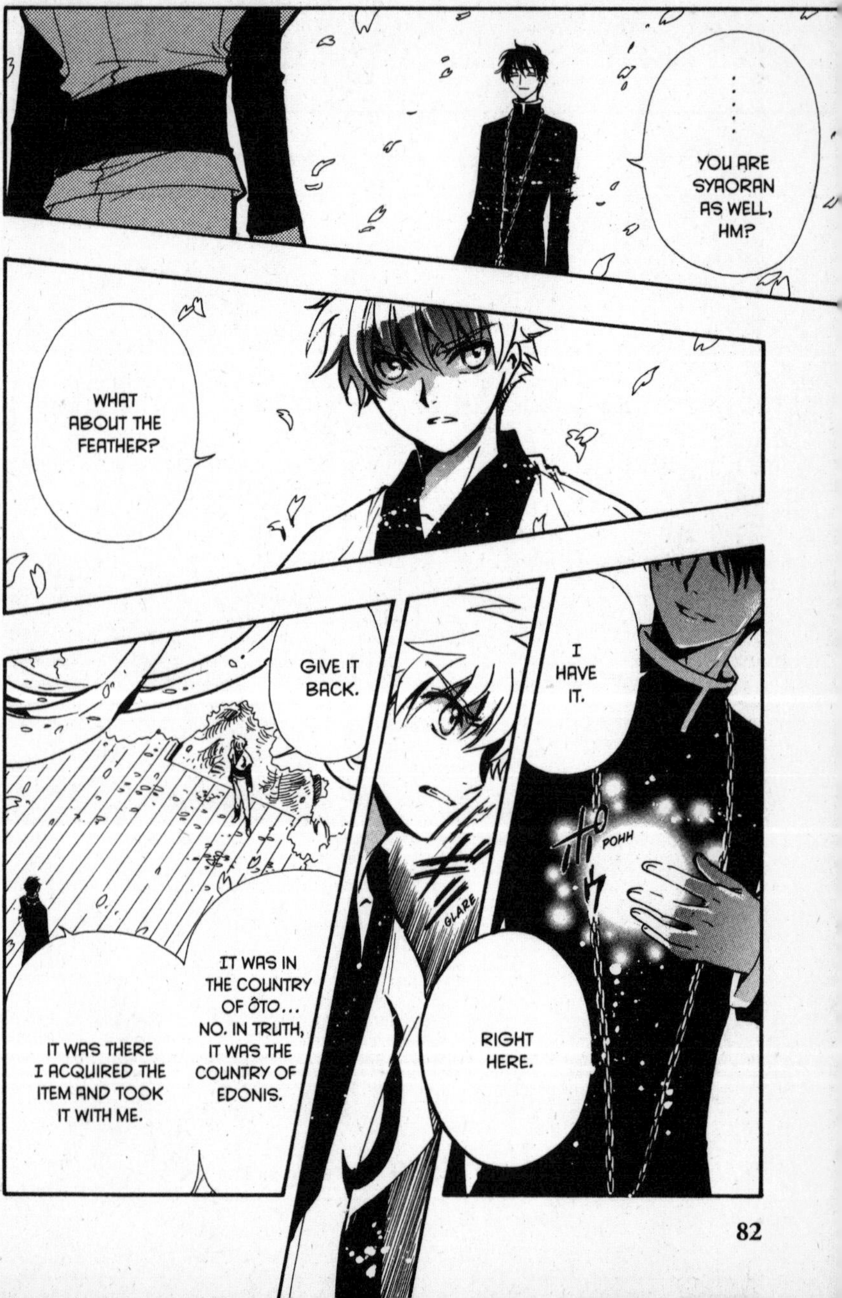
......
YOU ARE SYAORAN AS WELL, HM?
WHAT ABOUT THE FEATHER?
I HAVE IT.
POHH
RIGHT HERE.
GIVE IT BACK.
GLARE
IT WAS IN THE COUNTRY OF ÔTO... NO. IN TRUTH, IT WAS THE COUNTRY OF EDONIS.
IT WAS THERE I ACQUIRED THE ITEM AND TOOK IT WITH ME.

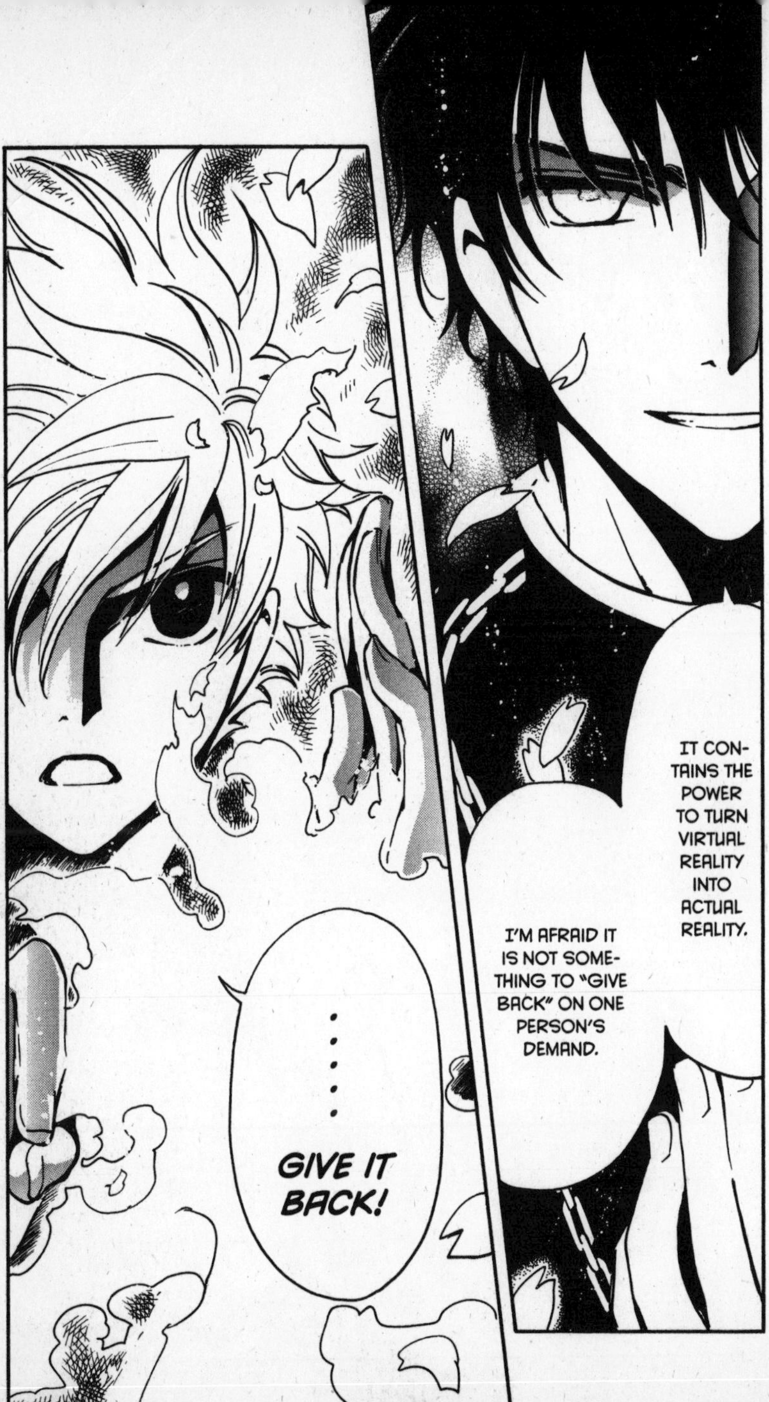
IT CONTAINS THE POWER TO TURN VIRTUAL REALITY INTO ACTUAL REALITY.
I'M AFRAID IT IS NOT SOMETHING TO "GIVE BACK" ON ONE PERSON'S DEMAND.
..... GIVE IT BACK!

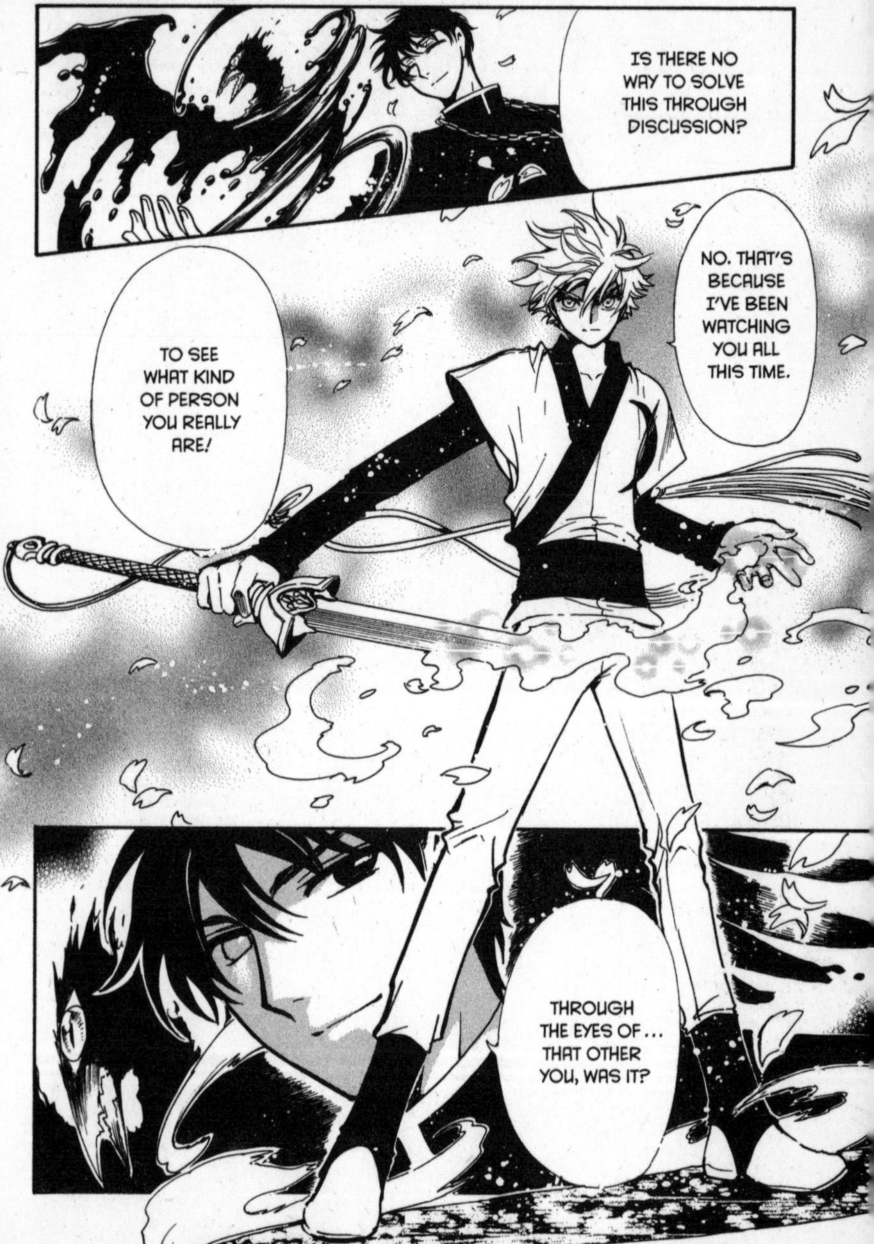
IS THERE NO WAY TO SOLVE THIS THROUGH DISCUSSION?
NO. THAT'S BECAUSE I'VE BEEN WATCHING YOU ALL THIS TIME.
TO SEE WHAT KIND OF PERSON YOU REALLY ARE!
THROUGH THE EYES OF... THAT OTHER YOU, WAS IT?

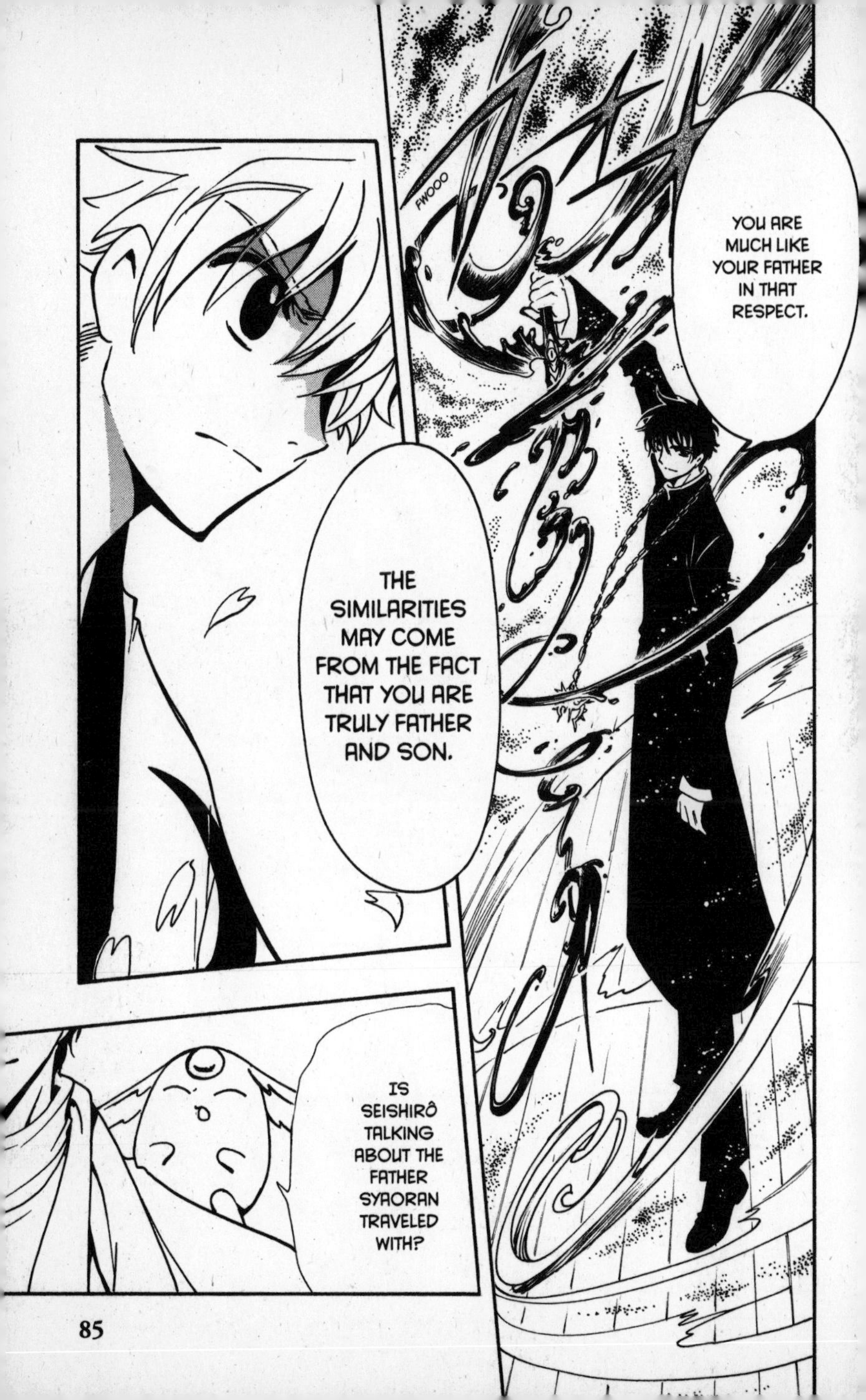
YOU ARE MUCH LIKE YOUR FATHER IN THAT RESPECT.
FWOOO
THE SIMILARITIES MAY COME FROM THE FACT THAT YOU ARE TRULY FATHER AND SON.
IS SEISHIRÔ TALKING ABOUT THE FATHER SYAORAN TRAVELED WITH?

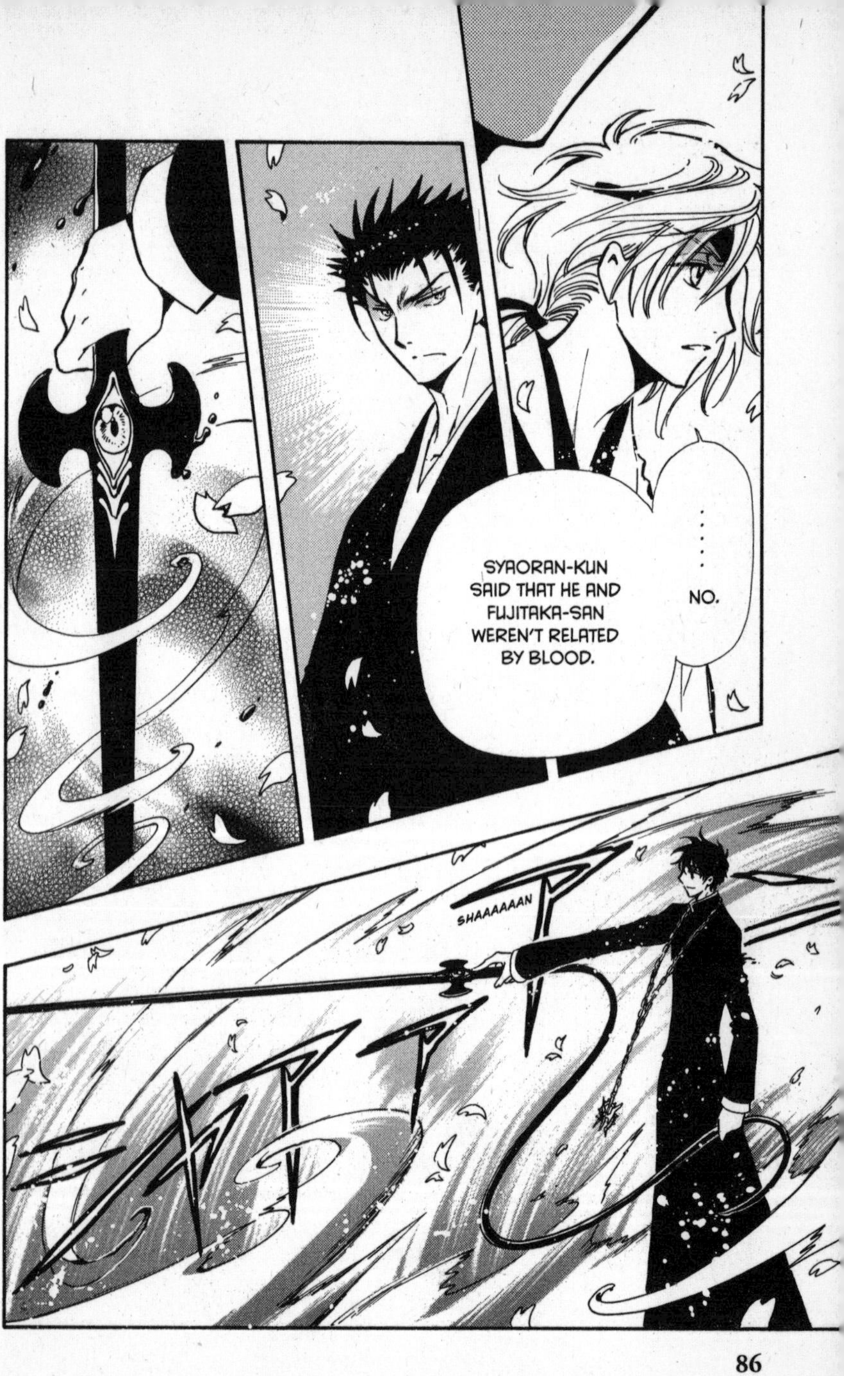
......
NO.
SYAORAN-KUN SAID THAT HE AND FUJITAKA-SAN WEREN'T RELATED BY BLOOD.
SHAAAAAAN

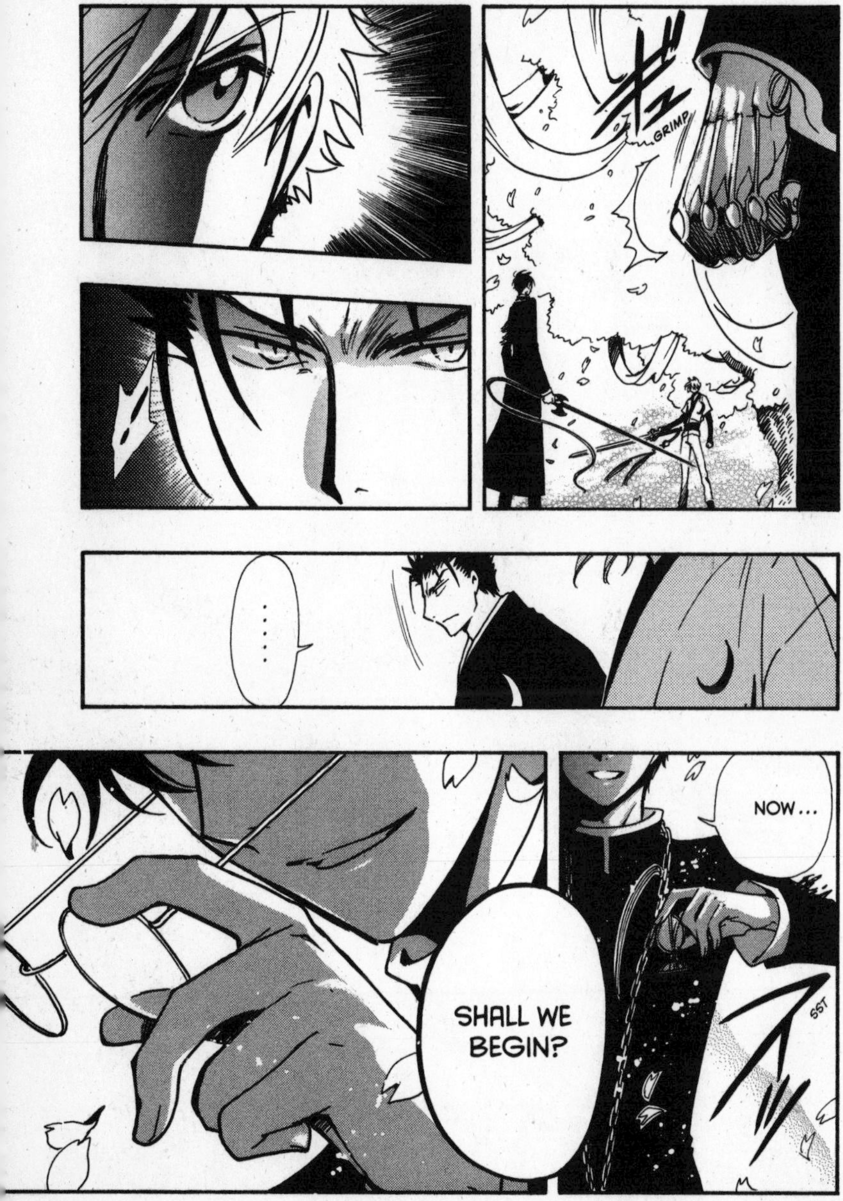
GRIMP
.....
NOW...
SST
SHALL WE BEGIN?

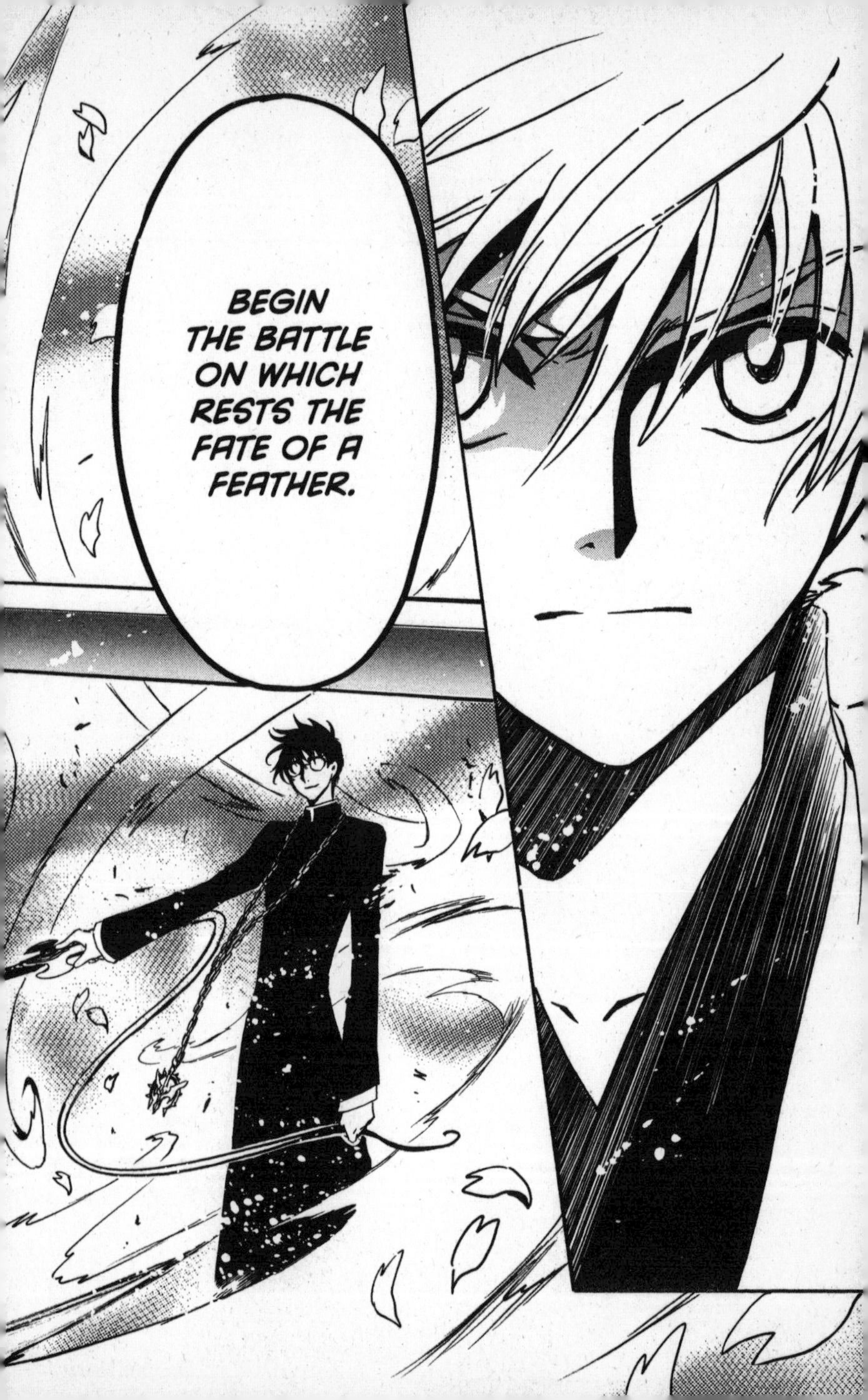
BEGIN THE BATTLE ON WHICH RESTS THE FATE OF A FEATHER.

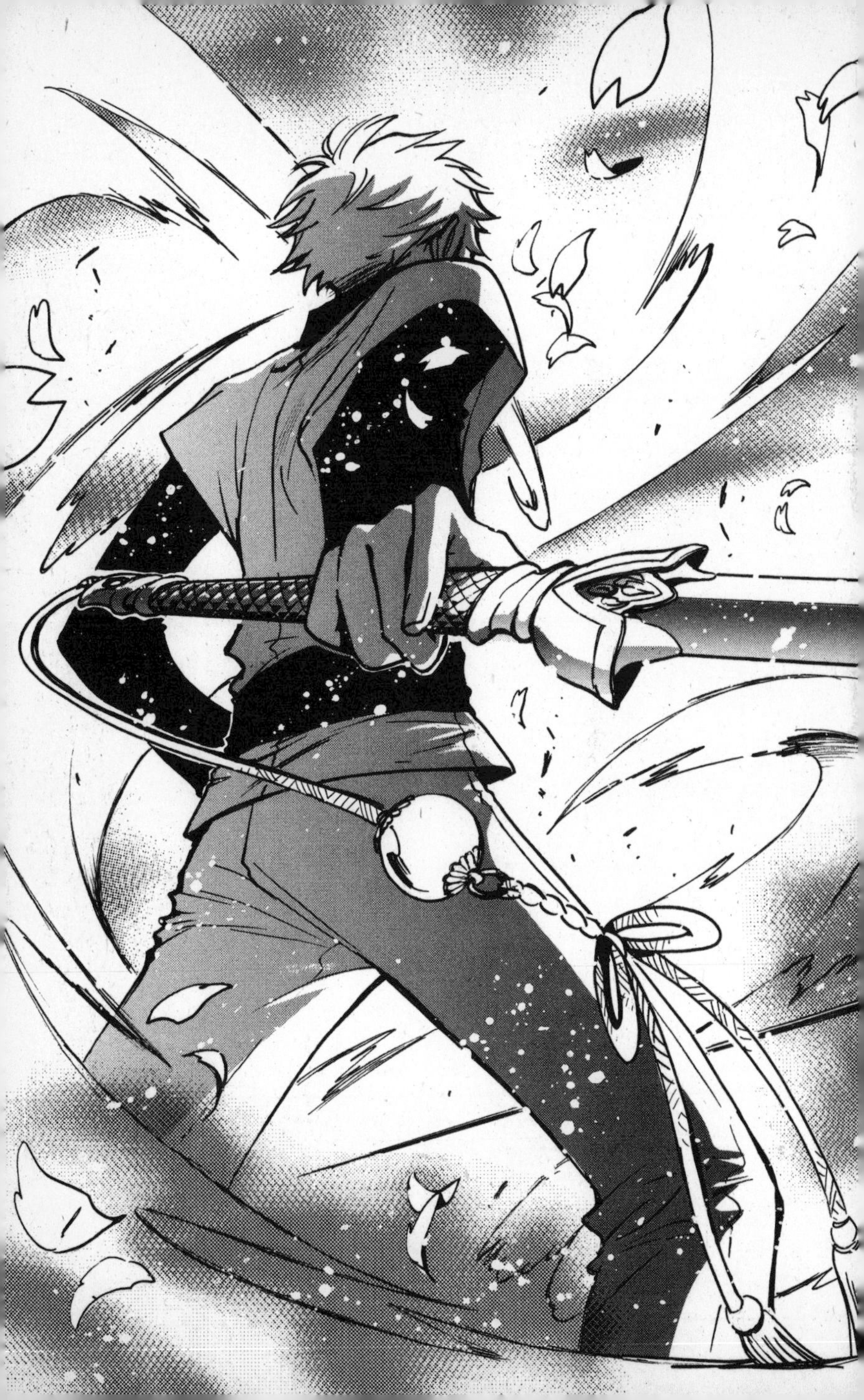

RESERVoir CHRoNiCLE

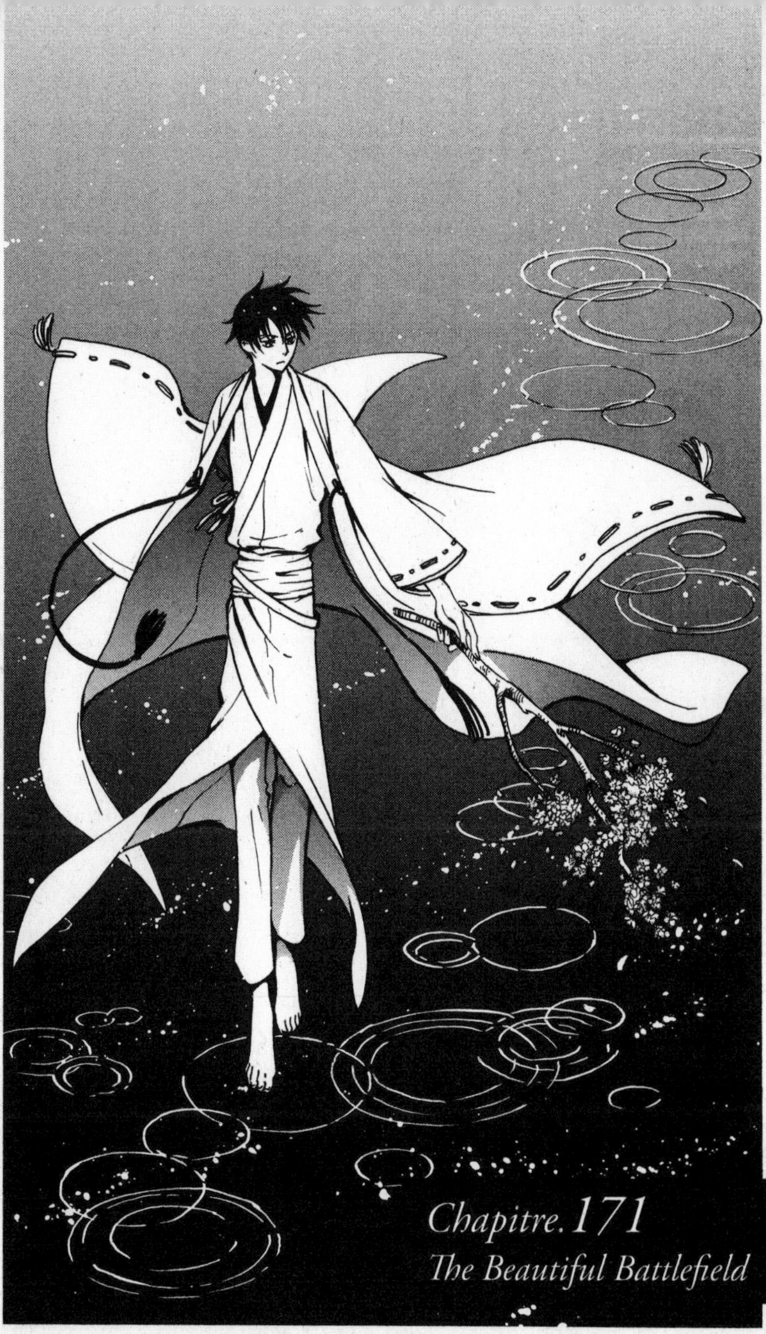
Chapitre. 171
The Beautiful Battlefield

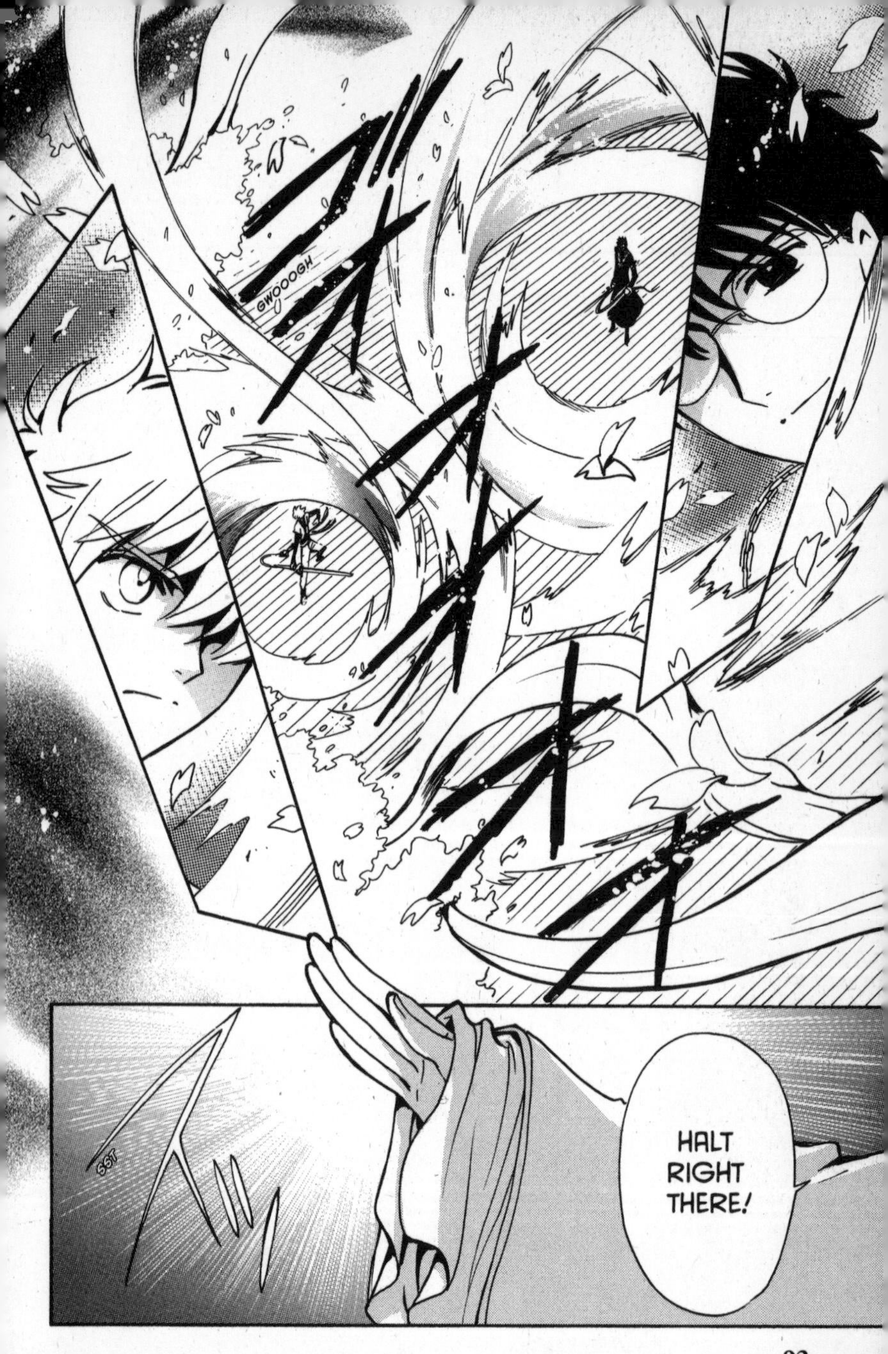
GWOOOGH
SSST
HALT RIGHT THERE!

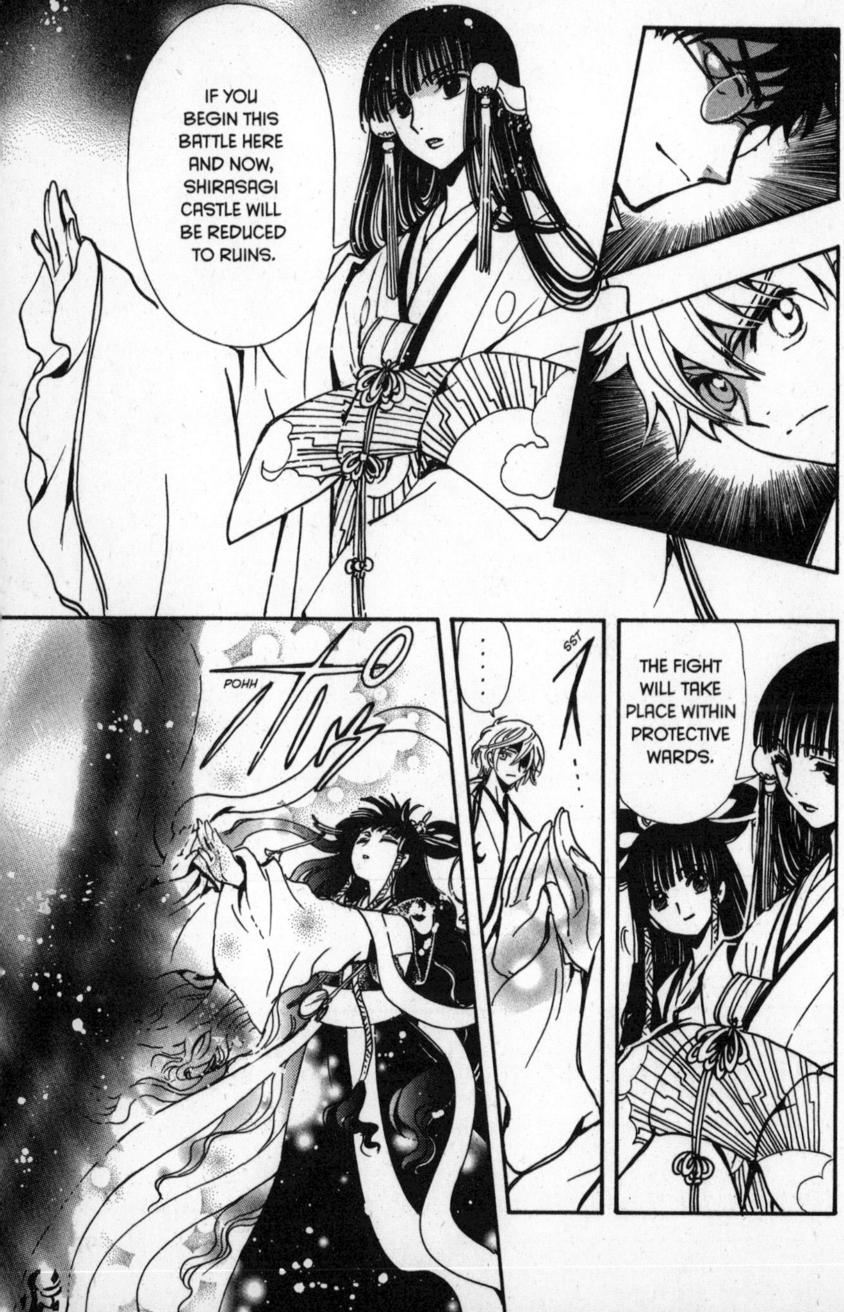
IF YOU BEGIN THIS BATTLE HERE AND NOW, SHIRASAGI CASTLE WILL BE REDUCED TO RUINS.
THE FIGHT WILL TAKE PLACE WITHIN PROTECTIVE WARDS.
......
SST
POHH

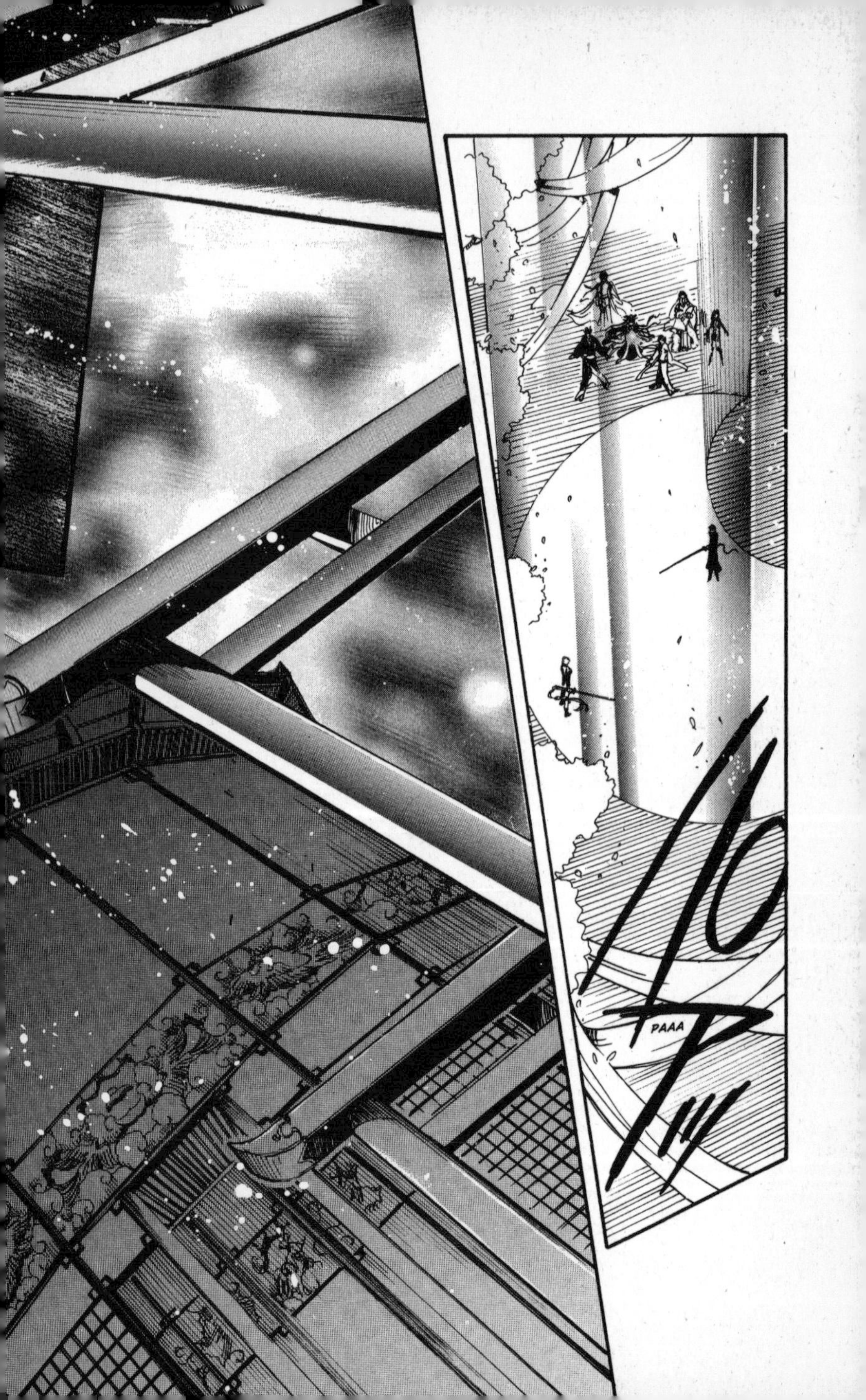
PAAA

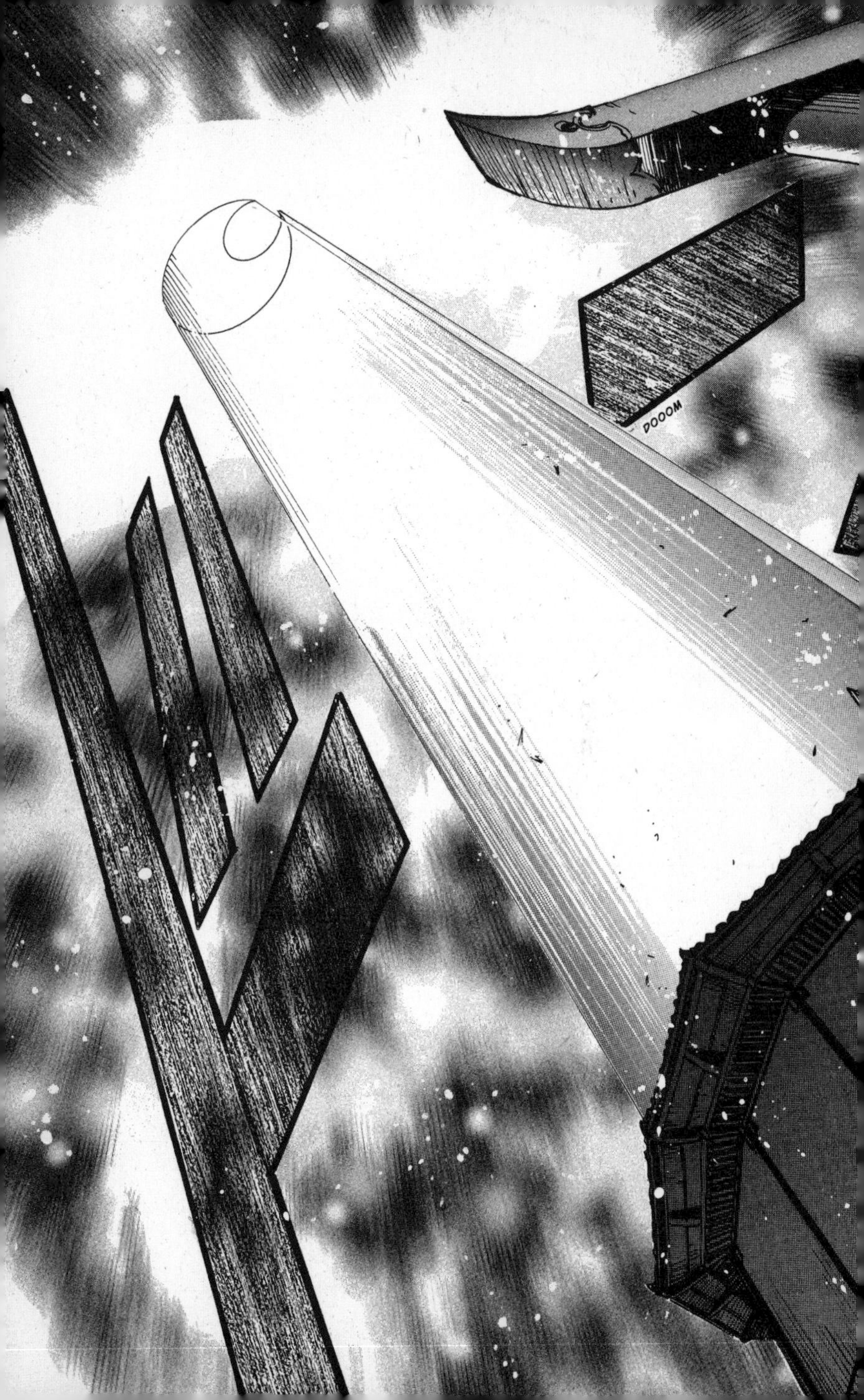
DOOOM

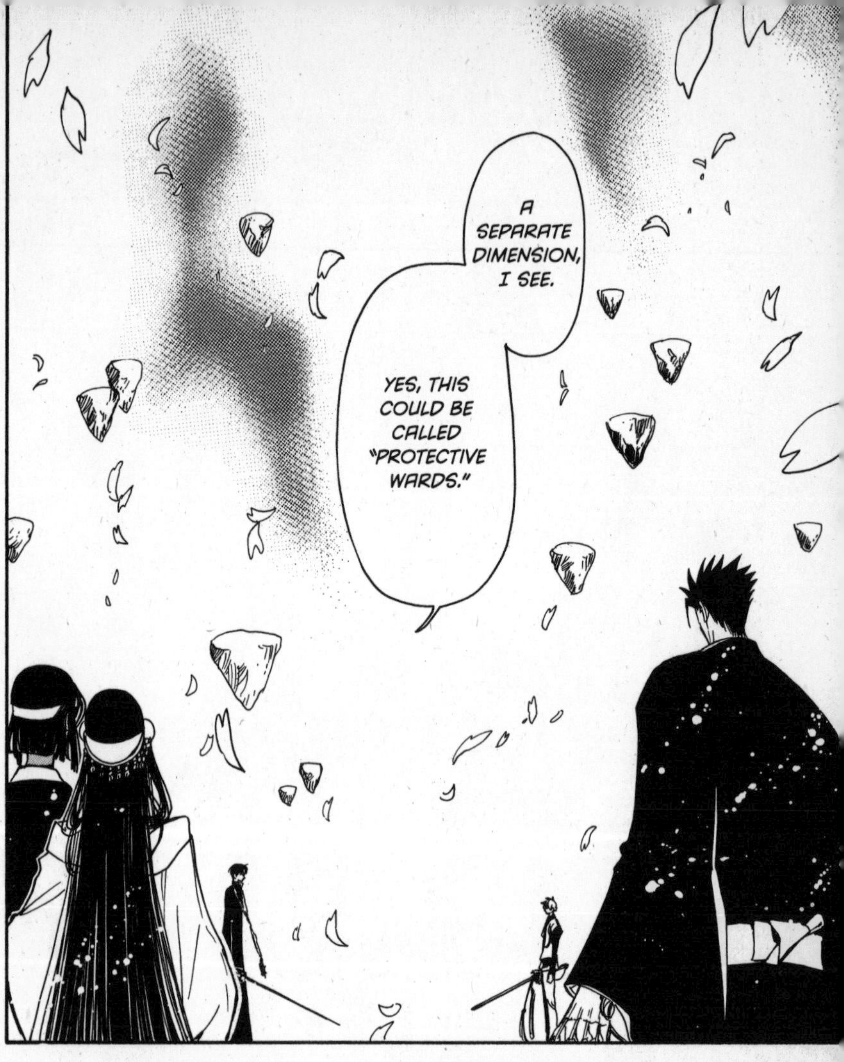
A SEPARATE DIMENSION, I SEE.
YES, THIS COULD BE CALLED "PROTECTIVE WARDS."

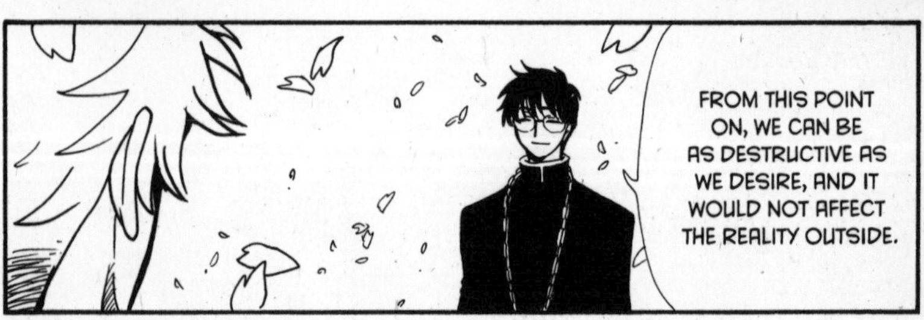
FROM THIS POINT ON, WE CAN BE AS DESTRUCTIVE AS WE DESIRE, AND IT WOULD NOT AFFECT THE REALITY OUTSIDE.

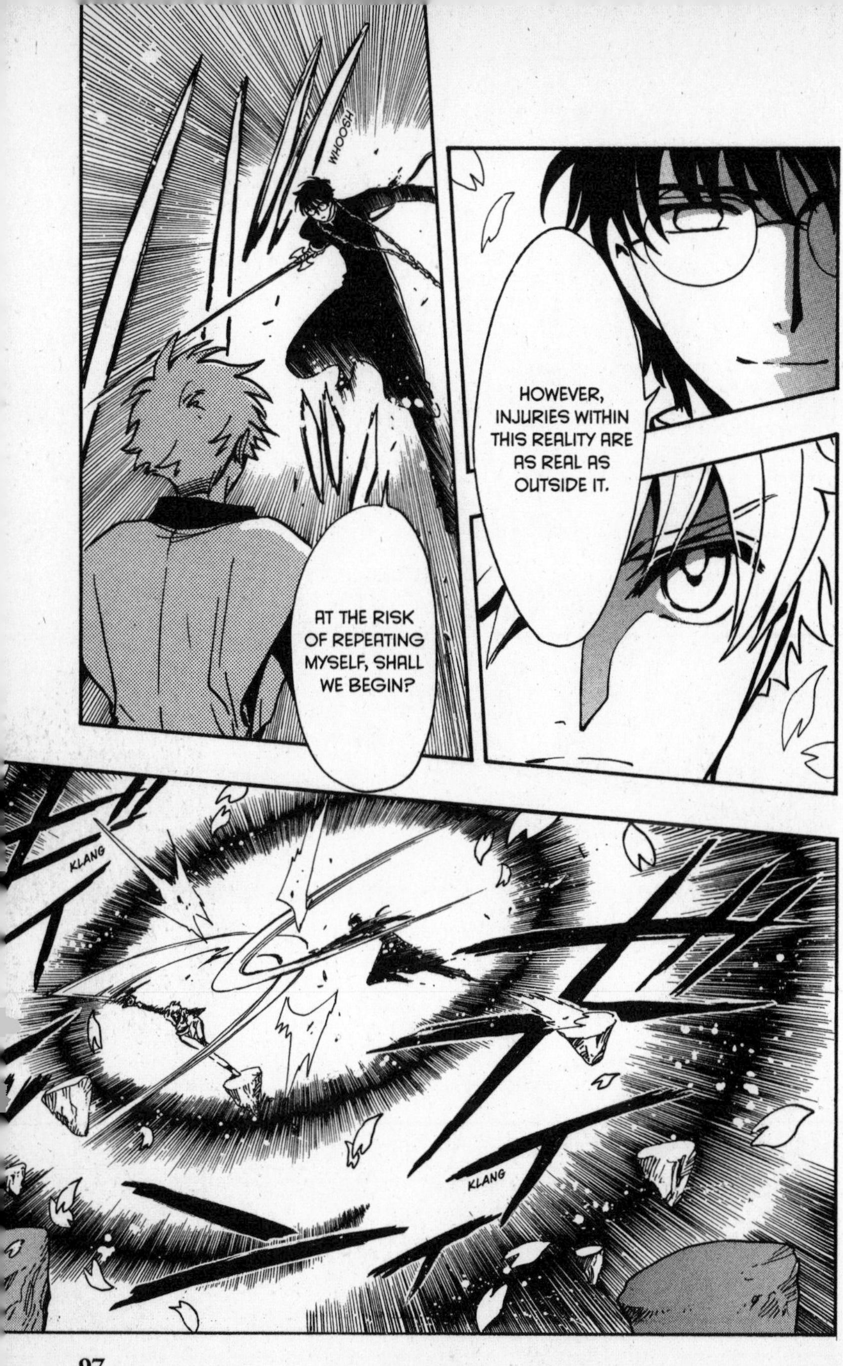
HOWEVER, INJURIES WITHIN THIS REALITY ARE AS REAL AS OUTSIDE IT.
WHOOSH
AT THE RISK OF REPEATING MYSELF, SHALL WE BEGIN?
KLANG
KLANG

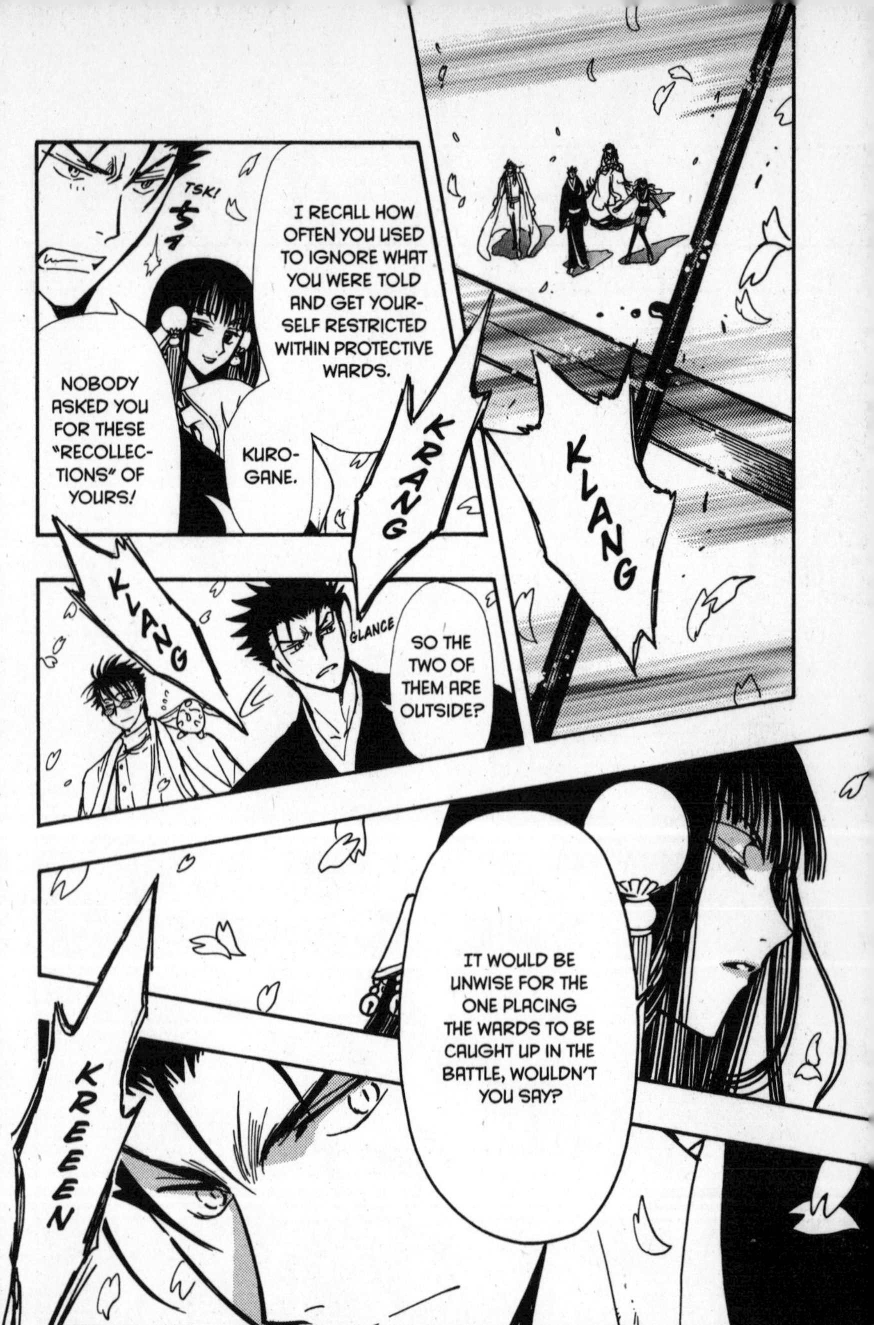
KVANG
I RECALL HOW OFTEN YOU USED TO IGNORE WHAT YOU WERE TOLD AND GET YOUR-SELF RESTRICTED WITHIN PROTECTIVE WARDS.
KURO-GANE.
TSK!
NOBODY ASKED YOU FOR THESE "RECOLLEC-TIONS" OF YOURS!
KRANG
GLANCE
SO THE TWO OF THEM ARE OUTSIDE?
KVANG
IT WOULD BE UNWISE FOR THE ONE PLACING THE WARDS TO BE CAUGHT UP IN THE BATTLE, WOULDN'T YOU SAY?
KREEEN

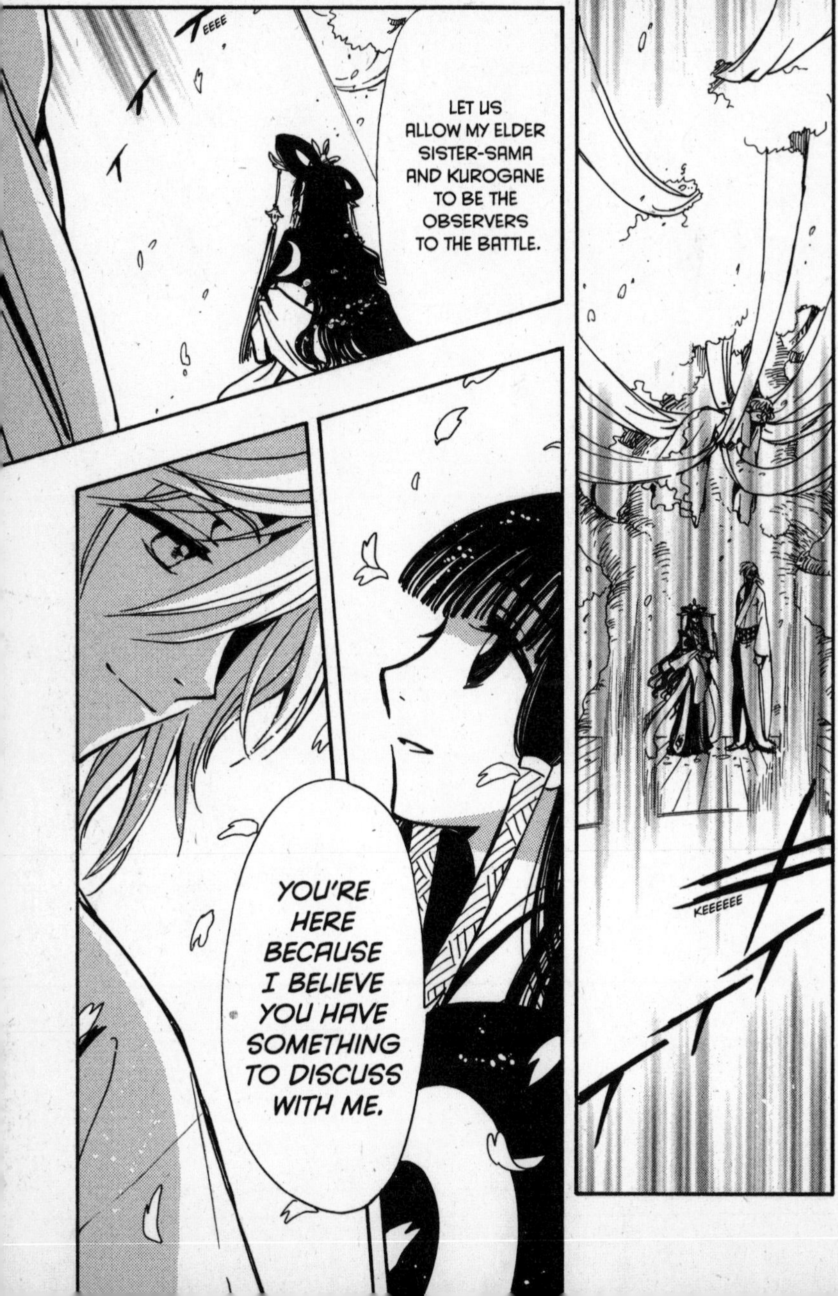
KEEEEEE
TEEEE
LET US ALLOW MY ELDER SISTER-SAMA AND KUROGANE TO BE THE OBSERVERS TO THE BATTLE.
YOU'RE HERE BECAUSE I BELIEVE YOU HAVE SOMETHING TO DISCUSS WITH ME.

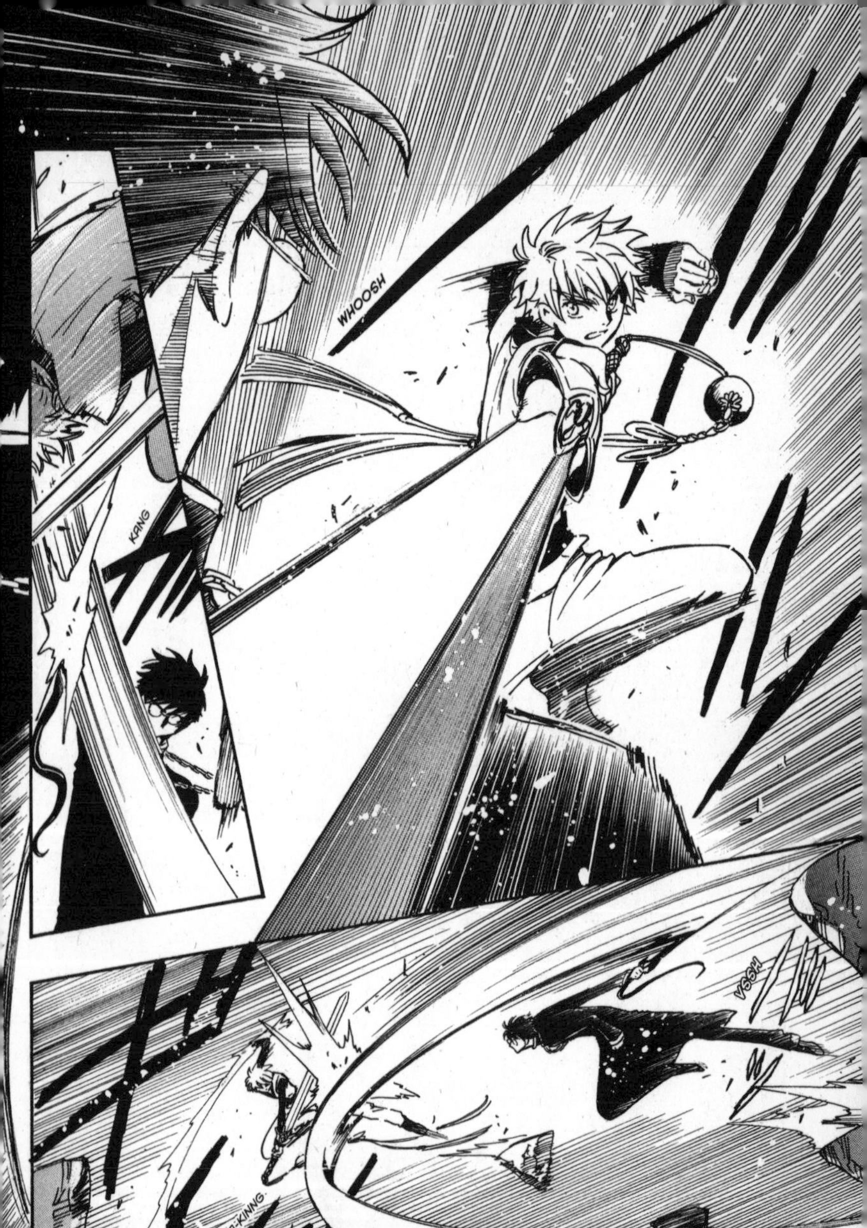
WHOOSH
KANG
VSSH
KA-KINNG

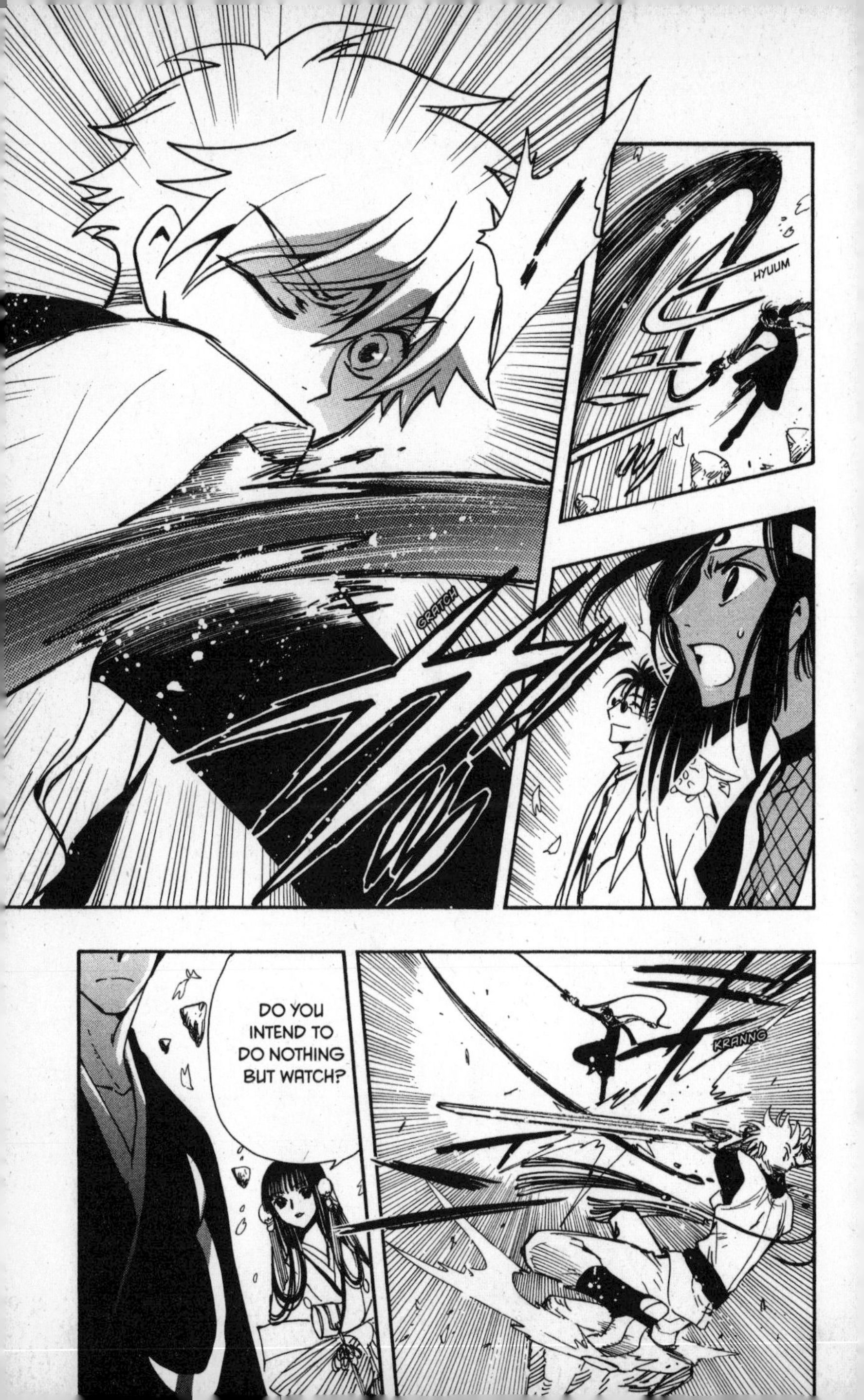
HYUUM
GRATCH
KRANNG
DO YOU INTEND TO DO NOTHING BUT WATCH?

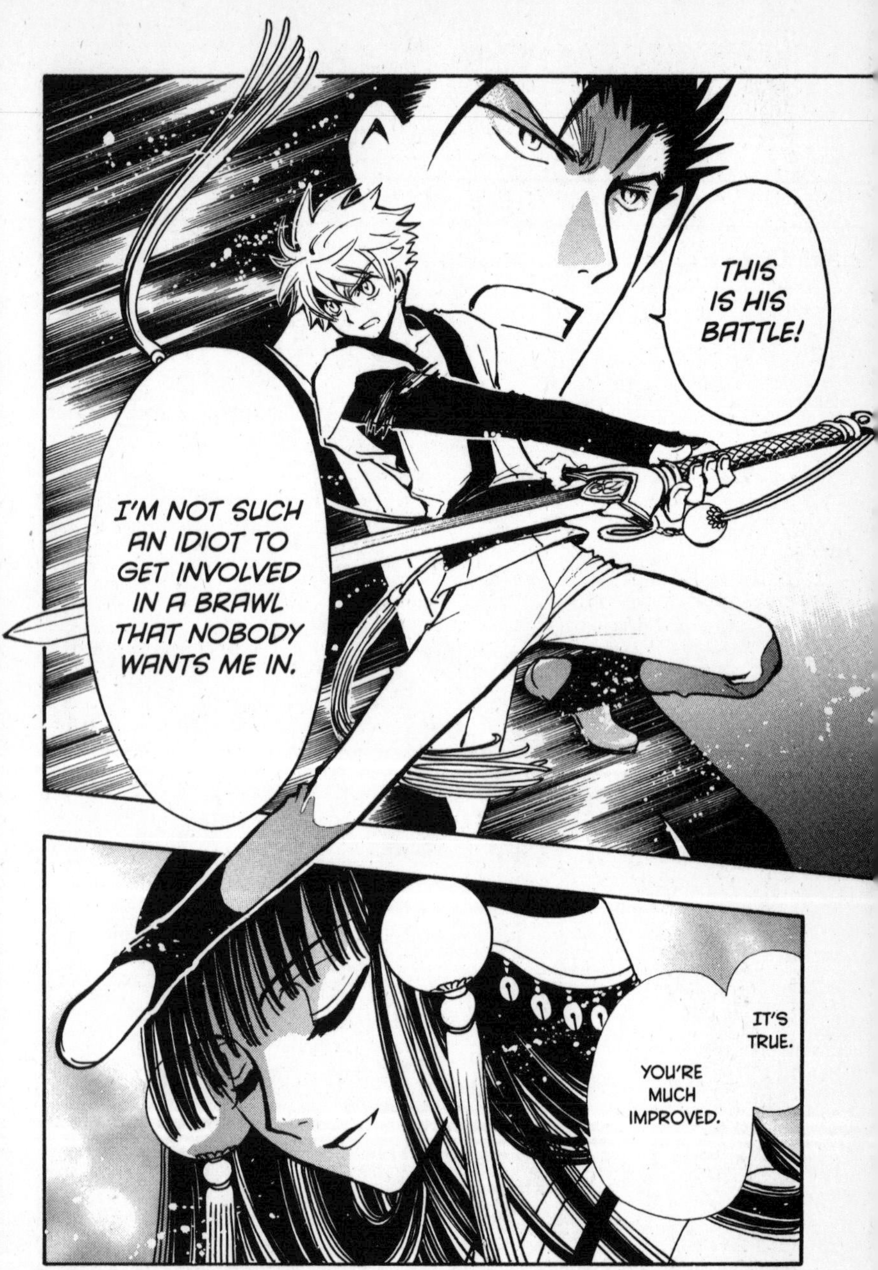
THIS IS HIS BATTLE!
I'M NOT SUCH AN IDIOT TO GET INVOLVED IN A BRAWL THAT NOBODY WANTS ME IN.
IT'S TRUE.
YOU'RE MUCH IMPROVED.

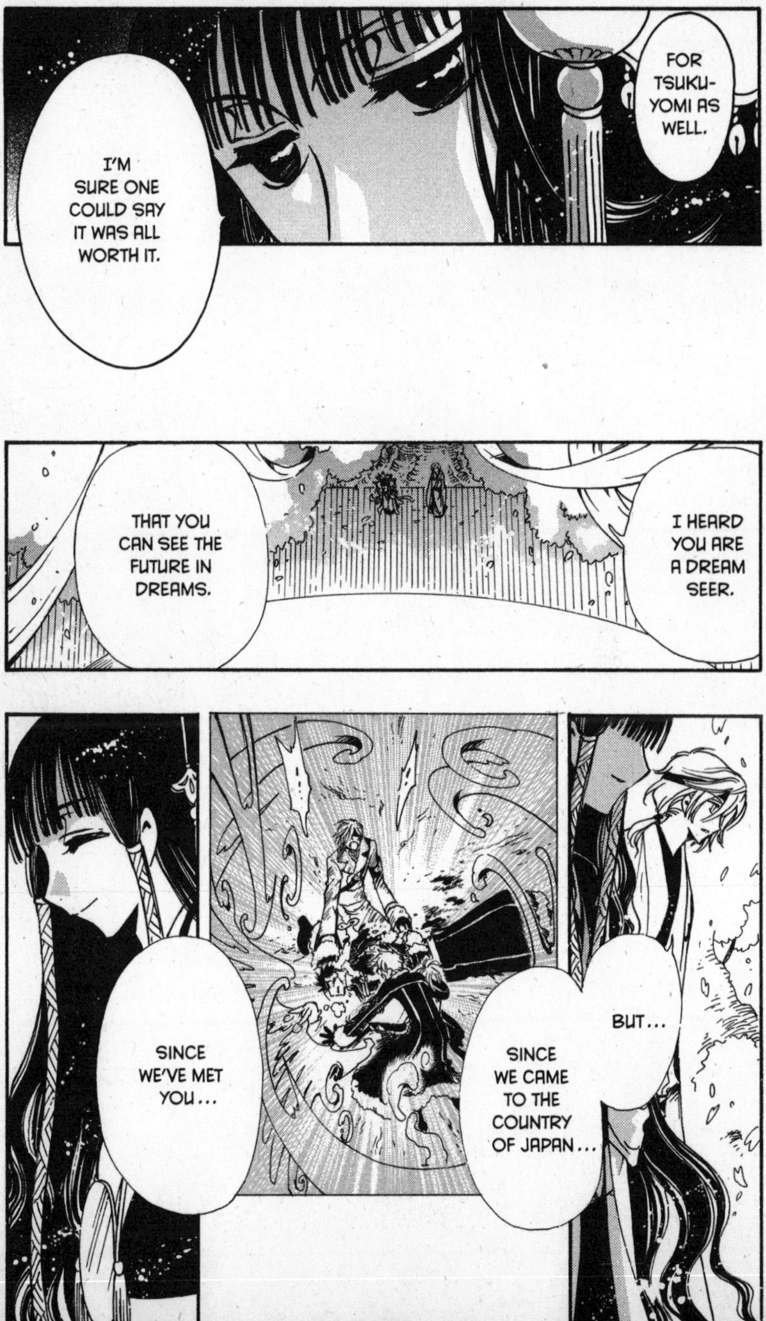

FOR TSUKU-YOMI AS WELL.
I'M SURE ONE COULD SAY IT WAS ALL WORTH IT.
I HEARD YOU ARE A DREAM SEER.
THAT YOU CAN SEE THE FUTURE IN DREAMS.
BUT...
SINCE WE CAME TO THE COUNTRY OF JAPAN...
SINCE WE'VE MET YOU...

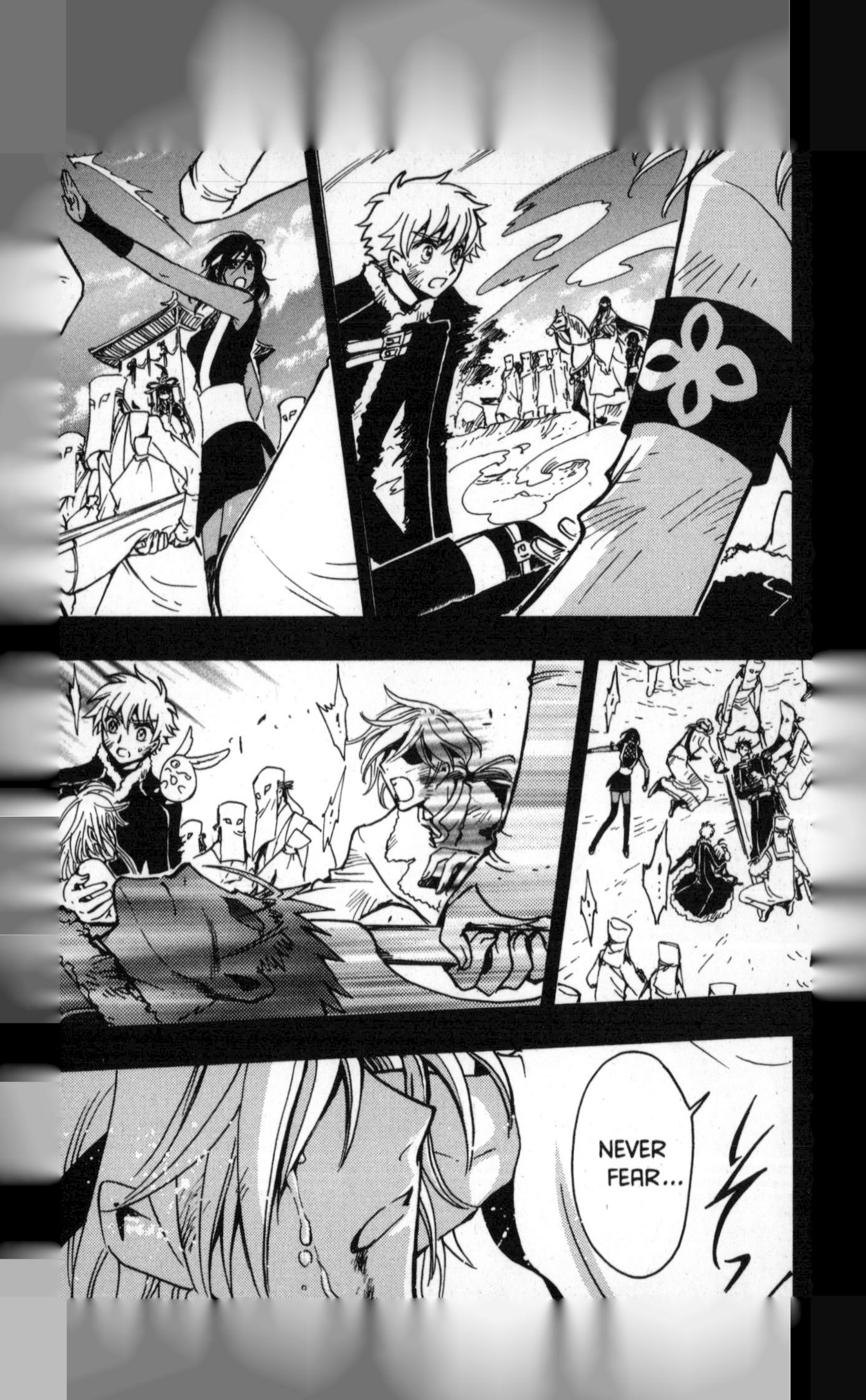
NEVER FEAR...

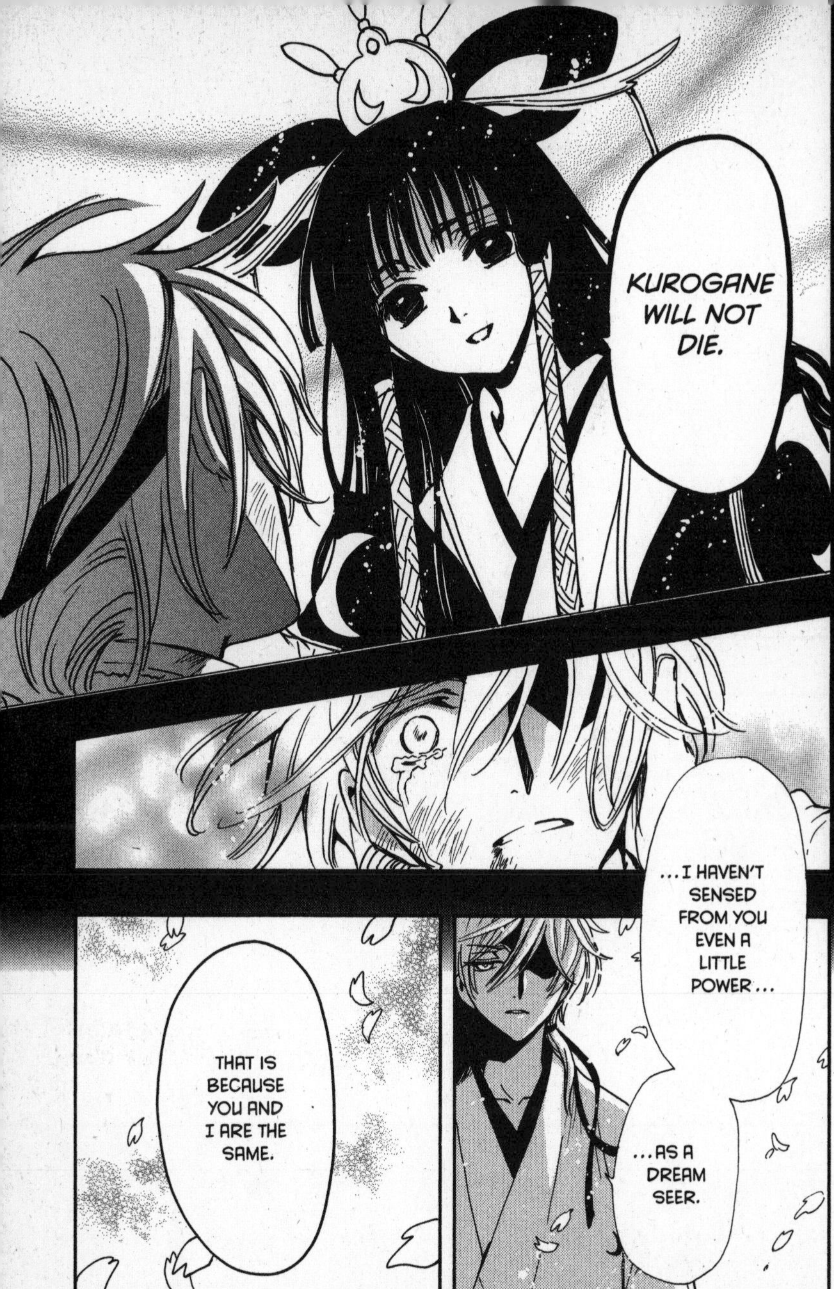
KUROGANE WILL NOT DIE.
...I HAVEN'T SENSED FROM YOU EVEN A LITTLE POWER...
...AS A DREAM SEER.
THAT IS BECAUSE YOU AND I ARE THE SAME.

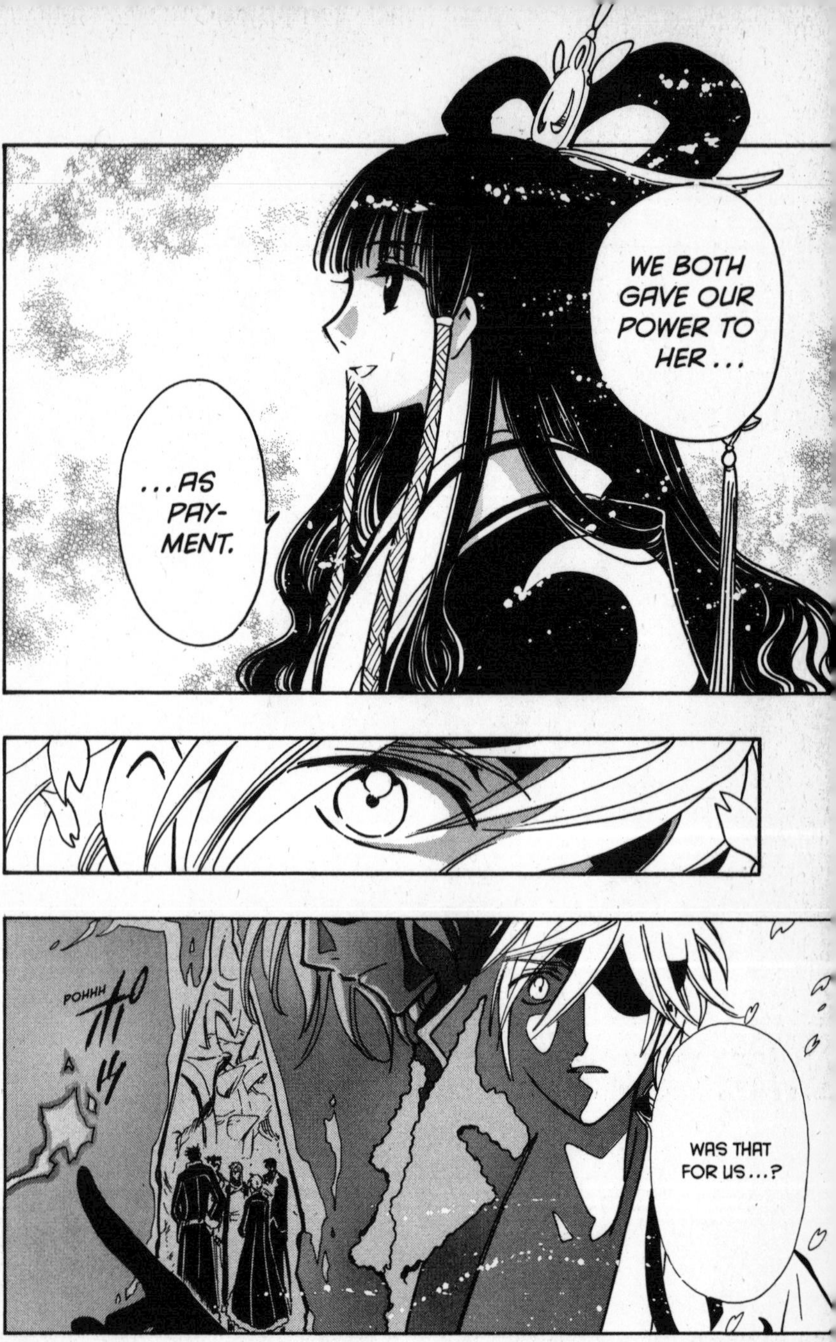
WE BOTH GAVE OUR POWER TO HER...
...AS PAY-MENT.
WAS THAT FOR US...?
POHHH

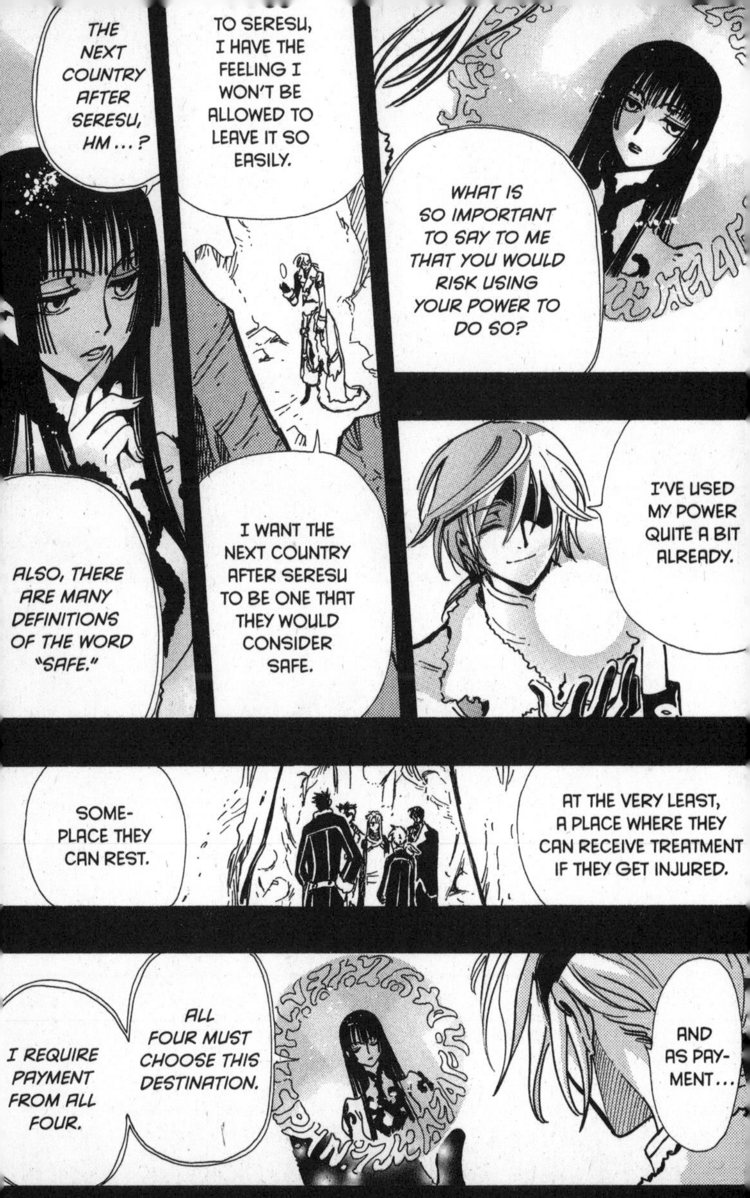
WHAT IS SO IMPORTANT TO SAY TO ME THAT YOU WOULD RISK USING YOUR POWER TO DO SO?
I'VE USED MY POWER QUITE A BIT ALREADY.
TO SERESU, I HAVE THE FEELING I WON'T BE ALLOWED TO LEAVE IT SO EASILY.
I WANT THE NEXT COUNTRY AFTER SERESU TO BE ONE THAT THEY WOULD CONSIDER SAFE.
THE NEXT COUNTRY AFTER SERESU, HM ...?
ALSO, THERE ARE MANY DEFINITIONS OF THE WORD "SAFE."
AT THE VERY LEAST, A PLACE WHERE THEY CAN RECEIVE TREATMENT IF THEY GET INJURED.
SOME-PLACE THEY CAN REST.
AND AS PAY-MENT...
ALL FOUR MUST CHOOSE THIS DESTINATION.
I REQUIRE PAYMENT FROM ALL FOUR.

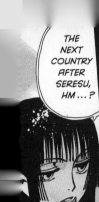

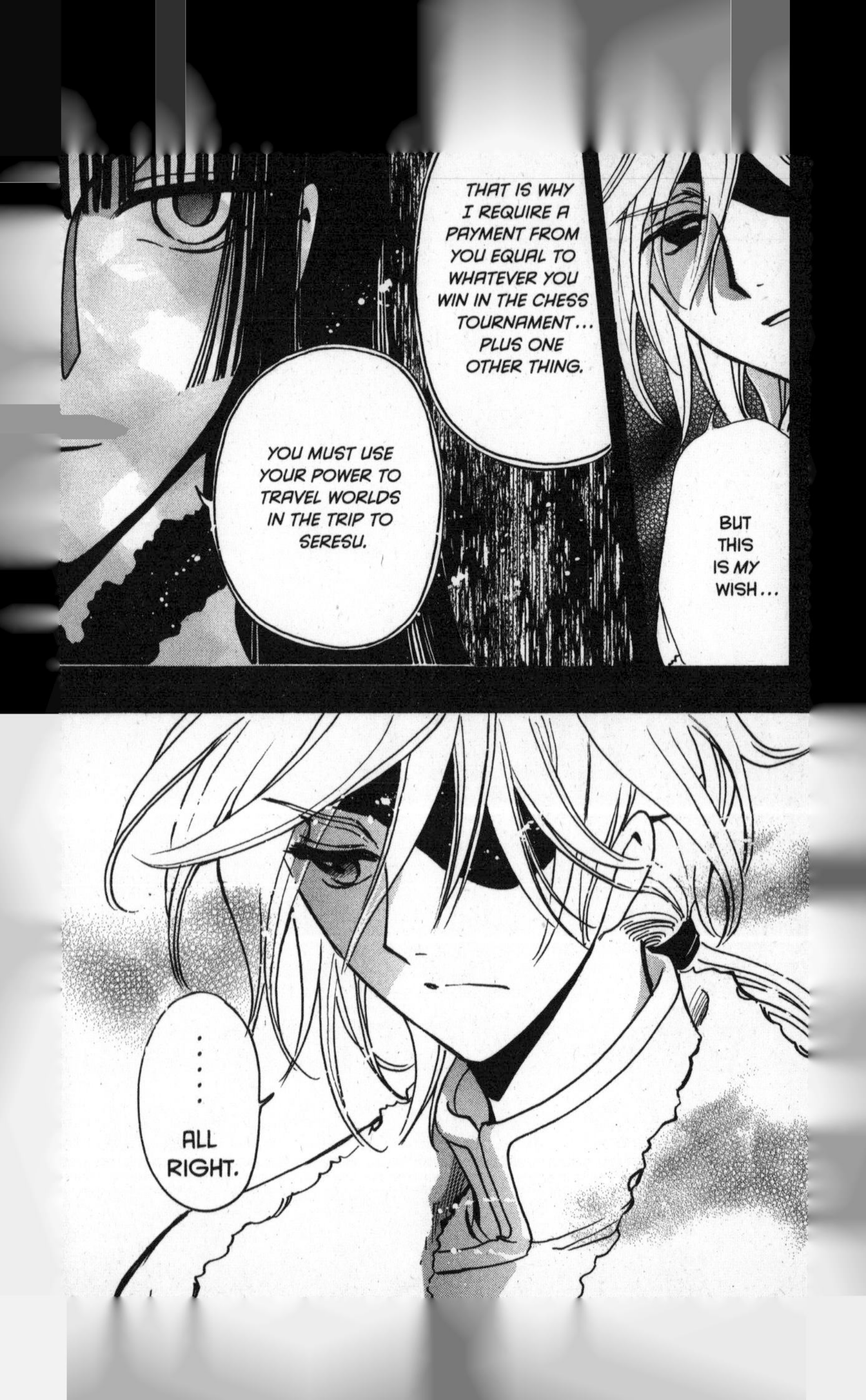
BUT THIS IS MY WISH...
THAT IS WHY I REQUIRE A PAYMENT FROM YOU EQUAL TO WHATEVER YOU WIN IN THE CHESS TOURNAMENT... PLUS ONE OTHER THING.
YOU MUST USE YOUR POWER TO TRAVEL WORLDS IN THE TRIP TO SERESU.
..... ALL RIGHT.

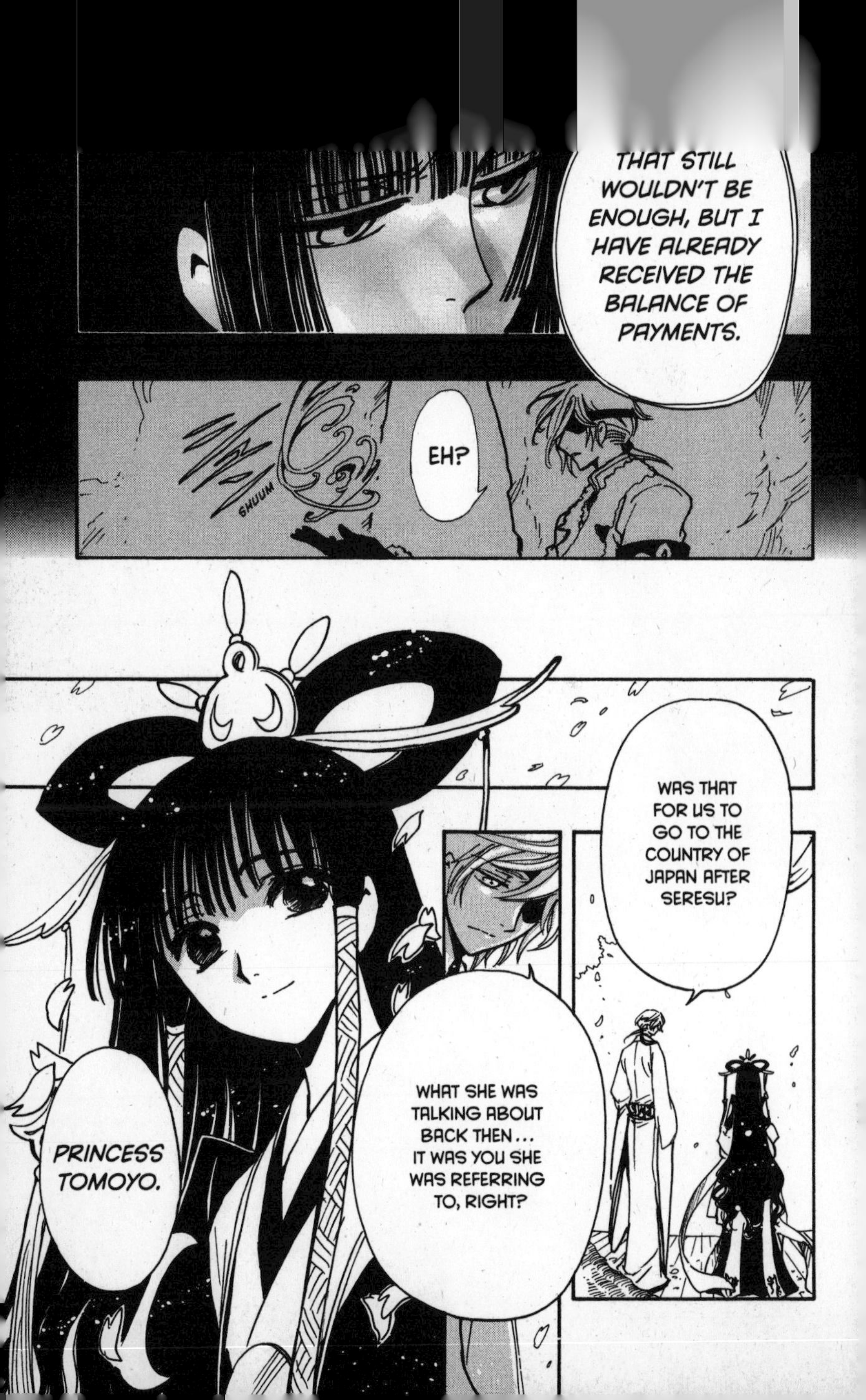
THAT STILL WOULDN'T BE ENOUGH, BUT I HAVE ALREADY RECEIVED THE BALANCE OF PAYMENTS.
EH?
SHUUM
WAS THAT FOR US TO GO TO THE COUNTRY OF JAPAN AFTER SERESU?
WHAT SHE WAS TALKING ABOUT BACK THEN... IT WAS YOU SHE WAS REFERRING TO, RIGHT?
PRINCESS TOMOYO.

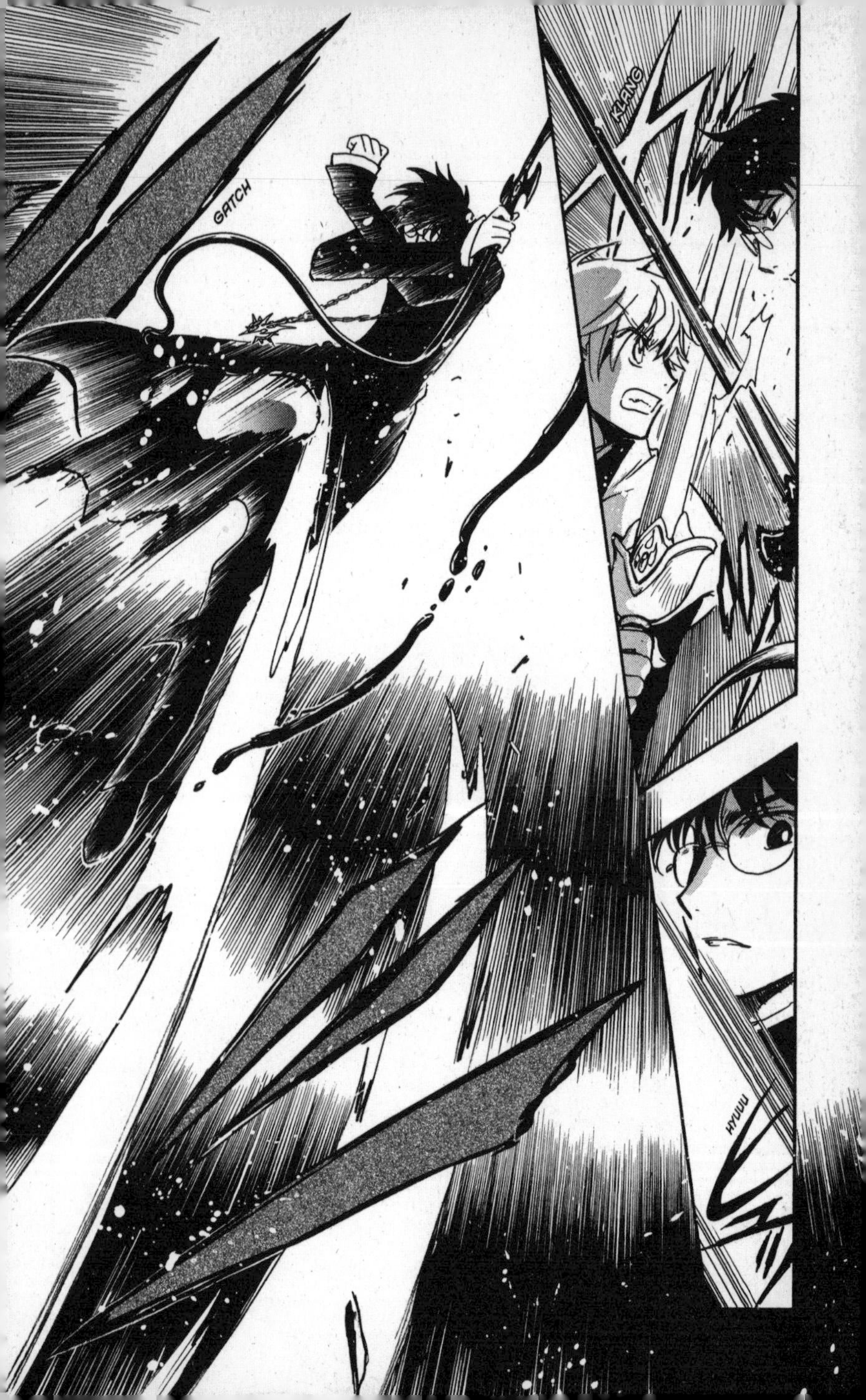
KLANG
HYUUU
GATCH

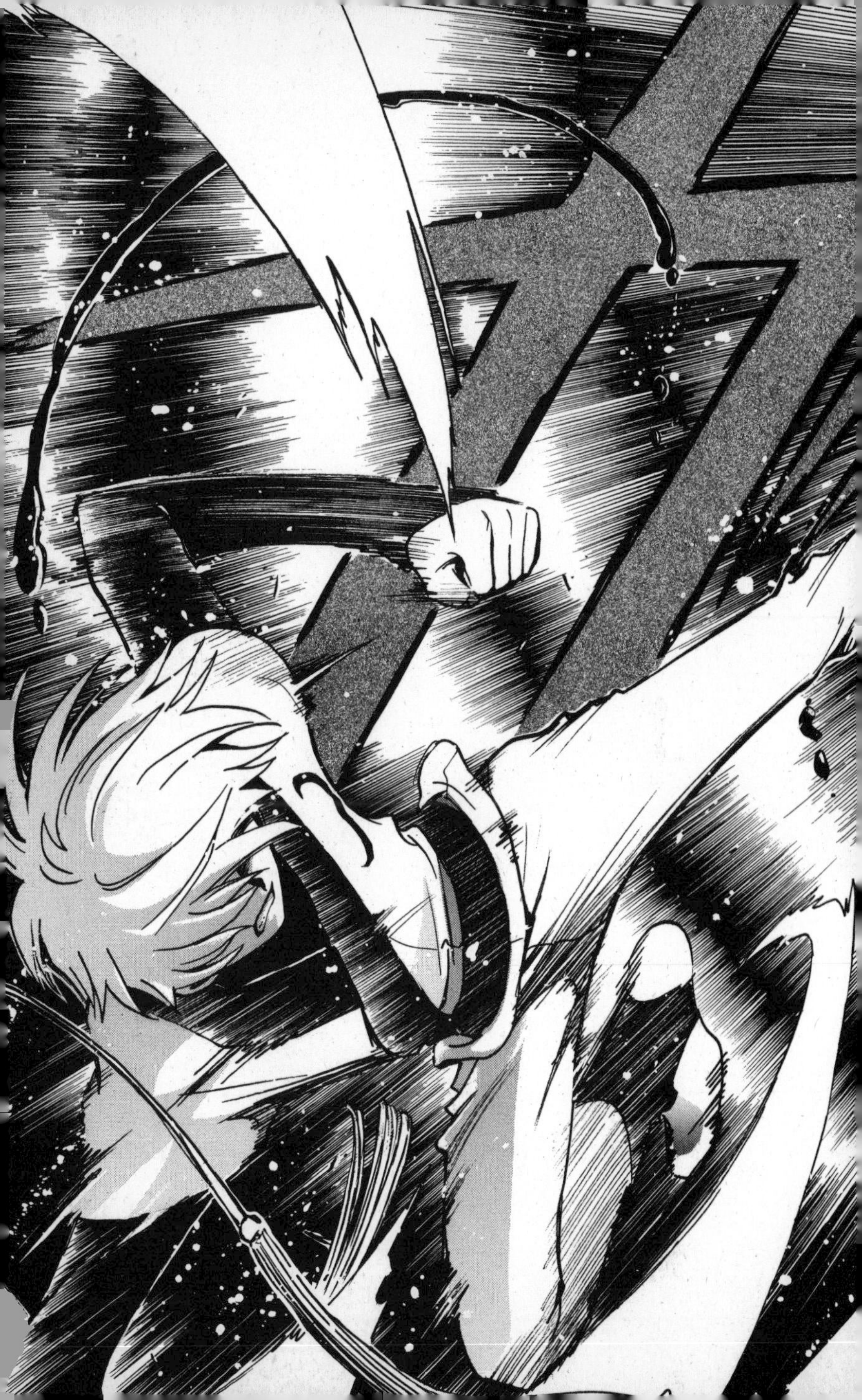

ツバサ

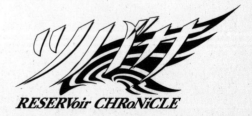

RESERVoir CHRoNiCLE

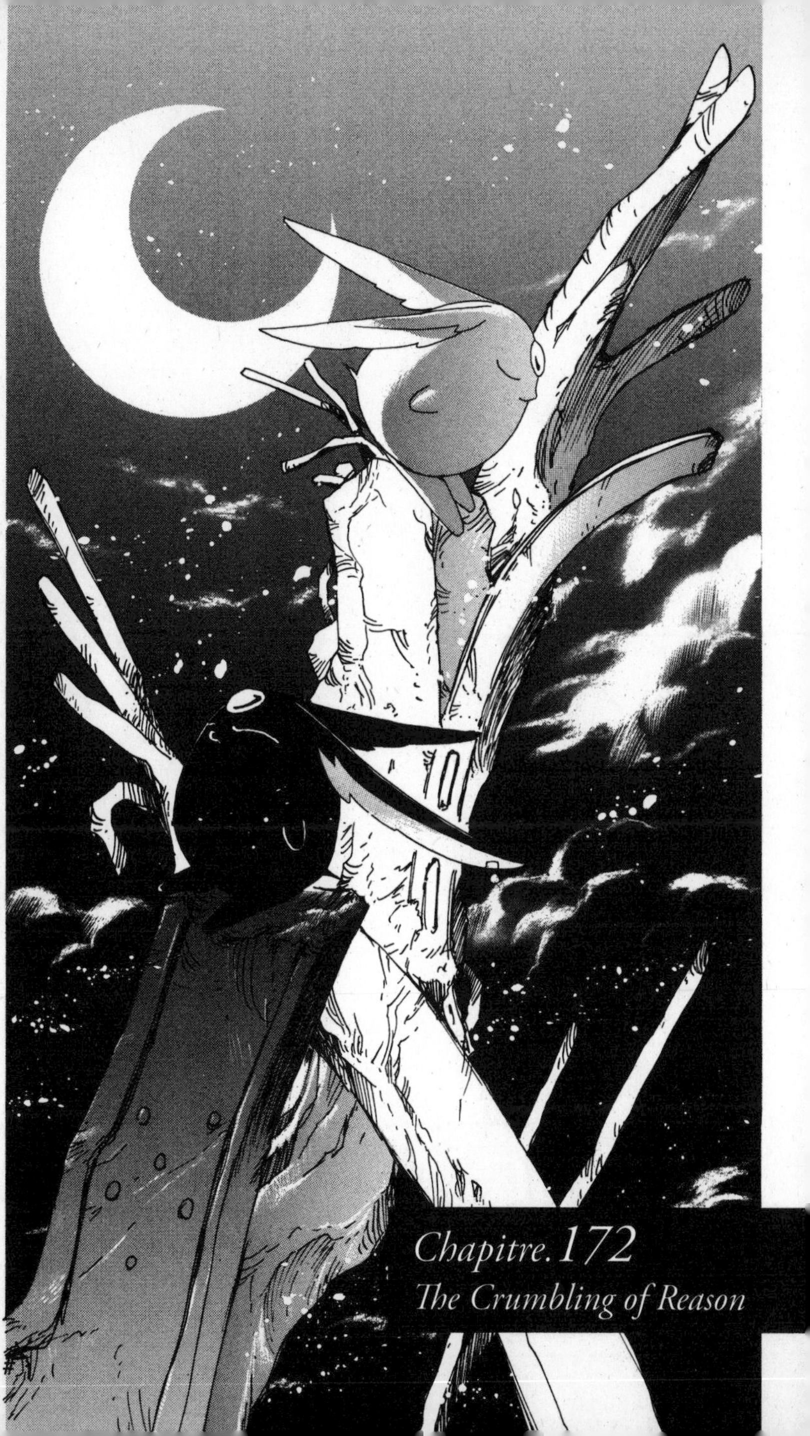
Chapitre. 172
The Crumbling of Reason

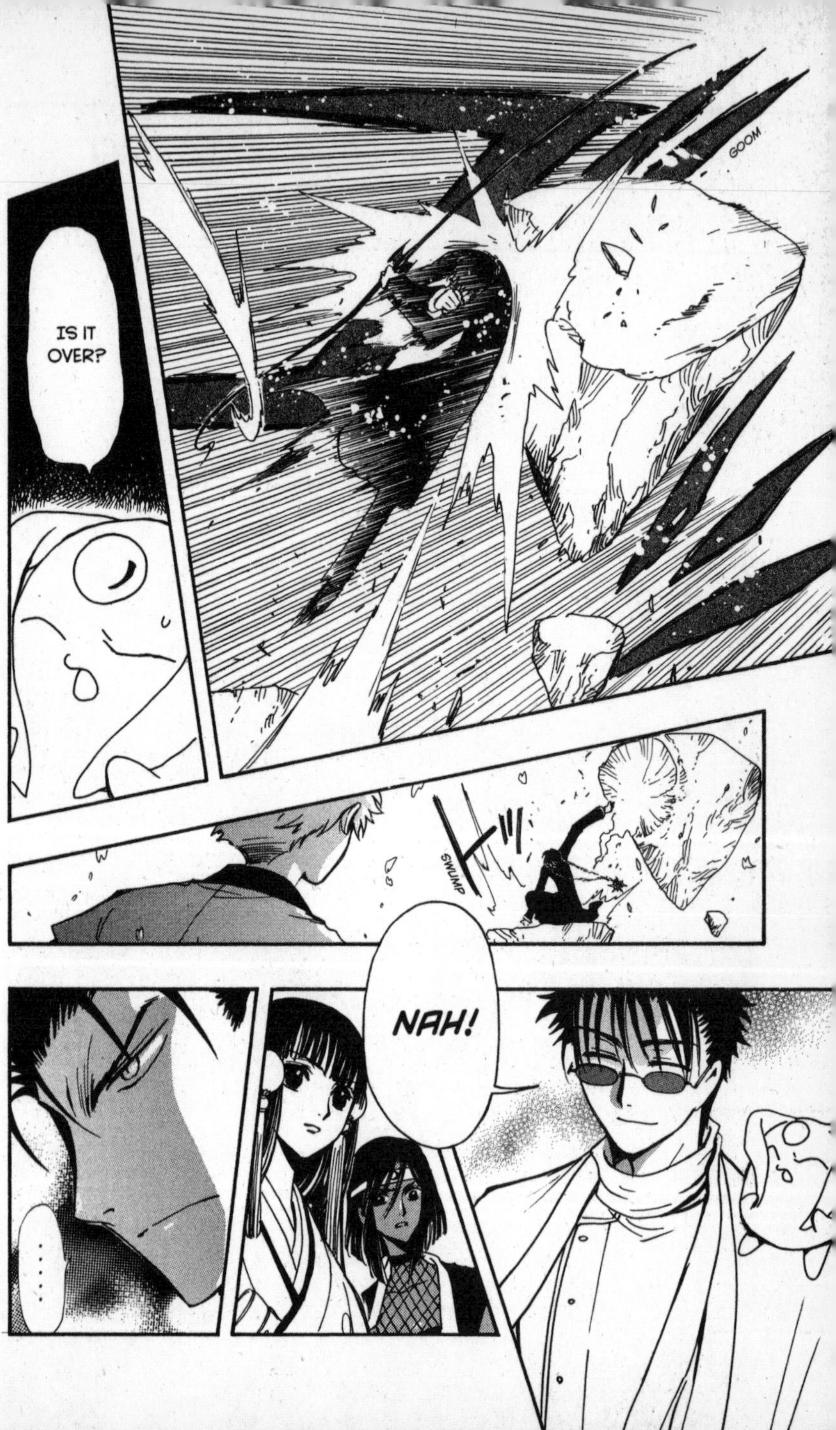
GOOM
IS IT OVER?
SWUMP
NAH!
......

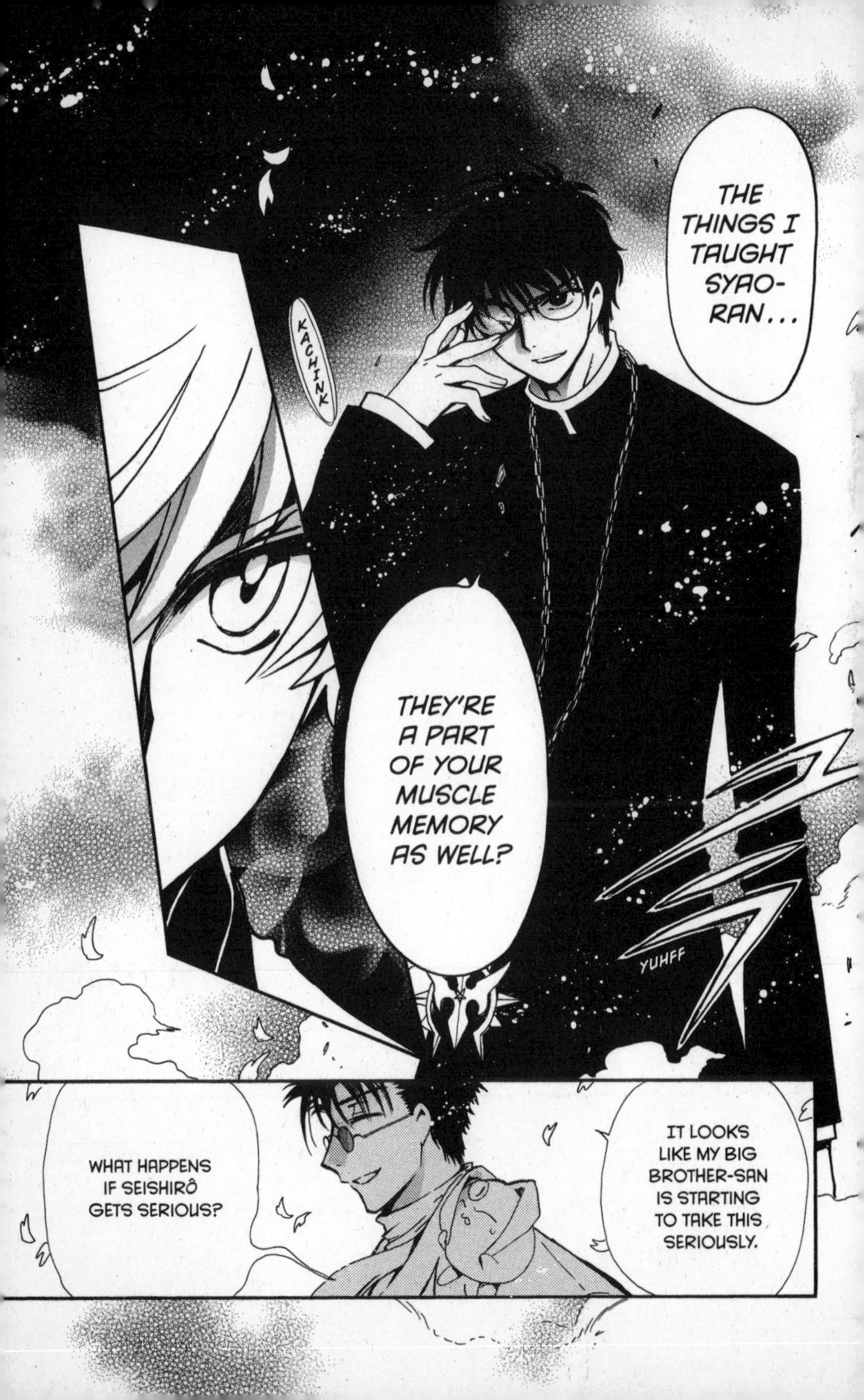
THE THINGS I TAUGHT SYAO-RAN...
KACHINK
THEY'RE A PART OF YOUR MUSCLE MEMORY AS WELL?
YUHFF
IT LOOKS LIKE MY BIG BROTHER-SAN IS STARTING TO TAKE THIS SERIOUSLY.
WHAT HAPPENS IF SEISHIRÔ GETS SERIOUS?

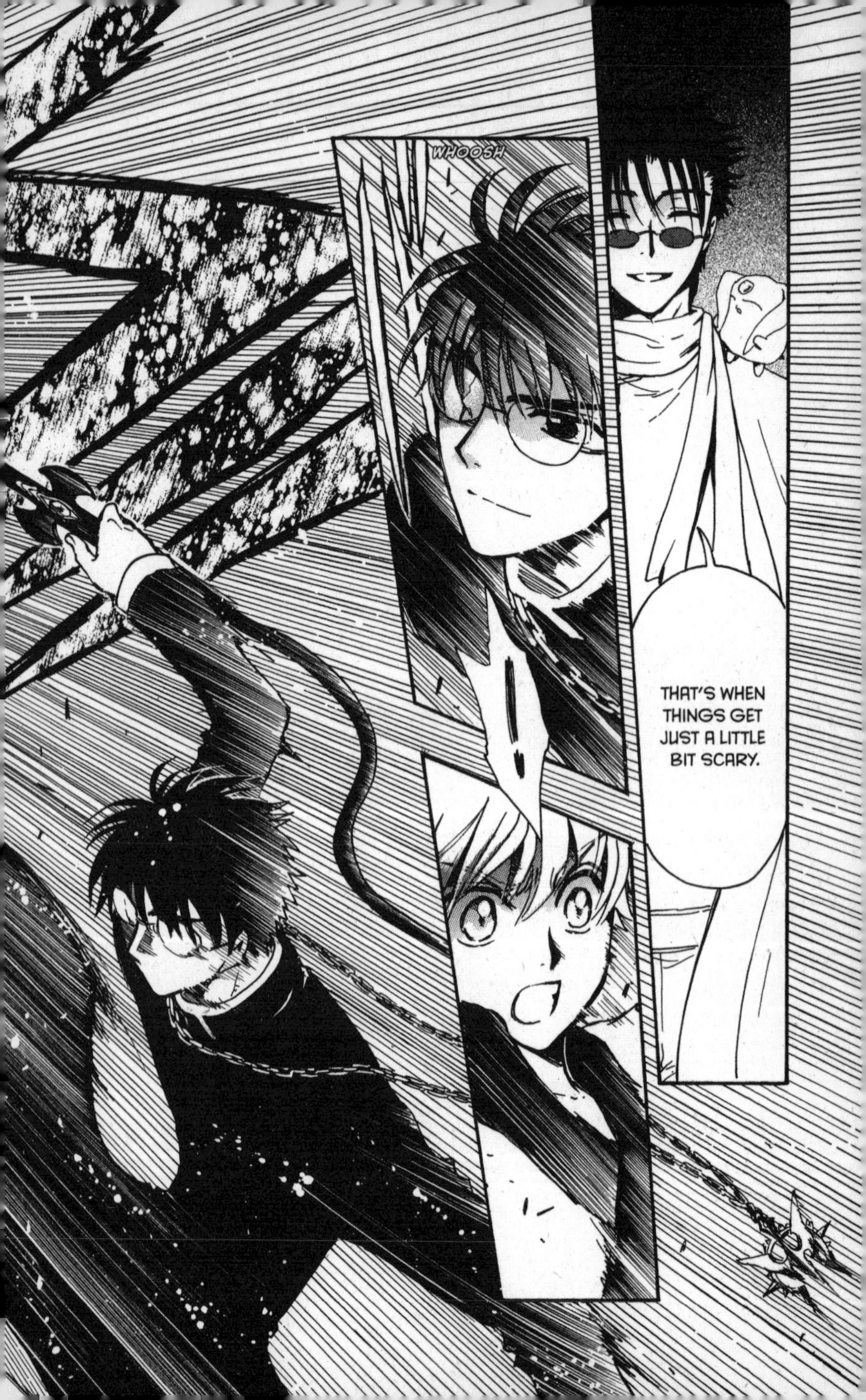
WHOOSH
THAT'S WHEN THINGS GET JUST A LITTLE BIT SCARY.

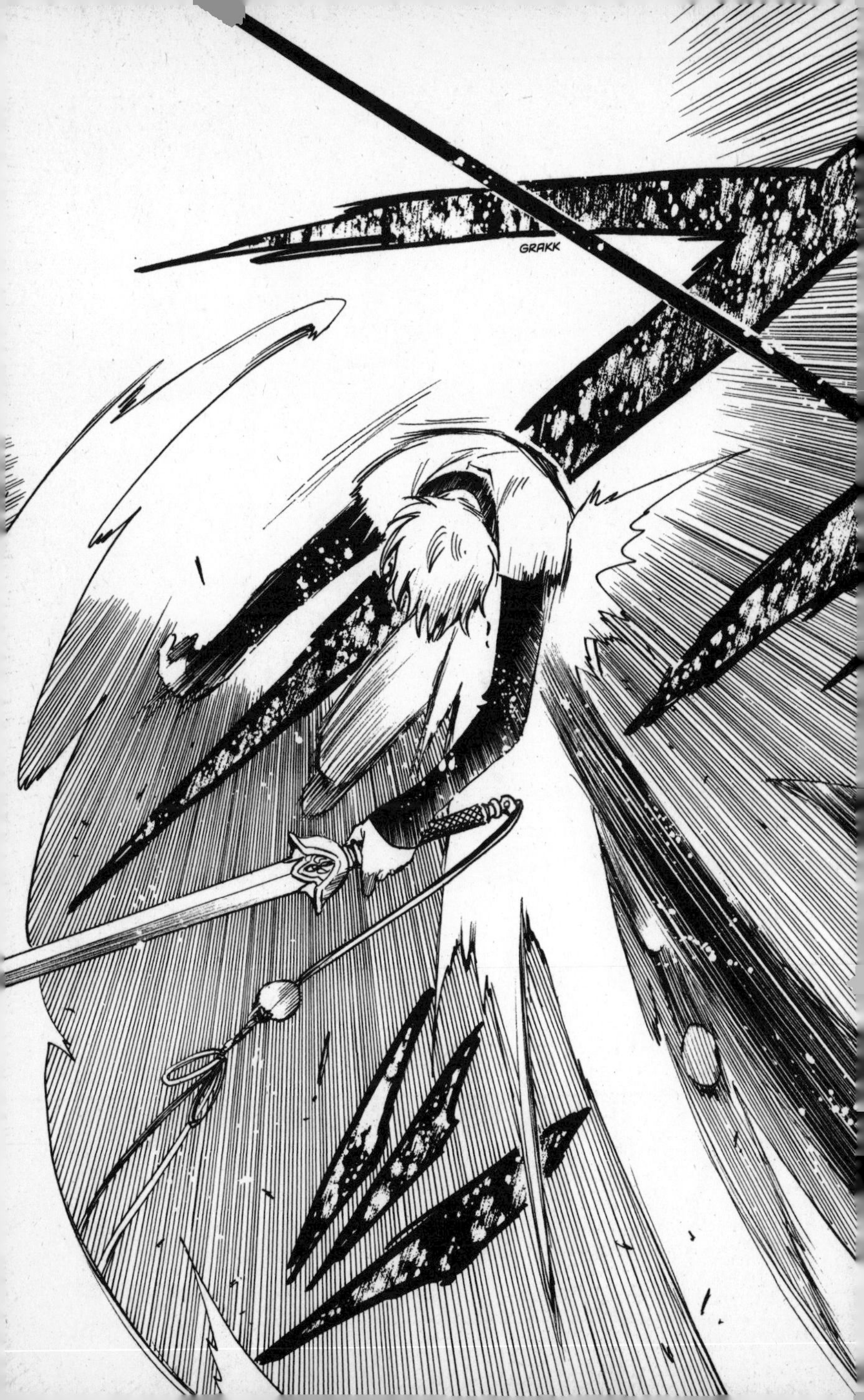
GRAKK

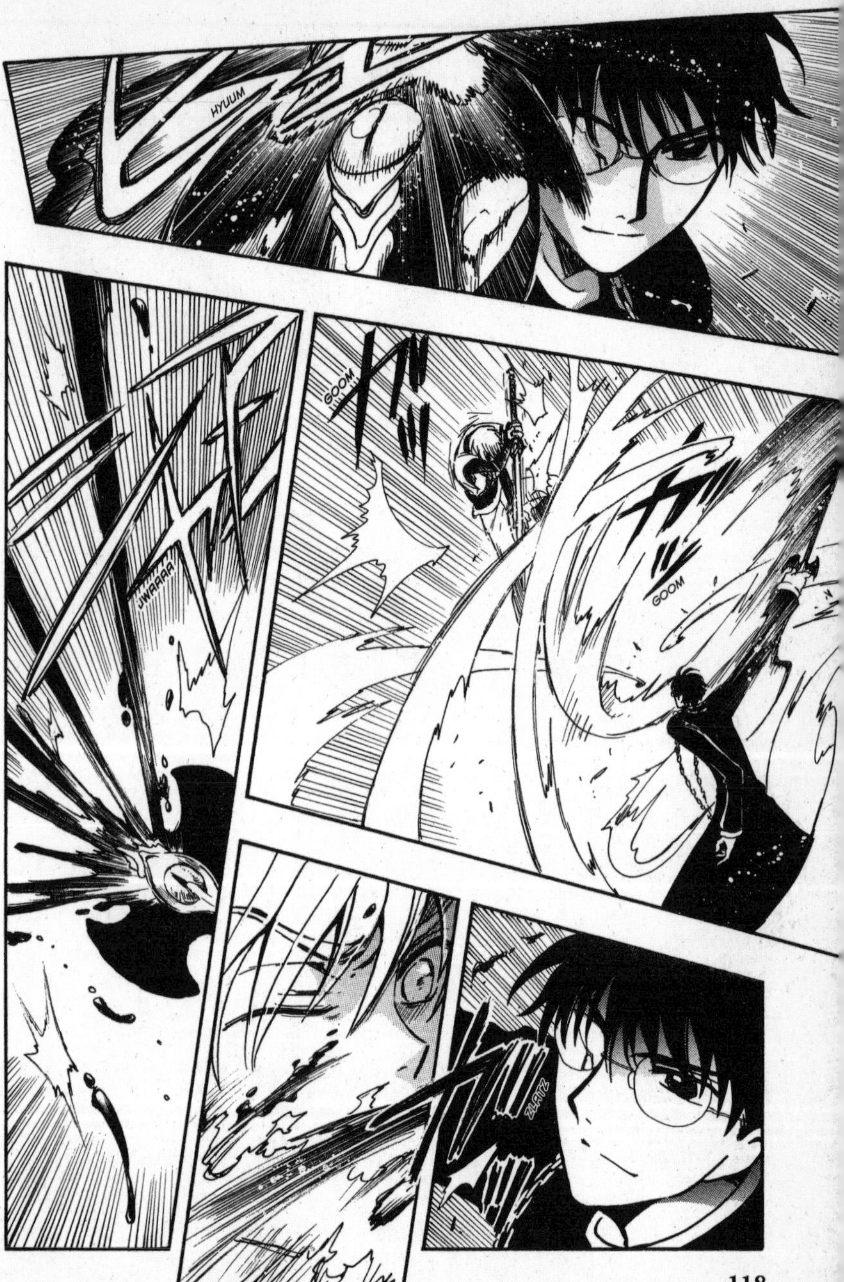
HYUUM
GOOM
GOOM
ZLATZ
JWARRR

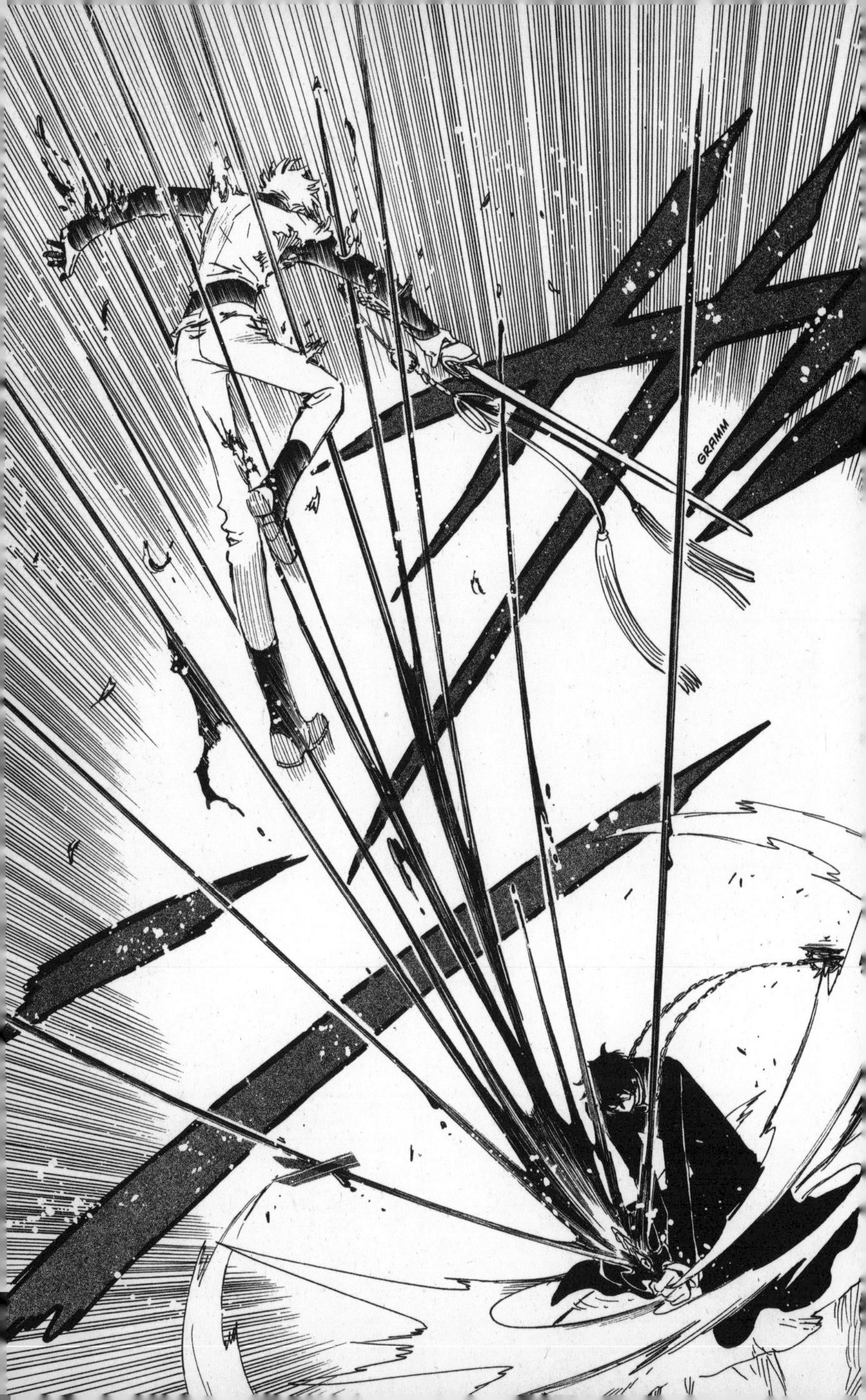
GRAMM

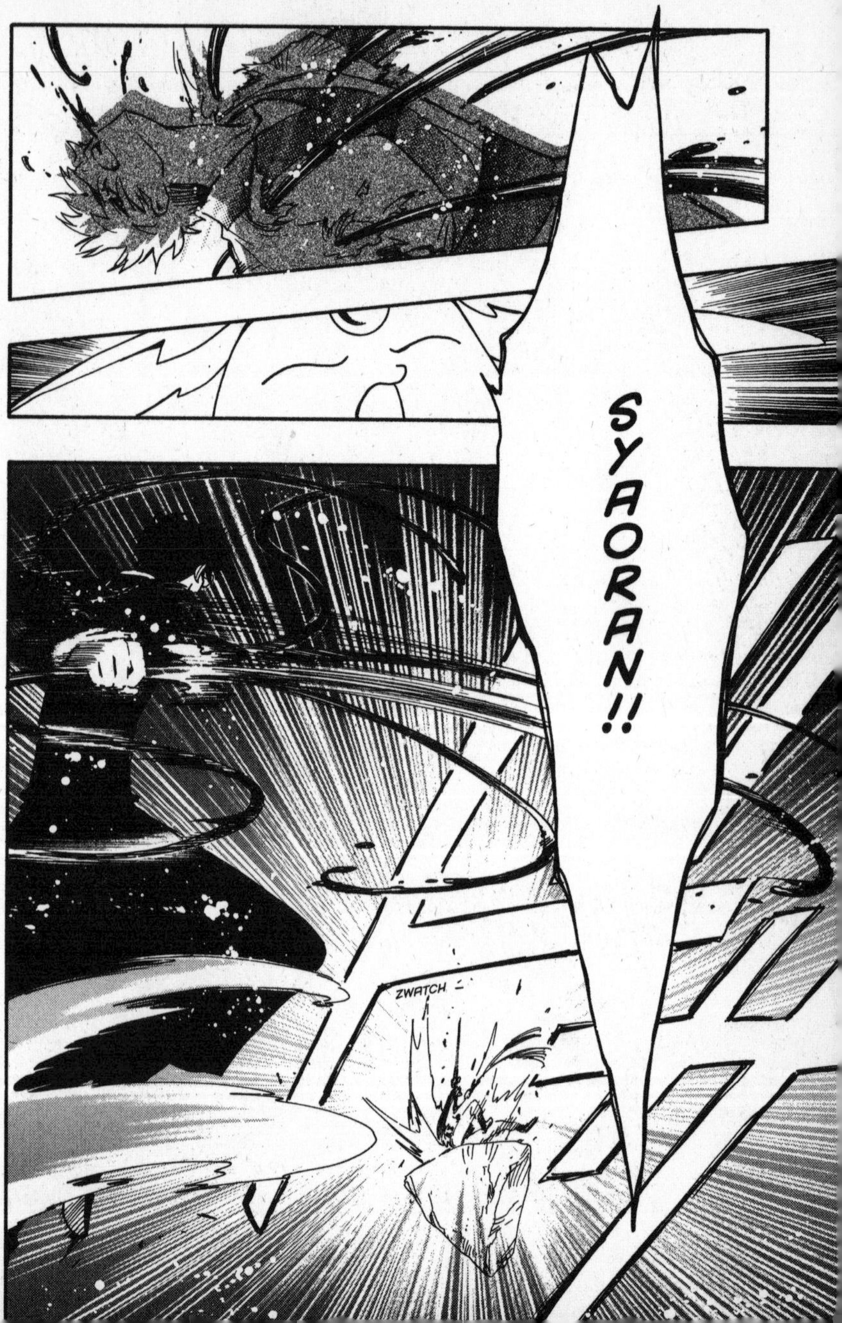
SYAORAN!!
ZWATCH

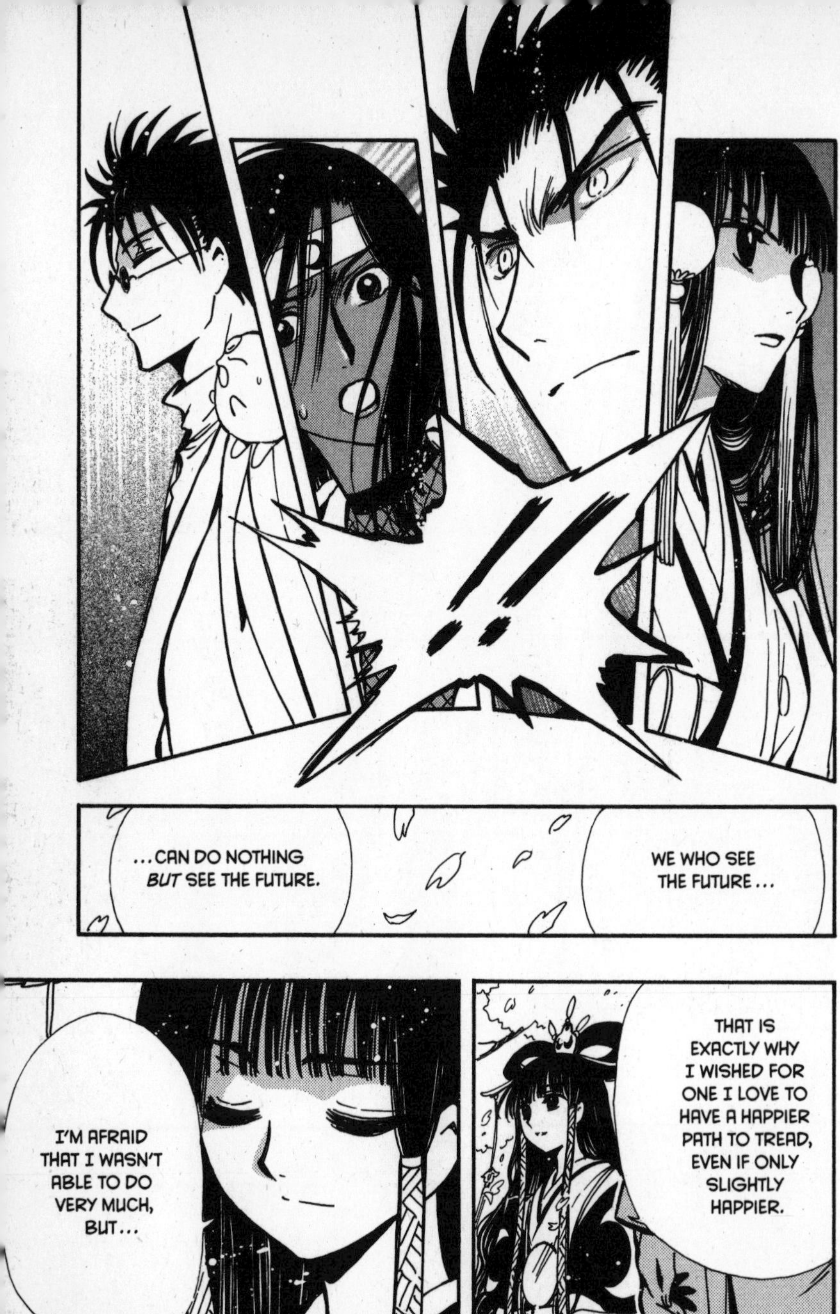
WE WHO SEE THE FUTURE...
...CAN DO NOTHING *BUT* SEE THE FUTURE.
THAT IS EXACTLY WHY I WISHED FOR ONE I LOVE TO HAVE A HAPPIER PATH TO TREAD, EVEN IF ONLY SLIGHTLY HAPPIER.
I'M AFRAID THAT I WASN'T ABLE TO DO VERY MUCH, BUT...

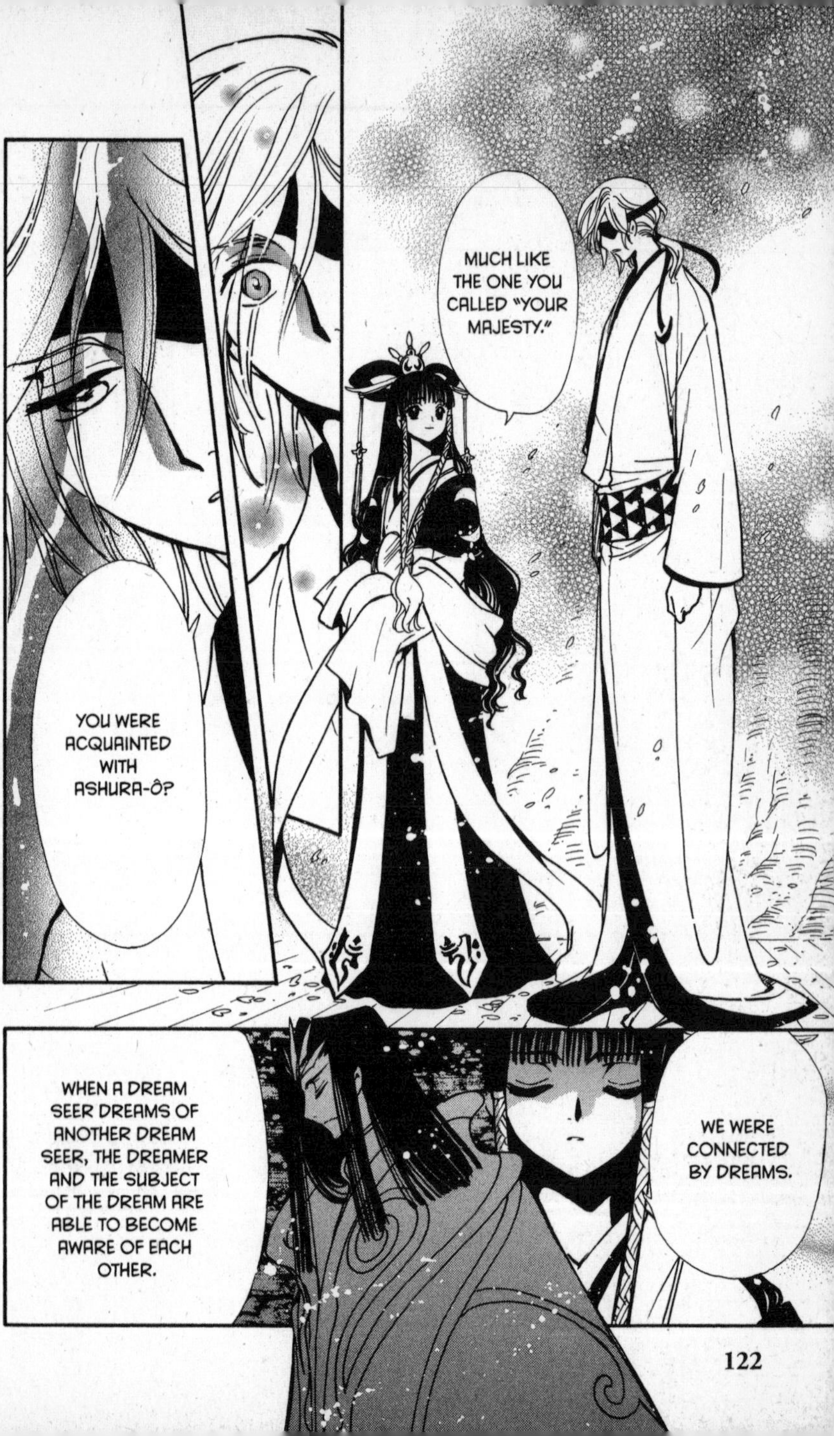
MUCH LIKE THE ONE YOU CALLED "YOUR MAJESTY."
YOU WERE ACQUAINTED WITH ASHURA-Ô?
WE WERE CONNECTED BY DREAMS.
WHEN A DREAM SEER DREAMS OF ANOTHER DREAM SEER, THE DREAMER AND THE SUBJECT OF THE DREAM ARE ABLE TO BECOME AWARE OF EACH OTHER.

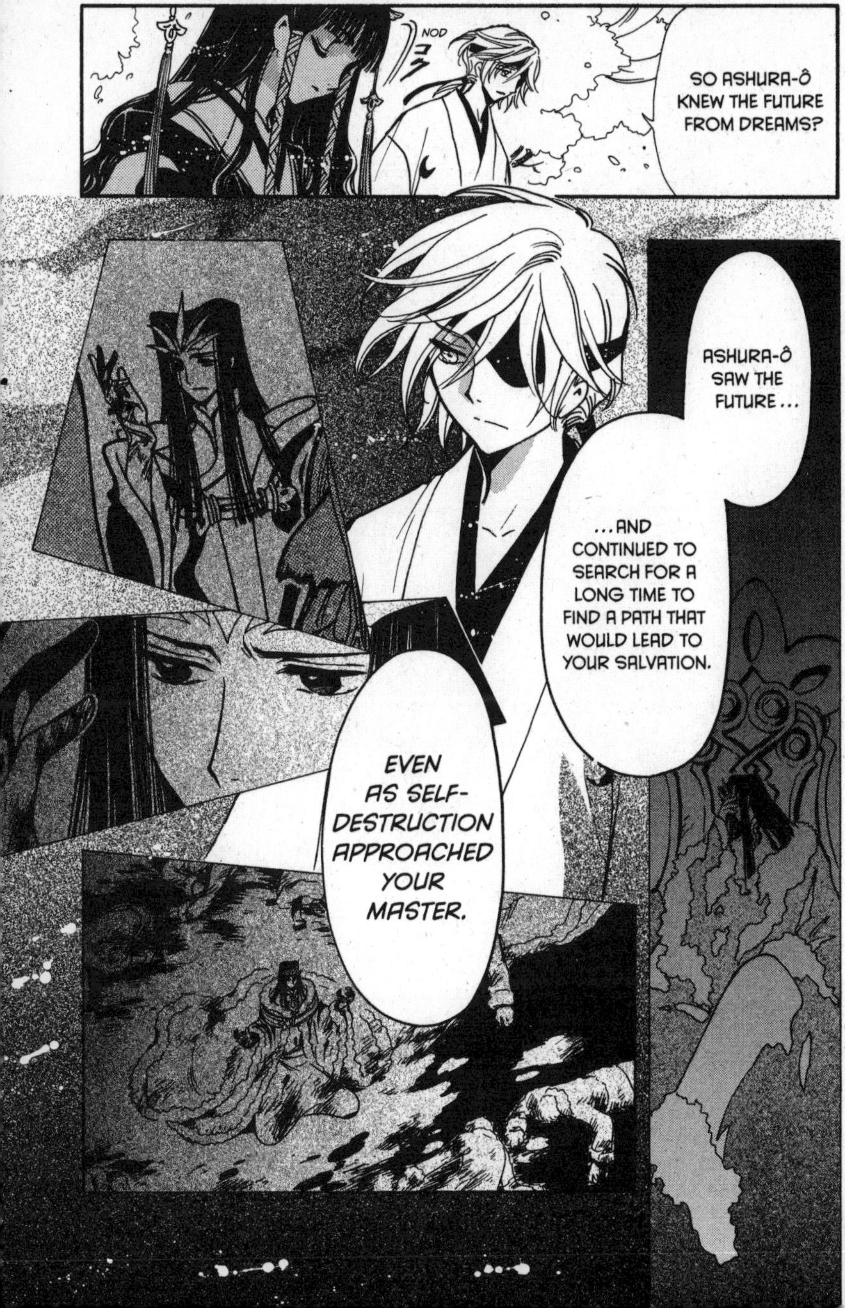
SO ASHURA-Ô KNEW THE FUTURE FROM DREAMS?
NOD
ASHURA-Ô SAW THE FUTURE...
...AND CONTINUED TO SEARCH FOR A LONG TIME TO FIND A PATH THAT WOULD LEAD TO YOUR SALVATION.
EVEN AS SELF-DESTRUCTION APPROACHED YOUR MASTER.

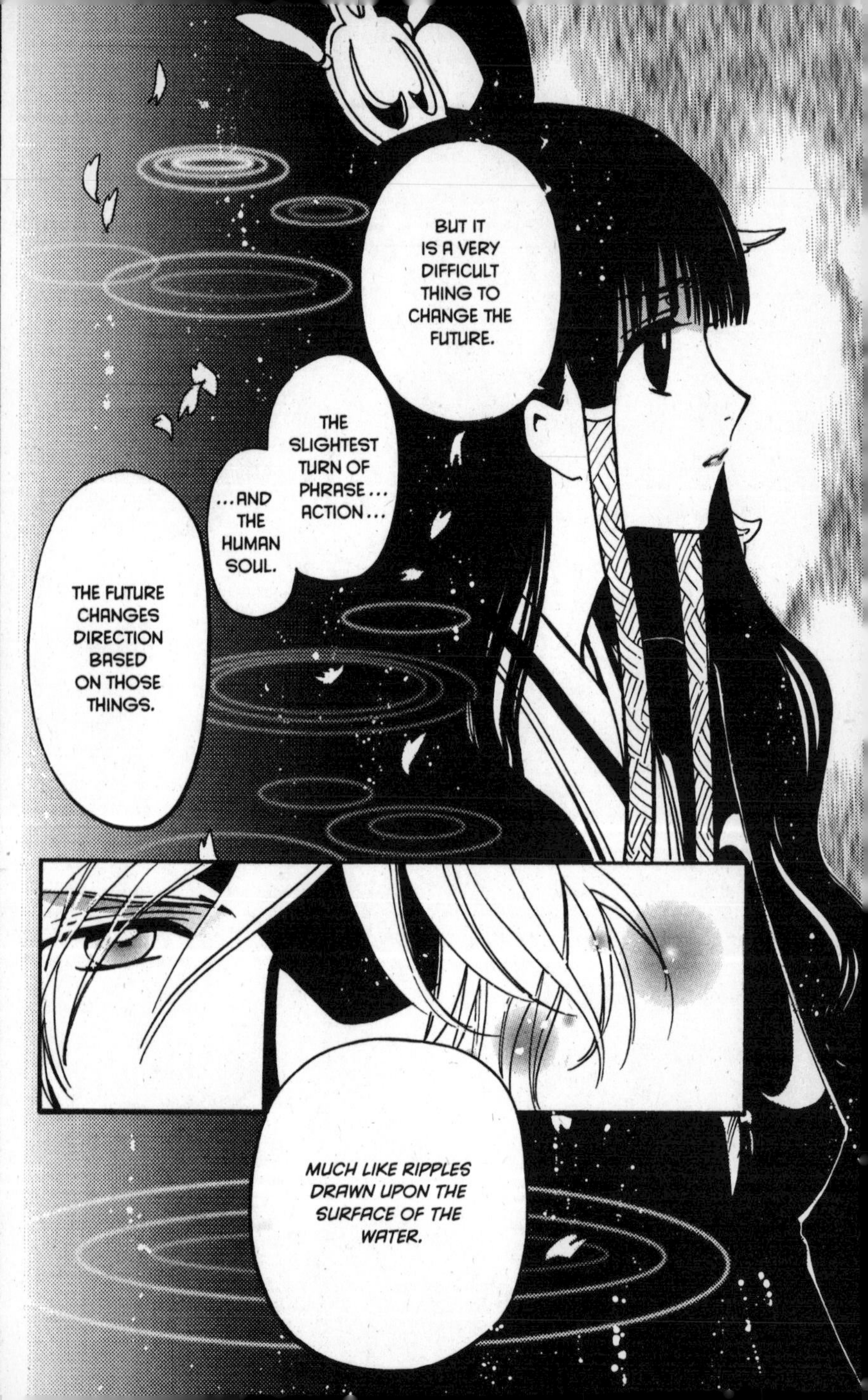
BUT IT IS A VERY DIFFICULT THING TO CHANGE THE FUTURE.
THE SLIGHTEST TURN OF PHRASE... ACTION...
...AND THE HUMAN SOUL.
THE FUTURE CHANGES DIRECTION BASED ON THOSE THINGS.
MUCH LIKE RIPPLES DRAWN UPON THE SURFACE OF THE WATER.

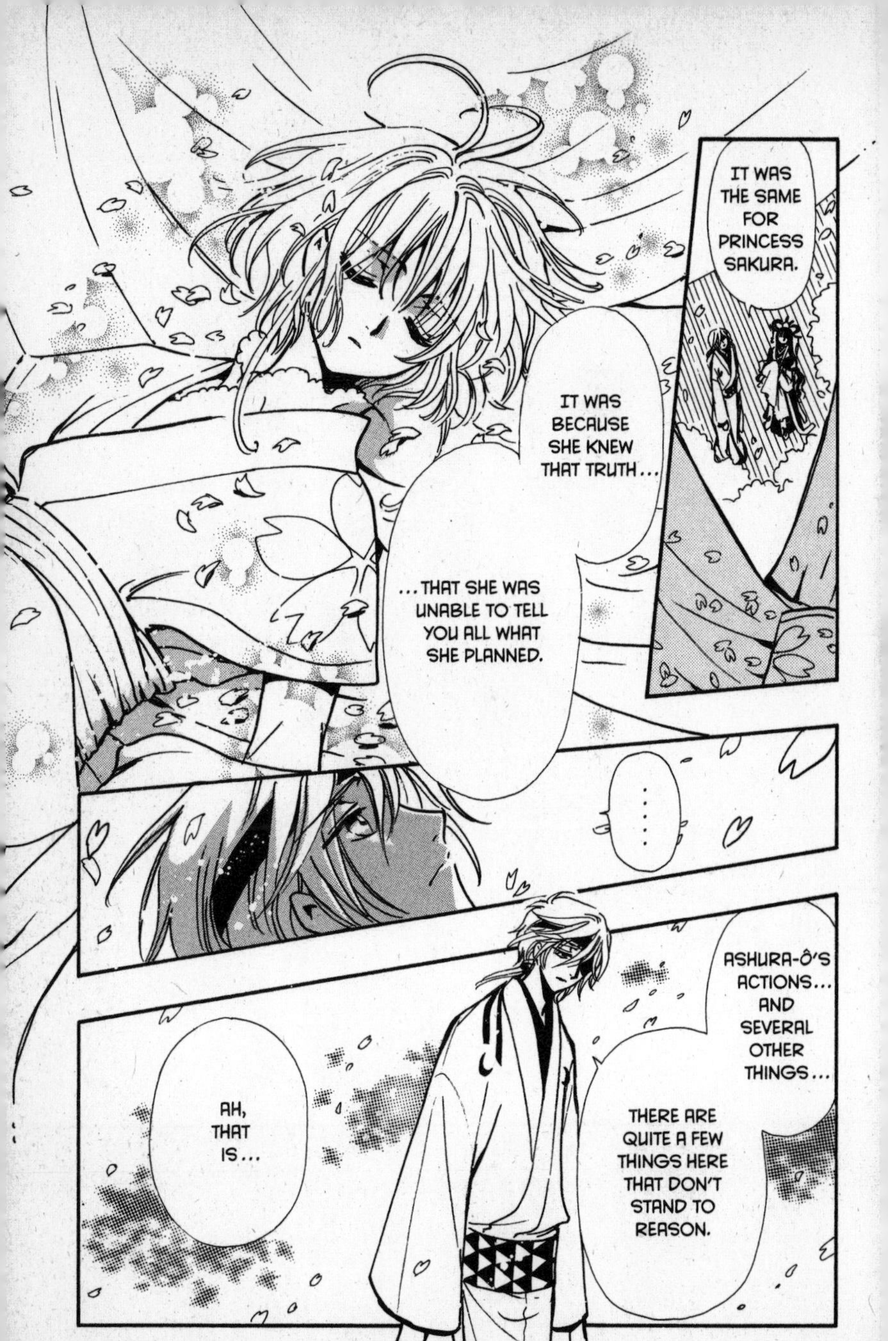
IT WAS THE SAME FOR PRINCESS SAKURA.
IT WAS BECAUSE SHE KNEW THAT TRUTH...
...THAT SHE WAS UNABLE TO TELL YOU ALL WHAT SHE PLANNED.
.....
ASHURA-Ô'S ACTIONS... AND SEVERAL OTHER THINGS...
THERE ARE QUITE A FEW THINGS HERE THAT DON'T STAND TO REASON.
AH, THAT IS...

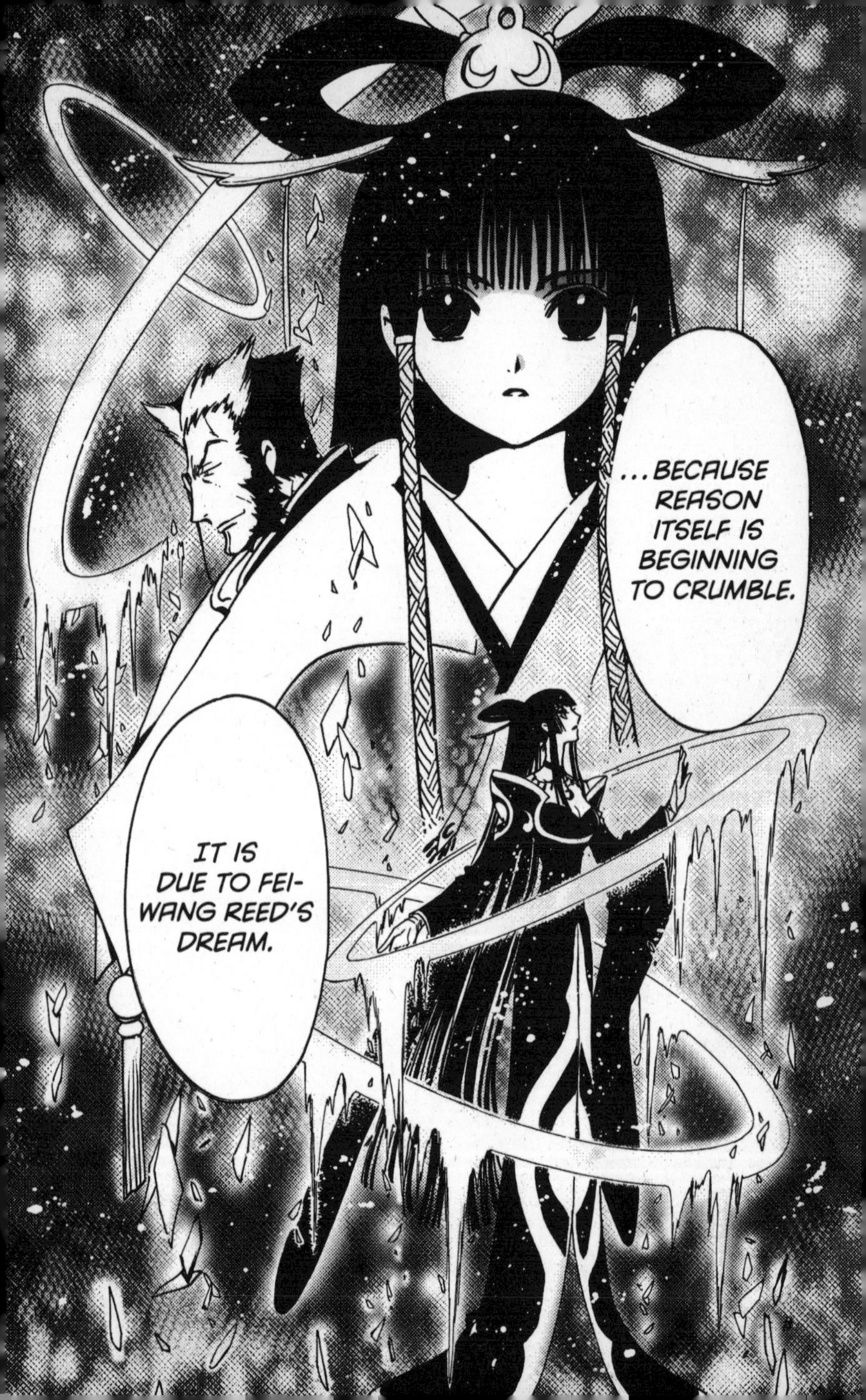
...BECAUSE REASON ITSELF IS BEGINNING TO CRUMBLE.
IT IS DUE TO FEI-WANG REED'S DREAM.

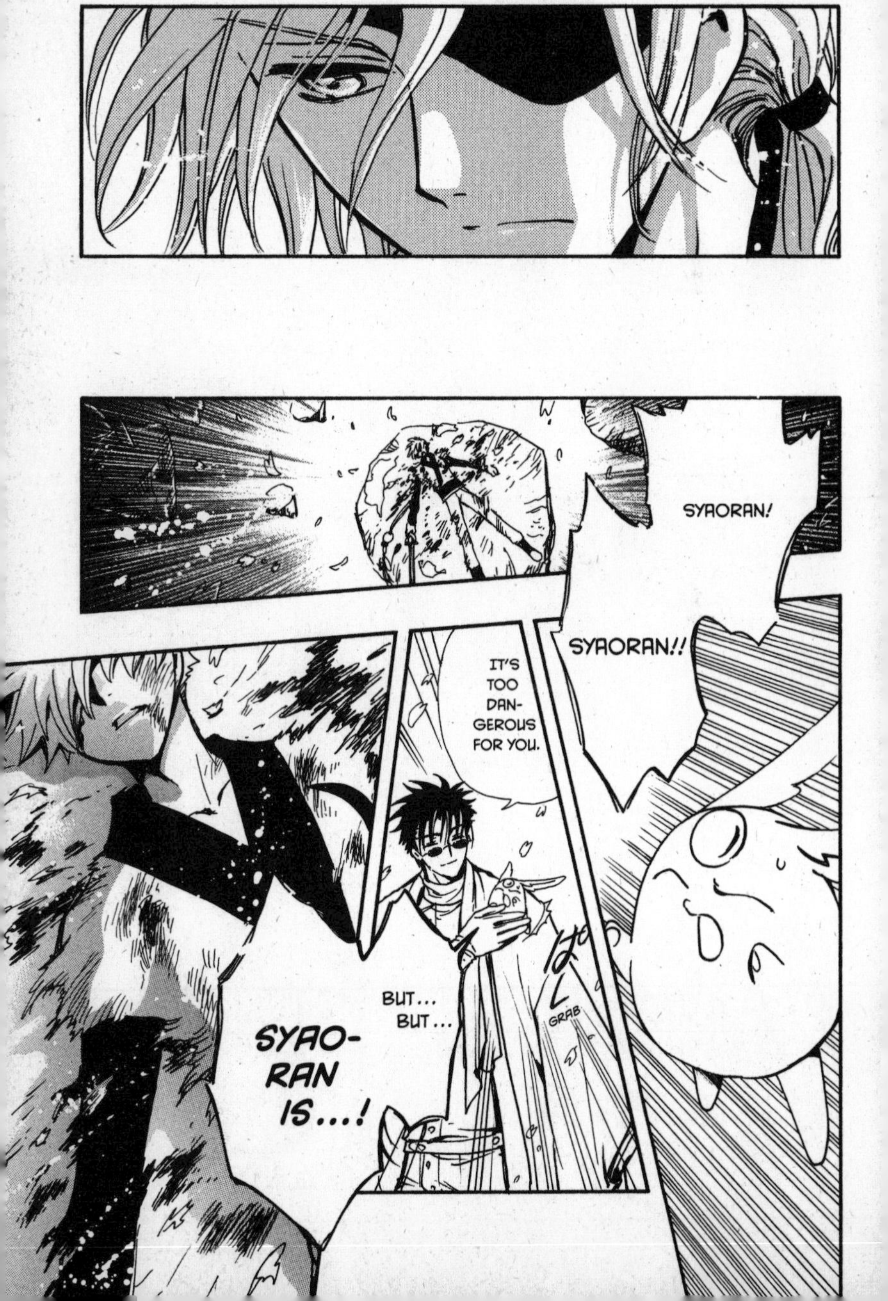
SYAORAN!
SYAORAN!!
IT'S TOO DAN-GEROUS FOR YOU.
GRAB
BUT... BUT...
SYAO-RAN IS...!

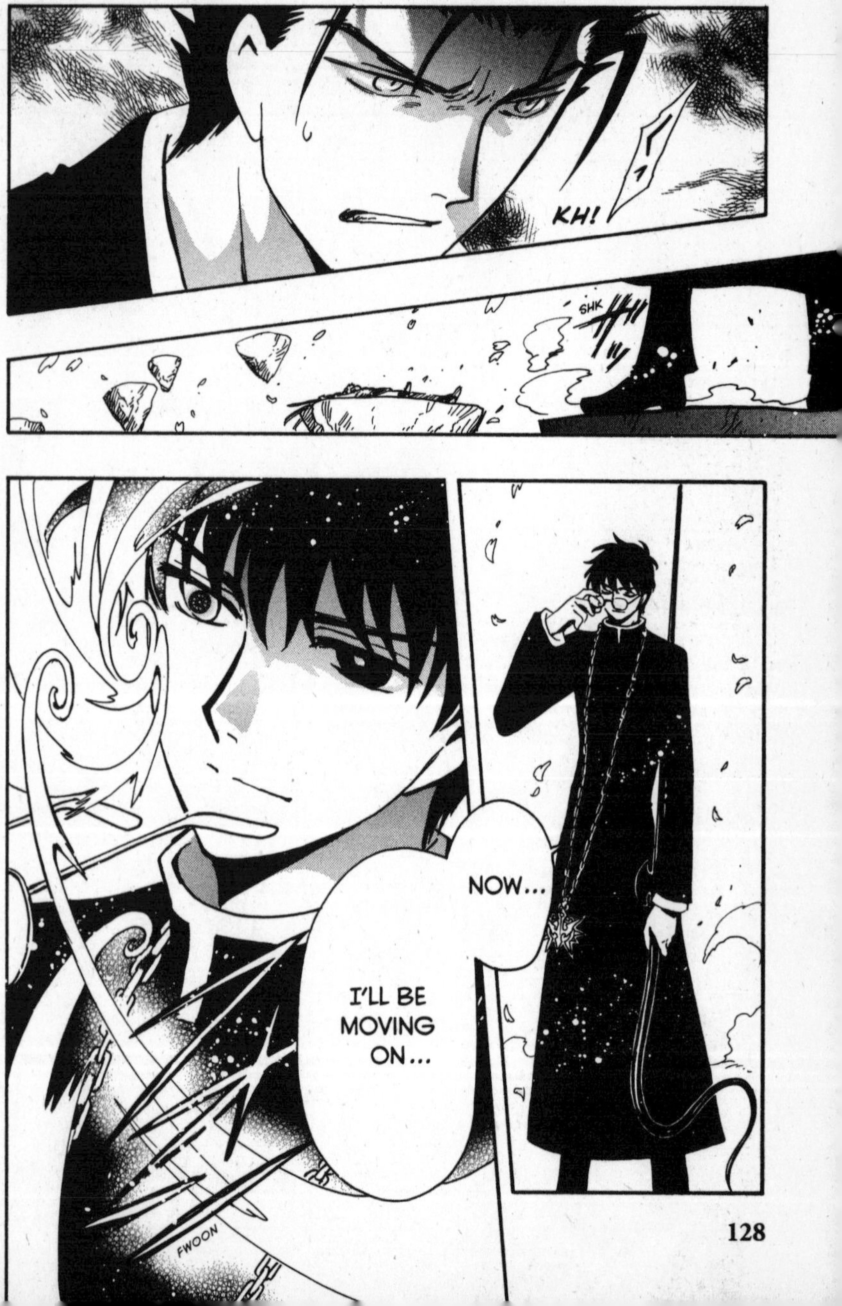
KH!
SHK
NOW...
I'LL BE MOVING ON...
FWOON

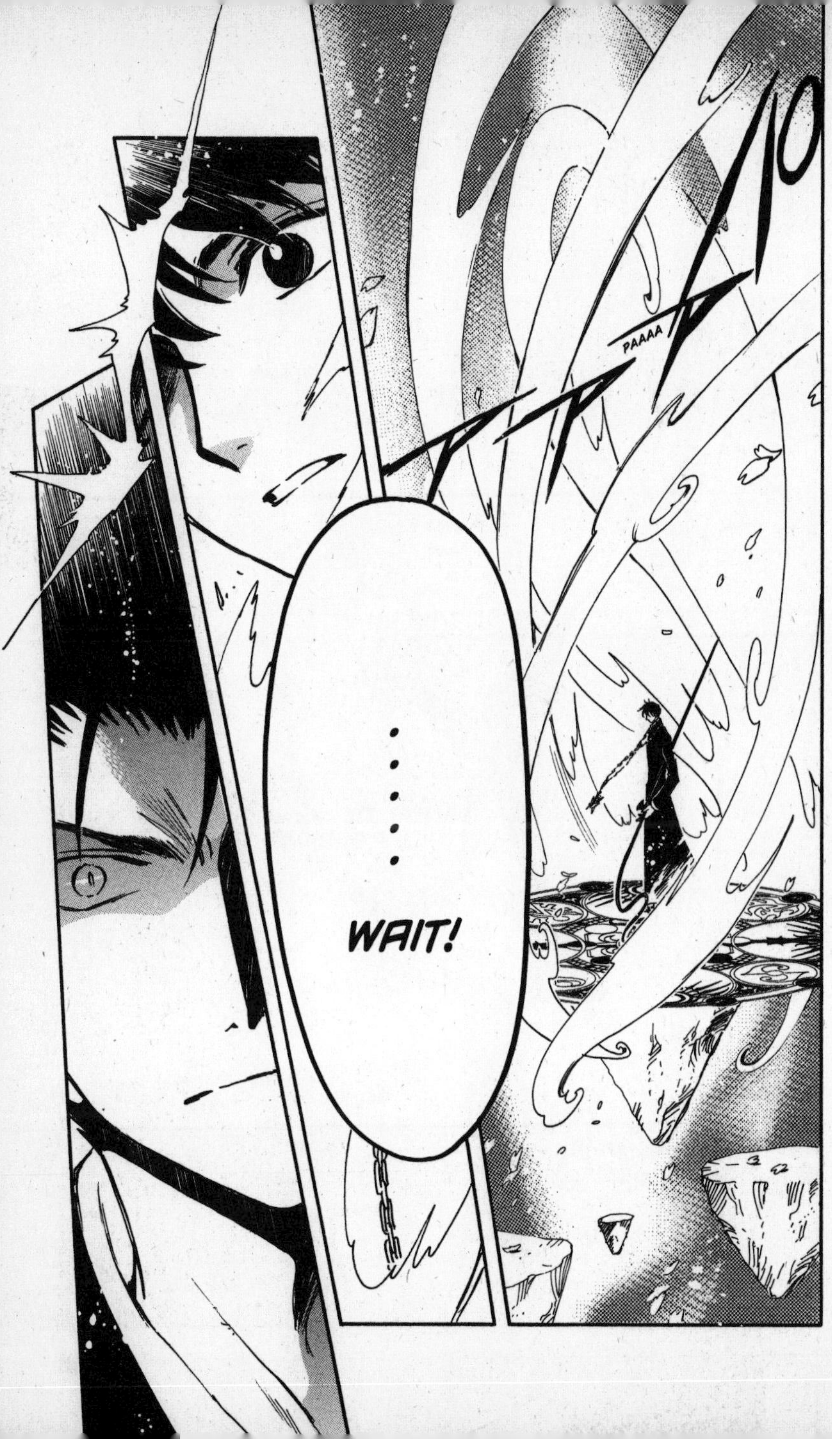
PAAAA
.....
WAIT!

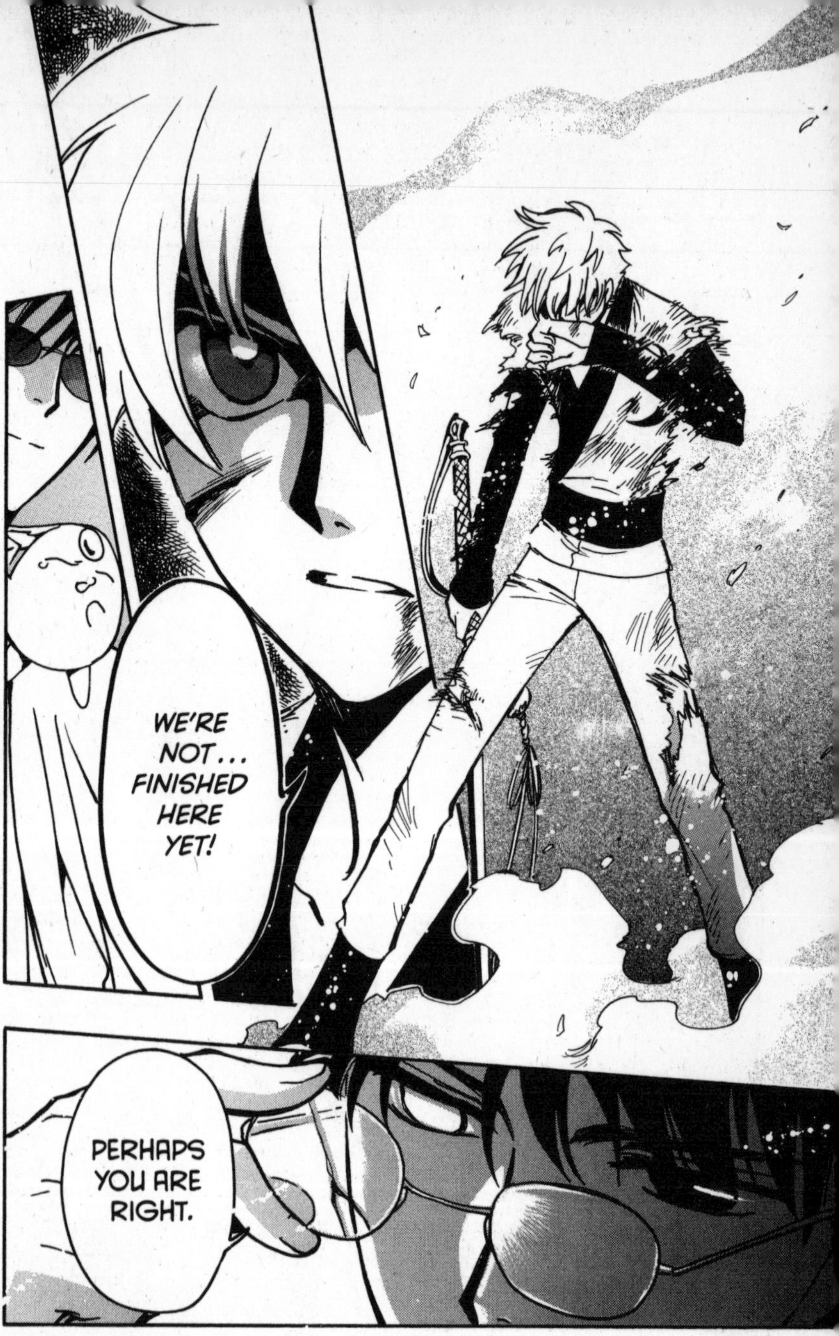
WE'RE NOT... FINISHED HERE YET!
PERHAPS YOU ARE RIGHT.

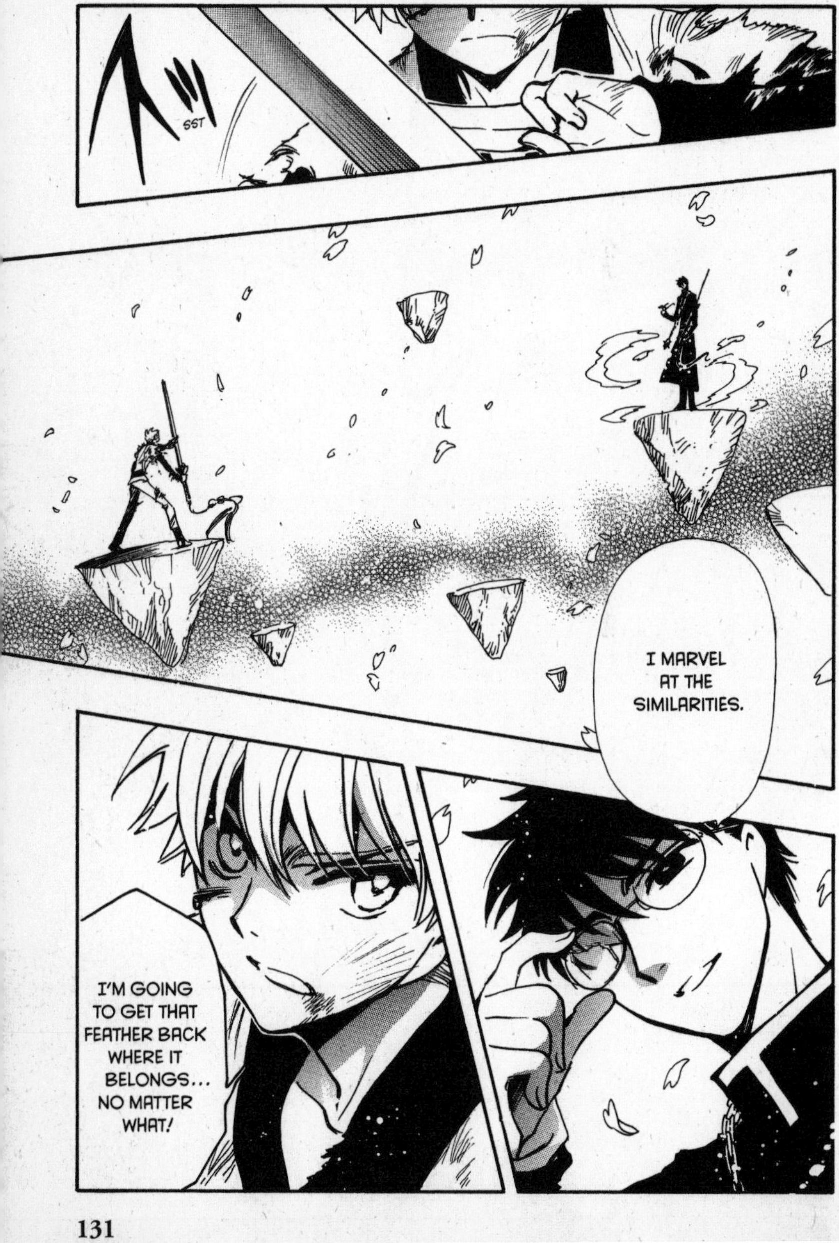
SST
I MARVEL AT THE SIMILARITIES.
I'M GOING TO GET THAT FEATHER BACK WHERE IT BELONGS... NO MATTER WHAT!

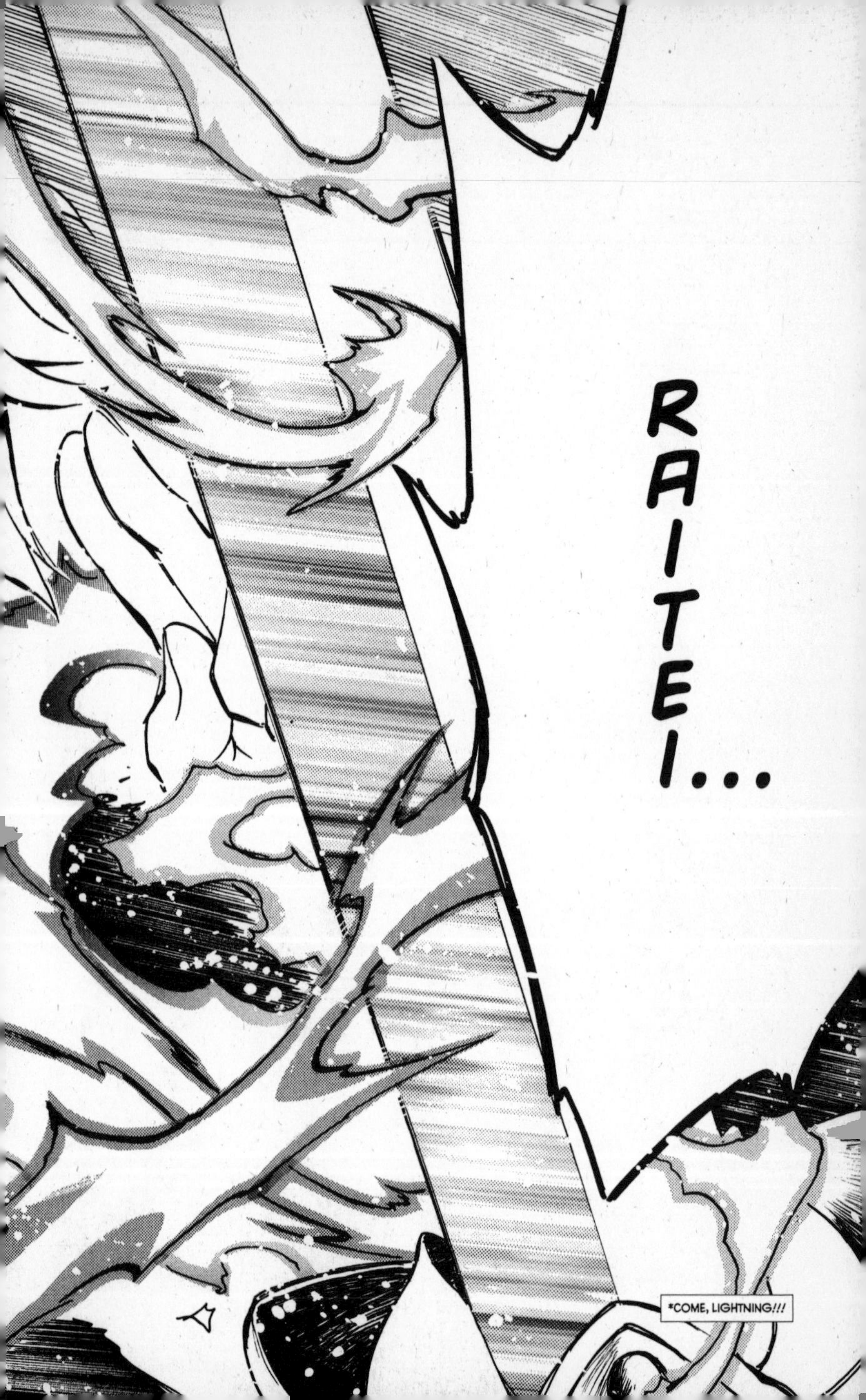
RAITEI...
*COME, LIGHTNING!!!

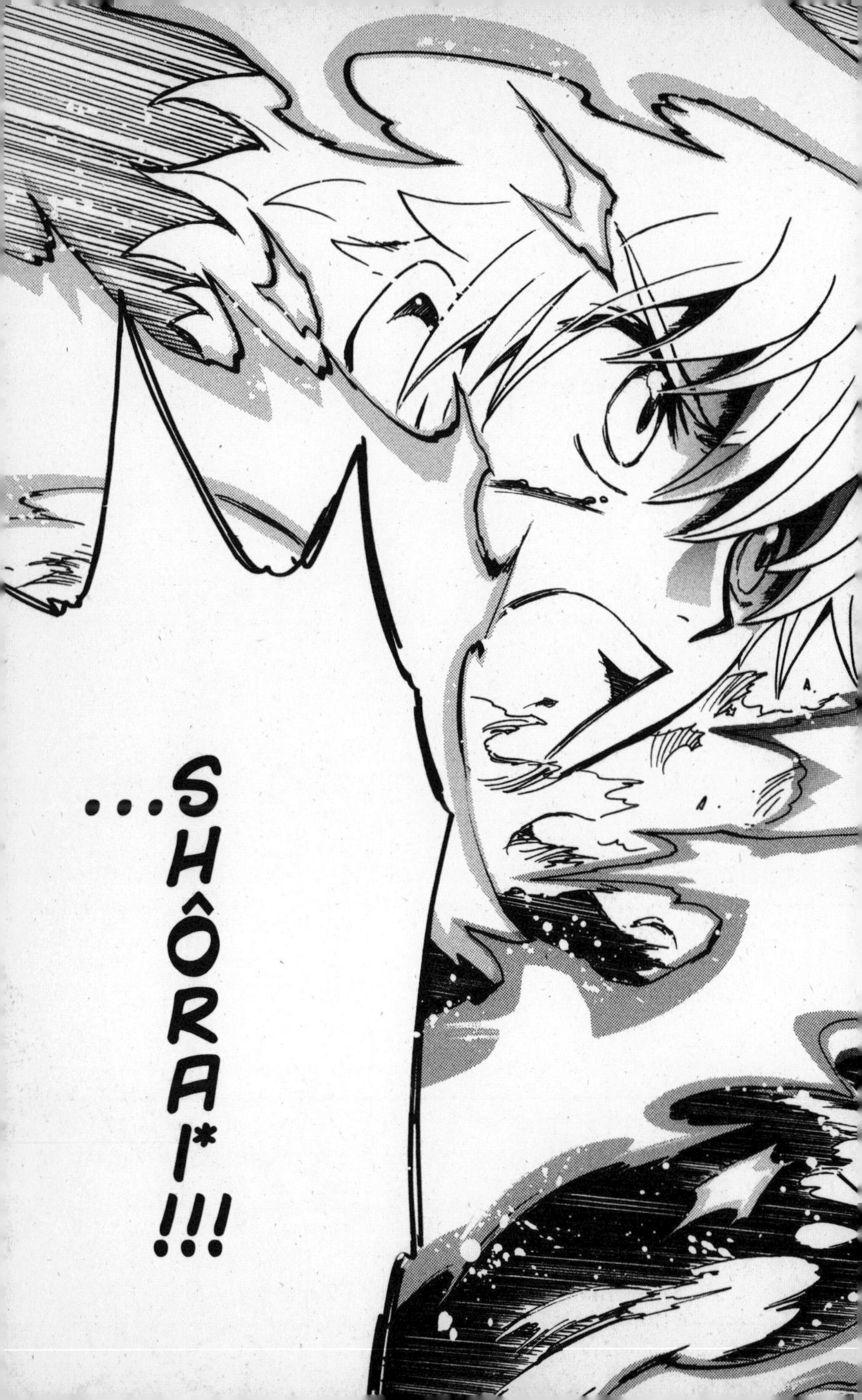
...SHÔRAI*!!!

ツバサ
RESERVoir CHRoNiCLE

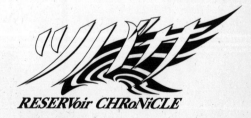

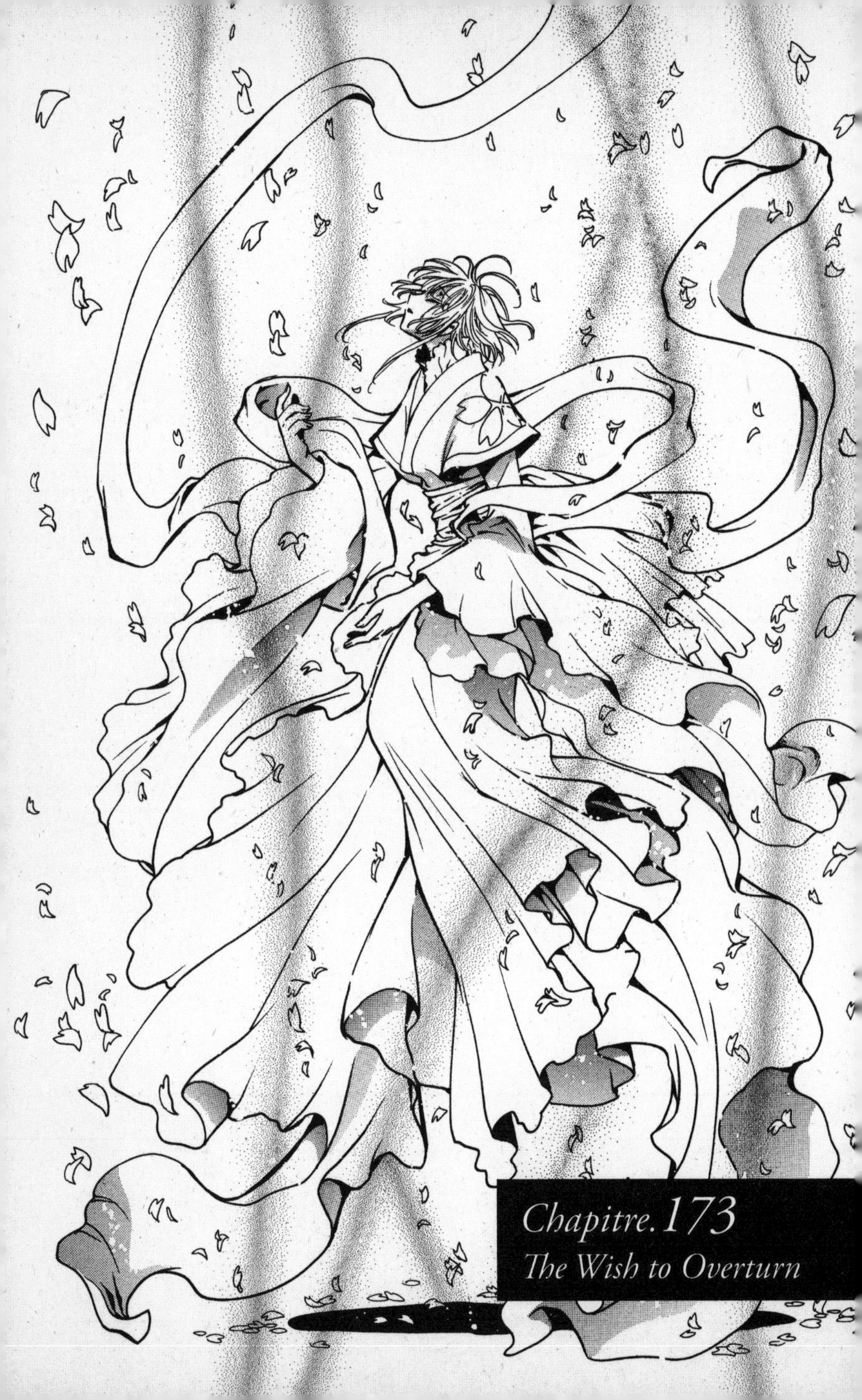
Chapitre. 173
The Wish to Overturn

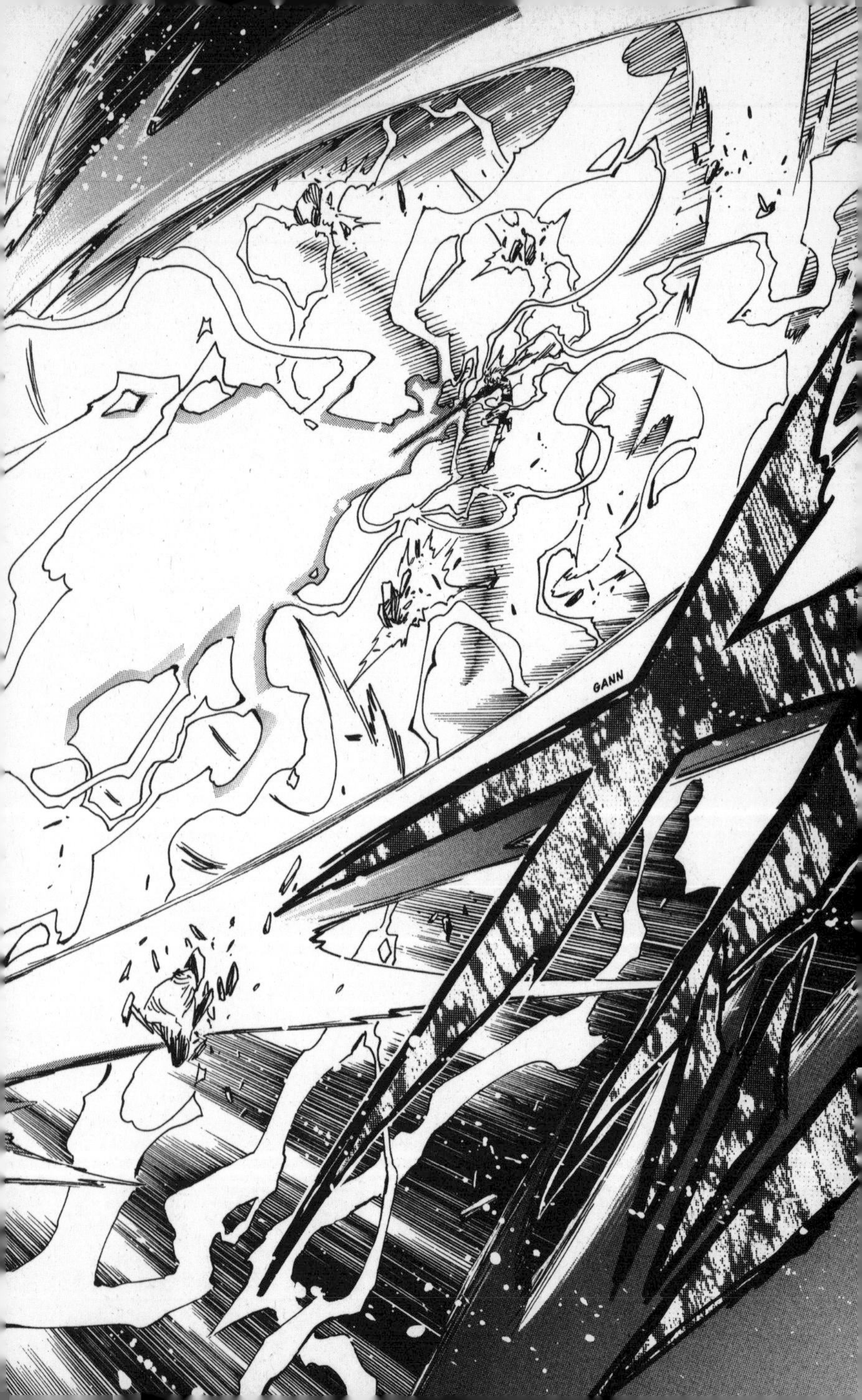
GANN

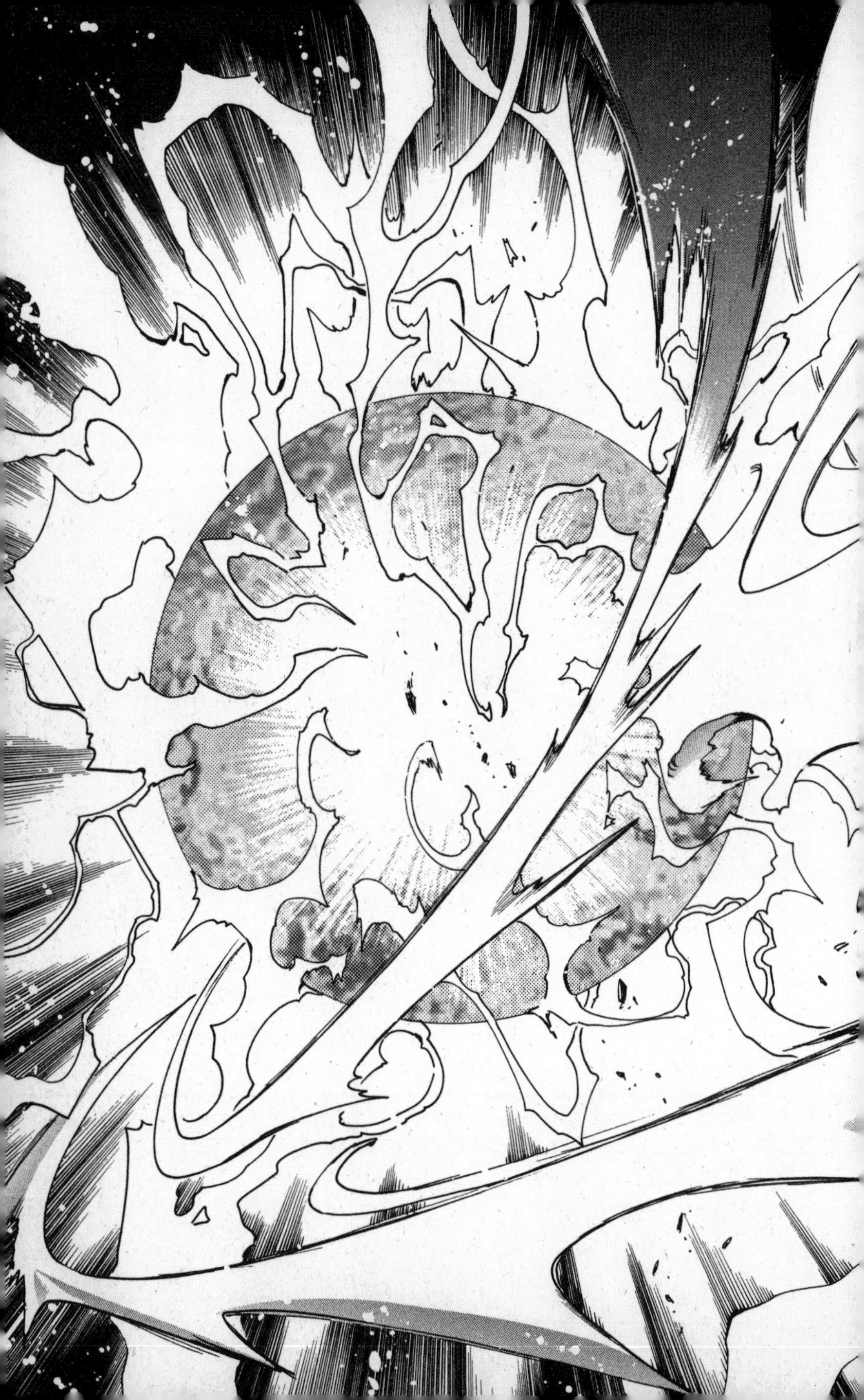

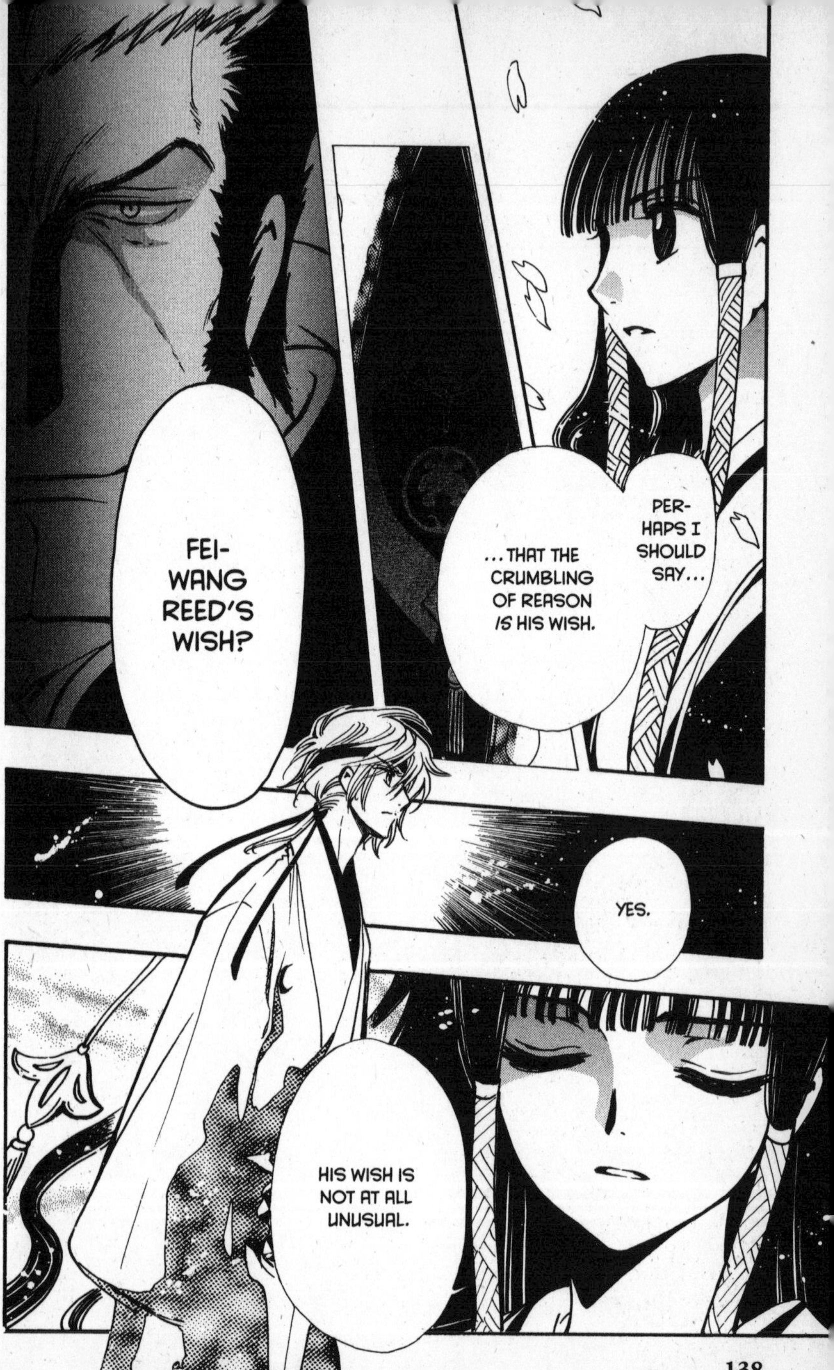
PER-HAPS I SHOULD SAY...
...THAT THE CRUMBLING OF REASON *IS* HIS WISH.
FEI-WANG REED'S WISH?
YES.
HIS WISH IS NOT AT ALL UNUSUAL.

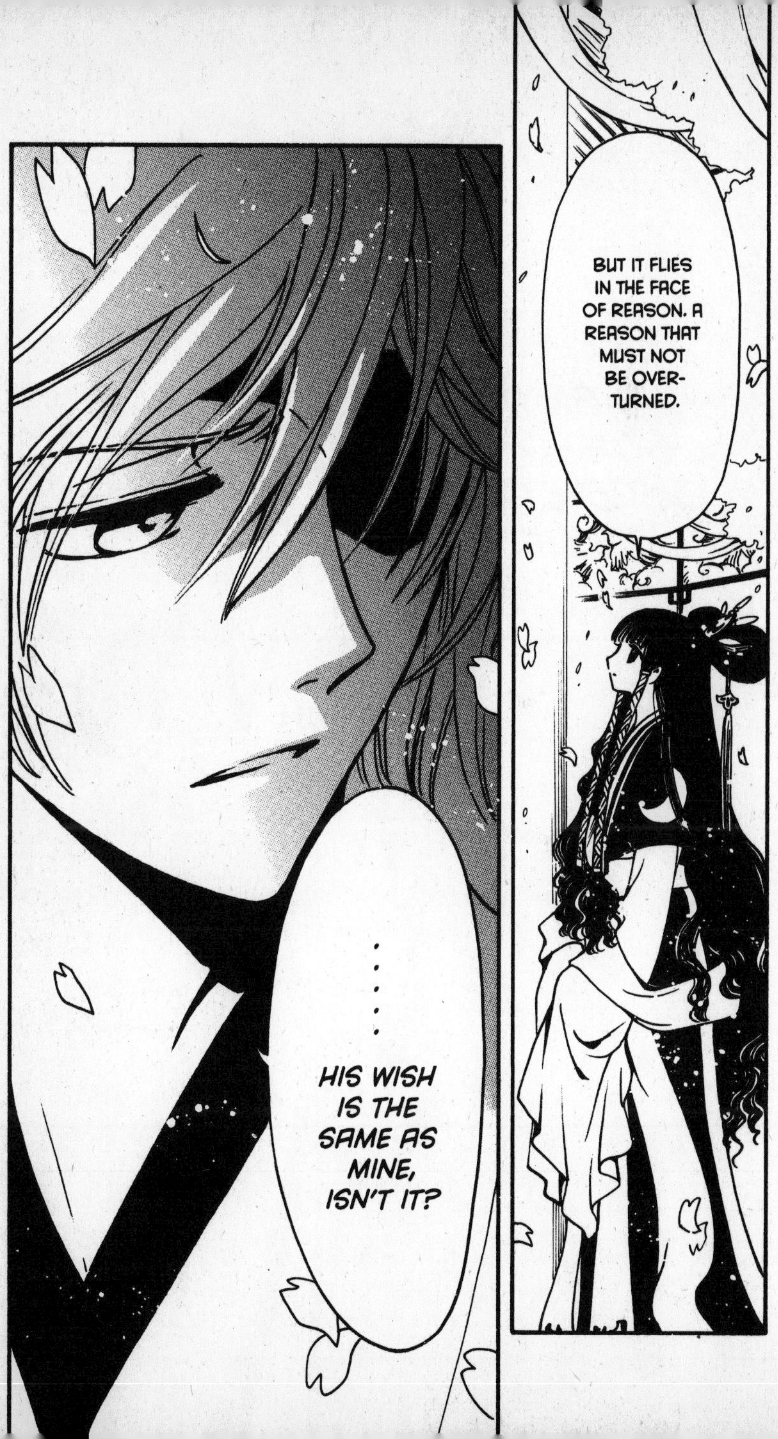
BUT IT FLIES IN THE FACE OF REASON. A REASON THAT MUST NOT BE OVER-TURNED.
..... HIS WISH IS THE SAME AS MINE, ISN'T IT?

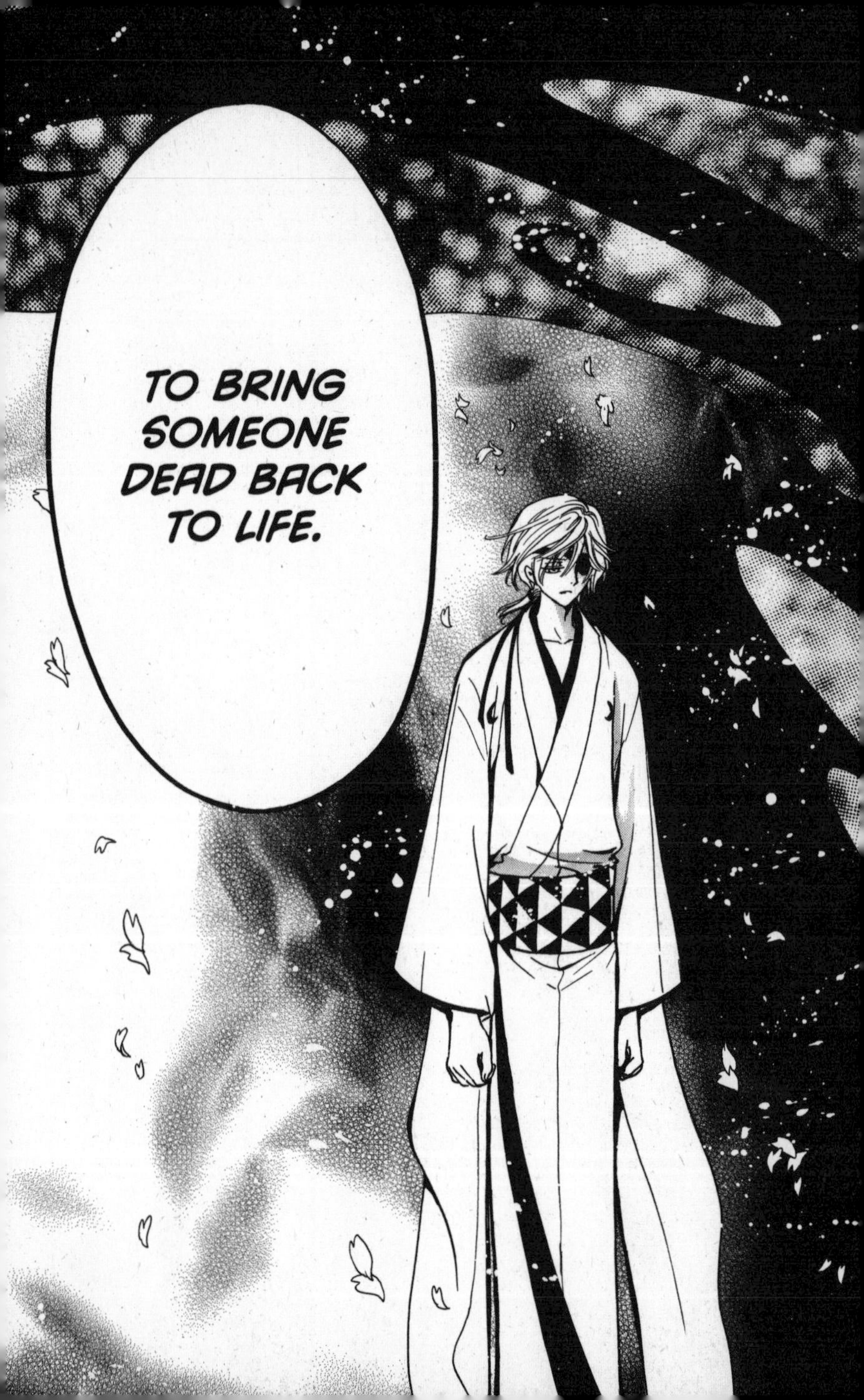
TO BRING SOMEONE DEAD BACK TO LIFE.

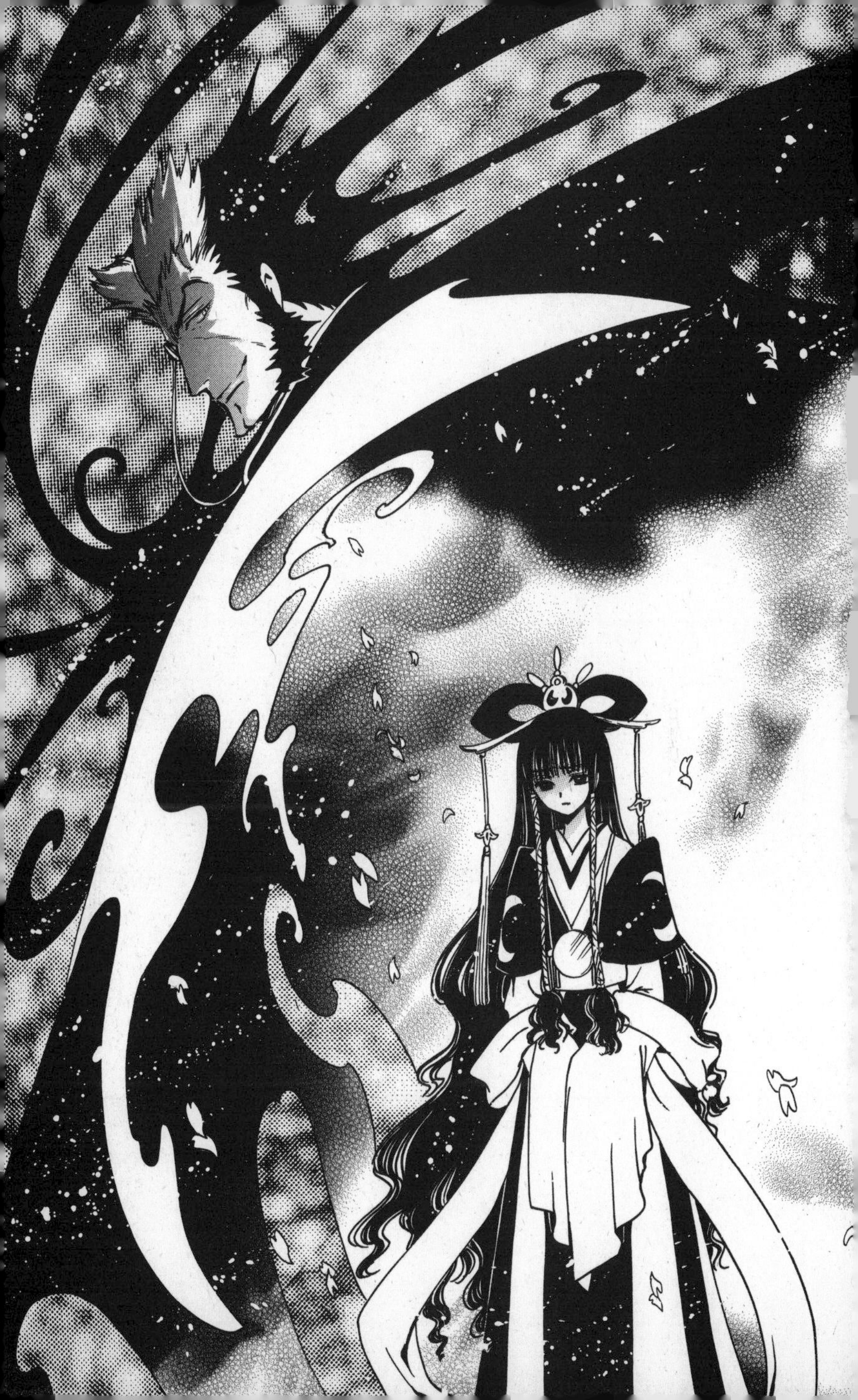

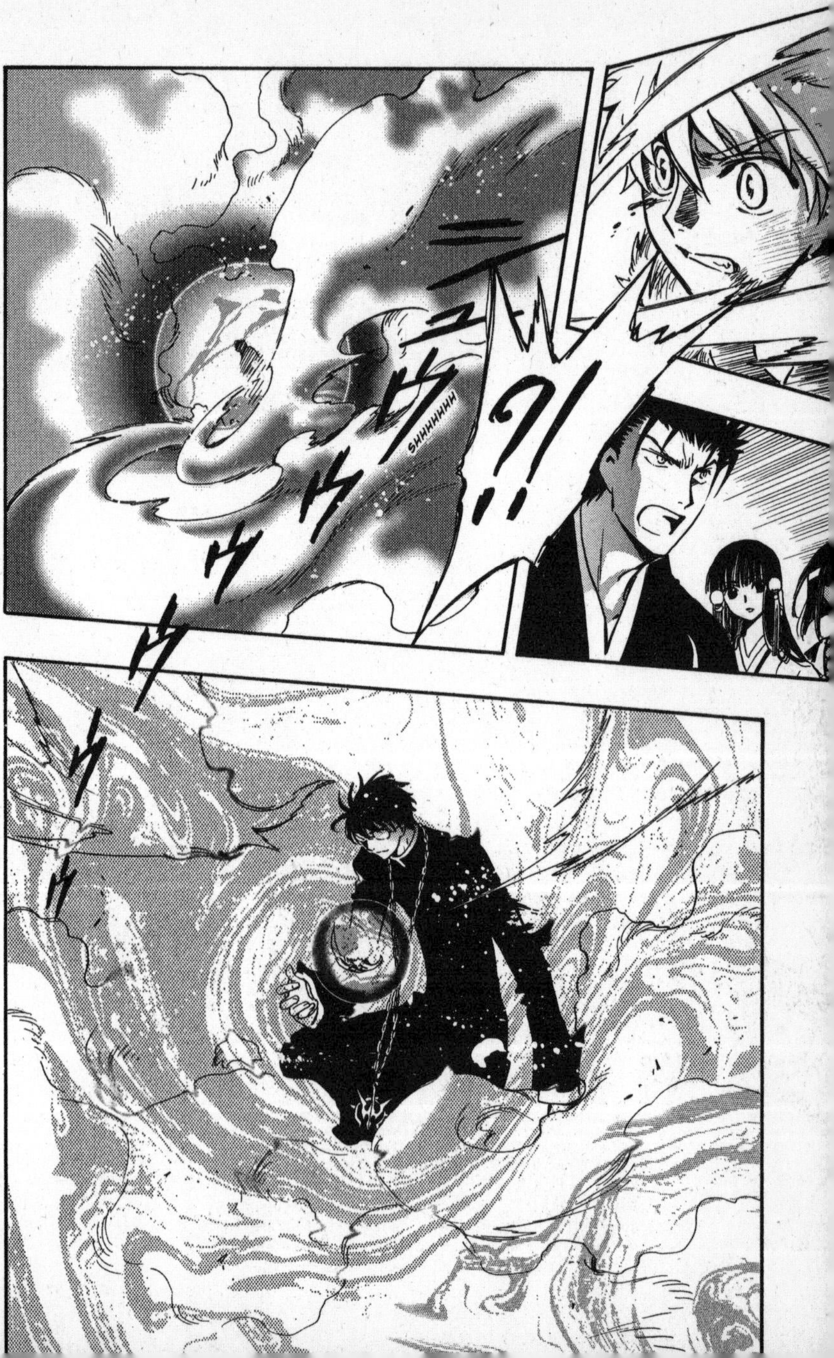
?!!
SHHHHHHH

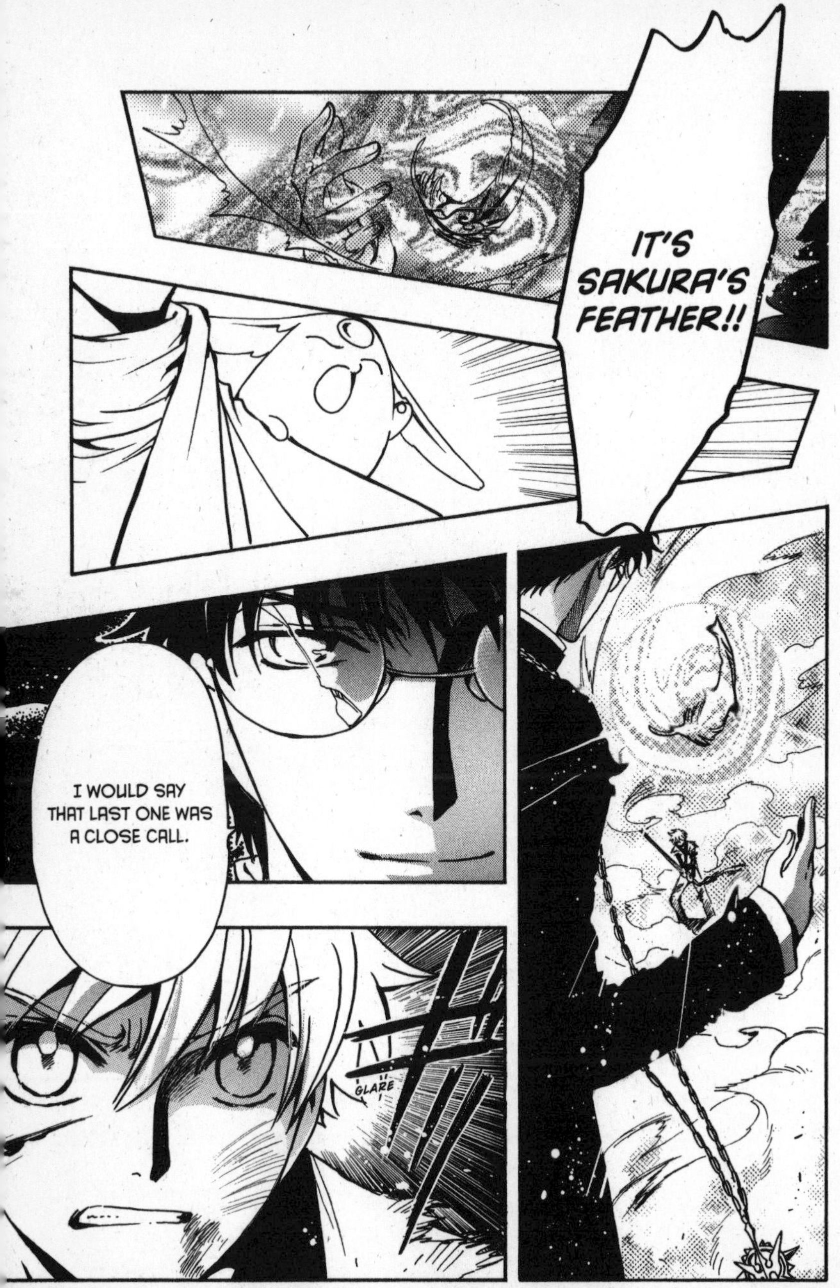
IT'S SAKURA'S FEATHER!!
I WOULD SAY THAT LAST ONE WAS A CLOSE CALL.
GLARE

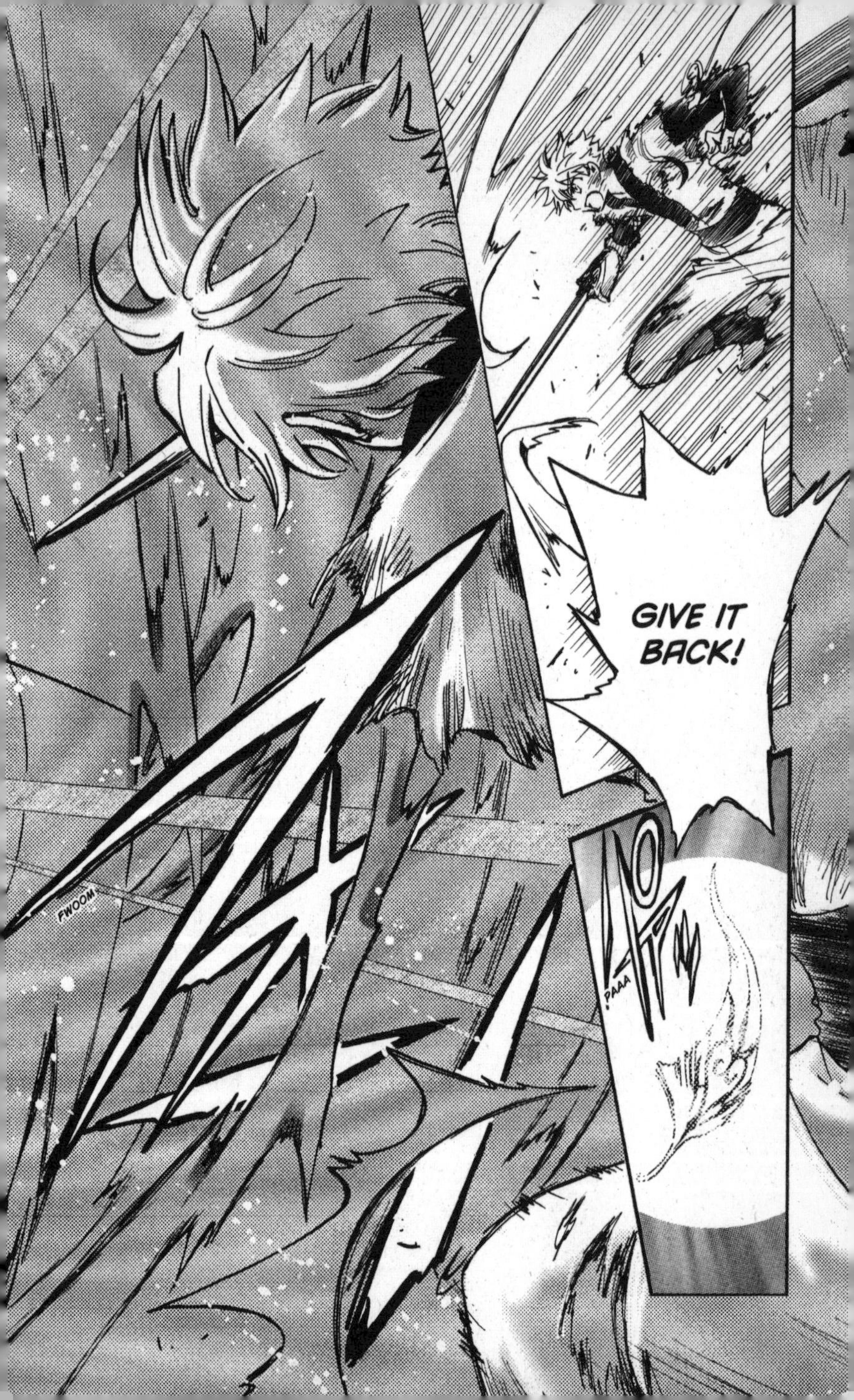
GIVE IT BACK!
PAAA
FWOOM

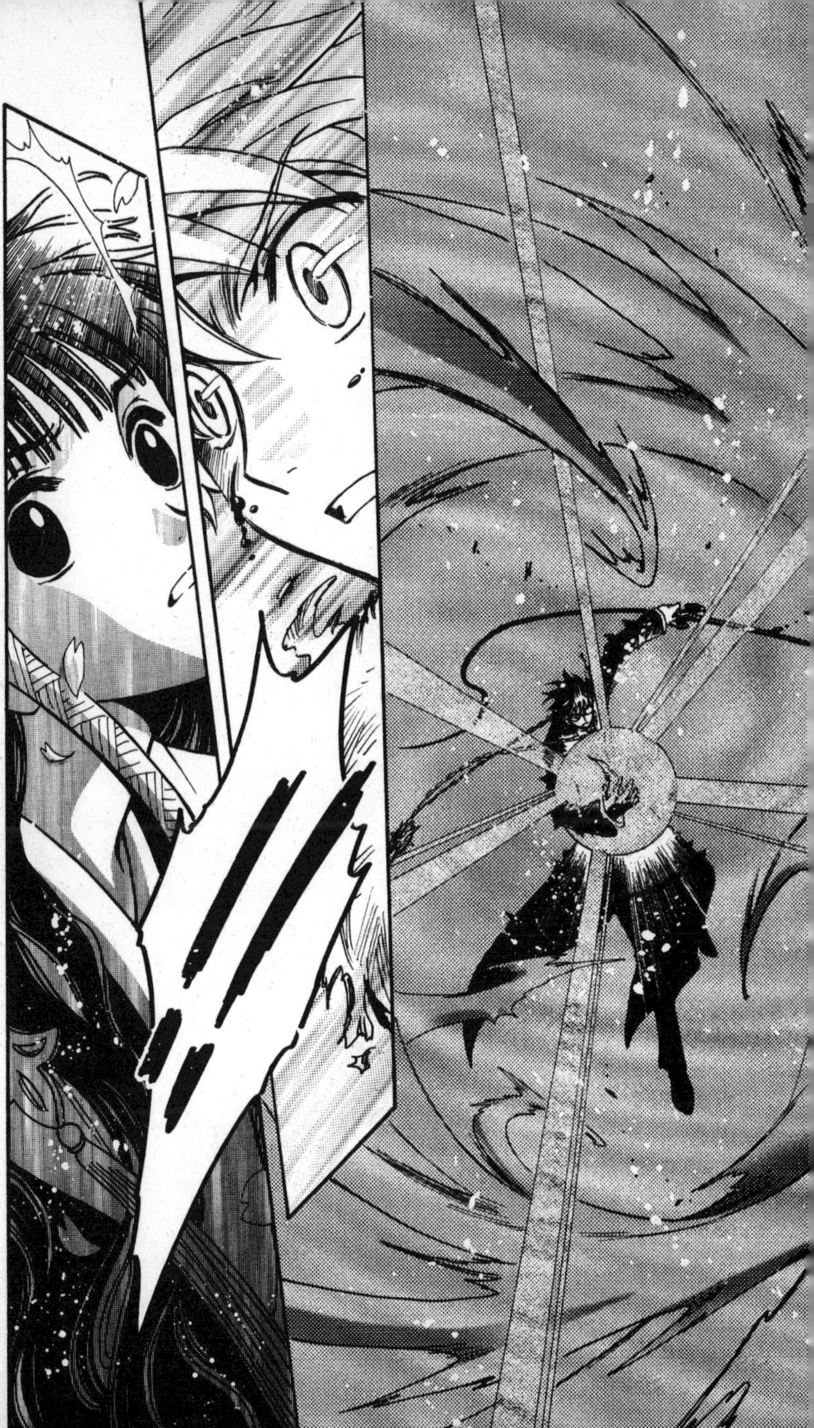

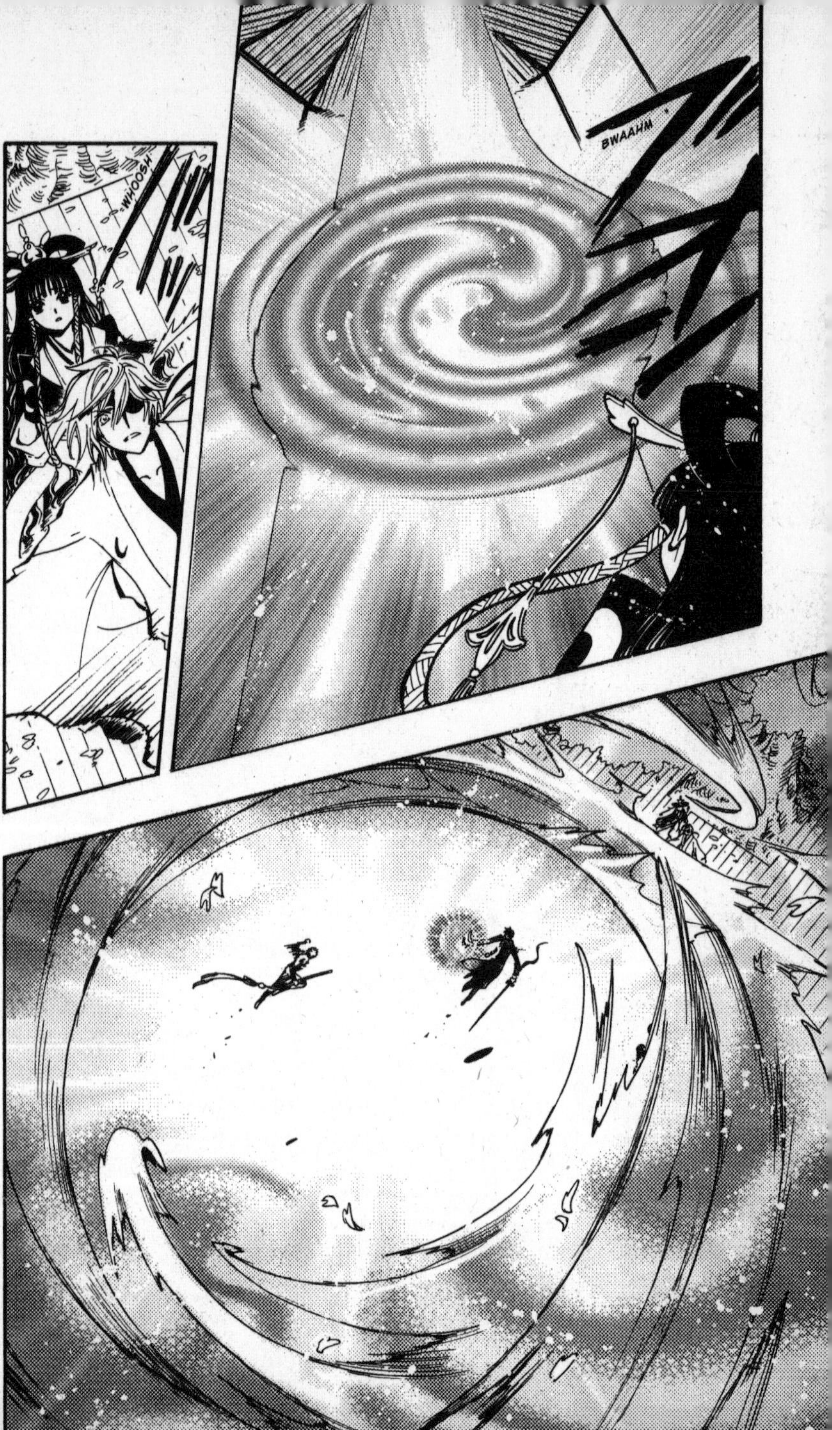
BWAAHM
WHOOSH

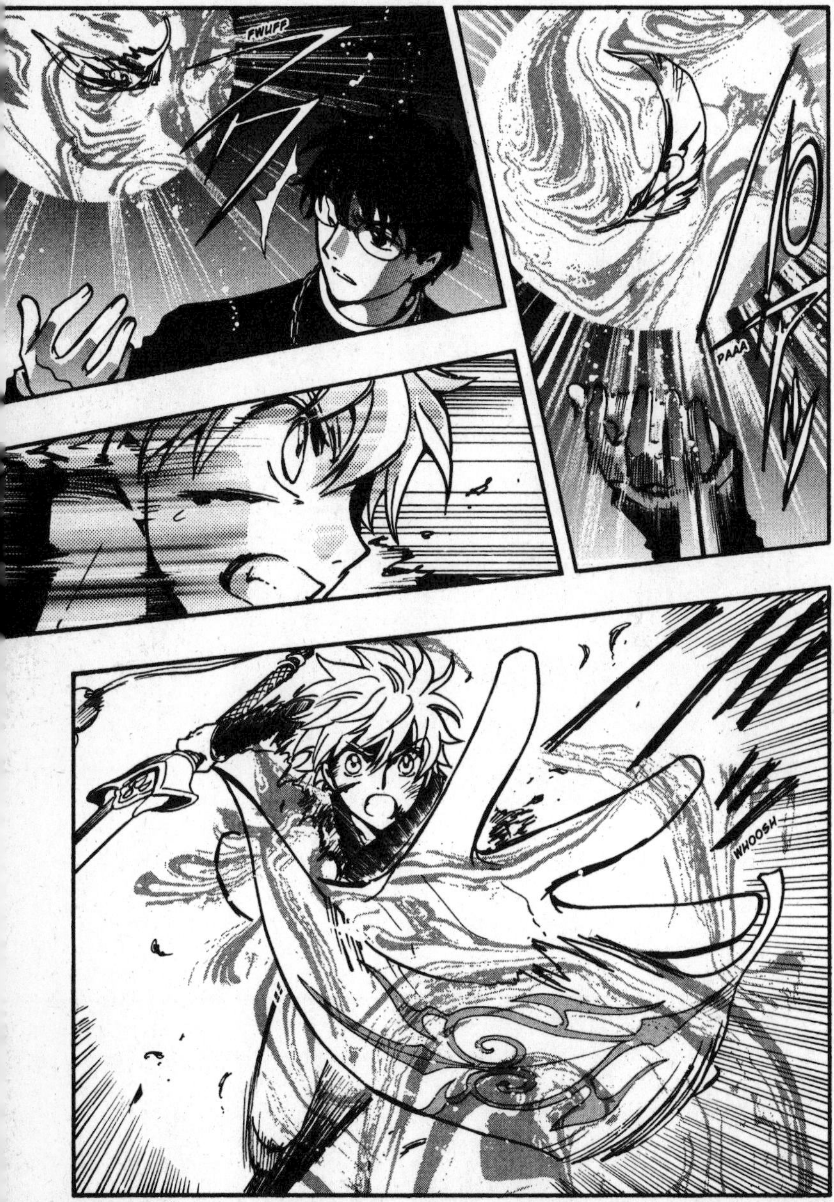
PAAA
FWUFF
WHOOSH

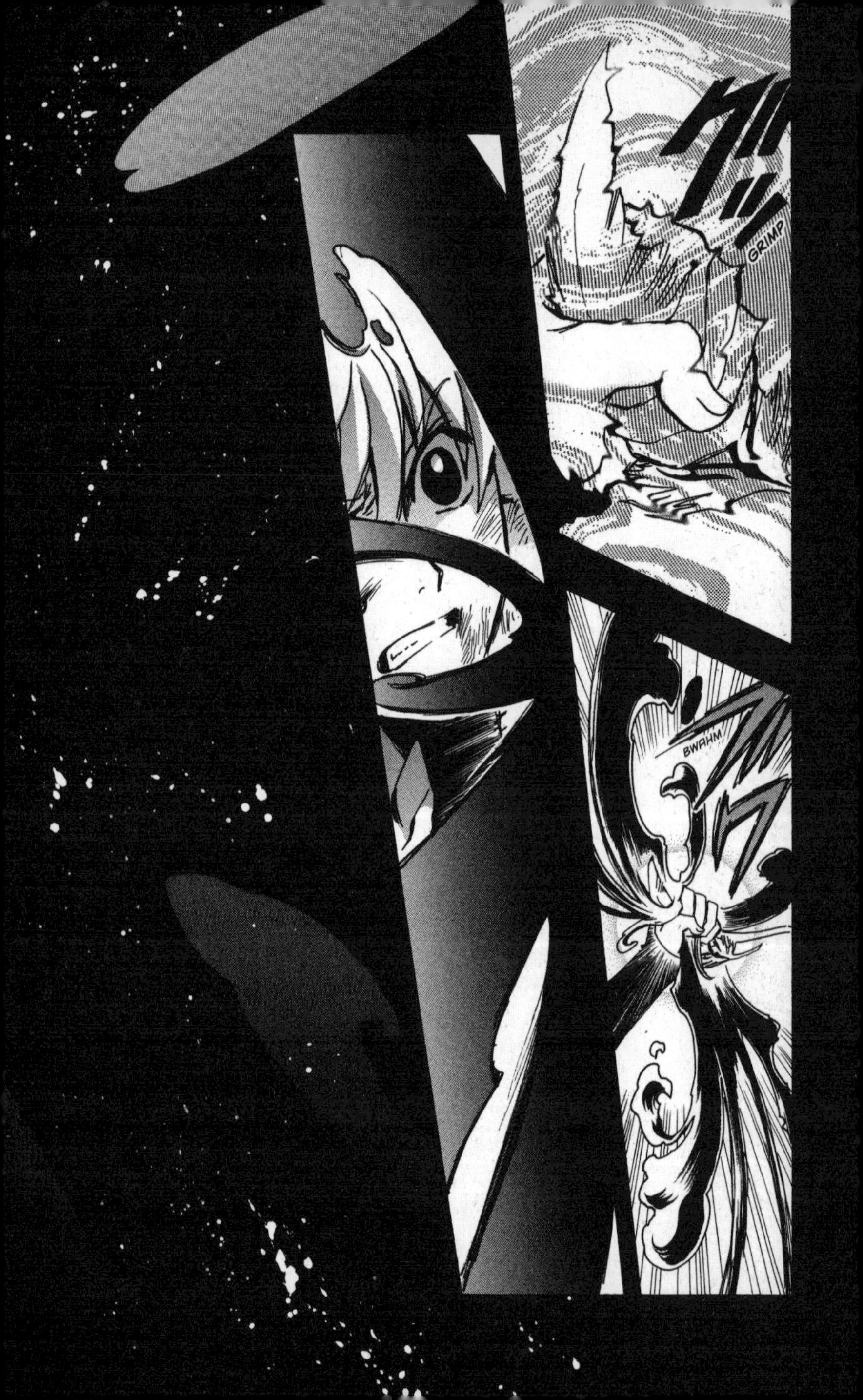
GRIMP
BWAHM

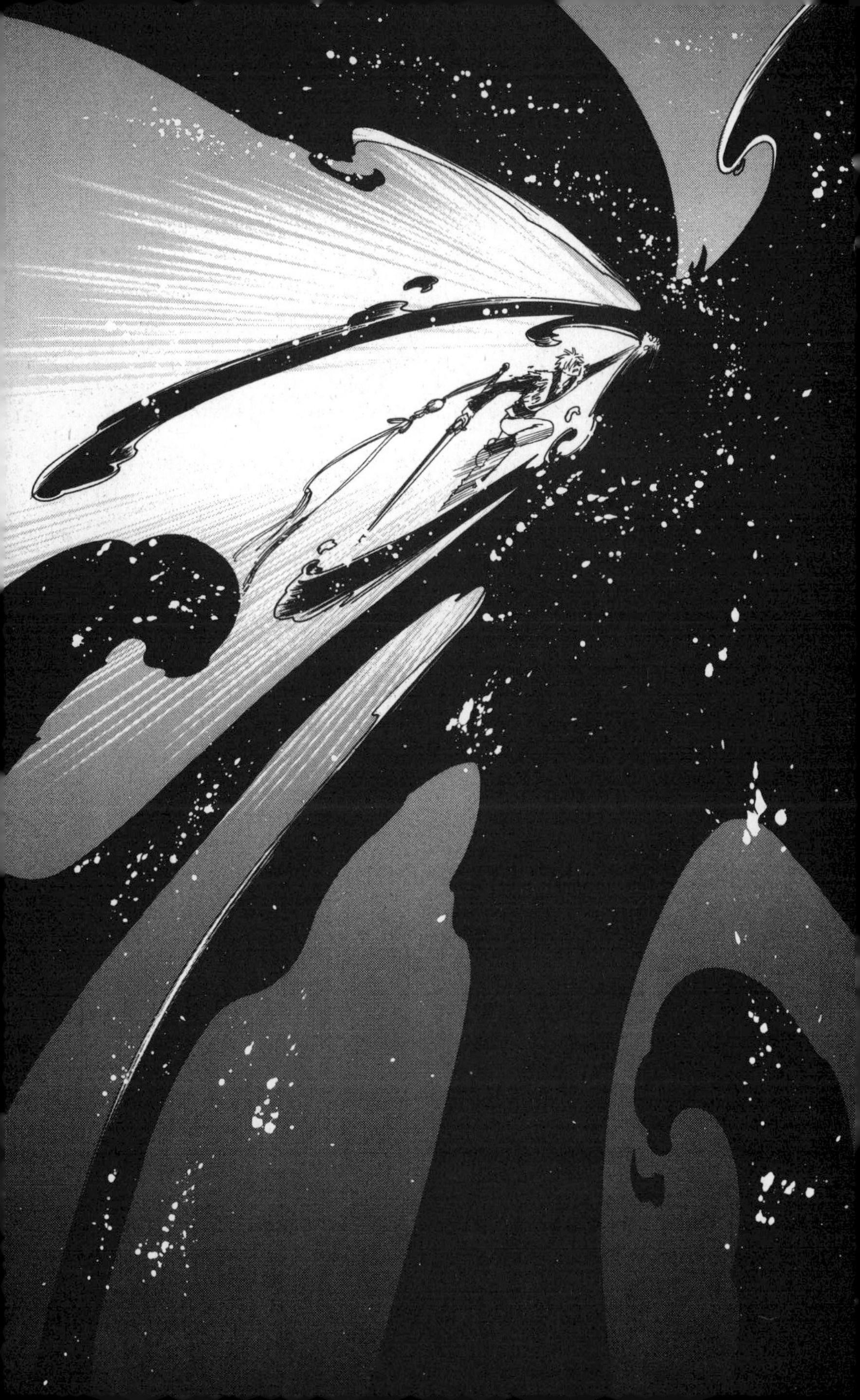

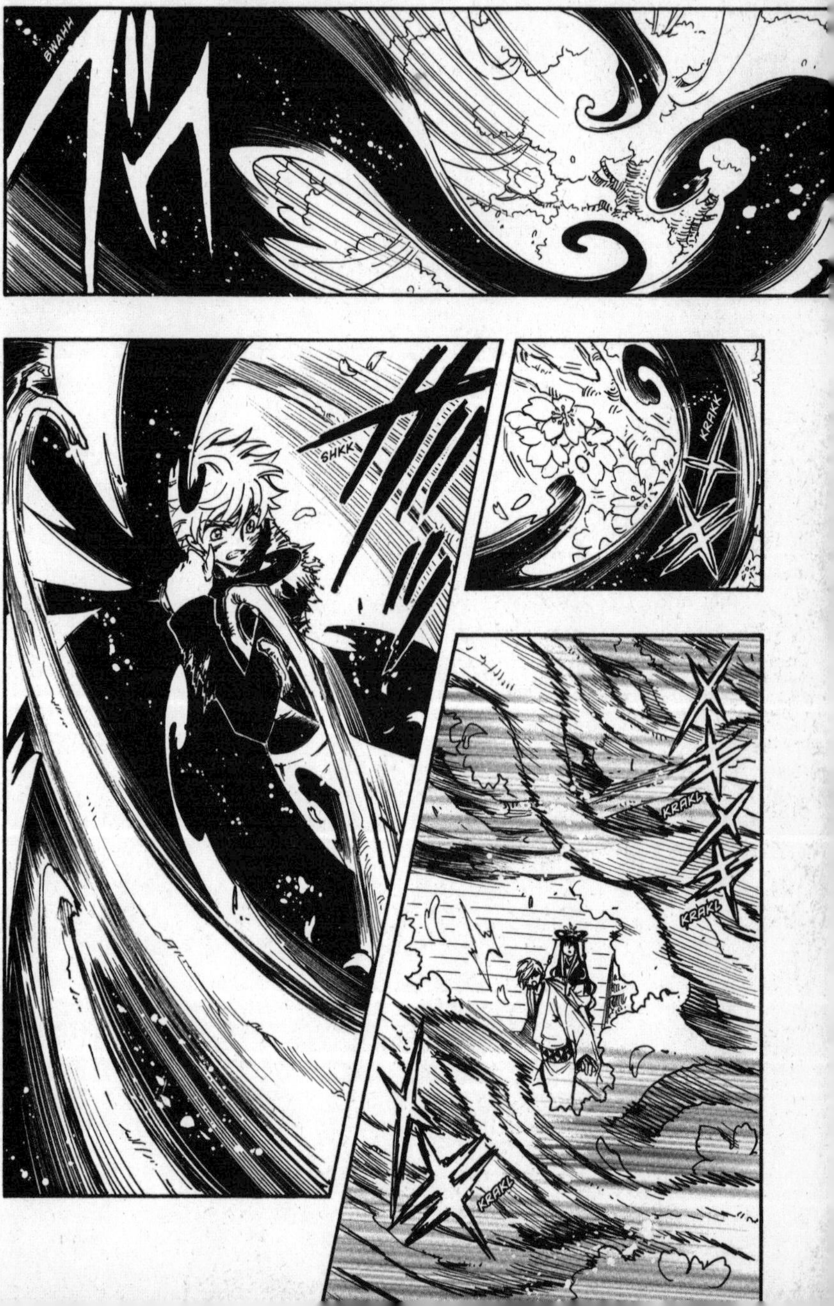
BWAHH
KRAKK
KRAKL
KRAKL
KRAKL
SHKK

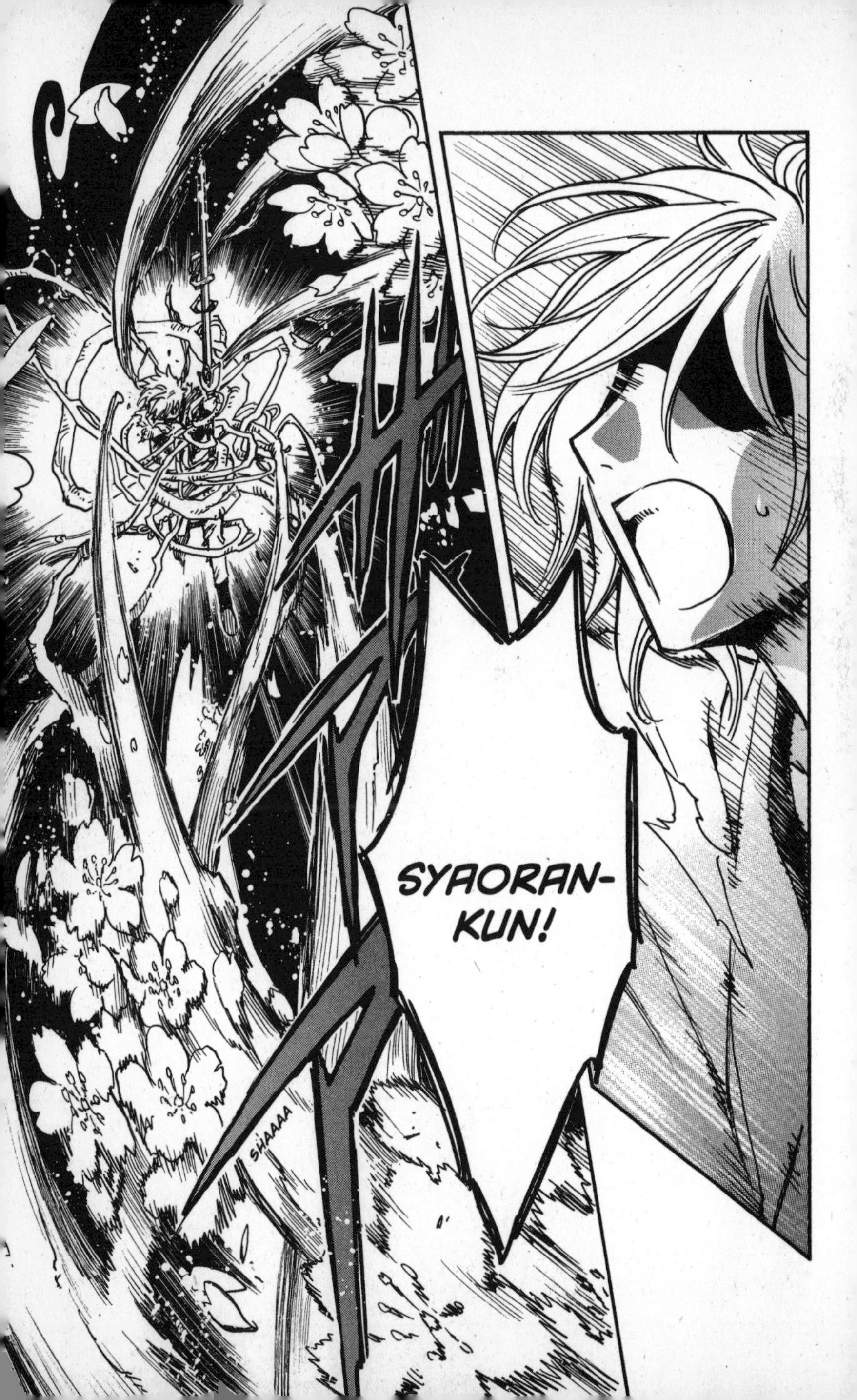
SYAORAN-KUN!
SHAAAA

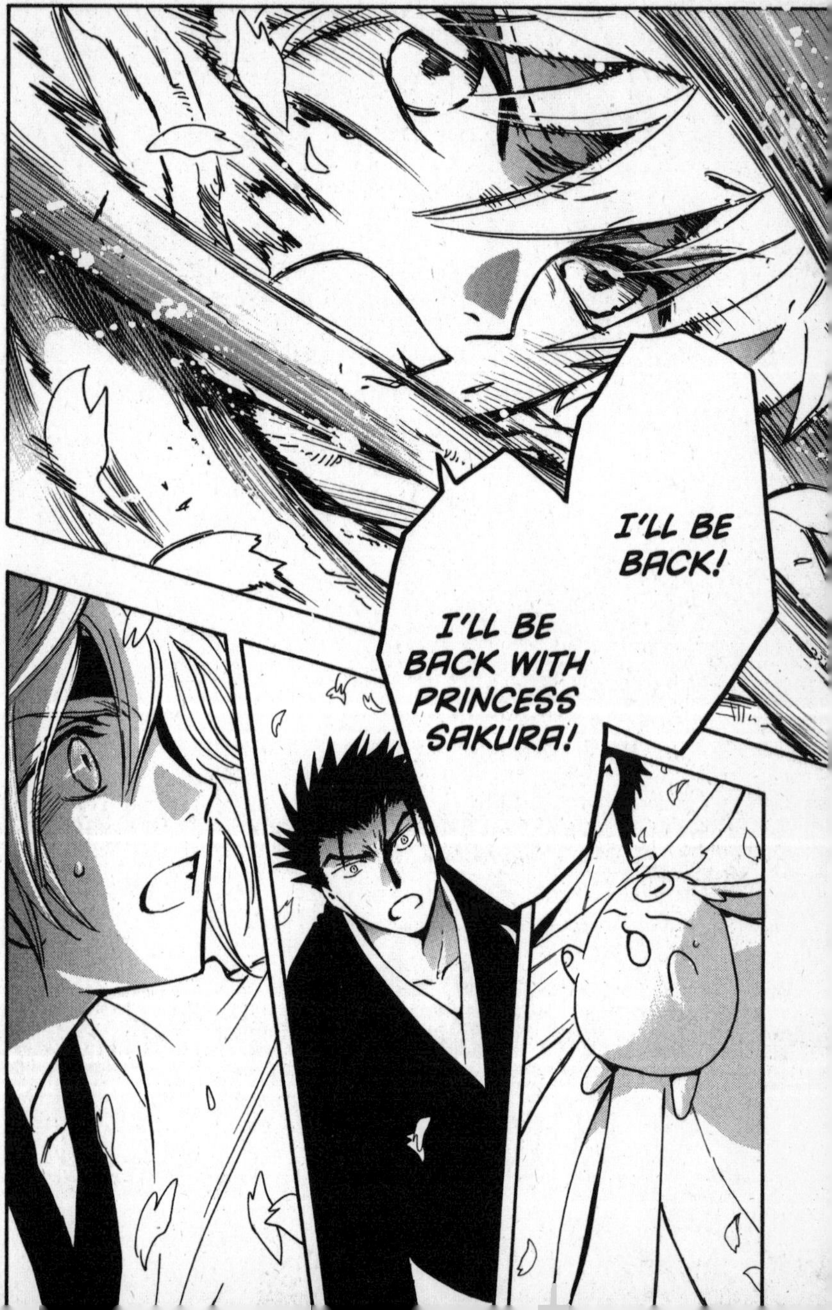
I'LL BE BACK!
I'LL BE BACK WITH PRINCESS SAKURA!

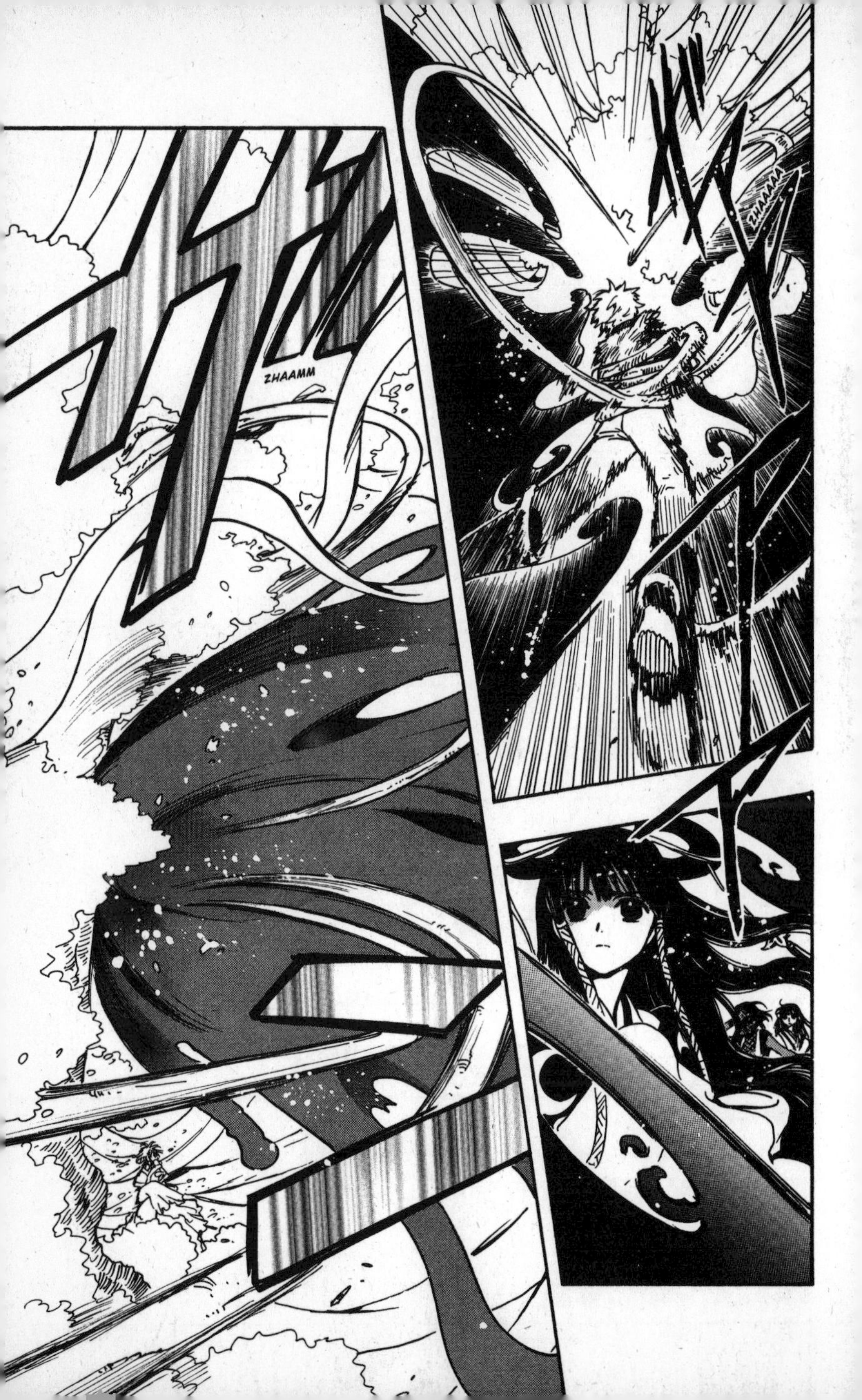
ZHAAAAA
ZHAAMM

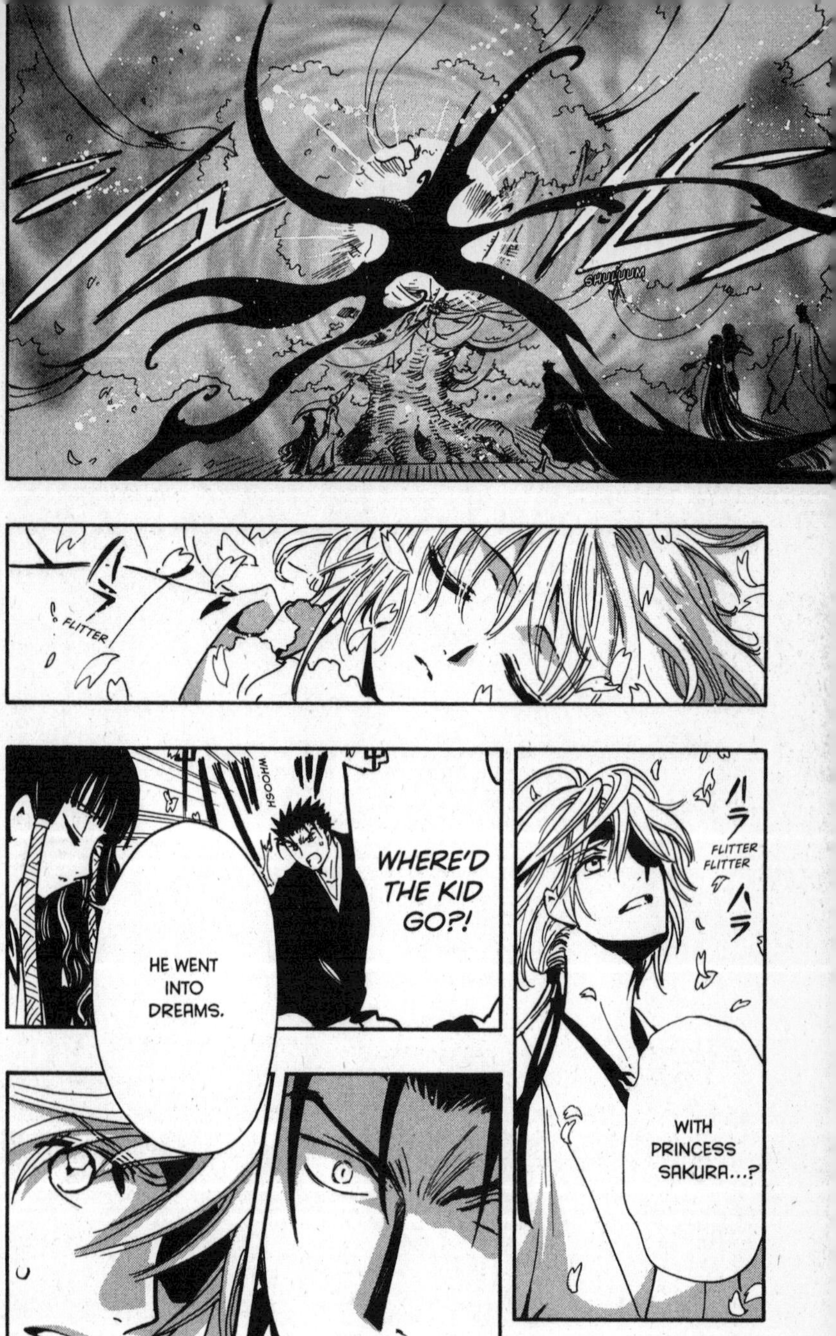
SHULUUM
FLITTER
ハラ
FLITTER
FLITTER
ハラ
WITH PRINCESS SAKURA...?
WHOOSH
WHERE'D THE KID GO?!
HE WENT INTO DREAMS.

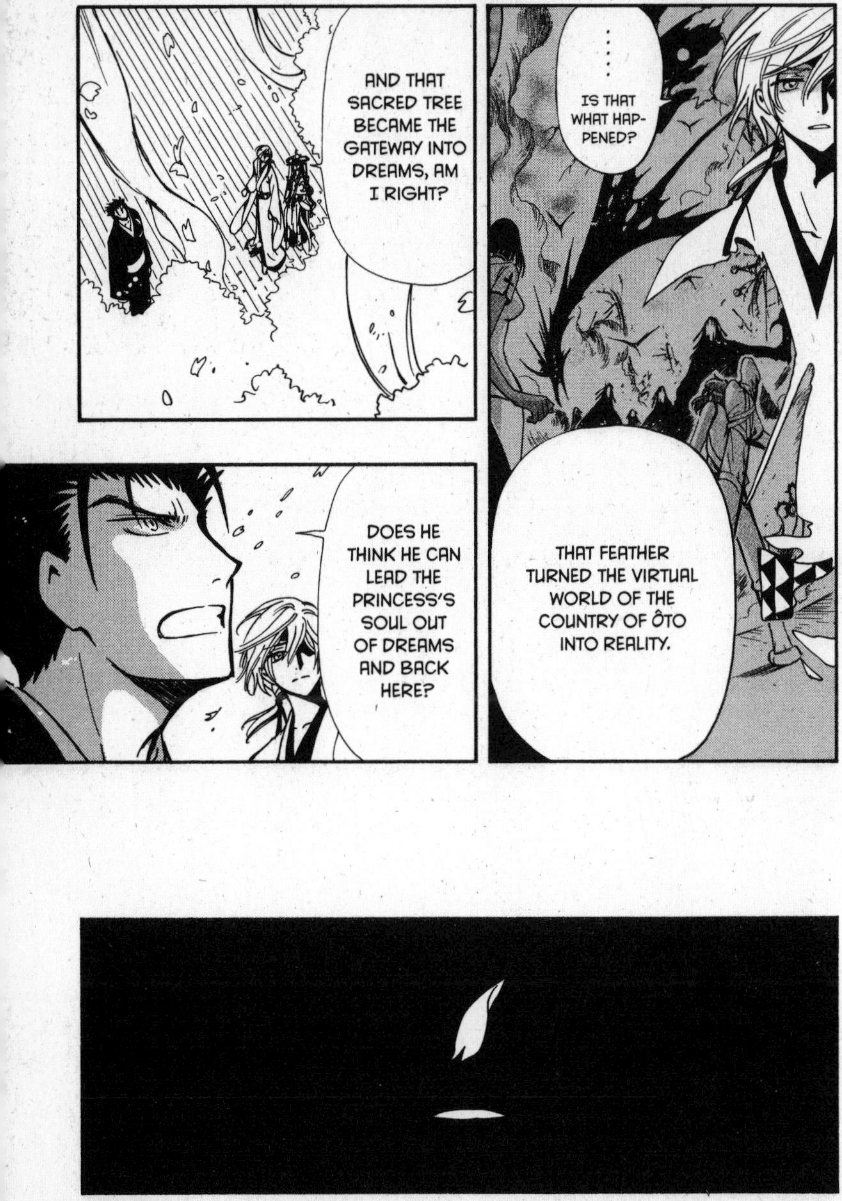

..... IS THAT WHAT HAP-PENED?
THAT FEATHER TURNED THE VIRTUAL WORLD OF THE COUNTRY OF ÔTO INTO REALITY.
AND THAT SACRED TREE BECAME THE GATEWAY INTO DREAMS, AM I RIGHT?
DOES HE THINK HE CAN LEAD THE PRINCESS'S SOUL OUT OF DREAMS AND BACK HERE?

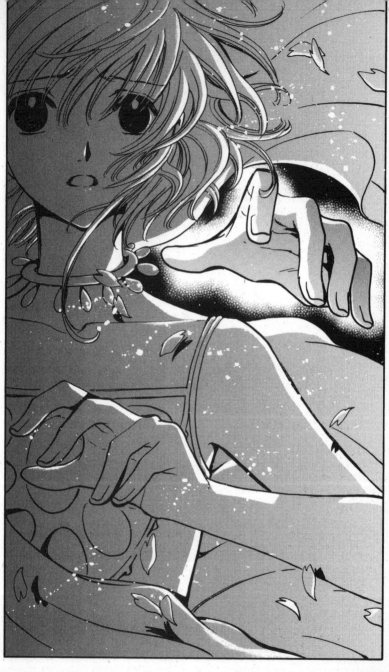

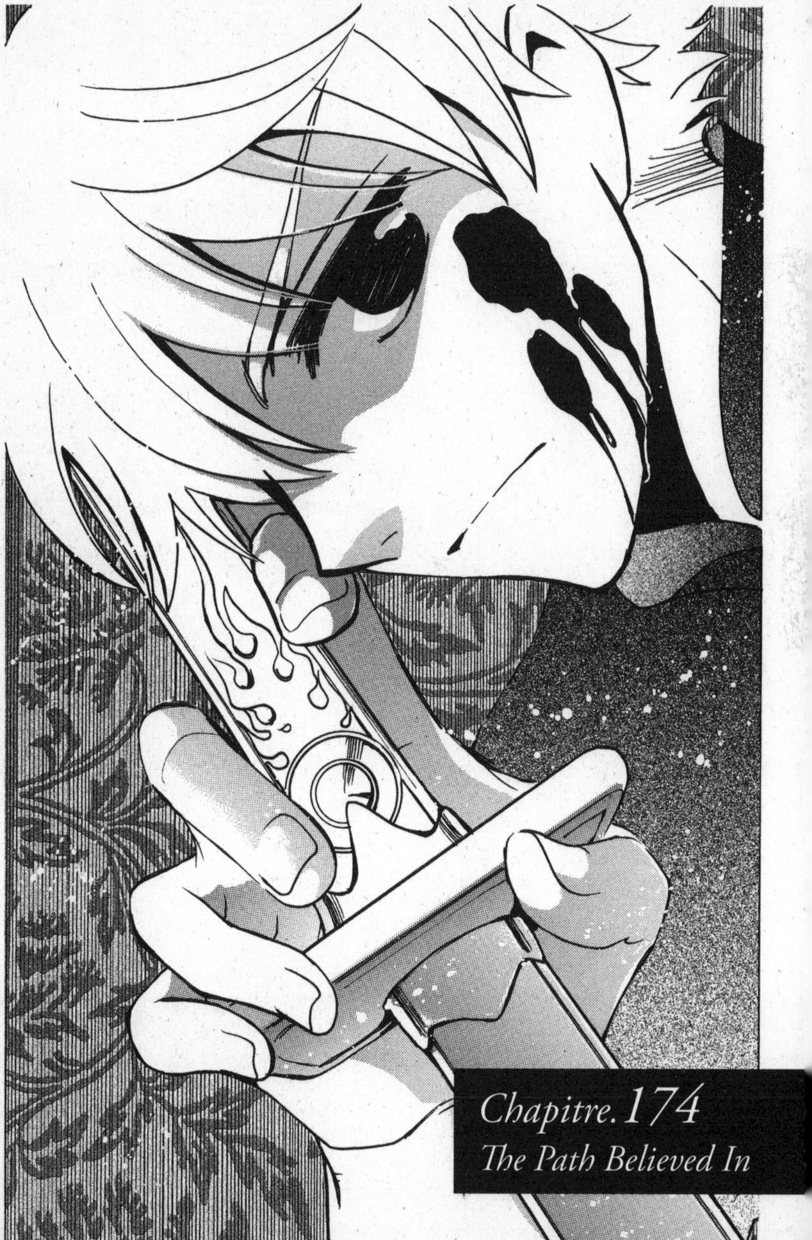
Chapitre. 174
The Path Believed In

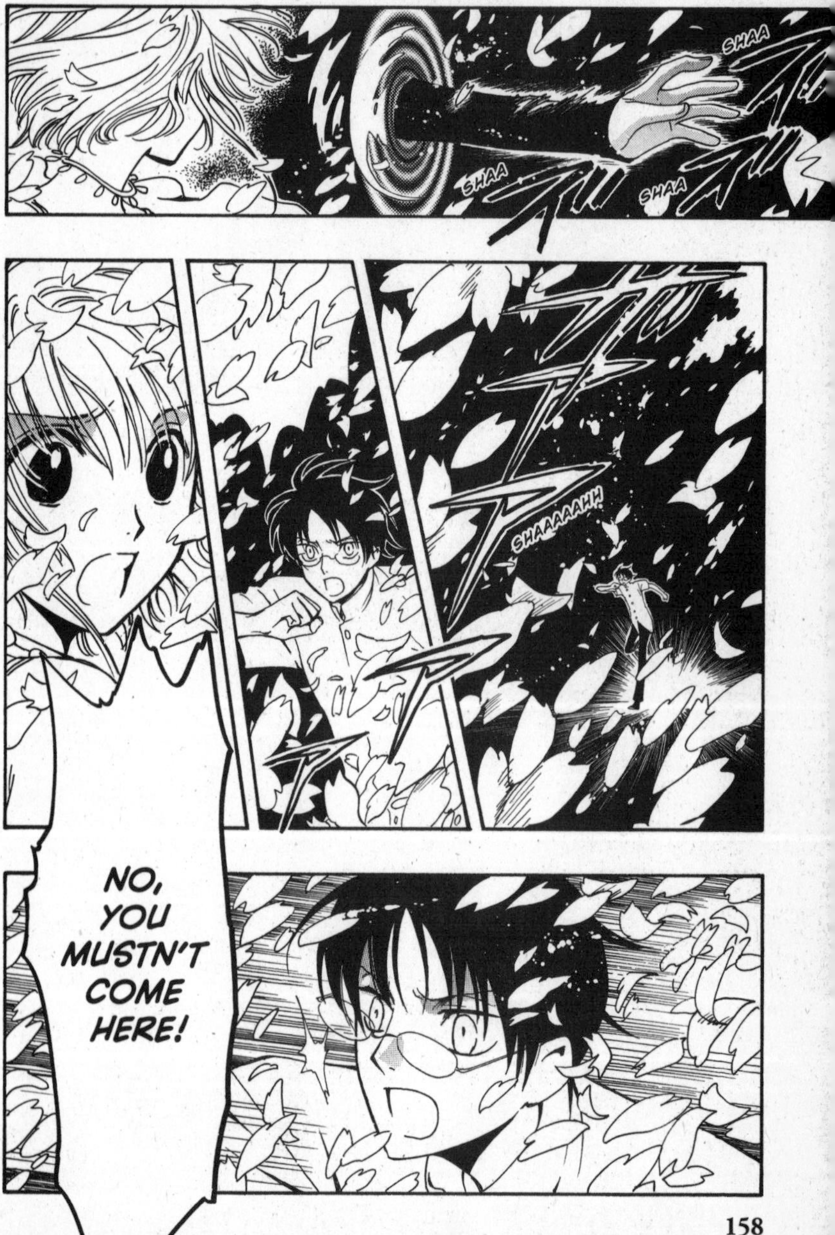
SHAA
SHAA
SHAA
SHAAAAAHH!
NO, YOU MUSTN'T COME HERE!

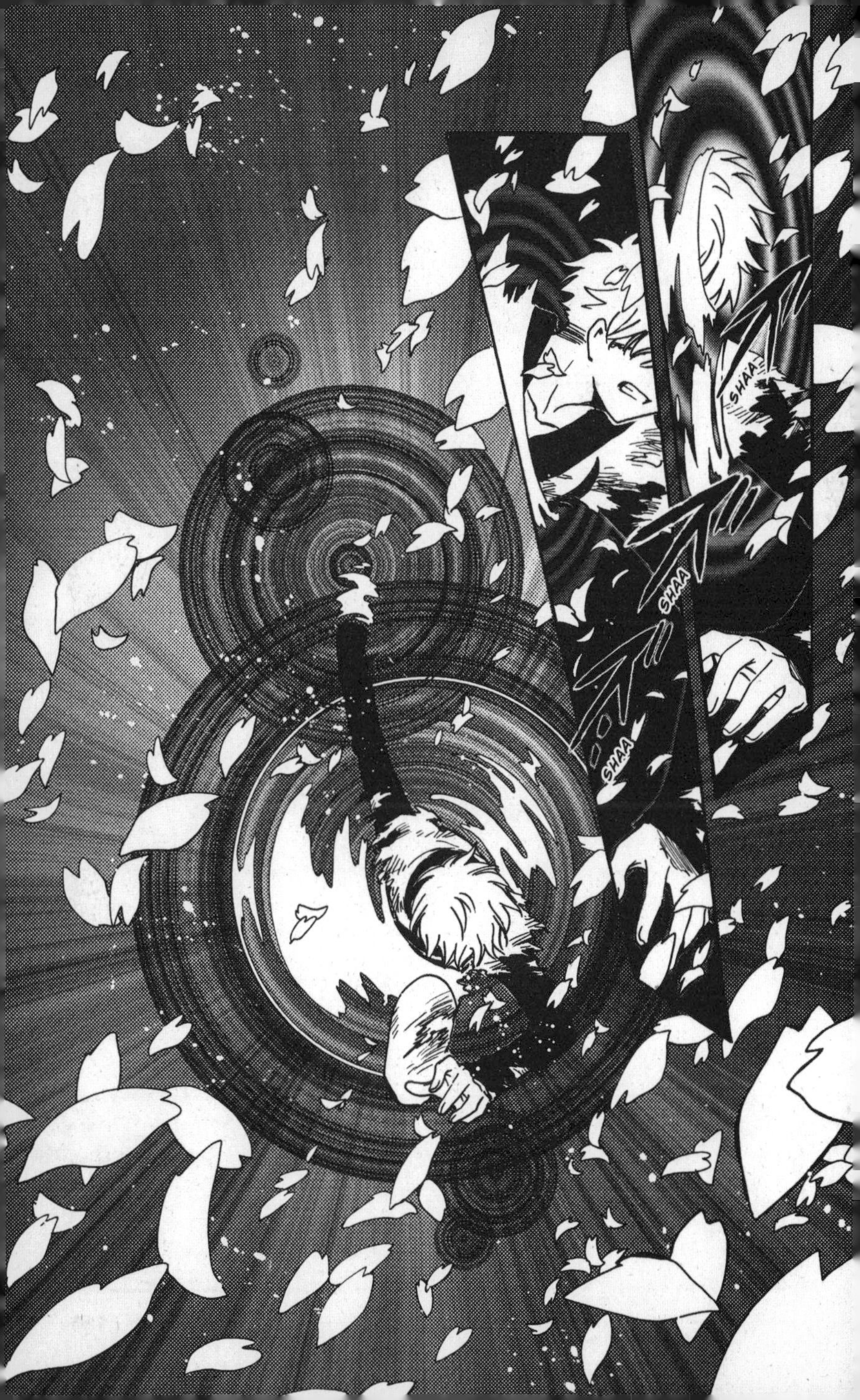
SHAA
SHAA
SHAA

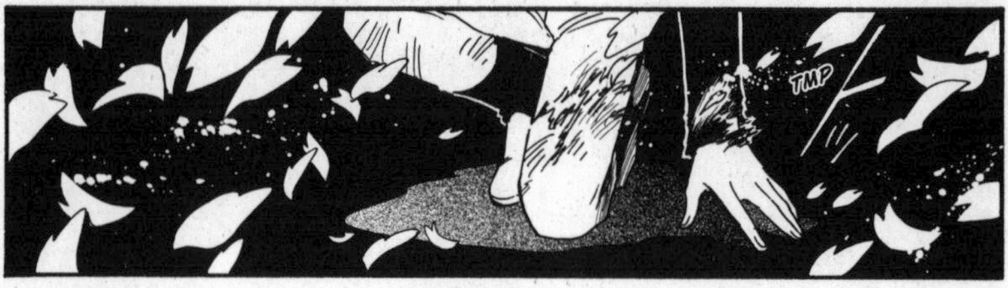
TMP
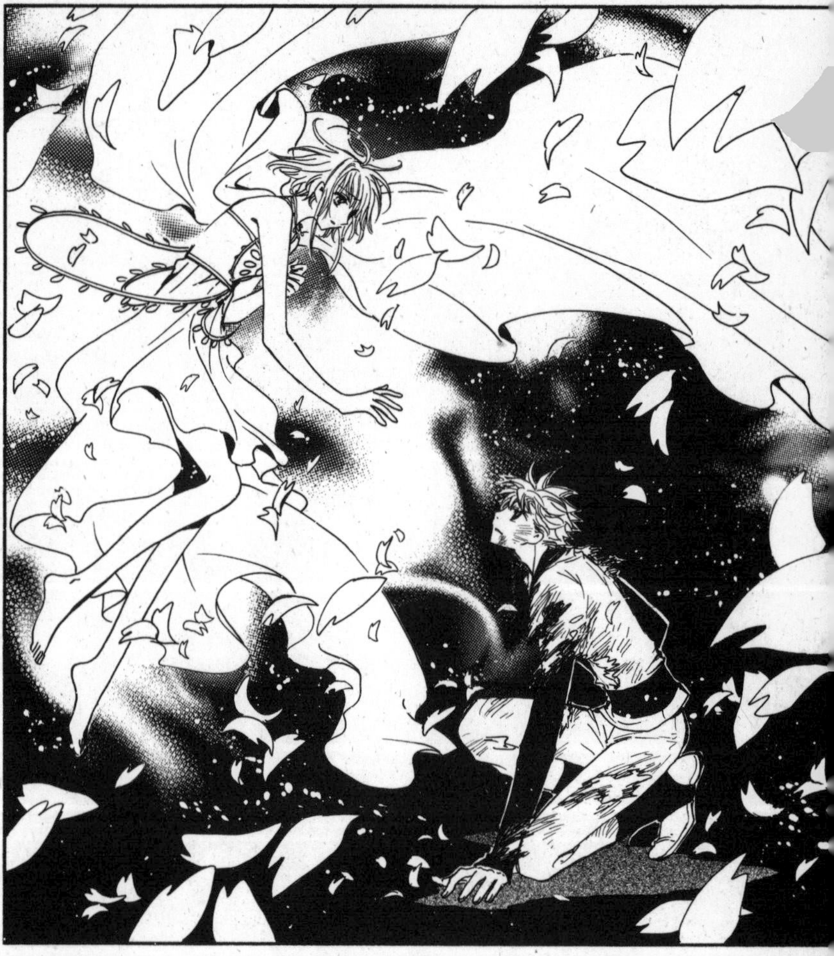

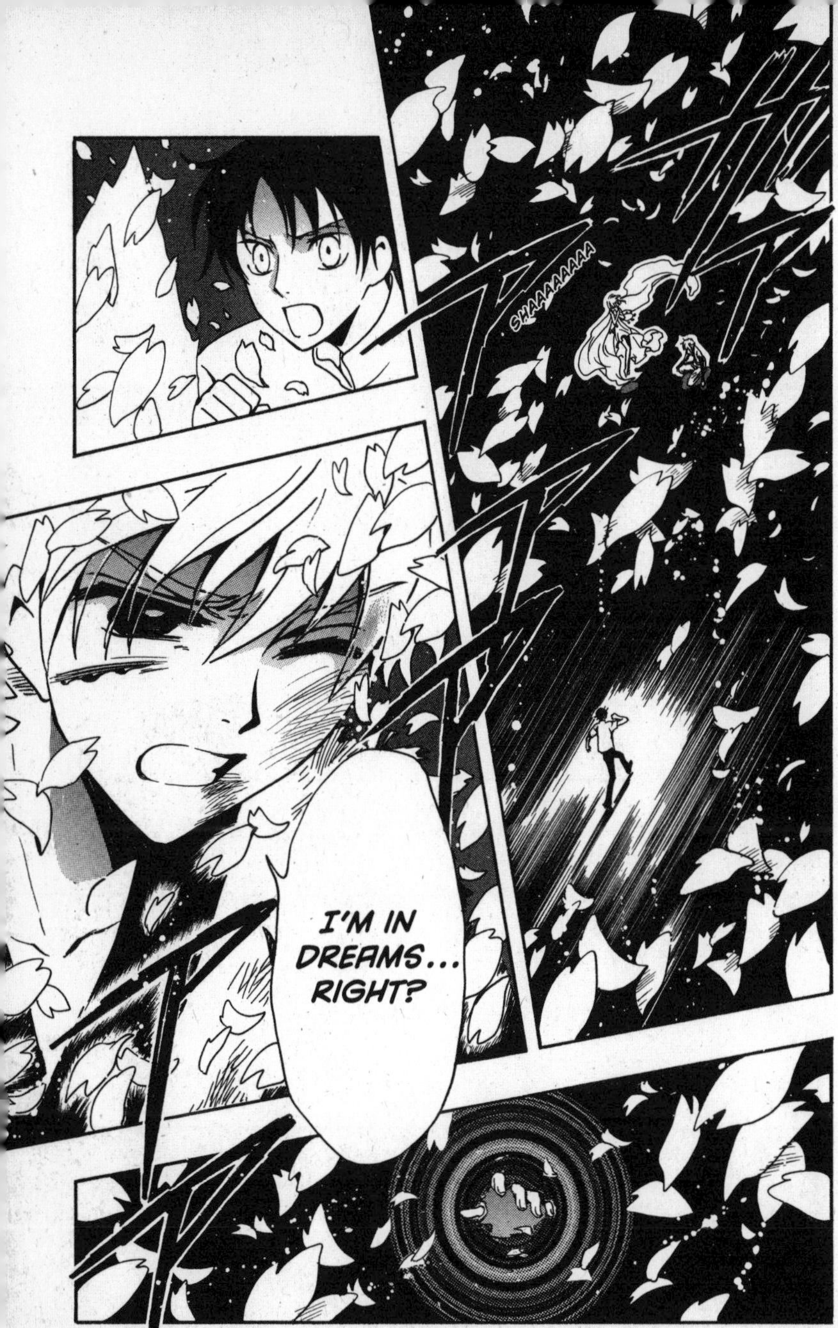
SHAAAAAAAA
I'M IN DREAMS... RIGHT?

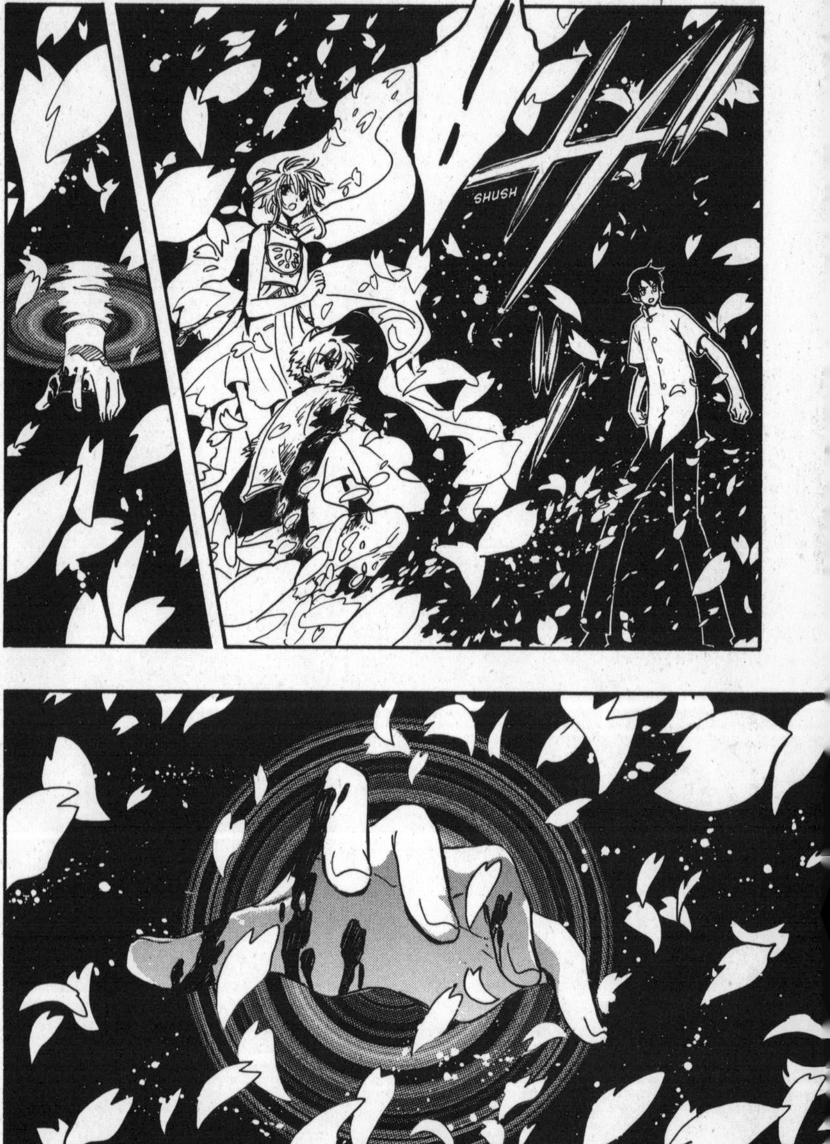
SHUSH

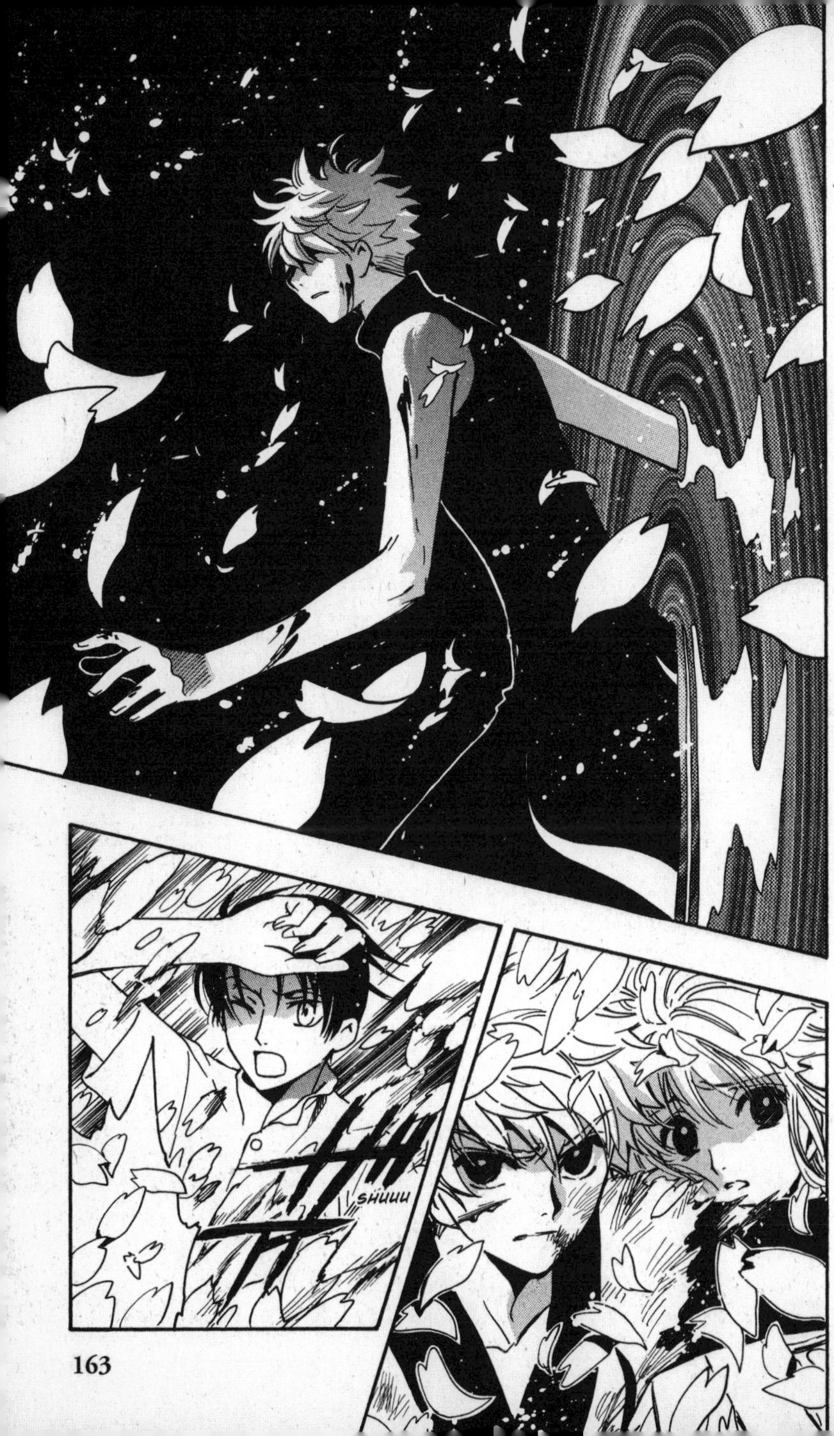
SHUUU

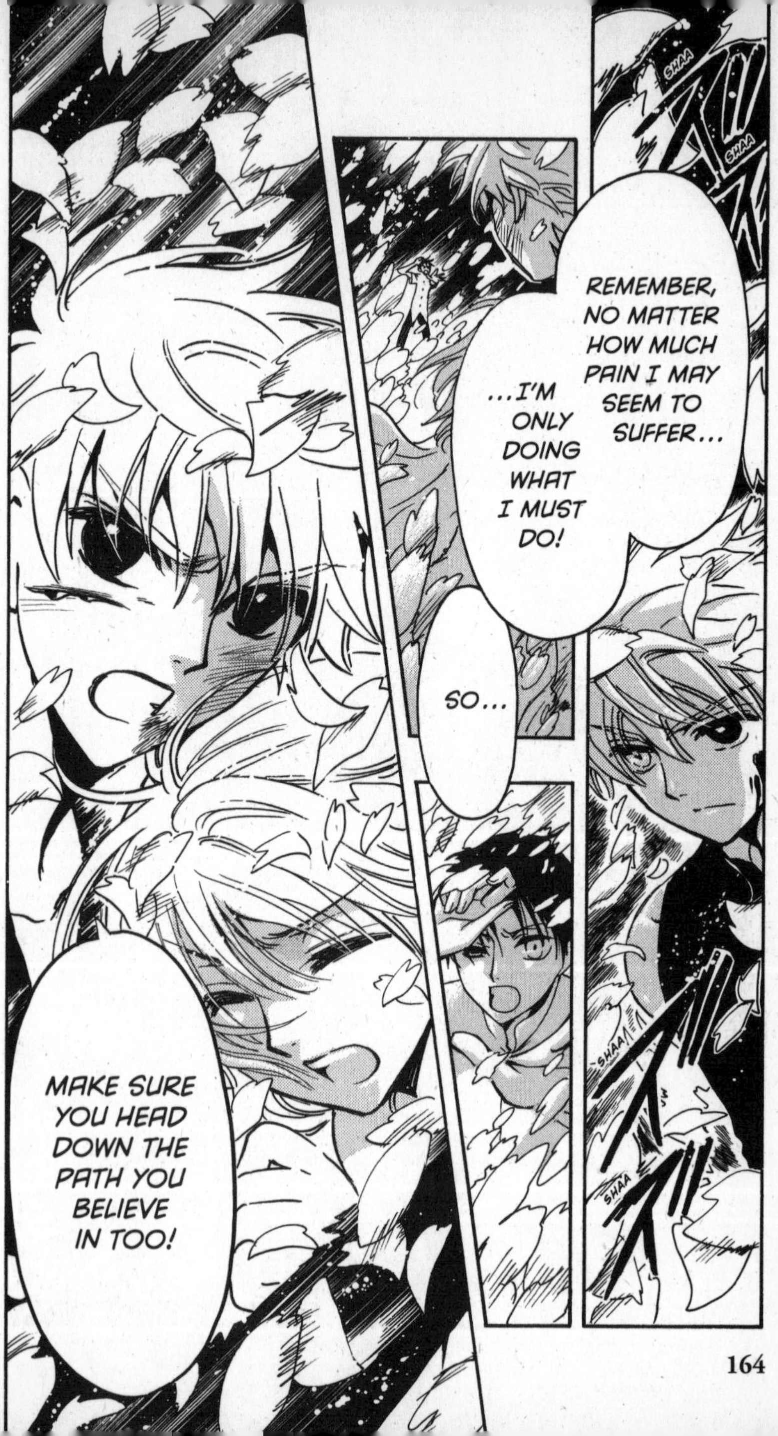
SHAA SHAA
REMEMBER, NO MATTER HOW MUCH PAIN I MAY SEEM TO SUFFER...
...I'M ONLY DOING WHAT I MUST DO!
SO...
SHAA
SHAA
MAKE SURE YOU HEAD DOWN THE PATH YOU BELIEVE IN TOO!

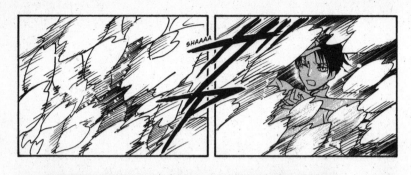

SHAAAA

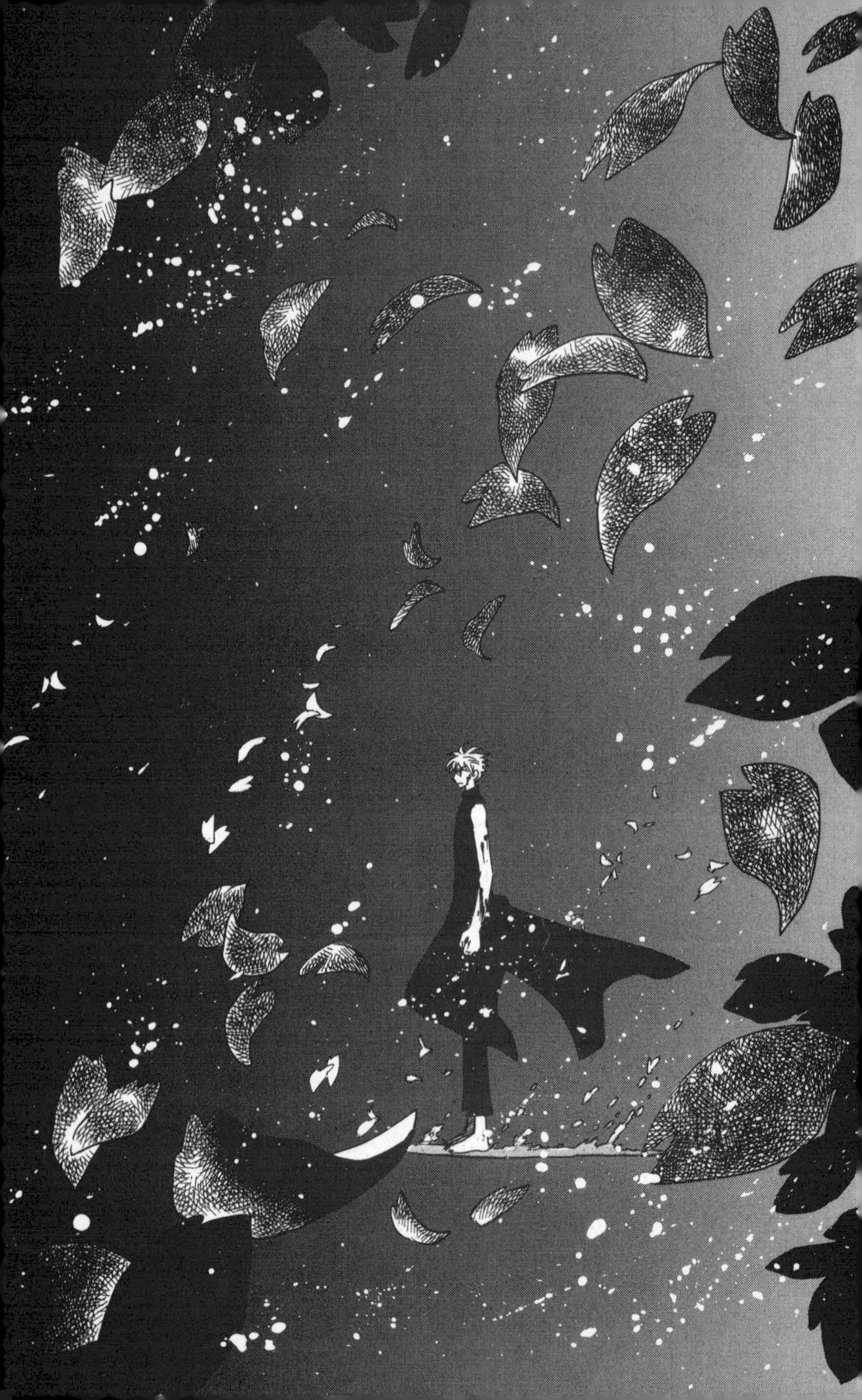

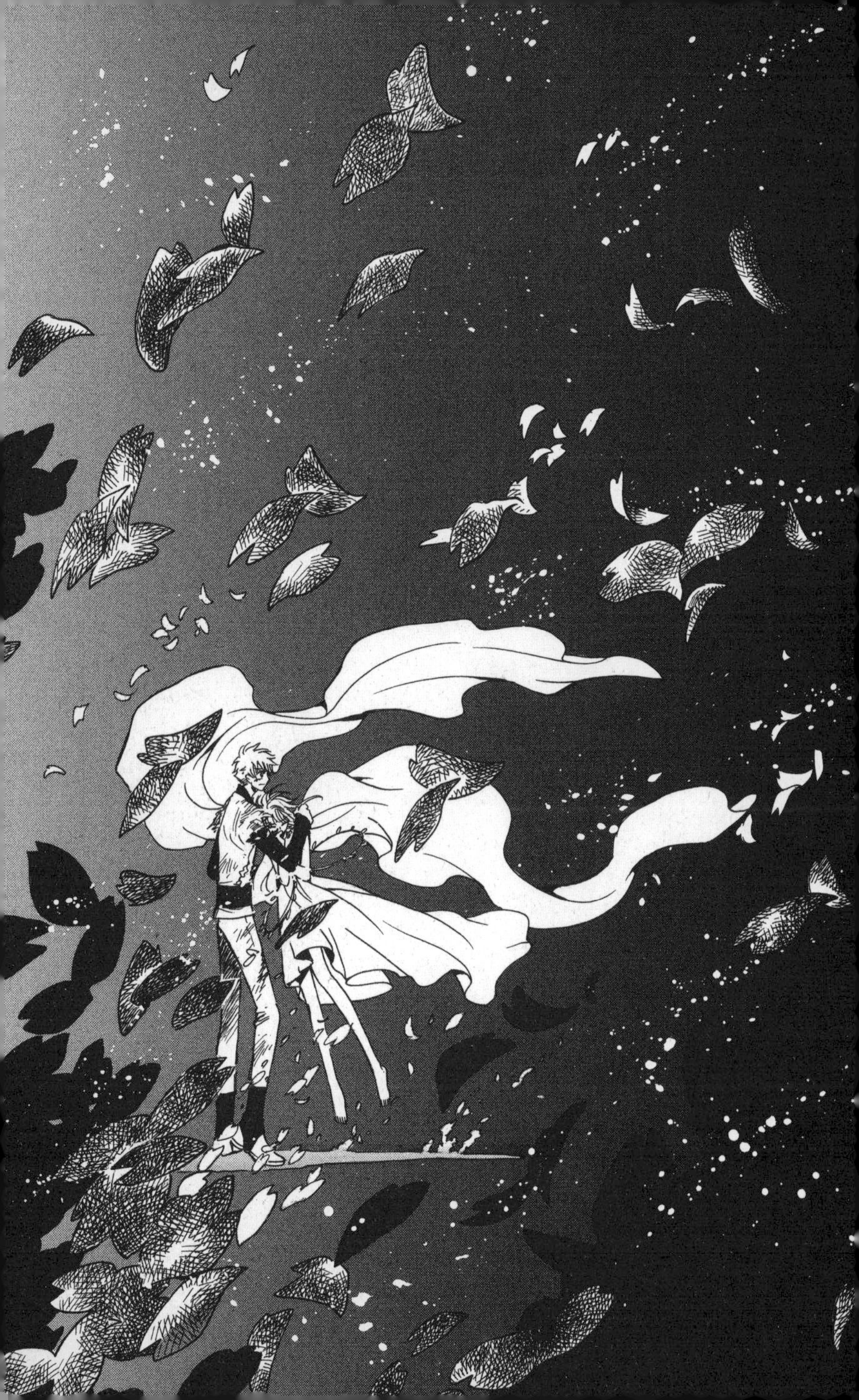

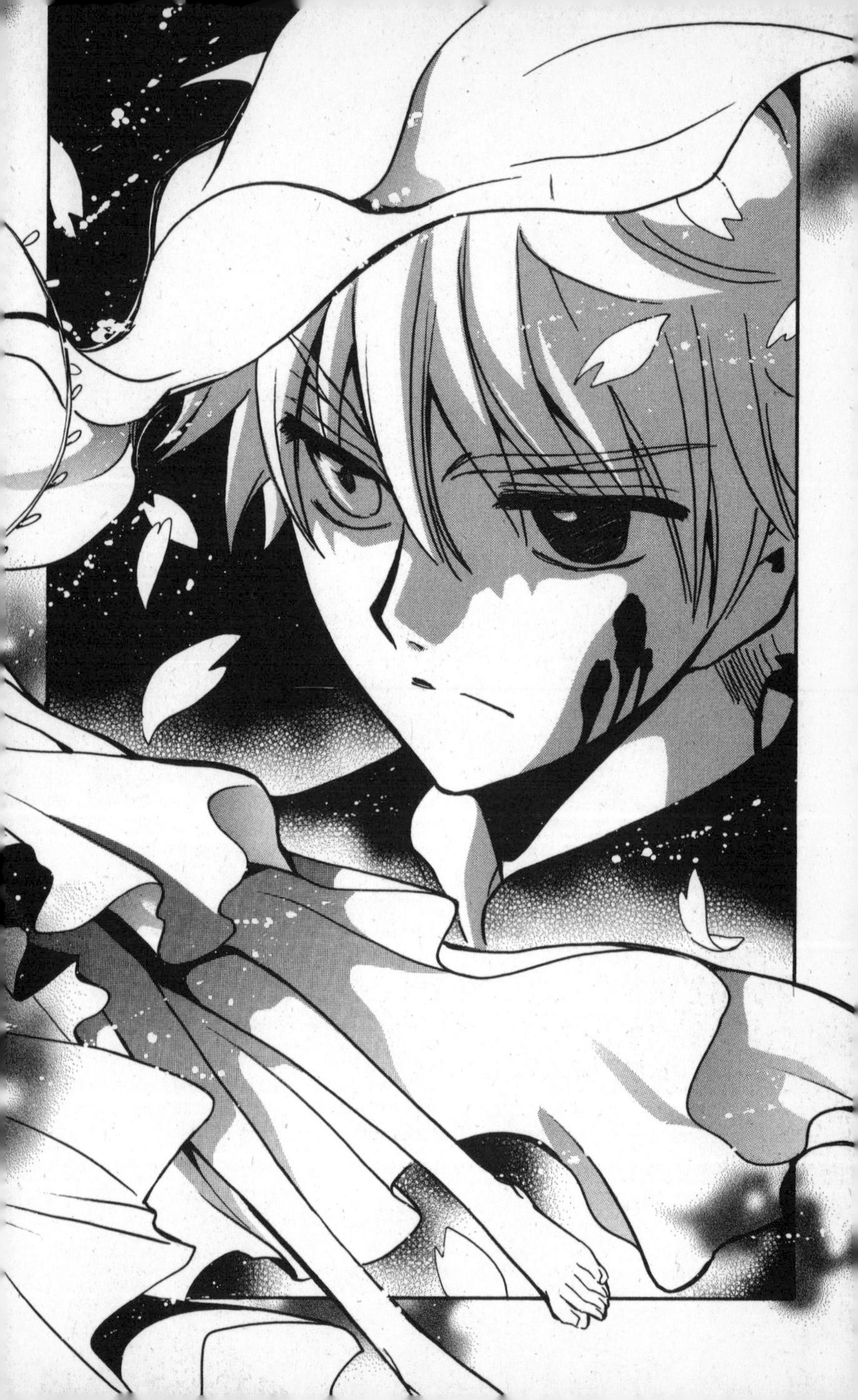

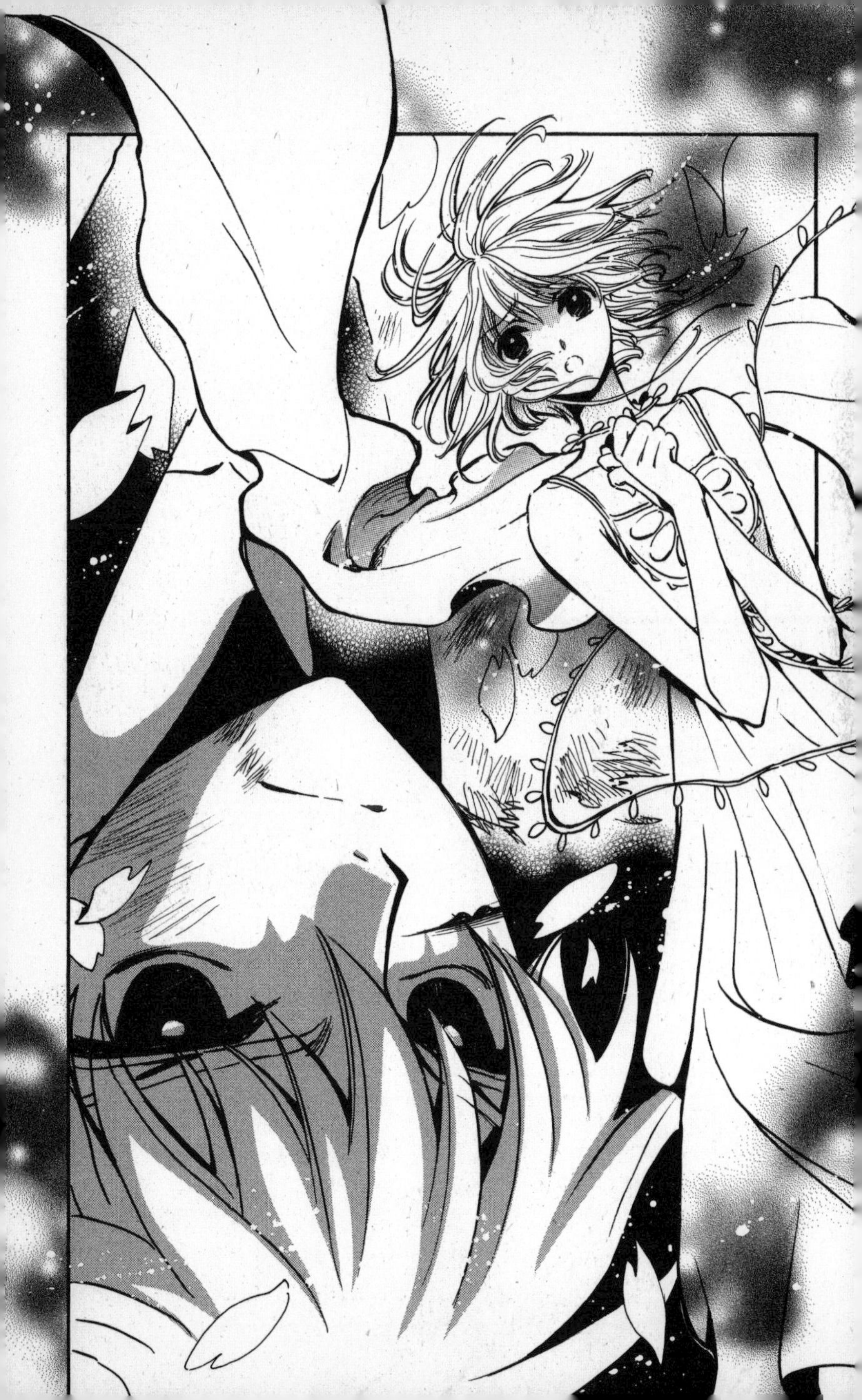

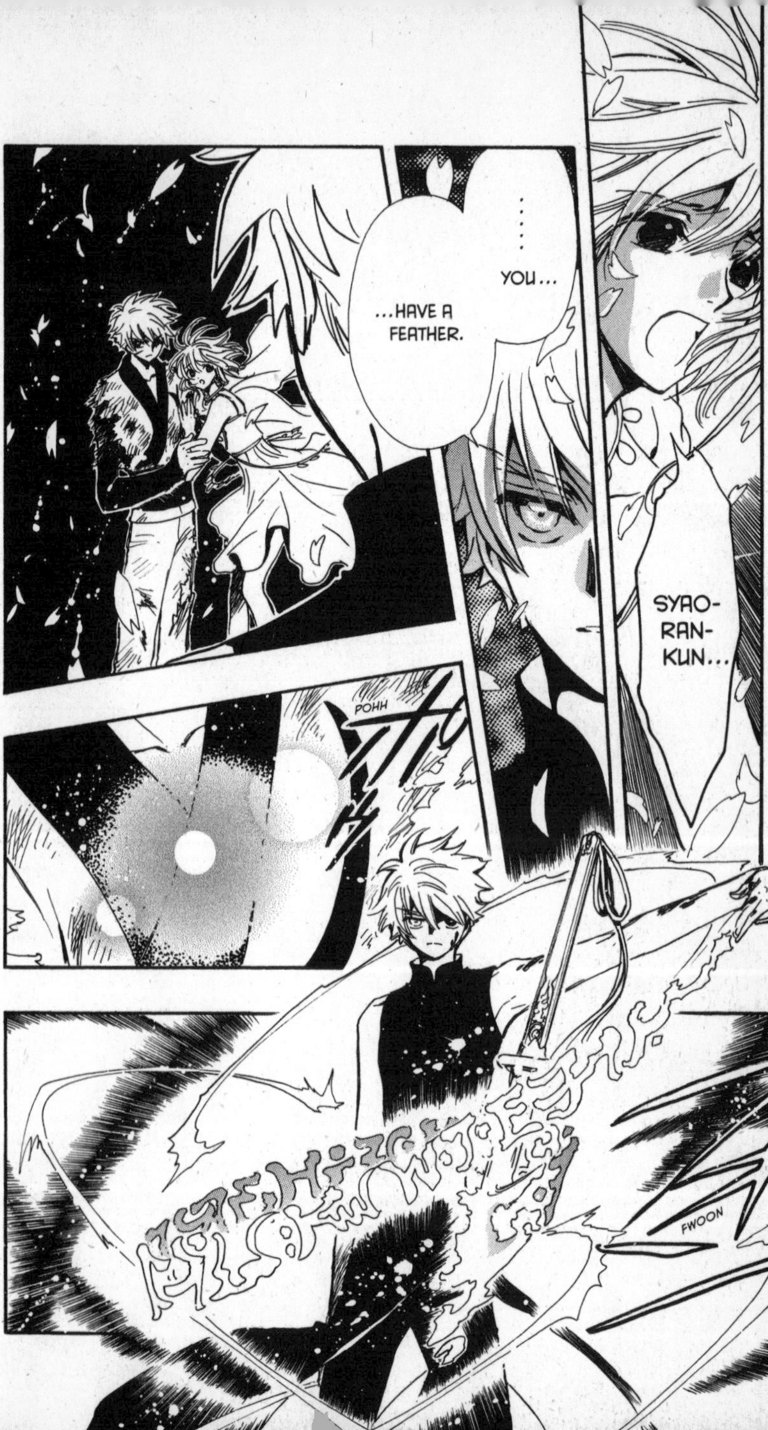
SYAO-RAN-KUN...
......
YOU...
...HAVE A FEATHER.
POHH
FWOON

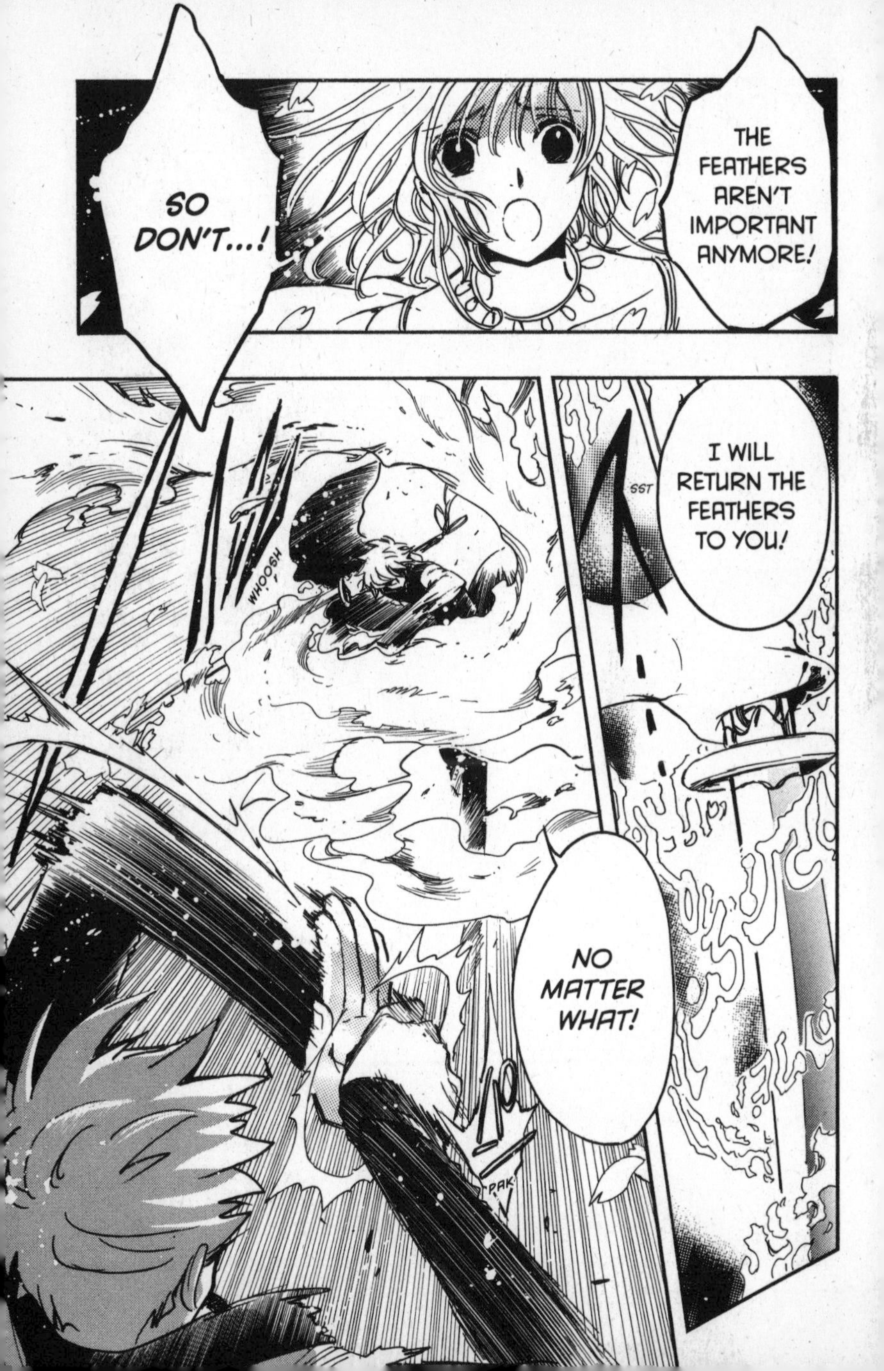
THE FEATHERS AREN'T IMPORTANT ANYMORE!
SO DON'T...!
SST
I WILL RETURN THE FEATHERS TO YOU!
WHOOSH
NO MATTER WHAT!
PAK

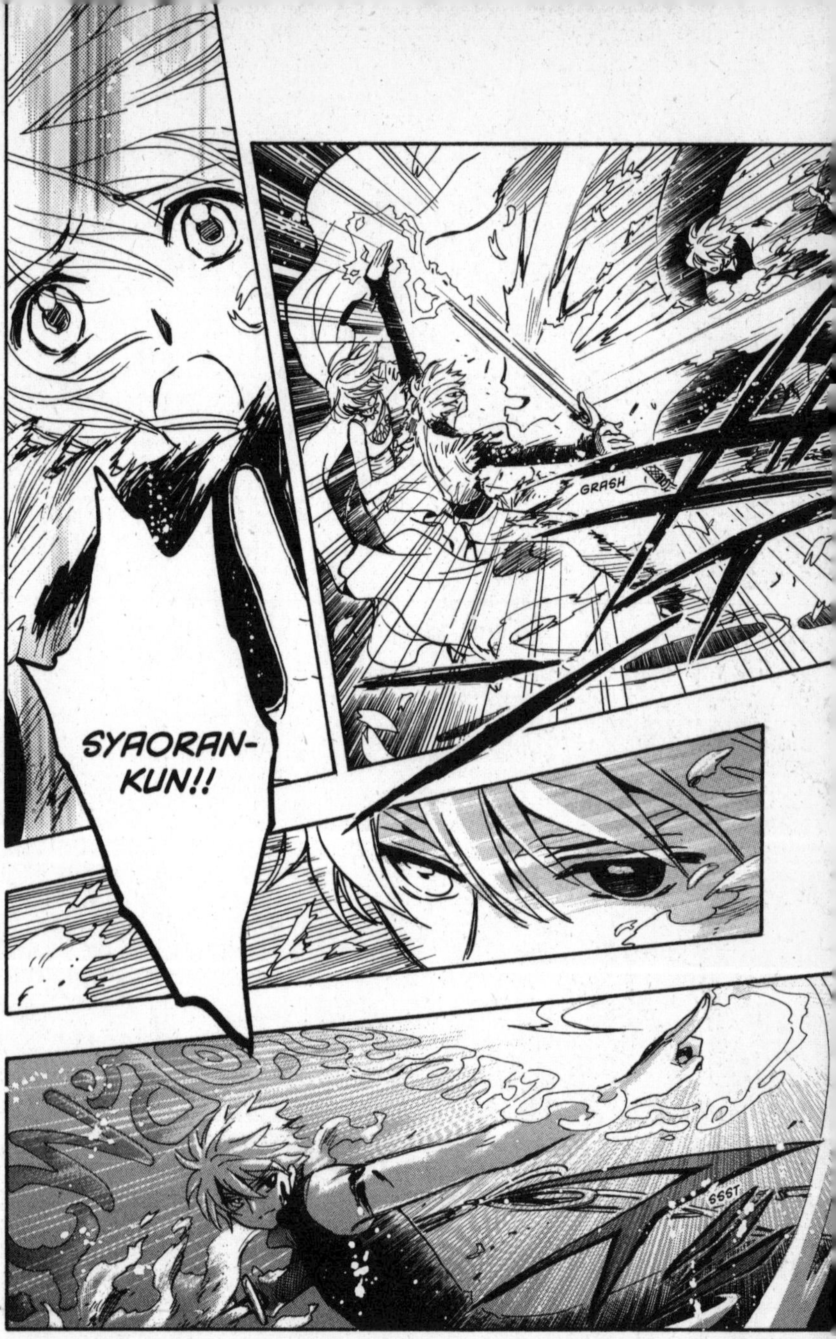
GRASH
SYAORAN-KUN!!
SSST

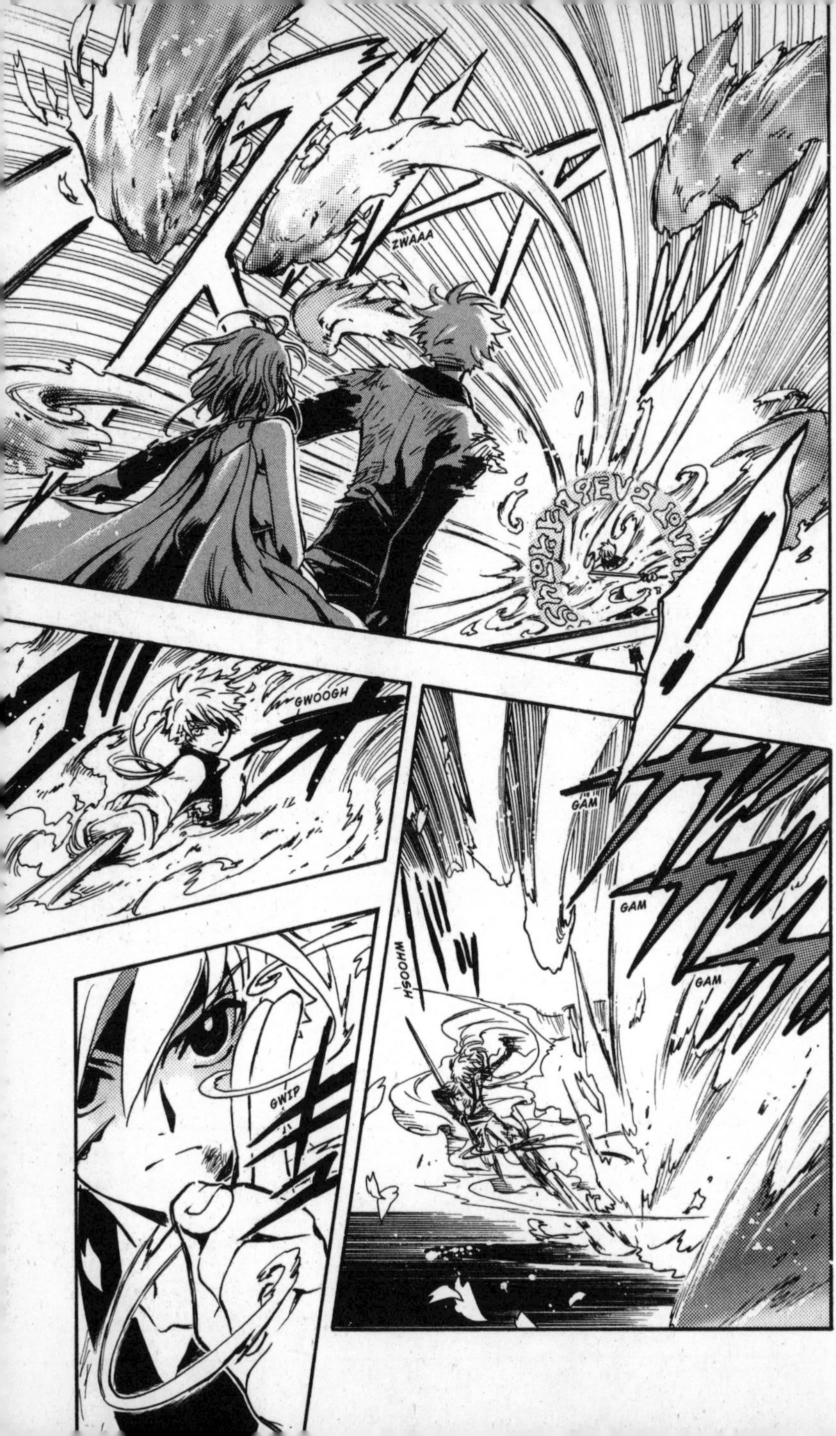
ZWAAA
GAM
GAM
GAM
WHOOSH
GWOOGH
GWIP

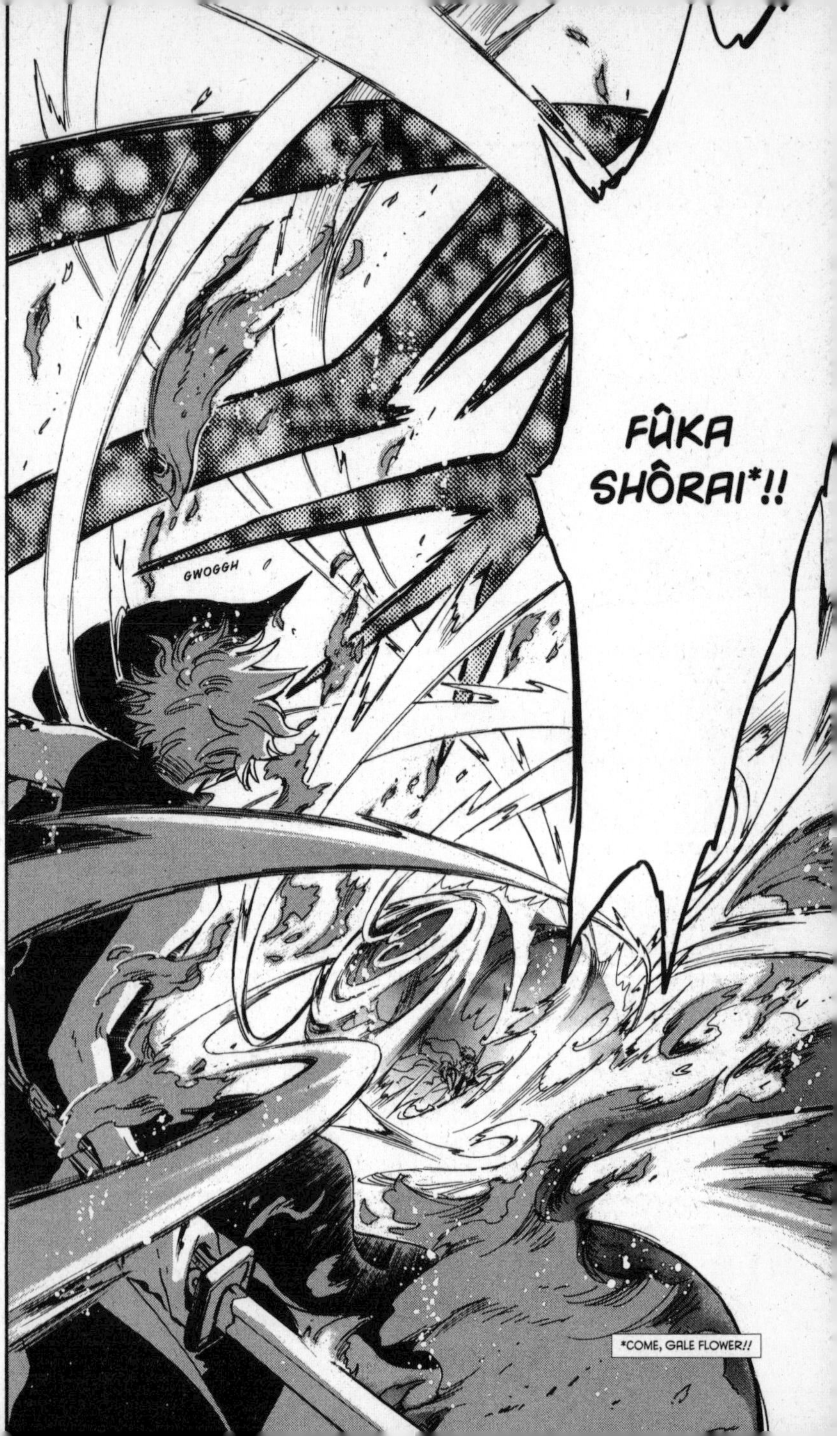
FÛKA SHÔRAI*!!
GWOGGH
*COME, GALE FLOWER!!

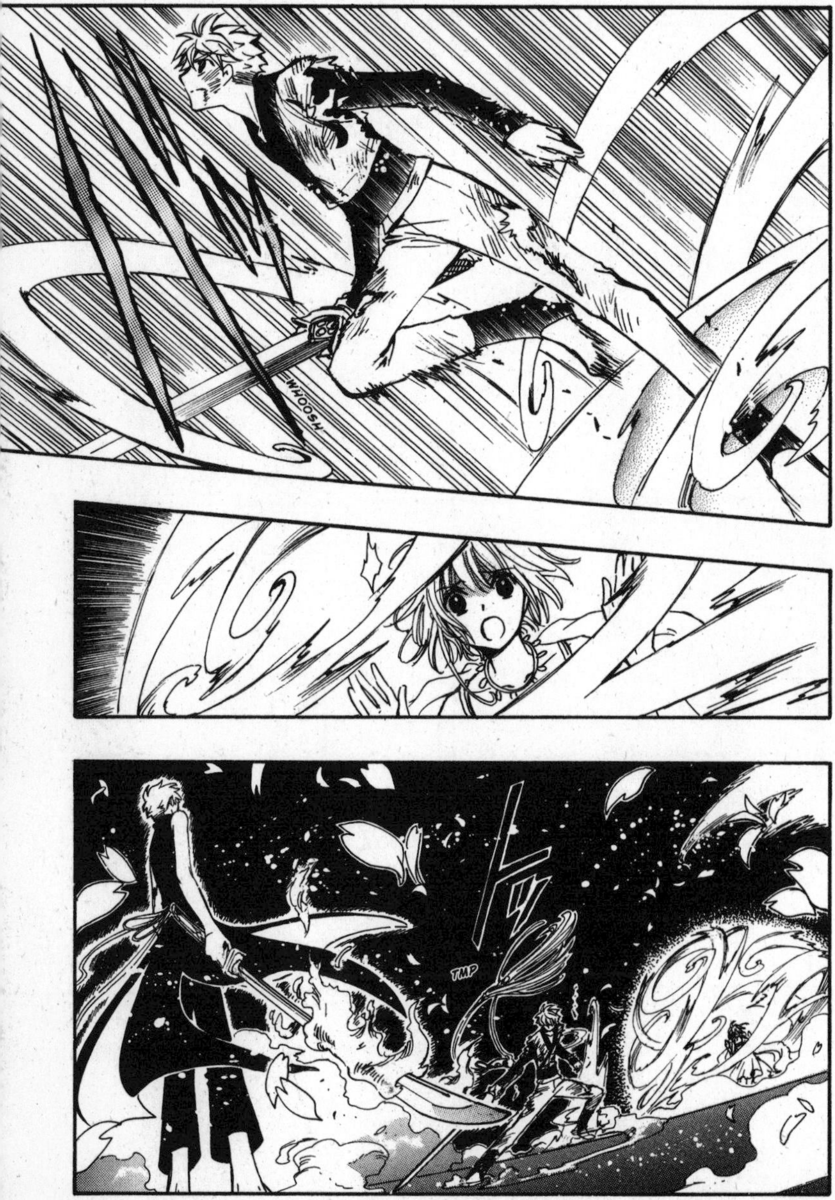
WHOOSH
TMP

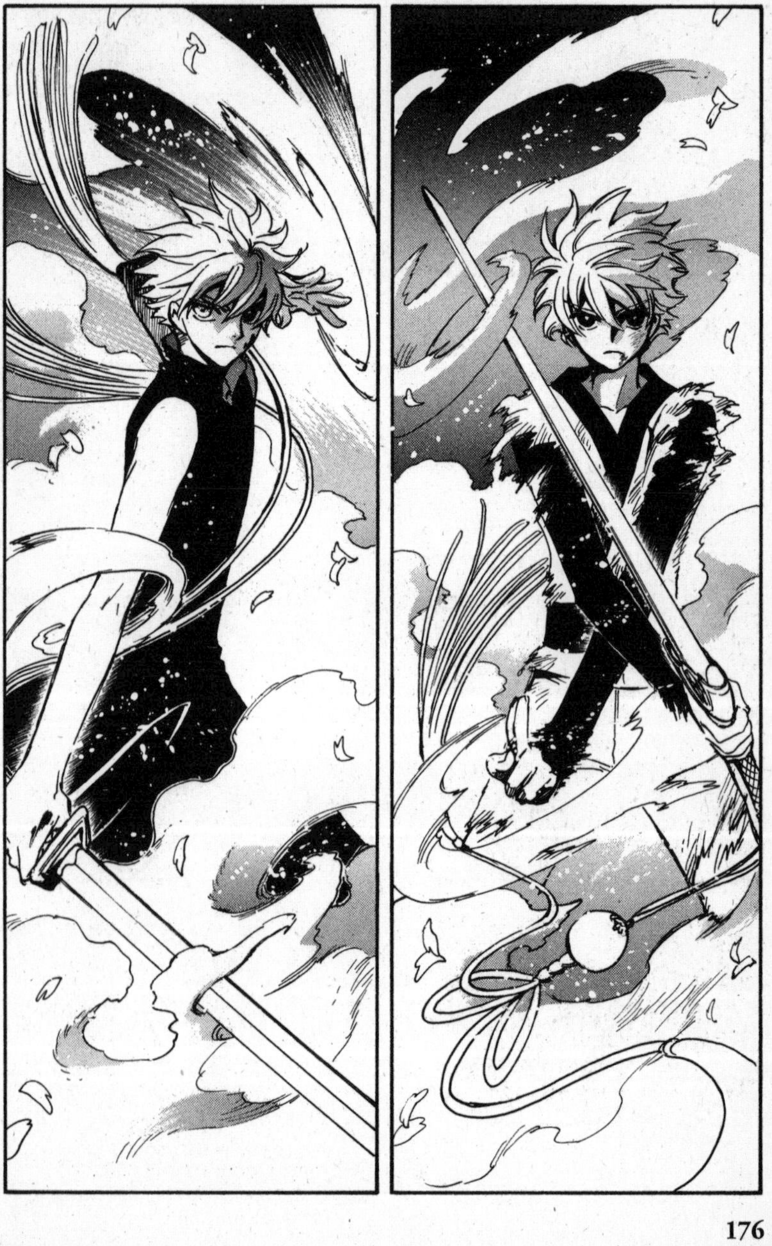

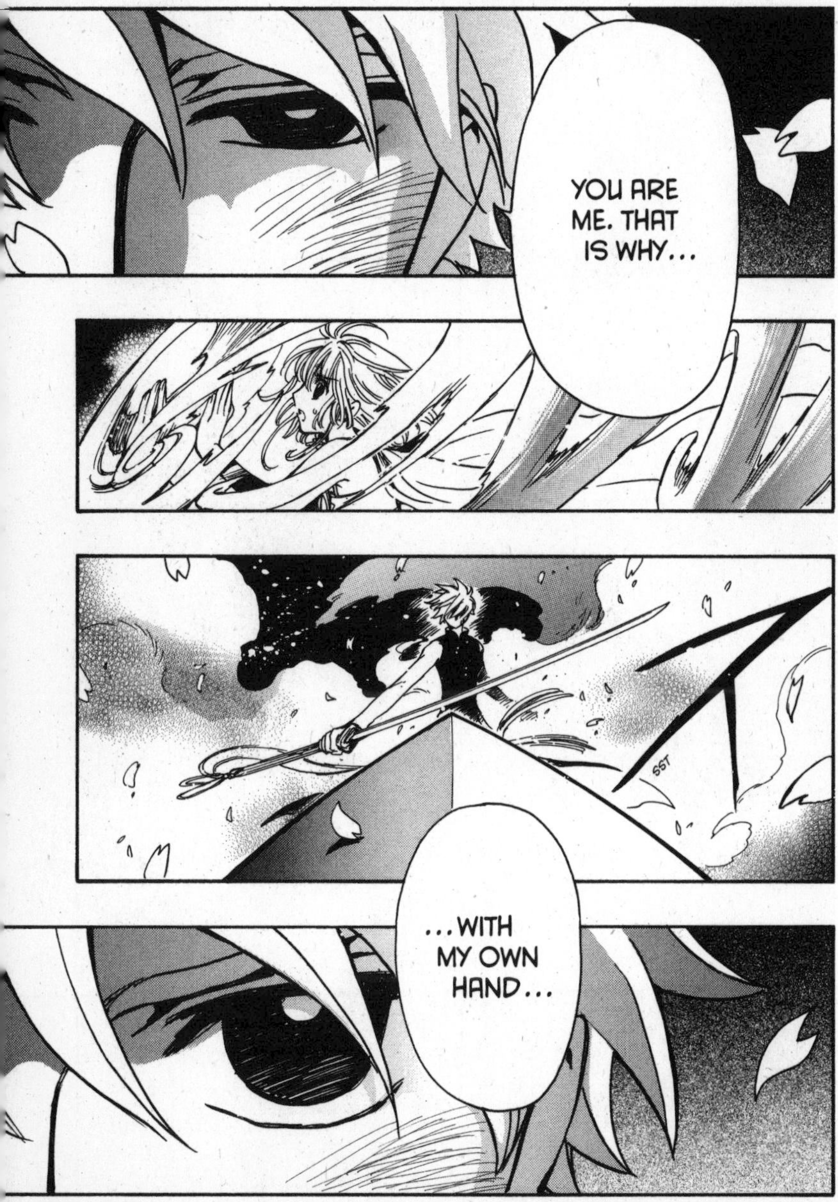
YOU ARE ME. THAT IS WHY...
SST
...WITH MY OWN HAND...

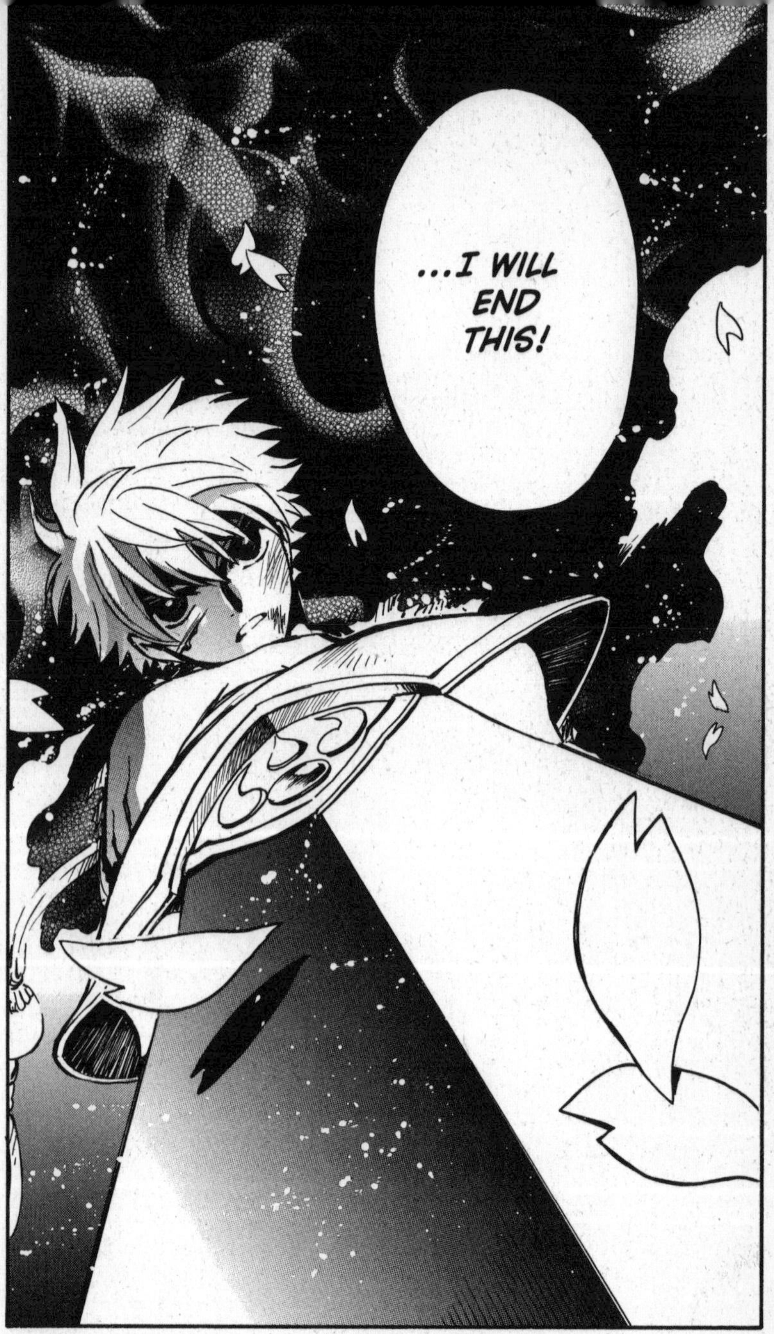
...I WILL
END
THIS!

To Be Continued

About the Creators

CLAMP is a group of four women who have become the most popular manga artists in America—Nanase Ohkawa, Mokona, Satsuki Igarashi, and Tsubaki Nekoi. They started out as *doujinshi* (fan comics) creators, but their skill and craft brought them to the attention of publishers very quickly. Their first work from a major publisher was *RG Veda*, but their first mass success was with *Magic Knight Rayearth*. From there, they went on to write many series, including Cardcaptor Sakura and Chobits, two of the most popular manga in the United States. Like many Japanese manga artists, they prefer to avoid the spotlight, and little is known about them personally.

CLAMP is currently publishing three series in Japan: Tsubasa and xxxHOLiC with Kodansha and Gohou Drug with Kadokawa.

Translation Notes

Japanese is a tricky language for most Westerners, and translation is often more art than science. For your edification and reading pleasure, here are notes on some of the places where we could have gone in a different direction in our translation of the work, or where a Japanese cultural reference is used.

Body Double, page 13

In the original Japanese, Kurogane referred to a term that isn't exactly "body double" (which is *kagemusha* in Japanese), but instead a ninja technique called *migawari*, where the ninja disguises some other object to look like him and take the attack for him. In concept, it's very much like a body double; however, this decoy need not necessarily be a living person.

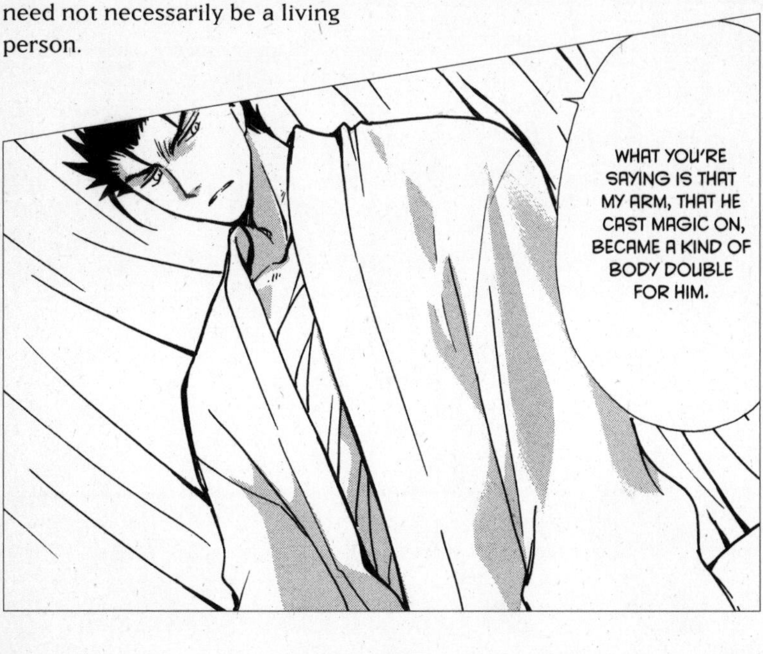
WHAT YOU'RE SAYING IS THAT MY ARM, THAT HE CAST MAGIC ON, BECAME A KIND OF BODY DOUBLE FOR HIM.

Flashback to Fûma's dialogue, page 57

Attentive readers with early printings of Tsubasa, volume 18 will notice that the dialog doesn't quite match. This is because volume 18 was printed in the United States before the translator could get his paws on this volume (vol. 22) to read it and correct the translation. CLAMP writes dialogue the meaning of which only becomes clear with flashbacks to the dialogue in later volumes. In this case the original dialogue in volume 18 included a sentence in which it wasn't clear just who Fûma was doing the other work for. Taken on its own, my original translation is not a bad interpretation. But given the new information, it is clear that my original translation is in error. Later printings of Tsubasa 18 will reflect this new, more accurate translation.

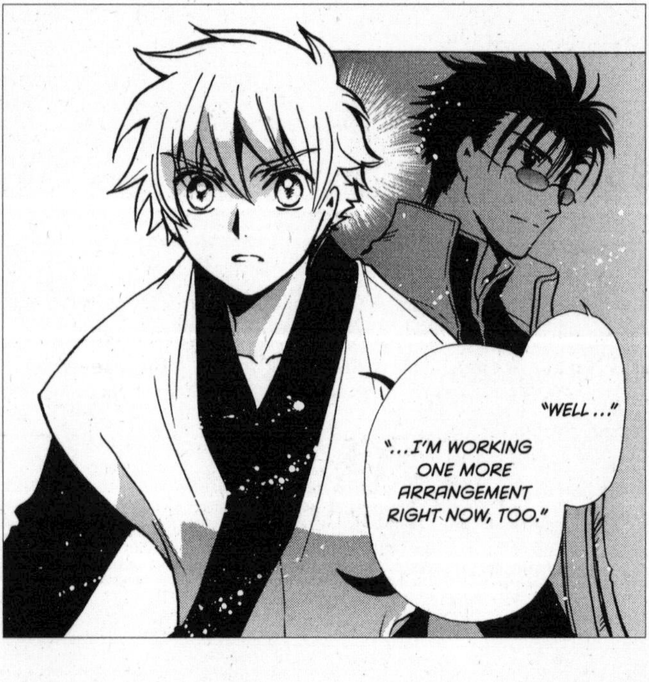
"WELL ..."
"...I'M WORKING ONE MORE ARRANGEMENT RIGHT NOW, TOO."

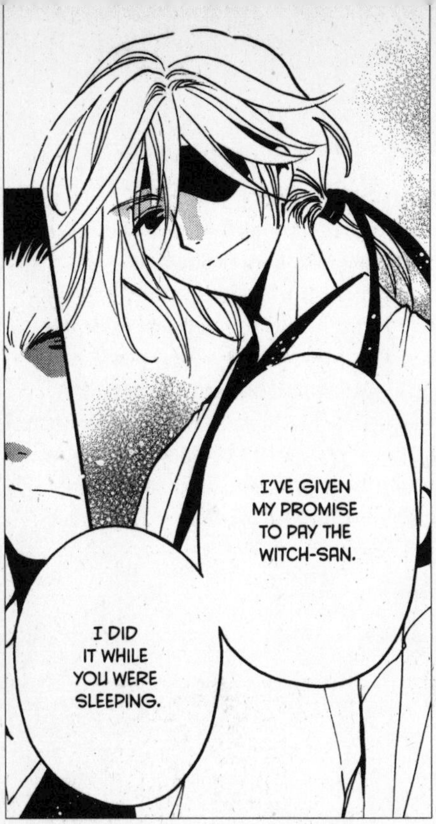
I'VE GIVEN MY PROMISE TO PAY THE WITCH-SAN.
I DID IT WHILE YOU WERE SLEEPING.

Witch-san, page 60

Honorifics can go at the end of job titles as a means of address just as they can go at the end of names. If you work in an electronics store, you could be referred to as *denkiya-san.* Of course, this doesn't work where the job title is an honorific in itself such as the word *sensei* for teachers, doctors, and artists. One would never say *Sensei-san.* In this case, the original was *majo-san* (witch-san).

Haven't changed, page 71

This is a standard greeting in Japan when one meets up with a person again after a long time. Like "how are you doing" in English, the phrase is hardly noticed for its real meaning in Japanese—it is simply a greeting. But the fact that the main characters of Tsubasa have changed so much since the Country of Ôto/Edonis, the idea of who has changed and who hasn't becomes very significant.

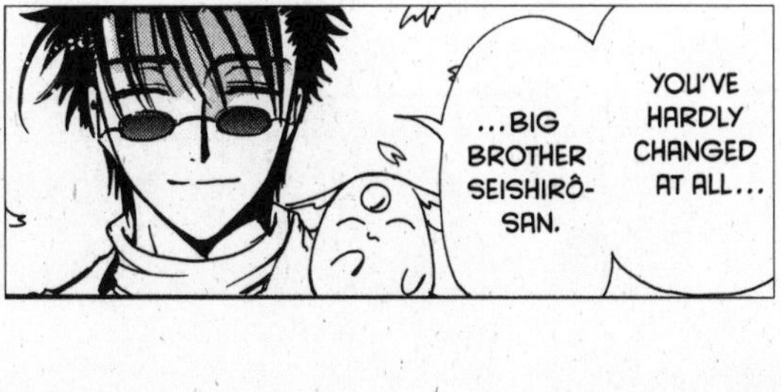
YOU'VE HARDLY CHANGED AT ALL...
...BIG BROTHER SEISHIRÔ-SAN.

Peanut Gallery (anachronism), page 76

Some may balk at Kurogane, who comes from a feudal-Japan-style world, using slang like "peanut gallery" in his dialogue. Normally, I wouldn't translate his dialogue using words the character wouldn't know, but in this case, the Japanese version of his line of dialogue was about criticisms being shouted from the outfield—a baseball reference. Since the Japanese was anachronistic, it left room for the English to be equally anachronistic. That being the case, aside from the fact that the Japanese was a reference to baseball, and the English translation was a reference to vaudeville, "peanut gallery" is a near exact translation of the original Japanese line.

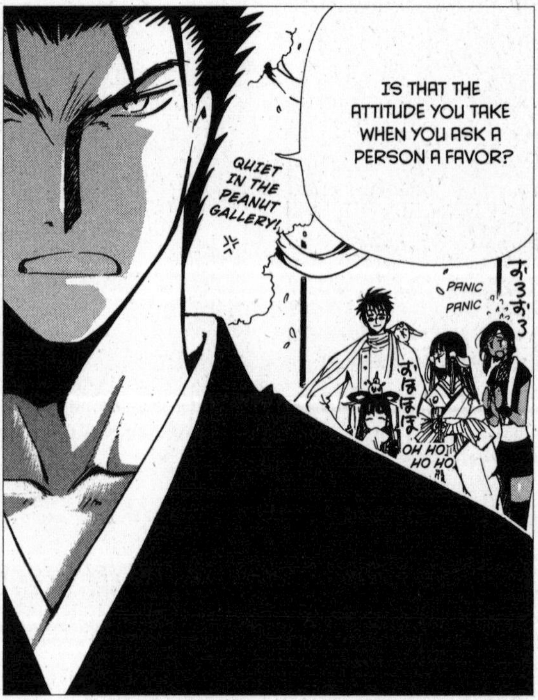
IS THAT THE ATTITUDE YOU TAKE WHEN YOU ASK A PERSON A FAVOR?
QUIET IN THE PEANUT GALLERY!
PANIC PANIC
OH HO HO HO

TOMARE!

[STOP!]

You're going the wrong way!

Manga is a completely different type of reading experience.

To start at the *beginning,* go to the *end!*

That's right! Authentic manga is read the traditional Japanese way—from right to left. Exactly the *opposite* of how American books are read. It's easy to follow: Just go to the other end of the book, and read each page—and each panel—from right side to left side, starting at the top right. Now you're experiencing manga as it was meant to be!